# TEACHING SOCIAL–EMOTIONAL SKILLS AT SCHOOL AND HOME

Linda K. Elksnin

Nick Elksnin

The Citadel

**LOVE PUBLISHING COMPANY®**

Denver • London • Sydney

*With love and appreciation to*

Bob Kitchen
Ann and Hank Elksnin

*And in loving memory of*

Polly Kitchen
David Kitchen
Bob Ingle
and
Dick Rogers

Published by Love Publishing Company
P.O. Box 22353
Denver, Colorado 80222
www.lovepublishing.com

Library of Congress Control Number: 2005901218

ISBN 0-89108-316-2

# Contents

**3** **Teaching Children and Youth to Understand and Regulate Emotions** **69**

**4** **Teaching Children and Youth Social–Emotional Problem-Solving Strategies** **103**

**5** **Teaching Children and Youth Peer-Pleasing Social–Emotional Skills** **131**

**6** **Teaching Children and Youth**
**Teacher-Pleasing Social–Emotional Skills** **161**

**7** **Teaching Occupational Social–Emotional Skills** **191**

**8** **Parents as Teachers** **219**

## Figures and Tables

# Preface

Adults who have attained a fairly high level of social skills often have a difficult time conceiving of the need to directly teach social–emotional skills such as maintaining a conversation, introducing oneself, or identifying a "social problem." But when these same socially competent adults are asked to think of situations in which they feel socially taxed, they recall their stress during cocktail parties, job interviews, formal dinners, funerals, and social situations when they were the ethnic or cultural minority. Many children and youth will not reach social–emotional competence unless they are directly taught requisite social–emotional skills. This text was written to help teachers and parents teach these skills.

In Chapter One, "The Importance of Social–Emotional Competence," we define some of the terms that appear throughout the book and emphasize the importance of children and youth becoming competent socially and emotionally. We close the chapter by discussing children and youth who are at risk for social–emotional problems.

Chapter Two, "Identifying Children and Youth Who Need Social–Emotional Skills Instruction," emphasizes the importance of determining the *reason* for the problem with social–emotional skills. Knowing whether the problem is related to acquisition, performance, or interfering behaviors will drive instructional planning. Instructional approaches vary, depending upon whether the social–emotional problem is the result of lack of knowledge, lack of opportunity, lack of feedback, lack of sensitivity to environmental cues, or lack of reinforcement. We describe specific assessment approaches that teachers and parents can use to obtain critical information about children's social–emotional skills. These approaches include rating scales, tests of emotional intelligence and nonverbal communication abilities, sociometric techniques, interviews, observation, role-play assessment, and functional behavioral assessment.

In Chapter Three, "Teaching Children and Youth to Understand and Regulate Emotions," we provide teachers and parents with strategies for helping children and youth develop nonverbal communication skills, including understanding and using paralanguage, facial expressions, postures and gestures, interpersonal space, rhythm and time, and objectics. We also describe strategies to help children and youth understand emotions and become more empathetic toward others. Because an inability to manage anger can lead to school violence and other tragic outcomes, we also include strategies for helping children and youth to effectively control anger.

Chapter Four, "Teaching Children and Youth Social–Emotional Problem-Solving Strategies," presents social problem-solving approaches. Teachers and parents learn about problem-solving routines such as FIG TESPN and programs such as PATHS, Think Aloud, and I Can Problem Solve, which they can use to help children and youth become competent social–emotional problem solvers. We also describe ways to use children's literature to teach social–emotional problem solving. Finally, conducting social skill autopsies offers teachers and parents an effective means of helping children and youth identify and solve interpersonal problems. We conclude the chapter with a discussion of how problem-solving routines may be applied to academic subjects as well as to social–emotional problems.

The theme of Chapter Five, "Teaching Children and Youth Peer-Pleasing Social–Emotional Skills," is friendship. It is hard to overestimate the importance of children's friendships. Friendship provides children and youth safety and security, and having friends is a good predictor of success in school. We begin this chapter by considering the developmental aspects of friendship and suggest ways to promote friendship during early childhood, middle childhood, and adolescence. Conversational skills, which are vital across all ages, also receive careful attention. We close the chapter by describing strategies for recruiting peer support.

In Chapter Six, "Teaching Children and Youth Teacher-Pleasing Social–Emotional Skills," we turn our attention to teacher-pleasing skills that relate to success in the classroom. These are not always the same skills that are valued by peers. After identifying specific skills that teachers value for early childhood, middle childhood, and adolescence, we describe a five-step sequence for students to use to learn teacher-pleasing skills. We end the chapter by discussing the importance of explicitly teaching children and youth classroom routines.

Chapter Seven focuses on its title, "Teaching Occupational Social–Emotional Skills." These skills are related to getting and keeping a job beyond the school years. Compelling data suggest that social–emotional skills are more critical for employment success than are academic or technical skills. We begin this chapter by identifying the social–emotional skills that employers highly value. Then we describe ways by which teachers and parents can assess and teach occupational social–emotional skills.

Throughout the text, we emphasize the importance of teacher and parent involvement in teaching social–emotional skills. In Chapter Eight, "Parents as Teachers," we describe more specific ways in which parents can teach their children social–emotional skills. Parents learn how to become "emotion coaches" and to teach social–emotional skills incidentally. For parents of children with special needs, we offer tips for how to ensure that social–emotional objectives are included in individualized education programs (IEPs). We also describe specific strategies that parents can use to support children's friendships. The chapter concludes with a discussion of how parents can use children's literature to support social–emotional learning.

In Chapter Nine, "Getting Children and Youth to Use Social–Emotional Skills," we discuss factors that affect generalization of skills across individuals, settings, and situations and offer strategies to promote the use of these skills. Specifically, we recommend that teachers infuse social–emotional skills instruction within the academic curriculum, engage in co-teaching, adopt cooperative learning strategies, and assign homework in social–emotional skills. We suggest that parents and teachers use incidental, coincidental, and opportunistic teaching strategies, and that they teach children and youth self-management strategies to encourage generalization. Finally, we suggest that home–school–community collaboration offers the best chance of encouraging children and youth to use social–emotional skills where and when they count.

The prognosis for children and youth who lack social–emotional competence is not encouraging: Social problems become more debilitating over time and exert a powerful, and negative, influence on adult adjustment. We hope that, after reading this book, teachers and parents will become more able and willing to teach children critical social–emotional skills.

# Acknowledgments

We would like to express our thanks to individuals who provided support and encouragement throughout the preparation of this book. Creighton Eddings, our graduate assistant, aided in the preparation of the manuscript by checking references and securing permissions. Stan Love was enthusiastic about the project from the beginning and patiently awaited its completion. We also offer our thanks to Susan Warhover, a.k.a. "Turbo Editor." Finally, we are grateful to the Citadel Foundation for funding the research that made the project possible.

LKE
NE

# CHAPTER 1

# The Importance of Social–Emotional Competence

## Goals of This Chapter

In this chapter you will learn

- ▶ the difference between social competence and social–emotional skills
- ▶ the types of social–emotional skills
- ▶ how social–emotional skills relate to the construct of emotional intelligence, or emotional literacy
- ▶ various approaches for teaching social–emotional skills
- ▶ the principles of social–emotional learning
- ▶ the reasons why today's children may fail to develop social–emotional skills
- ▶ negative outcomes of not developing adequate social–emotional skills
- ▶ which children and youth are most at risk for developing problems with social–emotional skills

# Terms to Know

Asperger syndrome (AS)

attention deficit/hyperactivity disorder (ADHD)

autism

autism spectrum disorders (ASD)

body basics

cognitive–behavioral approach

emotional/behavioral disorders (E/BD)

emotional intelligence (EI)

emotional literacy

emotional quotient (EQ)

learning disabilities (LD)

mental retardation/developmental disabilities (MR/DD)

nonverbal learning disabilities (NLD)

operant approach

social competence

social–emotional learning (SEL)

social–emotional skills

social learning theory approach

# A Tale of Two Children

*Third-grade teacher Donna smiled to herself. Jeff was a pleasure to have in her class. Although his academic skills were not quite at grade level, he was getting along well with his classmates and was the first to be chosen for teams during recess. Jeff seemed to have an intuitive understanding of others' feelings, he was considerate of children and adults, and he knew how to start a conversation and keep it going. In addition, he had all of the student behaviors that teachers desire: He was cooperative, he listened, he worked independently, and he dealt with frustration well. Donna wouldn't mind teaching a roomful of "Jeffs," even if every one of them was struggling in reading and math. Actually, she would gladly trade Allen for five "Jeffs."*

*Allen was academically gifted and excelled in every subject. He read at the eighth-grade level, and his math skills were 3 years above grade level. Unlike Jeff, however, Allen was not well liked by his classmates. He dominated cooperative groups and whined when he didn't get his way. He could be counted on to say the wrong thing at the wrong time. Donna recalled that he called Maria, a member of his spelling team, "stupid" when she couldn't spell the word* respond. *Maria had joined the class 2 months ago and was learning to speak, read, and write English. In those short months she had made tremendous progress, but she was a quiet girl lacking self-confidence. What she didn't need was an obnoxious child like Allen calling her names! Donna hoped her dislike of Allen wasn't apparent to him and the rest of the class, but she had her doubts.*

A fter reading the opening vignette, it is easy to guess which child in Donna Zahn's class is more likely to be successful in school, at home, and in life. The vignette underscores the importance of social–emotional competence, which is related to academic success. Jeff and children like him are more likely to succeed in school despite their academic difficulties because teachers are more willing to work with them. The social support of classmates goes a long way in keeping students who struggle academically in school.

With the increasing numbers of children and youth who have social–emotional difficulties, teachers and parents face unique challenges. Approximately 20% of young children demonstrate emotional problems before the age of 5 (Mugno & Rosenblitt, 2001). School adjustment problems are evident in 25% of children ages 10 to 17, and 35% of adolescents engage in high-risk behaviors such as substance abuse and unprotected sex (J. Cohen, 2001). Between 15% and 22% of youth in the United States have social–emotional problems that are severe enough to warrant mental health services, but 80% fail to receive these services (J. Cohen, 2001).

The antithesis of social–emotional problems is social–emotional competence, the subject of this book. In the discussion that follows, we define some of the terms that appear throughout the book. Then we explain why social and emotional competence is crucial. Finally, we identify just who is at risk for social–emotional problems.

## ▶ Defining Our Terms

### Social Competence and Social–Emotional Skills

*Social competence* is an evaluative term. Teachers, parents, employers, or peers judge an individual to be adequately skilled in social situations based on a number of widely agreed-upon behaviors (Gresham, Sugai, & Horner, 2001). In addition to possessing adequate social skills, a socially competent individual also must read a social situation accurately, select the appropriate social-emotional skill to use, and be motivated to use it. Social competence results in positive social outcomes such as peer acceptance, making friends, and getting along with co-workers (Elliott & Gresham, 1993; Foster & Ritchey, 1979; McFall, 1982).

*Social–emotional skills* are specific abilities that allow an individual to perform competently in social situations. These skills include physiological, cognitive, and overt motor behaviors (McFall, 1982). For example, the ability to focus attention, control impulsivity, or manage stress affects how we learn and use social–emotional skills. The cognitive ability to understand the feelings of others, dynamics of the group, or expectations of a culture determines when and how to use certain skills. Further, being able to perform the skill requires certain verbal and nonverbal behaviors.

Schumaker and Hazel's (1984) definition of social–emotional skills includes both the cognitive and behavioral aspects.

> A social skill is any cognitive function or overt behavior in which an individual engages while interacting with another person or persons. Cognitive functions include such capacities as empathizing with or understanding another person's feelings, discriminating and evaluating consequences for social behavior. Overt behaviors include the nonverbal (e.g., head nods, eye contact, facial expression) and verbal (e.g., what the person says) components of social performance. (p. 422)

For example, the verbal, nonverbal, and cognitive components of the skill "accepting criticism" include these ordered steps:

1. Listening to the other person
2. Thinking about what the person said
3. Giving your side, if appropriate
4. Saying you will change if you think you should, and/or thanking the person

Notice the important cognitive, or decision-making, components involved in this skill. The individual must process what the other person says, evaluate whether the person makes good point(s), and decide if behavior change is warranted based on these points. Other cognitive components of this skill include knowing when and where to use it, and how to evaluate its effectiveness (e.g., did using the skill result in a positive outcome?).

The skill involves additional, nonverbal behaviors, which Hazel, Schumaker, Sherman, and Sheldon (1996) call *body basics*, including

▶ staying close to the person,
▶ facing the person and maintaining eye contact,
▶ having a serious facial expression,
▶ maintaining a relaxed but serious body posture,
▶ using a serious tone of voice.

We organize social–emotional skills within six clusters:

1. Interpersonal behaviors
2. Peer-related social skills
3. Teacher-pleasing social skills
4. Self-related behaviors
5. Assertiveness skills
6. Communication skills

Figure 1.1 includes examples of skills for each cluster.

To gain a better understanding, it is useful to consider the relationship of social competence and social–emotional skills to that of literacy and reading. Literate individuals are able to draw on a variety of reading and writing skills—decoding, skimming, scanning, spelling, punctuating, and so forth. Similarly, the socially competent

| | |
|---|---|
| **Interpersonal Behaviors** | These behaviors are "friendship-making skills," such as introducing yourself, joining in, asking a favor, offering to help, giving and accepting compliments, and apologizing. |
| **Peer-Related Social Skills** | These skills, valued by classmates, are associated with peer acceptance. Examples include working cooperatively, asking for and receiving information, and correctly assessing another's emotional state. |
| **Teacher-Pleasing Social Skills** | Behaviors associated with success in school include following directions, doing your best work, and listening to the teacher. |
| **Self-Related Behaviors** | These skills allow a child to assess a social situation, select an appropriate skill, and determine the effectiveness of the skill. Other self-related behaviors include following through, dealing with stress, understanding feelings, and controlling anger. |
| **Assertiveness Skills** | These behaviors allow children to express their needs without resorting to aggression. |
| **Communication Skills** | Communication skills include listener responsiveness, taking turns, maintaining conversational attention, and giving feedback to the speaker. |

Source: From "Teaching Social Skills to Students with Learning and Behavior Problems," by L. K. Elksnin and N. Elksnin, in *Intervention in School and Clinic, 33*, p. 132. Copyright © 1998 by Pro-Ed Inc. Reprinted with permission.

**FIGURE 1.1** ▶ Types of Social–Emotional Skills

individual has a wide range of social–emotional skills in his or her repertoire and the cognitive ability to read a social situation and act accordingly.

## Emotional Intelligence

In recent years articles about the large role emotional intelligence plays in life success have appeared frequently in newspapers and magazines. Mayer, DiPaolo, and Salovey introduced the term *emotional intelligence* (EI) in 1990.

> Emotional intelligence is a type of emotional information pro-
> cessing that includes accurate appraisal of emotions in one-
> self and others, appropriate expression of emotion, and adap-
> tive regulation of emotion in such a way as to enhance living.
> (p. 773)

The psychologists revised their definition in 1999.

> Emotional intelligence refers to an ability to recognize the
> meanings of emotions and their relationships, and to reason
> and problem-solve on the basis of them. Emotional intelligence
> is involved in the capacity to perceive emotions, assimilate emo-
> tion-related feelings, understand the information of those emo-
> tions, and manage them. (Mayer, Caruso, & Salovey, 1999, p. 267)

Although Mayer and colleagues may have coined the term *EI,* Daniel Goleman, a science journalist, popularized it with the publication of his 1995 book, *Emotional Intelligence: Why It Can Matter More Than IQ.* Interest in the topic was so high that *Time* magazine featured EI as a cover story.

Whereas Mayer et al. restricted their construct of EI to the first three domains, Goleman added motivation and interpersonal skills as core components. Thus, the five social–emotional domains correlated with life success became: knowing one's emotions, managing emotions, recognizing emotions, motivating oneself, and handling relationships.

More recently, in his book *Working with Emotional Intelligence,* Goleman (1998) revised his model to include these domains:

▶ Self-awareness (emotional awareness, self-confidence)
▶ Self-regulation (self-control, trustworthiness, conscientiousness, adaptability, innovation)
▶ Motivation (achievement drive, commitment, initiative, optimism)
▶ Empathy (understanding others, developing others, service orientation, leveraging diversity, political awareness)
▶ Social skills (influence, communication, conflict management, leadership, serving as change catalyst, building bonds, collaboration and cooperation, team capabilities)

Reuven Bar-On (1997), an Israeli clinical psychologist, first used the term *EQ,* or *emotional quotient,* to place emotional intelligence on the same footing as cognitive intelligence, which is commonly referred to as IQ. The BarOn Emotional Quotient Inventory is based on his model. It includes five scales: Intrapersonal (subscales: self-actualizing, independence, emotional self-awareness); Interpersonal (subscales: empathy, social responsibility); Adaptability (subscales: problem solving, reality testing); Stress Management (subscales: impulse control, stress tolerance); and General Mood (subscales: happiness, optimism).

Although emotional intelligence is important, it likely is less important than IQ. As Mayer (2001) succinctly points out:

> Why? Intelligence regularly predicts academic grade point average at $r = .50$ level; moreover, the prestige of an occupation (as rated by independent observers) correlates about $r = .80$ with the average IQ of people in the occupation. To claim that EI out-predicts intelligence means that it should have correlations above those $r = .50$ and $r = .80$—a stiff hurdle. (p. 23)

A correlation coefficient (i.e., $r$) quantifies the relationship between two variables (grade-point average and intelligence, and occupational prestige and intelligence in the above example). Coefficients range from .00 to +1.00 or –1.00. A correlation coefficient of .00 means that there is no relationship between two variables. The closer to +1.00 the correlation coefficient, the higher the degree of relationship between two variables. A coefficient of .80 is considered high.

The good news is that emotional intelligence appears to be less genetically determined than IQ, which means that EI can be taught. It also seems that many EQ skills overlap, so teaching one skill has a spillover effect on others. For this reason, emotional intelligence can be taught relatively efficiently. Children begin to learn emotional skills through nurturing parent–child interactions. Parents can accelerate the process by helping their children identify and label their emotions, as will be discussed in Chapter Three.

## Emotional Literacy

*Emotional literacy*, a term used by many European researchers and practitioners, is in many ways equivalent to emotional intelligence (Joseph & Strain, 2003). Weare (2004) defines emotional literacy as

> the ability to understand ourselves and other people, and in particular to be aware of, understand, and use information about the emotional states of ourselves and others with competence. It includes the ability to understand, express and manage our own emotions, and respond to the emotions of others, in ways that are helpful to ourselves and others. (p. 2)

## Social–Emotional Skills Instruction and Social–Emotional Learning

Instruction in social–emotional skills involves teaching specific social–emotional skills, social–emotional problem-solving skills, or a combination of both (see L. K. Elksnin & N. Elksnin, 1995). Briefly, parents and teachers model the skill steps, provide learners with practice opportunities, and reinforce use of the skills in school and at home. When teaching specific skills such as joining a group, asking for help, sharing, or negotiating, each skill is task-analyzed, or broken down into its constituent parts. Children learn by watching the teacher or parent perform the skill, by practicing the skill during role-playing exercises, and by performing the skill in real-life social situations.

Problem-solving approaches are used to teach children to solve interpersonal problems using a routine that requires them to define the problem (e.g., "I want to join the pick-up basketball game"); come up with potential solutions ("I could just take the ball and start to play," or "I could wait until the girls take a break and ask to play," or "I could stand around and wait until someone asks me to play"); select a solution ("I'll wait until a break, then I'll ask if I can play"); implement a solution ("I waited and asked, but the players said to wait until tomorrow"); and finally, evaluate the effectiveness of the chosen solution ("Well, I didn't get to play today, but I might tomorrow. If I show up and they still won't let me in the game, I'll wait until after the game and try to make friends with one of the girls").

*Social–emotional learning (SEL)* grew out of the interest in fostering emotional intelligence. As evidence of the perceived importance of EI, two years after Goleman published *Emotional Intelligence: Why It Can Matter More Than IQ,* 700 school districts implemented programs designed to teach students social–emotional skills (Ratnesar, 1997). Social–emotional learning programs now are part of the elementary and secondary curricula in many school districts, with all students receiving instruction in skills, emotional understanding, and values. J. Cohen (2001) emphasized that the majority of programs focus on

▶ awareness of self and others;
▶ emotional self-regulation;
▶ communication;
▶ self-motivation;
▶ problem solving and decision making;
▶ collaboration;
▶ formation of a more realistic, positive sense of self. (p. 8)

Elias (2004) emphasized that three essential principles support SEL programs:

1. Caring relationships are the foundation of all lasting learning.
2. Emotions affect how and what we learn.
3. Goal setting and problem solving provide focus, direction, and energy for learning. (p. 54)

Social–emotional skills may be taught to individual children or to groups of children. Instruction can be formal (i.e., a regularly scheduled part of the school day) or informal (i.e., seizing opportunities during the day to teach a needed skill). Special education teachers and school psychologists developed many of the instructional strategies that have proven to be effective for teaching children with social–emotional problems. These programs are designed to prevent behaviors such as drug and alcohol use, unsafe sex practices, violent behavior, and so forth.

## ▷ Why Teach Social–Emotional Skills?

Parents and teachers must provide instruction in social–emotional skills for several reasons. The landscape of American life has changed, and poorly developed social–emotional skills are related to undesirable outcomes such as dropping out of school and developing mental health problems as adults. By contrast, well-developed social–emotional skills are associated with positive outcomes such as academic competence and self-confidence.

In the past, social–emotional skills were passed on from generation to generation as extended family life enabled children to interact with parents, grandparents, other relatives, and neighbors. Many natural opportunities, including play, allowed children to learn and practice social–emotional skills. Now, rather than remaining close to extended family, more than a fifth of families move annually (Marano, 1998a). Thus, parents can no longer rely on relatives to help pass on skills but must assume total responsibility for their children's social–emotional education. Parents today have greater demands placed on their time than ever before. In the rush to meet job responsibilities and keep the household running, social interactions are likely to be the first casualties and often are looked upon as "time wasters."

This attitude is communicated from parents to children, who observe their parents avoiding social interactions with neighbors, friends, and service personnel. Children see parents not taking time to talk with people as they go about their daily business. Single-focused parents are all about "getting the job done" as quickly as possible, leaving little room for conversation with shop clerks, bank tellers, and neighbors. Less family time means fewer opportunities for parents to help their children learn and practice social and problem–solving skills.

Some authors speculate that children's reduced opportunities to play affect their social–emotional development adversely (Marano, 1998a). Frequent moves may make it difficult for children to form friendships. Many parents are afraid of letting their children have "free range" in the neighborhood after school, preferring that they remain inside. Further, opportunities to play with siblings are reduced significantly because many children are *only* children: The U.S. Census Bureau reported that the average number of children decreased from 2.3 to 1.8 between 1970 and 1991 (Marano, 1998a, 1998b).

Technology (e.g., television and computers) also may reduce children's opportunities to learn and practice social–emotional skills (Goleman, 1995; Shapiro, 1997). Shapiro allows that television has great potential for teaching social–emotional skills, but passive TV watching "stunts the growth of EQ skills" (p. 35). Although computers enable people to keep in touch, e-mail is no substitute for face-to-face contact. Phillip Zimbardo of Stanford University tracked children's use of computers for two decades and reported that more children than ever said their computer was their best friend (Marano, 1998a, 1998b).

Despite the deck being stacked against them in the traditional avenues for social–emotional development, many children develop social–emotional skills on their own, just as many children teach themselves to read. Still, a large group of children need both formal and informal social–emotional skills instruction if they are to become emotionally intelligent. Further, a small number have what Elias, Tobias, and Friedlander (1999) call "social dyslexia." The emotional intelligence of these children will improve only through persistence and hard work. This is a necessary endeavor as the failure of children to become socially and emotionally competent is linked to numerous negative lifelong outcomes, as described in the sections that follow.

## Outcomes of Inadequate Social–Emotional Skills

Children and youth who demonstrate adequate social–emotional skills are likely to be successful academically, be accepted by their peers, be emotionally well adjusted, and have high levels of self-esteem and self-confidence (Merrell & Gimpel, 1998). Conversely, children and youth who fail to acquire social–emotional skills are likely to be rejected by their peers, have difficulty in school, leave school early, have mental health problems, and be underemployed or unemployed.

### Peer Rejection

Between 10% and 15% of children have serious peer relationship problems (Asher & Rose, 1997). Poorly developed social–emotional skills are related to lack of peer acceptance (Craig-Unkefer & Kaiser, 2002). Social–emotional skills deficits do not necessarily *cause* a child to be ignored or disliked by peers; other within-child characteristics (e.g., physical appearance, disability) can trigger negative peer reaction. Still, children who are well accepted "are far more likely to display prosocial characteristics such as friendliness, cooperativeness, helpfulness, and kindness," whereas "poorly accepted children are less likely to display these prosocial characteristics and are more likely to exhibit aggressive, disruptive, or extremely withdrawn behavior" (Asher & Rose, 1997, p. 199).

If children lack social–emotional skills *and* are rejected by peers, they are denied opportunities to become more socially skilled. Peer rejection prevents children from interpersonal interactions that provide support and that help hone social–emotional skills. Worse yet, such rejection may be permanent. Asher and Rose (1997) reported that 30% to 50% of children rejected during middle childhood continued to be rejected five years later. On the positive side, we have strong evidence to suggest that children who receive social-emotional skills instruction experience increased peer acceptance (L. K. Elksnin & N. Elksnin, 2003).

### School Problems

Many children with deficient social–emotional skills have difficulty in the classroom (Craig-Unkefer & Kaiser, 2003). Despite the renewed emphasis on academics, we cannot ignore the reality that life in the classroom is social and emotional (Pianta, 1999). For this reason, children with strong social networks perform better in school (Marcus & Sanders-Reio, 2001). Results of several studies that followed children's transition to kindergarten and their experiences during the school year indicated that children who had friends at the beginning of the year and maintained these friendships performed better than children who were rejected by their peers (Ladd, 1990, 1991; Ladd, Kochenderfer, & Coleman, 1996). The best predictor of academic performance and attitude toward school was social adjustment, not intelligence or prior school performance. Similar results have been reported for children who made the transition from elementary to middle/junior high school (Berndt & Keefe, 1995; Berndt, Laychak, & Park, 1990; Wentzel, 1993; Wentzel & Caldwell, 1997; Wentzel, Barry, & Caldwell, 2004).

Because of the important role that social support plays in school, it is not surprising that youth without support are more likely to drop out of school, as well as engage in delinquent activities (LaGreca & Vaughn, 1992; Matson, Sevin, & Box, 1995; Merrell & Gimpel, 1998; Vaughn & Hogan, 1994). The drop-out rate for rejected youth is estimated to be at least three times that for other children (Asher & Rose, 1997; Ollendick, Weist, Borden, & Green, 1992, as cited in Marcus & Sanders-Reio, 2001; Shapiro, 1997).

### Mental Health Problems

Another negative outcome of poor social–emotional skills is the emergence of mental health problems. Thus, children and youth with social–emotional skills problems are at risk for externalizing and internalizing problems (Merrell & Gimpel, 1998). *Externalizing problems* include acting out, as well as aggressive and violent behavior. *Internalizing problems* include anxiety, withdrawal, and depression.

Social–emotional deficits affect children and youth long after they leave school. For example, as adults they are more likely to receive bad conduct discharges from the military (Gresham, 1982; Matson et al., 1995; Merrell & Gimpel, 1998) and to have mental health problems (Bender, Rosenkrans, & Crane, 1999; LaGreca & Vaughn, 1992; Matson et al., 1995; Merrell & Gimpel, 1998). Strain and Odom (1986) reported that poorly developed social–emotional skills during early childhood were the single best predictor of significant problems in adulthood. For these reasons, the impact of social–emotional competence cannot be underestimated.

> Today early appearing social relationships are believed to have a profound influence on many adult behaviors. For example, children who develop early social relationships with their peers have better employment records as adults, they are more likely to live independently, they live longer, are less likely to contract adult diseases, have better mental health, and have greater self-esteem. (Strain & Smith, 1996, p. 24)

### Underemployment and Unemployment

"Deficits in social skills have also been cited as a major factor in unsuccessful post-school adjustment for [students with disabilities] in employment and independent living contexts" (O'Reilly & Glynn, 1995, p. 187). Several researchers have reported that 90 percent of job loss is related to social–emotional problems rather than inability to do the job (Bullis, Nishioka-Evans, Fredericks, & Davis, 1992; Hagner, Rogan, & Murphy, 1992; D. W. Johnson & R. T. Johnson, 1990). Clearly, interpersonal skills are essential to employability, productivity, and career success (L. K. Elksnin, N. Elksnin, & Sabornie, 1994; L. K. Elksnin & N. Elksnin, 1996; N. Elksnin & L. K. Elksnin, 1991, 1998, 2001). (Chapter Seven addresses how to effectively teach occupational social–emotional skills.)

# ▶ Who Is at Risk for Problems With Social–Emotional Skills?

Approximately one fifth of children and youth in the United States have significant social–emotional problems (J. Cohen, 2001). Many of them are at risk for school failure or have diagnosed disabilities. For example, results of longitudinal studies conducted by Vaughn and her colleagues suggest that low-achieving students and students with learning disabilities are less well accepted than high-achieving and average-performing students (Vaughn, Elbaum, & Schumm, 1996; Vaughn & Hogan, 1994; Vaughn, Zaragoza, Hogan, & Walker, 1993). Similarly, Shapiro (1997) reported that 50% of children referred for special education services have problems with social skills that result in peer rejection. According to the U.S. Department of Education (1996), almost one third of adolescents with disabilities require social–emotional instruction following graduation from high school.

In the discussion that follows, we describe social–emotional problems among children within the following high-risk populations: attention deficit/hyperactivity disorder, autism spectrum disorders, emotional/behavioral disorders, learning disabilities, nonverbal learning disabilities, and mental retardation/development disabilities.

## Attention Deficit/Hyperactivity Disorder

Attention deficit/hyperactivity disorder (ADHD) is described in the *Diagnostic and Statistical Manual of Mental Disorders–IV–TR* (DSM–IV–TR) as a "persistent pattern of inattention and/or hyperactivity–impulsivity that is more frequently displayed and more severe than is typically observed in individuals of comparable development" (American Psychiatric Association, 2000, p. 84). Half of all children with ADHD demonstrate social–emotional skills problems (Frederick & Olmi, 1994; Gresham et al., 2001; Lopez, Forness, MacMillan, Bocian, & Gresham, 1996; Matson et al., 1995); and from 50% to 60% are rejected by their peers (Guevremont, 1990; Shapiro, 1997). Individuals with ADHD exhibit symptoms of inattention and/or hyperactivity–impulsivity, which may interfere with learning and using social–emotional skills.

In social situations, they may demonstrate inattention as failing to attend to the speaker, rapidly shifting conversational topics, introducing topics not related to the conversation at hand, and failing to follow the rules of games and activities. Hyperactivity–impulsivity may lead to lack of control and interruption of activities, including grabbing and touching others' things; failing to follow directions; continuously interrupting others; and making comments out of turn. Other children and adults regard children and youth who exhibit these behaviors extremely negatively (Frederick & Olmi, 1994; Landau & Moore, 1991). These same turn-off behaviors also make it difficult for children and youth with ADHD to learn positive, peer-pleasing behaviors (Barkley, 1990; DuPaul & Stoner, 1994; Landau & Moore, 1991).

## Autism Spectrum Disorders

Deficits in social–emotional skills among individuals with autism spectrum disorders (ASD) are widely known (Celani, Battacchi, & Arcidiacono, 1999; Hobson & Lee, 1998; Loveland, Pearson, Tunali-Kotoski, Ortegon, & Gibbs, 2001; Yang, Schaller, Huang, Wang, & Tsai, 2003). ASD encompasses children and youth with autism, high-functioning autism (i.e., verbal and nonverbal intelligence quotients above 70), Asperger syndrome, and pervasive developmental disorders—not otherwise specified. Although these disorders vary in severity (from mental retardation to normal range of intelligence), common characteristics include "social impairment, verbal and nonverbal communication deficits, and stereotypic behaviors and restricted range of interests" (Myles & Adreon, 2001–2002, p. 3).

Kanner described autism in 1943 (Meyer, 2001–2002). The *DSM–IV–TR* (APA, 2000) describes the primary features of autism as "the presence of markedly abnormal or impaired development in social interaction and communication and a markedly restricted repertoire of activity and interests" (p. 70).

Asperger syndrome (AS) was identified 1944 by the Austrian physician for whom it is named. Asperger noted that although AS is similar to autism, it differs in several respects. For example, unlike autism, AS seems to present itself later and does not seem to result in delayed speech; however, motor problems are more prevalent. The *DSM–IV–TR* (2000) describes the primary features of AS as

> severe and sustained impairment in social interaction and the development of restricted, repetitive patterns of behavior, interests, and activities. In contrast to Autistic Disorder, there are no clinically significant delays or deviance in language acquisition, although more subtle aspects of social communication may be affected. In addition, during the first 3 years of life, there are no clinically significant delays in cognitive development as manifested by expressing normal curiosity about the environment or in the acquisition of age-appropriate learning skills and adaptive behaviors (other than social interaction). (p. 80)

Children and youth with AS engage in many socially off-putting behaviors such as standing or sitting too close to people, carrying on one-sided conversations that focus on restricted topics (i.e., weather, maps, transportation timetables, facts about TV stations), and making inappropriate comments (Klin, Volkmar, Sparrow, Cicchetti, & Rourke, 1995; Marks et al., 1999). In addition, they are unable to read nonverbal cues and have difficulty recognizing and understanding others' emotions (Marks et al., 1999).

## Emotional/Behavioral Disorders

Children and youth with emotional/behavior disorders (E/BD) in schools account for 10% of the school-aged population (Heward, 2003). The problems in social–emotional skills for this group are widely acknowledged (Center & Wascom, 1987; Connolly, 1987; Gresham et al., 2001; Hallahan & Kauffman, 2003; Hollinger, 1987; Lane et al., 2003; Lopez et al., 1996; Nickerson & Brosof, 2003; Panacek & Dunlap, 2003; Panella & Henggeler, 1986; Rahill & Teglasi, 2003; Sabornie & Kauffman, 1985; P. J. Schloss, C. N. Schloss, Wood, & Kiehl, 1986; Schonert-Reichi, 1993; Scott & Nelson, 1998).

Kauffman (2001) defined children and youth with E/BD as "those who chronically and markedly respond to their environment in socially unacceptable and/or personally unsatisfying ways" (p. 23). Merrell and Gimpel (1998) reported that "social skills deficits . . . tend to be more pronounced with [E/BD] children than with any other educational group" (p. 50). One of the characteristics, "an inability to build or maintain satisfactory relationships with peers and teachers," is part of the definition that public schools use to identify students as E/BD.

Children and youth with E/BD are often described as falling at either end of the behavioral continuum. That is, they engage in externalizing behaviors such as verbal and/or physical aggression, or in internalizing behaviors such as withdrawal or anxiety (Hallahan & Kauffman, 2003). Both externalizing and internalizing behaviors may interfere with learning and using social–emotional skills, as well as limit opportunities for the individual to practice social–emotional skills (Schonert-Reichi, 1993). Internalizers tend to be neglected by peers and teachers because of their withdrawn behaviors, and externalizers usually are regarded negatively by teachers and outwardly rejected by peers (Schonert-Reichi, 1993).

## Learning Disabilities

Children and youth with learning disabilities (LD) make up the largest number of students with disabilities. Although the federal definition and criteria used to identify LD in public schools do not explicitly address their social–emotional problems, it is well known that they are less socially skilled and less well accepted by peers than nondisabled students. In 1974, Tanis Bryan's article, "Peer Popularity of Learning Disabled Children," promoted interest beyond the academic problems of children and youth with LD (Donahue & Wong, 2002). The resulting body of research has offered convincing evidence that children and youth with LD are less well accepted by their peers (e.g., Coleman, McHam, & Minnett, 1992; L. K. Elksnin, 1989; Gresham, 1992; Olmeda & Trent, 2003; Reiff & Gerber, 1990; Sabornie, Kauffman, Ellis, Marshall, & Elksnin, 1988; Swanson & Malone, 1992; Toro, Weissberg, Guare, & Liebenstein, 1990; Vaughn & Hager, 1994; Vaughn & Hogan, 1994; Vaughn, Zaragoza, Hogan, & Walker, 1993).

The poorly developed social–emotional skills of children and youth with LD may account for their rejection by peers and others (Bryan, 1994; Bryan, Burstein, & Ergul, 2004; Court & Givon, 2003; Gresham, MacMillan, & Bocian, 1996; Gresham et al., 2001; Kuhne & Wiener, 2000; Lopez et al., 1996; Margalit, 1998; McIntosh, Vaughn, & Zaragoza, 1991; Sabornie, 1994; Wiener & Harris, 1997; Wiener & Tardif, 2004). Several researchers estimate that 75% of children and youth with LD have social–emotional problems (Kavale & Forness, 1996; LaGreca & Vaughn, 1992). After conducting an extensive review of the literature, Bender and Wall (1994) concluded that children and youth with LD exhibited deficits in social competence, had difficulty establishing interpersonal relationships with peers, and experienced adult maladjustment related to social–emotional skills problems.

The reasons for the social–emotional problems of children and youth with LD are less clear (L. K. Elksnin & N. Elksnin, 2004). Possible explanations include

▶ poor language and communication skills (Bryan, Donahue, Pearl, & Sturm, 1981; Donahue & Bryan, 1983; Mathinos, 1991; Vallance, Cummings, & Humphries, 1998);

▶ difficulty recognizing and understanding others' emotions (Stone & LaGreca, 1983; Wiig & Harris, 1974);

▶ cognitive processing and social–emotional problem-solving difficulties (Conte & Andrews, 1993; Hartas & Donahue, 1997; Tur-Kaspa & Bryan, 1995);

▶ central nervous system dysfunction (Denckla, 1986; Little, 1993; Rourke, 1987; Vogel & Forness, 1992);

▶ co-morbid psychiatric disorders such as ADHD, depression, and dysthymia (Forness, Kavale, San Miguel, & Bauman, 1998; San Miguel, Forness, & Kavale, 1996);

▶ academic problems and educational isolation that produce social–emotional problems as a side effect (LaGreca & Stone, 1990; Siperstein & Bak, 1988; Siperstein & Rickards, 2004);

▶ history of repeated failure and low self-esteem. (Vogel & Forness, 1992)

## Nonverbal Learning Disabilities

The field of learning disabilities initially focused on academic difficulties. More recently, neuropsychologists have identified nonverbal learning disabilities (NLD), a subset of LD, thereby expanding the notion of LD beyond academic performance (Rourke, 1989, 1991; Rourke & Fuerst, 1991, 1992). Other terms used for the condition include *right-hemisphere learning disabilities* (as nonverbal communication is governed by the right hemisphere of the brain), *visual–spatial and graphomotor learning disabilities,* and *social–emotional learning disabilities.*

Telzrow and Bonar (2002) have estimated that approximately one third of children and youth with LD also have nonverbal learning disabilities. They identified characteristics of NLD as

- ▶ stronger verbal than perceptual cognitive skills,
- ▶ weak psychomotor and perceptual motor skills,
- ▶ deficiency in arithmetic,
- ▶ difficulty with novel and complex tasks,
- ▶ poor problem-solving skills,
- ▶ social and interpersonal deficits. (p. 9)

Examples of social–emotional problems within this population include misinterpreting social cues, speaking in a mechanical, "robot-like" fashion, being impulsive and inappropriately familiar, failing to "get the joke" or recognize sarcasm, and exhibiting limited self-awareness (Telzrow & Bonar, 2002). Morris (2002) reported that children with NLD also had problems being empathetic, talking and playing with peers, working in groups, managing frustration, and resolving conflict. The overriding difficulty faced by individuals with NLD is their inability to pick up on nonverbal cues such as facial expression, posture, gaze, gesture, and tone of voice, which are so essential to effective interpersonal communication. (See Chapter Three for strategies for teaching nonverbal skills.)

## Mental Retardation and Developmental Disabilities

Greenspan and Granfield (1992) consider an individual's ability "to perform certain crucial social roles (e.g., worker, friend, neighbor) more than ability to master academic tasks" (p. 443) as the most important consideration when diagnosing *mental retardation/development disabilities* (MR/DD). To make a diagnosis of mental retardation, the American Association on Mental Retardation (AAMR, 1992) requires limitations in two or more adaptive skill areas, including social skills, in addition to low cognitive ability. The AAMR defines social skills as

> skills related to social exchanges with other individuals, including initiating, interacting, and terminating interaction with others; receiving and responding to pertinent situational cues; recognizing feelings; providing positive and negative feedback; regulating one's own behavior; being aware of peers and peer acceptance; gauging the amount and type of interaction with others; assisting others; forming and fostering of friendships and love; coping with demands from others; making choices; sharing; understanding honesty and fairness; controlling impulses; conforming conduct to laws. (AAMR, 1992, p. 40)

The problems with social–emotional skills of children and youth with MR/DD are well known (Gresham et al., 2001; Merrell & Gimpel, 1998). Briefly, these children often have difficulty making friends and tend to be less well accepted than their typically achieving peers (Freeman & Alkin, 2000; Gresham et al., 1996). Reasons for their problems in this area may be attributable to cognitive deficits related to social, practical, and conceptual intelligence, and in information processing (Greenspan & Granfield, 1992; Gumpel, 1994; Margalit, 1993, 1995; Moffatt, Hanley-Maxwell, & Donnellan, 1995).

# ► Social–Emotional Skills Interventions

Considering the importance of social–emotional competence, the good news is that these skills can be taught. A 1996 Public Agenda Survey reported that 80% of teachers thought it was "absolutely essential" to teach good work habits, honesty, and tolerance. Overwhelmingly, parents of children with disabilities rank developing social relationships as the number-one skill they want their children to learn in early childhood programs, placing social–emotional skills above academic skills (Strain & Smith, 1996).

Elliott and Gresham (1993) have described three approaches to teaching social–emotional skills:

1. The *operant approach* teaches social–emotional skills through direct instruction and reinforcement of skill use.
2. The *social learning theory* approach uses modeling, role playing, and self-instruction to focus on observable behaviors and mediational processes.
3. The *cognitive–behavioral approach* teaches social–problem strategies.

Many commercial curricula combine all three approaches (L. K. Elksnin & N. Elksnin, 1995). Social–emotional intervention outcomes can be enhanced by

▶ matching treatment to specific social–emotional skills deficits (Gresham, 1998a, 1998b; Gresham et al., 2001);
▶ adopting interventions that combine modeling, coaching, and reinforcement (Gresham et al., 2001);
▶ delivering intervention of sufficient quantity and intensity (i.e., "more is more") (Forness & Kavale, 1996; Gresham et al., 2001; McIntosh et al., 1991);
▶ teaching social–emotional skills incidentally to promote generalization (Gresham, 1998a, 1998b; Kavale & Mostert, 2004).

# ► Chapter Summary

A person who is socially competent reads social situations accurately, selects the appropriate social–emotional skill to use, and is motivated to use the skill.

Social–emotional skills consist of specific functions and behaviors—physiological, cognitive, and overt motor—that allow people to perform competently in social situations.

Emotional intelligence, or emotional literacy, includes self-awareness, self-regulation, motivation, empathy, and social skills, and is regarded as essential for life success. Social–emotional learning programs were designed to teach emotional intelligence domains in order to prevent behaviors such as drug and alcohol use, violent behavior, and so forth.

Skills-specific and problem-solving approaches are two ways of teaching social–emotional skills. Skills-specific approaches teach each social–emotional skill by modeling each step, allowing children opportunities to practice, and rewarding children for using skills throughout the day. Children are taught to solve interpersonal problems using problem-solving routines.

It is crucial that children learn social–emotional skills if they are to succeed in school and in life. Children who lack these skills frequently are rejected by others and are at risk for developing mental health problems that persist during adulthood. As adults, the majority of them are underemployed or unemployed. Children and youth who are likely to have social–emotional problems include those with disabilities such as attention deficit/hyperactivity disorder, autism spectrum disorders, emotional/behavioral disorders, learning disabilities, and mental retardation.

Fortunately, children and youth can become socially competent through social–emotional skills instruction grounded in operant, social learning and cognitive-behavioral theories.

# CHAPTER 2

# Identifying Children and Youth Who Need Social–Emotional Skills Instruction

## Goals of This Chapter

In this chapter you will learn

▶ the difference between social–emotional skills acquisition, performance, and fluency problems

▶ the problem behaviors that interfere with acquisition and performance of social–emotional skills

▶ different approaches to assessing social–emotional skills and problem behaviors

▶ the importance of linking social–emotional skills assessment and intervention

# Terms to Know

acquisition problems

archival reviews

behavior intervention plans (BIPs)

behavioral observation

fluency problems

functional behavioral assessment (FBA)

interfering behaviors

interviews

performance problems

rating scales

role-play assessment

sociometric techniques

tests of emotional intelligence

# Thad

*An only child, 3-year-old Thad was wreaking havoc in his preschool class. His classmates, after repeatedly being poked, hit, pinched, and bitten, stayed clear of him. Thad's teacher, Sally, observed that he desperately wanted to play with his peers, but that he had no idea how to go about it. Thad would go to an activity center and grab objects and toys away from other children, then act surprised when they moved away and ignored him. Infuriated, he sought their attention by hitting or pinching them. Sally planned to meet with Thad's mom, Rita, to tell her about the difficulties in managing her son. If Thad's behavior didn't improve, Sally intended to recommend that he be removed from the preschool.*

# Sarah

*Sarah's mom, Julie, met with her seventh-grade teacher, Marcia, to talk about her daughter's difficulty in making friends. The family had moved 3 months earlier from a small town where they lived for more than 15 years. Mount Airy was the only home Sarah had known, and she terribly missed her friends, teachers, and school. Sarah had always been a quiet child, shy and reticent, but she had a likeable personality and an innate sense of fairness. These traits endeared her to her peers once they took time to get to know her. When her family lived in Mount Airy, Sarah was one of the most popular girls in her class. It just took Sarah a bit of time to connect with people. Julie hoped that she and the teacher could come up with a plan to help Sarah make a better transition from Mount Airy to Vista Park Middle School.*

# David

*Thirteen-year-old David dreaded going to school. He had a reading disability, which made middle school extremely difficult for him. But his reading problems paled in comparison to his difficulty in being accepted by the boys in the seventh grade. He kept trying to make friends, but his overtures were met with ridicule. David's LD teacher, Ricardo, ached for David and wanted to develop an intervention plan that would help him get along better with his classmates. This afternoon, Ricardo, three of David's teachers, and David's parents were scheduled to meet to put their heads together and come up with a plan for David.*

A s illustrated in the vignettes, Thad, Sarah, and David are all having social–emotional problems. They each require an intervention designed to help them get along with their peers. Before planning social–emotional skills intervention, however, the *reason* for the child's social–emotional skills problems must be determined. Knowing *why* a child fails to engage in appropriate social–emotional behavior will determine the instructional strategies to be used.

We begin this chapter by discussing types of social–emotional skills problems, and review approaches used to assess social–emotional skills. We describe functional behavioral assessment (FBA), which incorporates many assessment approaches. Teachers must become familiar with different assessment approaches because rarely will a single approach answer all of our questions about a child's social–emotional skills, nor will one approach provide sufficient information about behaviors that interfere with social–emotional competence. Reliable assessment of social–emotional skills requires use of multiple assessment approaches by multiple evaluators across a variety of settings (L. K. Elksnin & N. Elksnin, 1997; Martin, 1988).

## ► Types of Social–Emotional Problems

As shown in Figure 2.1, social–emotional problems are of two major types: acquisition problems and performance problems (Gresham, 1981, 1990, 2001). On the one hand, children and youth with *acquisition problems* do not have the social–emotional skills necessary to interact appropriately with others. Children and youth with *performance problems*, on the other hand, know how to use social–emotional skills but choose not to do so. Either type of problem may occur because of *interfering behaviors* (Elliott & Gresham, 1991).

### Acquisition Problems

It is critical to determine which of the two types of problems—the child *cannot* perform or the child *chooses not* to perform the social–emotional skill—is being demonstrated. The "can't" versus "won't" distinction is important because it dictates the instructional approach to be used. Children and youth with acquisition problems may not be able to perform the skill at all, perform only part of the skill, or not be able to perform the skill in a convincing manner.

For example, a child does not know how to negotiate and instead relies on physical force to get his way. Another child performs only some of the steps of the skill "accepting criticism," listening to what the other person has to say but not giving her side when appropriate. Or a child has learned all of the steps to deal with teasing but does not use a "brave" voice when he asks his classmates to stop the teasing. In each case, our task as teachers and parents is to teach the child the skill.

Chapter Six presents a five-step strategy for teaching social–emotional skills. Social–emotional skills are effectively taught using modeling, role playing, coaching, and feedback. Many children and adolescents with acquisition problems benefit

| | Acquisition Problem | Performance Problem |
|---|---|---|
| **Interfering problem behaviors absent** | Social–emotional skills acquisition problem <br><br> ("Can't do") | Social–emotional skills performance problem <br><br> ("Won't do") |
| **Interfering problem behaviors present** | Social–emotional skills acquisition problem with interfering problem behaviors | Social–emotional skills performance problem with interfering problem behaviors |

Source: *Social Skills Problems: Acquisition or Performance Deficits?* in *Best Practices in Social Skills Training* (1990, p. 61), by F. M. Gresham, in *Best Practices in School Psychology—II* (pp. 695–709) by A. Thomas and J. Grimes (Eds.) (Washington, DC: National Association of School Psychologists). Copyright 1990 by the National Association of School Psychologists, Bethesda, MD. Reprinted with permission of the publisher.

**FIGURE 2.1** ▶ Types of Social–Emotional Skills Problems

from direct instruction of social skills in small groups (Elliott & Gresham, 1993; Gresham et al., 2001; Gumpel & Golan, 2000). In addition to teaching specific skills instruction, children and youth with acquisition problems often are aided by learning social–emotional problem-solving strategies, and by having teachers and parents conduct social-skills autopsies. Table 2.1 offers examples of interventions designed to address acquisition problems.

## Performance Problems

Children and youth who have performance problems know how to use a skill but for some reason choose not to do so. Rather than teach the skill, we must create situations that encourage children to use the skill. Performance problems require that teachers and parents manipulate events that occur *before* a child performs the social–emotional skill (i.e., *antecedents*) and events that *follow* skill performance (i.e., *consequences*) (Elliott & Gresham, 1991). As seen in Table 2.1, *antecedent interventions* include peer mediation, incidental teaching, and self-management strategies. An example of a *consequence intervention* is a behavior contract. Finally,

**TABLE 2.1** ►Social–Emotional Problems and Examples of Interventions

| Problems | Interventions |
| --- | --- |

**Acquisition**    *Teach social skill*[1] (6)

1. Define/describe skill.
2. Provide rationale for learning skill.
3. Describe situations in which to use skill.
4. Teach skill:
   a. Teacher/parent models skill.
   b. Students role-play skill.
   c. Teacher/parent coaches child.
   d. Teacher/parent provides feedback.

*Teach social–emotional problem-solving routines*[2] (4, 8)

1. STOP and CALM DOWN.
2. Identify the PROBLEM.
3. Identify the FEELINGS.
4. Decide on a GOAL.
5. Think of lots of SOLUTIONS.
6. Think about the CONSEQUENCES.
7. Choose the BEST solution.
8. Make a good PLAN.
9. TRY MY plan.
10. EVALUATE—How did I do?
11. If you need to, TRY AGAIN.

*Conduct social skill autopsy by discussing:* (4, 8, 9)

1. What the child did or said.
2. What happened when he/she did or said it.
3. The direction (i.e., positive, negative, neutral) of the social outcome, and what the child will do in a similar situation.

**Performance**    *Antecedent Interventions*

1. Use *peer mediation*—recruit peers to initiate, prompt social interaction, and to reinforce appropriate social-emotional responses. (5)
2. Use *incidental teaching*—capitalize on "teaching opportunities." (4, 8, 9)
3. Use *self-management* strategies—teach child to self-talk, self-monitor, self-reinforce, self-record. (6, 9)

*Consequence Interventions*[2]

1. Use *behavior contracts*—specify what student must do/not do to result in positive/negative consequences; have everyone sign/date contract, renegotiate contract if necessary.

Note: Numbers in parentheses designate the chapter(s) in this book that focus on these interventions.

**TABLE 2.1** ▶(Continued)

| Problems | Interventions |
|---|---|
| **Performance** | *Reinforcement-Based Strategies* (7, 8, 9)<br>1. Identify social reinforcers, reinforce frequently and immediately, decrease reinforcement as skill develops.<br>2. Teach social–emotional skills that are highly valued by others.<br>3. Teach others to reinforce child.<br>4. Teach child to recruit own reinforcement.<br>5. Teach child to self-reinforce. |
| **Intefering Behaviors** | *Applied Behavior Analysis Strategies* [2]<br>1. Use *differential reinforcement:* Reinforce progressively lower rates of the problem behavior.<br>2. Use *response cost:* Give points when appropriate behavior occurs, immediately take away points following inappropriate behavior, allow child to exchange points for reinforcers on daily/weekly basis.<br>3. Use *positive practice:* Have child practice appropriate behavior immediately after student engages in inappropriate behavior.<br><br>*Anger Management Strategies* [3] (3)<br>1. Stop and count to 10.<br>2. Think about your choices:<br>  a. Tell the person in words why you are angry.<br>  b. Walk away for now.<br>  c. Do a relaxation exercise.<br>3. Act out your best choice. |
| **Fluency Problems** | *Provide practice opportunities:* (5, 6, 8, 9)<br>1. Include unstructured classroom activities.<br>2. Invite other children home.<br>3. Encourage child to participate in school/home extracurricular activities.<br>4. Assign homework to promote skill practice.<br><br>*Provide specific informative feedback:* (5, 6, 8, 9)<br>1. Provide feedback after role play and after skill is performed.<br>2. Teach peers, parents, teachers, coworkers, employers, and supervisors to provide feedback. |

[1] *The PATHS (Promoting Alternative Thinking Strategies) Curriculum* by C. A. Kusche and M. T. Greenberg (Seattle: Developmental Research and Programs, 1994).

[2] It is beyond the scope of this text to provide a complete discussion of applied behavior analysis principles. The reader is urged to consult these texts: *Applied Behavior Analysis for Teachers* (6th ed.), by P. A. Alberto and A. C. Troutman (Englewood, NJ: Merrill/Prentice Hall, 2003); *Social Skills Intervention Guide: Practical Strategies for Social Skills Training,* by S. N. Elliott and F. M. Gresham (Circle Pines, MN: American Guidance Service, 1991).

[3] *Skillstreaming the Elementary School Child* (rev. ed.), by E. McGinnis and A. P. Goldstein (Champaign, IL: Research Press, 1997).

children and youth with performance problems respond to reinforcement-based strategies such as those listed in Table 2.1.

## Interfering Behaviors

Interfering behaviors range on a continuum from *internalizing behaviors* such as anxiety, withdrawal, and depression to *externalizing behaviors* such as inattention, aggression, impulsivity, and hyperactivity. For example, many highly anxious children and youth avoid social situations, thereby decreasing their opportunity to learn appropriate interaction skills. Similarly, children who are inattentive may not learn appropriate social–emotional behaviors through observing competent peers and adults.

When behaviors interfere with acquisition or performance of social–emotional skills, we must address the interfering behaviors while teaching social–emotional skills. As shown in Table 2.1, interfering behaviors may be reduced or eliminated through applied behavior analysis strategies such as differential reinforcement of lower rates of behavior, response cost, positive practice, and timeout (Elliott & Gresham, 1993). In addition, the failure of many children and youth to control their anger interferes with their performance of social–emotional skills. Anger-control strategies can go a long way toward helping them manage their angry feelings and use more socially appropriate ways of expressing their feelings. These strategies are described in Chapter Three.

## Fluency

In addition to acquisition and performance problems, some children and youth have difficulty performing a social–emotional skill in an effortless, polished manner (Gresham et al., 2001). In this case, the child knows how to perform the skill and recognizes when it is appropriate to use the skill but performs it gracelessly.

As shown in Table 2.1, fluency problems are addressed by providing plenty of practice opportunities and by giving children specific, informative feedback detailing what they are doing well and what they are doing not so well. Teachers and parents can help by making sure children practice the skills until they reach a level of acceptable fluency. Just as musicians need plenty of rehearsal time to learn a new piece, children and youth need time to practice their newly acquired social–emotional skills.

The *Social Skills Intervention Guide* (Elliott & Gresham, 1991) is an excellent resource for additional intervention strategies for addressing acquisition and performance problems, and problem behaviors that interfere with acquisition and performance of social–emotional skills.

In the following discussion, we review assessment approaches, including rating scales, tests of emotional intelligence and nonverbal communication abilities, sociometric techniques, interviews, behavioral observation, role-play assessment, and functional behavioral assessment.

## ▶ Rating Scales

# David

*David's teachers and his parents invited the school psychologist, Tom, to meet with them to discuss David's social–emotional problems. Tom suggested that results from a social skills rating scale would help the team gain greater understanding of David's skills. The* Social Skills Rating System (SSRS) *would be a good choice because it includes rating scales that David, his teachers, and his parents could complete.*

*After the scales were completed, Tom scored each scale and related the results to the team. David earned social skills percentile rankings of 12, 15, and 20 on the teacher questionnaires, 25 on the parent questionnaire, and 8 on the student questionnaire. Tom explained that a percentile rank of 12 meant that 88% of students in the seventh grade earned a score higher than David's score. The scores indicated that David's rating of his social skills was lower than either his teachers' or his parents' ratings, and that David's parents rated his skills higher than the other raters. David's scores from all ratings indicated that he had more internalizing problem behaviors such as anxiety, sadness, loneliness, and poor self-esteem than other children his age. Further, his academic competence ratings were below average for children of his grade level.*

*Tom and the other members of the team decided that the ratings gave them a good place to start. They also recognized that they needed to gather more information about David's social–emotional skills.*

When using a rating scale, teachers, parents, or students make qualitative judgments about the extent to which a given behavior occurs. For example, the Preschool and Kindergarten Behavior Scales–2 (Merrell, 2002a) (shown as Figure 2.2) asks the rater to assess a young child's behavior as occurring "never," "rarely," "sometimes," or "often." Ratings of social behaviors such as sharing, cooperating, and apologizing, and problem behaviors such as teasing, bullying, and complaining are converted to standard scores and percentile ranks to compare the ratings to those of other children of the same age. Information collected using rating scales can be considered as "summaries of observations of the relative frequency of specific behaviors" (Gresham, 2001, p. 339). Following is a discussion of several rating scales and checklists designed to assess children's social–emotional skills and problem behaviors.

### Social–Emotional Skills Rating Scales

#### *Matson Evaluation of Social Skills with Youngsters–2d ed*

The MESSY (Matson, 1994) is designed to assess the use of appropriate and inappropriate social skills by children and youth ages 8 to 18. It consists of a 62-item

**PKBS-2**      **Summary/Response Form**

## Preschool and Kindergarten Behavior Scales
Second
Edition

| Section I. Child Information | Section II. Rater Information |
|---|---|

Child's Name _Austin Green_

Rated By _Maria Aguilar_

Age: __5__ Years __2__ Months   Sex: M ☑   F ☐

Relationship to Child _Head Start Teacher_

Is this child receiving services in a school or in a school-related program (e.g., Preschool, Head Start)? _✓_ Yes _____ No

Date Completed _____

If Yes, what is the name of the school and the program?
_Washington Heights Head Start_

List the setting(s) in which you observe or interact with this child: _As his teacher at Washington Heights_ _Head Start Program_

If this child has a disability, please list the special education service category or classification: _____

_____

_____

_____

### Section III. Instructions and Scales

Please rate the child on each of the items on pages 2 and 3 of this rating form. Ratings should be based on your observations of this child's behavior **during the past 3 months.** The rating points after each item appear in the following format:

|  | Never | Rarely | Sometimes | Often |
|---|---|---|---|---|
|  | 0 | 1 | 2 | 3 |

**Never**      If the child does not exhibit a specified behavior, or if you have not had an opportunity to observe it, circle 0, which indicates *Never.*

**Rarely**      If the child exhibits a specified behavior or characteristic, but only very infrequently, circle 1, which indicates *Rarely.*

**Sometimes**      If the child occasionally exhibits a specified behavior characteristic, circle 2, which indicates *Sometimes.*

**Often**      If the child frequently exhibits a specified behavior or characteristic, circle 3, which indicates *Often.*

Please complete all items and do not circle between numbers.

Source: *Page 1 of a Sample PKBS–2 Summary/Response Form* from the *Preschool and Kindergarten Behavior Scales (2d ed.) Examiner's Manual* (p. 15), by K. W. Merrell (Austin, TX: Pro-Ed). Copyright © 2002 by Pro-Ed Inc. Reprinted with permission.

**FIGURE 2.2** ▶Summary/Response Form, Face Page of the PKBS–2

Self-Rating scale to be completed by the child, and a 64-item Teacher Rating scale. Practitioners and researchers can use the MESSY to identify children and youth with social–emotional skills problems and to determine the effectiveness of social–emotional skills intervention.

The Self-Rating includes five subscales: appropriate social skills, inappropriate assertiveness, impulsive, overconfident, and jealous. Nine items form a "miscellaneous items scale." Children are asked to rate each item as "a little," "not at all," "very much," "somewhat like me," or as like me "much of the time." Teachers evaluate appropriate and inappropriate social skills using the same 5-point scale.

### Preschool and Kindergarten Behavior Scale–2

The PKBS–2 (Merrell, 2002a) may be used to screen young children who are at risk for serious behavioral, social, and emotional problems, as well as to obtain information for planning effective interventions. The Social Skills scale consists of 31 items grouped within three subscales: social cooperation, social interaction, and social independence. The Problem Behavior scale consists of 38 items grouped within externalizing and internalizing subscales. Home and school raters who know the child well determine if he or she exhibits the behaviors described "never," "rarely," "sometimes," or "often" (see Figure 2.2).

### School Social Behavior Scales–2

Like the PKBS, the SSBS–2 (Merrell, 2002b) is designed to screen at-risk children and to identify children needing social skills intervention. The SSBS–2 is comprised of 64 items in two scales. The Social Competence Scale (Scale A) has three subscales composed of 32 items total: Peer Relations (14 items that describe behaviors needed to establish positive peer relationships), Self-Management/Compliance (10 items that describe behaviors related to self-constraint, cooperation, and compliance that are valued by teachers), and Academic Behavior (8 items that describe behaviors related to academic competence). Scale B, Antisocial Behavior, has 32 items with the subscales of Hostile/Irritable (14 items), Antisocial/Aggressive (10 items), and Defiant/Disruptive (8 items), which includes items that describe behaviors that place unreasonable demands on others and interfere with classroom activities.

### Social Behavior Assessment Inventory

The SBAI (Stephens & Arnold, 1992) is designed to complement *Social Skills in the Classroom* (Stephens, 1992), a social skills curriculum implemented using directive teaching. Although the SBAI can be used as a screening instrument, its authors recommend that results be used more appropriately to design social skills interventions. The inventory is composed of 136 social behaviors related to success in school, organized within four scales: Environmental Behaviors, Interpersonal Behaviors, Self-Related Behaviors, and Task-Related Behaviors. Raters use a 4-point scale to determine if the behavior is "not observed/not applicable," "exhibited at an acceptable level," "exhibited at a lower-than-acceptable level," or "never exhibited at an acceptable level."

### Social Competence and Behavior Evaluation–Preschool Edition

The SCBE–PE (LaFreniere & Dumas, 1995) is designed to assess social competence, affective expression, and adjustment problems of children ages 30 to 78 months. The three scales include dichotomous subscales:

Emotional Expression: Depressive–Joyful, Anxious–Secure, Angry–Tolerant
Social Interactions: Isolated–Integrated, Aggressive–Calm, Egotistical–Prosocial
Teacher–Child Relations: Oppositional–Cooperative, Dependent–Autonomous.

The teacher or other child-care professional completes the SCBE–PE by indicating if each item behavior "almost never occurs," "sometimes occurs," "often occurs," or "almost always occurs." Results may be used to identify young children requiring social and behavior intervention, as well as to assess intervention effects.

### Social Skills Rating System

The SSRS (Gresham & Elliott, 1990a, 1990b, 1990c) offers the most comprehensive social–emotional skills rating system available, spanning preschool through high school. The preschool scale of the SSRS has teacher and parent rating scales designed to assess the social skills and problem behaviors of children ages 3 to kindergarten. The 40-item Teacher Form is made up of three social skills subscales—cooperation, assertion, and self-control—and the problem behavior subscales of externalizing and internalizing. The 39-item Parent Form has four social skills subscales—cooperation, assertion, self-control, and responsibility—and the problem behavior subscales of externalizing and internalizing.

The elementary scale has Teacher, Parent, and Student Forms. The 57-item Teacher Form consists of three scales designed to provide a comprehensive social skills assessment of children in grades 3 through 6. The Social Skills Scale is composed of the cooperation, assertion, and self-control subscales. The Problem Behavior subscales include externalizing, internalizing, and hyperactivity. Academic Competence is determined by having the teacher rate the student in the lowest 10%, next lowest 20%, middle 40%, next highest 20%, or highest 10%, after reading academic-performance items such as "compared with other children in my classroom, the *overall academic performance* [authors' emphasis] of this child . . . ." The Parent Form has a responsibility subscale, in addition to the Social Skills subscales of cooperation, assertion, and self-control. Finally, the Student Form is a self-assessment scale with cooperation, assertion, empathy, and self-control subscales. Only the Student Form has an empathy subscale.

The secondary scale, designed to assess students in grades 7 through 12, is similar in construction to the elementary version. For example, the Teacher and Parent forms have the same Social Skills and Problem Behaviors subscales, except that the secondary scale does not include hyperactivity subscales. The Student form consists of the same subscales as the elementary form and highly similar developmentally appropriate items.

The Social Skills Rating System is unique in several respects: The system enables educators to obtain information from a variety of sources across a variety of settings. Academic performance and problem behaviors are assessed in addition to social skills. An Assessment–Intervention Record enables evaluators to summarize results from teacher, parent, and student ratings to identify social skills strengths, social skills performance deficits, social skills acquisition deficits, and problem behavior. The manual contains detailed information about how to use assessment results to plan instruction. *The Social Skills Intervention Guide: Practical Strategies for Social Skills Training* (Elliott & Gresham, 1991), which may be purchased separately, complements the preschool, elementary, and secondary scales.

### Waksman Social Skills Rating Scale

The WSSRS (S. A. Waksman, 1985) assesses a specific behavior cluster—assertiveness—generally thought to be related to social competence. The Aggression and Passive domains have 29 total items. Examples of items in the Aggression domain are "speaks too loudly," "hits rather than touches," and "speaks in demanding voice." Items in the passive domain include "dull or flattened voice," "stands too far when speaking," and "avoids joining groups." Individuals who are familiar with the student rate each behavior on a scale of 0 ("never") to 3 ("usually"). The WSSRS may be used for screening purposes, as well as to identify IEP objectives.

### Walker–McConnell Scale of Social Competence and School Adjustment

The WMS (Walker & McConnell, 1995a, 1995b) have elementary and secondary scales. The elementary scale, designed to assess children in grades K through 6, consists of 43 items forming three subscales. The subscale Teacher-Preferred Social Behaviors covers behaviors that classroom teachers highly value, such as "shows sympathy for others," "cooperates with peers in group activities or situations," and "controls temper." Items in the Peer-Preferred Social Behavior subscale describe interpersonal behaviors regarded by peers as essential in free-play settings: "plays or talks with peers for extended periods of time," "voluntarily provides assistance to peers who require it," and "plays games and activities at recess skillfully." Finally, the School Adjustment Behavior subscale is made up of items reflective of behaviors that teachers regard as essential for classroom success, such as "displays independent study skills," "attends to assigned tasks," and "listens carefully to teacher directions and instructions for assignments." The scale may be used to identify children who require social skills instruction, identify specific social skills deficits, and evaluate effects of intervention efforts. A 6- to 8-week observation period should occur before teachers complete the scale.

The adolescent scale, designed to assess students in grades 7 through 12, consists of 53 items that form four subscales. Three subscales—Self-Control, Peer Relations, and School Adjustment—are similar to those included in the elementary scale. The fourth subscale, Empathy, consists of items designed to assess the adolescent's concern

**TABLE 2.2** ►Social–Emotional Rating Scales

| Scale | Author(s)/Year | Grade/Age | Rater |
|---|---|---|---|
| Matson Evaluation of Social Skills with Youngsters | Matson (1994) | ages 8–18 | Teacher Self |
| Preschool and Kindergarten Behavior Scale–2 | Merrell (2002a) | ages 3–6 | Teacher Parent Others |
| School Social Behaviors Scales–2 | Merrell (2002b) | ages 5–18 | Teacher |
| Social Behavior Assessment Inventory | Stephens & Arnold (1992) | grades K–9 | Teacher |
| Social Competence and Behavior Evaluation–Preschool Edition | LaFreniere & Dumas (1995) | ages 30–78 months | Teacher or Child–Care Professional |
| Social Skills Rating System–Preschool | Gresham & Elliott (1990b) | ages 3–5 | Teacher Parent |
| Social Skills Rating System–Elementary | Gresham & Elliott (1990a) | grades K–6 | Teacher Parent Self |
| Social Skills Rating System–Secondary | Gresham & Elliott (1990c) | grades 7–12 | Teacher Parent Self |
| The Waksman Social Skills Rating Scale | Waksman (1985) | grades K–12 | Teacher |
| Walker–McConnell Scale of Social Competence and Social Adjustment–Elementary | Walker & McConnell (1995b) | grades K–6 | Teacher |
| Walker–McConnell Scale of Social Competence and Social Adjustment–Adolescent | Walker & McConnell (1995a) | grades 7–12 | Teacher |

for others: "is considerate of the feelings of others," "shows sympathy for others," and "is sensitive to the needs of others." Table 2.2 lists social–emotional skills rating scales.

### Problem-Behavior Rating Scales

Many of the rating scales just reviewed were designed to assess prosocial, adaptive skills. Of interest are also behaviors that may interfere with social–emotional skills acquisition or performance. Problem-behavior rating scales assess whether a child does or does not exhibit antisocial, maladaptive behaviors. General-purpose scales assess a wide variety of problem behaviors, whereas narrow-spectrum scales focus on a specific maladaptive behavior such as found in attention deficit/hyperactivity disorders or depression (Merrell, 2003). Table 2.3 lists commonly used general-purpose and narrow-spectrum problem behavior rating scales.

**TABLE 2.3** ▶Selected General-Purpose and Narrow-Spectrum Problem Behavior Rating Scales

| Scale | Author(s)/Year | Grade/Age | Rater |
|---|---|---|---|
| Attention Deficit Disorders Evaluation Scales | McCarney (1995a, 1995b) | ages 4–21 | Teacher Parent |
| ADHD Rating Scale–IV | DuPaul, Power, Anastopoulos, & Reid (1998) | ages 5–18 | Teacher Parent |
| Behavior Assessment System for Children | Reynolds & Kamphaus (1992) | ages 4–18 | Teacher Parent |
| Behavior Problem Checklist | Quay & Peterson (1996) | ages 5–16 | Teacher Parent |
| Behavior Rating Profile–2d ed. | Brown & Hammill (1990) | grades 1–12 | Teacher Parent Peer Self |
| Child Behavior Checklist | Achenbach (1991a) | ages 4–18 | Parent Others |
| The Children's Depression Inventory | Kovacs (1991) | ages 6–17 | Self |
| Revised Children's Manifest Anxiety Scale | Reynolds & Richmond (1985) | ages 6–17 | Self |
| Conners' Rating Scales–Revised | Conners (1997) | ages 3–17 | Parent Teacher Self |
| Devereux Behavior Rating Scale–School Form | Naglieri, LeBuffe, & Pfeiffer (1993) | ages 5–18 | Teacher Parent |
| Teacher's Report Form | Achenbach (1991b) | ages 5–18 | Teacher |

## Advantages and Disadvantages of Rating Scales

Rating scales are cost-efficient and time-efficient and allow us to obtain information from a variety of raters such as teachers, parents, employers, and peers (Demaray et al., 1995). Rating scales are particularly useful when the goal is to screen large numbers of students to determine who may benefit from social–emotional skills instruction. These scales provide a place to start before conducting other types of assessment. Thus, the results of rating scales will not pinpoint the *cause* of the social–emotional skills problem. For example, David earned a very low score (i.e., percentile score of 10) on the assertion subscale of the Social Skills Questionnaire of the SSRS, meaning that he earned a score lower than approximately 90% of his grade peers. But, we need more information to determine *why* David is so unassertive. Assessment approaches discussed subsequently help us obtain this information.

# ▶ Tests of Emotional Intelligence

# Sarah

*Sarah's teacher Marcia met with Sarah's other middle school teacher, Julie, as well as Melissa, the school psychologist, to talk about Sarah's difficulty making friends since her move to Vista Park Middle School. Melissa suggested that she administer the BarOn Emotional Quotient Inventory to get an overall idea of Sarah's emotional intelligence (EQ), and that the group meet 2 weeks later to discuss the results.*

*Sarah earned a total EQ standard score of 115, which means that she scored above average compared to other girls her age in areas that make up emotional intelligence. Specifically, the scores on the scales making up her EQ score indicated that she understood her emotions and those of others, was able to respond to stressful situations appropriately, and was good at solving everyday problems. Melissa planned to meet with Sarah to go over the BarOn results.*

## BarOn Emotional Quotient Inventory: Youth Version

The BarOn EQ–i: YV (Bar-On & Parker, 2000) assesses the emotional intelligence of children ages 7 to 18. The inventory shares the same theoretical foundation as the *BarOn Emotional Quotient Inventory* (EQ–I) (Bar-On, 1997), which is widely used with adults. Bar-On and Parker (2000) define emotional intelligence "as an array of emotional, personal, and interpersonal abilities that influence one's overall ability to cope with environmental demands and pressures" (p. 33).

The BarOn EQ–I: YV consists of 60 items that form seven scales:

Intrapersonal Scale (emotional self-awareness, ability to recognize and understand one's feelings, assertiveness, self-regard, self-actualization, and independence)

Interpersonal Scale (empathy, social responsibility, interpersonal relationship)
Adaptability Scale (reality testing, flexibility, problem solving)
Stress Management Scale (stress tolerance, impulse control)
Total EQ
General Mood (optimism, happiness)
Positive Impression (designed to determine if children are creating an exaggerated positive impression of themselves through their responses)

The Intrapersonal, Interpersonal Adaptability, and Stress Management scales are used to determine Total Emotional Intelligence. In addition, the BarOn EQ–I has an Inconsistency Index to determine if the responses are random. The manual includes treatment interventions for improving specific social and emotional skills. For example, BarOn recommends that, if scale scores are low, the child receive the Self Science and PATHS curricula (Kusche & Greenberg, 1994; Stone & Dillehunt, 1978).

## Mayer–Salovey–Caruso Emotional Intelligence Test

The MSCEIT (Mayer, Salovey, & Caruso, 2002) assesses the ability to perform social–emotional tasks and solve emotional problems. Designed to be used with individuals who are 17 years of age and older, the MSCEIT has eight subscales that assess the ability to perceive emotions, use emotions to aid and foster ideas, understand emotions, and manage emotions:

Subtest A (Faces Task): identifies how the assessed person feels based upon facial expression
Subtest B (Facilitation Task): asks the individual to identify moods that are useful when performing tasks such as composing, cooking, creating, and so forth
Subtest C (Changes Task): assesses understanding of how one emotion changes to another emotion (i.e., anger to rage)
Subtest D (Emotional Management Task): asks adolescents to evaluate effects of actions on emotions
Subtest E (Pictures Task): requires identifying emotions expressed by visual images
Subtest F (Sensations Task): asks adolescents to compare emotions to different sensations such as light, color, and temperature
Subtest G (Blends Task): assesses the ability to analyze blends of emotions into parts; for example, the adolescent is asked to identify emotions that combine to produce a feeling of concern
Subtest H (Emotional Relations Task): assesses the ability to make decisions involving other people while taking emotions into account

A scoring service must be used for the MSCEIT. Scores are reported as standard scores and percentiles for total emotional intelligence, experiential emotional intelligence, strategic emotional intelligence, perceiving emotion, facilitating thought, understanding emotion, and for the eight subtests.

# ► Assessing Nonverbal Communication Abilities

## Thad

*Thad's mother, Rita, left the meeting with Thad's preschool teacher, Sally, upset, yet determined to find out why her son had such a difficult time getting along with other children. Rita wasn't surprised to hear about Thad's behavior. She had seen it when other children visited, including Thad's young cousins. Because Thad was an only child, Rita worried that he didn't have as many opportunities as children in large families to interact with other children. But there must be other reasons for Thad's problems, she reasoned. Not all only children hit and punched other kids to get attention.*

*Rita decided to talk to Thad's speech and language pathologist, Maggie, from whom Thad had been receiving speech and language therapy. He had a slight lisp, but the biggest concern of both Rita and Maggie was that he did not have language skills consistent with other children his age. His vocabulary was smaller, and he lacked understanding of important concept words such as "first" and "last," "if" and "then," and "before" and "after."*

*When Maggie and Rita met, Maggie recommended that she administer a test designed to assess nonverbal communication abilities. She explained to Rita, "I'm concerned about Thad's spoken language, but I'm equally concerned about his nonverbal communication skills such as interpreting facial expressions, gestures, and postures of others. It could be that Thad's verbal and nonverbal language problems are making it hard for him to interact with other children appropriately." Rita readily agreed. "Anything that we can do to understand why Thad is having problems gets my vote. Maybe if we understand the reasons for his problems, we can help him."*

In Chapter Three we emphasize the importance of understanding and regulating emotions. Tests designed to assess nonverbal communication abilities should require children and youth to

- ► discriminate among nonverbal cues,
- ► identify the emotions presented in nonverbal communication,
- ► express emotions through various nonverbal channels,
- ► apply nonverbal information to interpret what is happening in diverse conversations. (Nowicki & Duke, 1992, p. 130)

The Diagnostic Analysis of Nonverbal Accuracy (DANVA) (Duke, Nowicki, & Martin, 1996) assesses receptive and expressive nonverbal social abilities. Although the DANVA was designed as a formal test for professionals to use, teachers and parents can adapt it to informally assess children's emotional understanding. The child's responses on the DANVA are compared to responses of other children of the same age. The DANVA includes nine subtests:

1. *Understanding facial expressions.* The child is shown 24 photos of adults and 24 photos of children depicting emotions of happiness, sadness, anger, or fear at low and high levels of intensity. The child matches each photo with one of the four emotions.

2. *Sending facial expressions.* The child is given a situation and asked to show one of four emotions (happy, sad, angry, fearful) while being videotaped. The examiner uses the videotape to rate the child's performance on a scale of 1 (not accurate) to 3 (very accurate).

3. *Understanding gestures.* The child identifies the emotions of anger, fear, happiness, or sadness depicted in photographs of a model making gestures.

4. *Sending gestures.* The child depicts one of the four emotions (i.e., anger, fear, happiness, or sadness) using arms and hands during 12 trials of three of each of the four emotions. Depictions are taped and later rated for accuracy.

5. *Understanding tone of voice.* The child is presented with an audiotape of another child saying, "I am going out of the room now, and I will be back later." During 16 trials, the child actor varies the tone of voice to indicate one of the four emotions (anger, fear, happiness, sadness). The child must match voice tone with the appropriate emotion.

6. *Sending tone of voice.* The child is instructed to say, "I am going to get my bike now and go for a ride" in an appropriate tone of voice when presented with eight situations representing two of each of the four emotions. The child's recorded responses are rated in terms of appropriateness.

7. *Understanding postures.* Each of the four emotions is presented as three photos of a model depicting various postures. The child is asked to match each posture with one of the four emotions.

8. *Sending postures.* Each of the four emotions is presented as three photos of a model depicting various postures. The child is asked to match each posture with one of the four emotions.

9. *Sending personal space.* The child is given a drawing (shown as Figure 2.3) that shows the center of a room with eight lines of equal length radiating from it. The child is asked to mark each line where he or she would want an individual to stop in each of the examples:

▶ a stranger who is the same age and sex as you
▶ a stranger who is the same age and opposite sex as you
▶ a stranger who is 5 years younger than you and the same sex
▶ a stranger who is 5 years older than you and the same sex
▶ your best friend

▶ your mother
▶ a schoolteacher who is a stranger to you
▶ the president of the United States (Duke et al., 1996, p. 27)

Teachers and parents also can informally assess nonverbal skills using these activities (Duke et al., 1996).

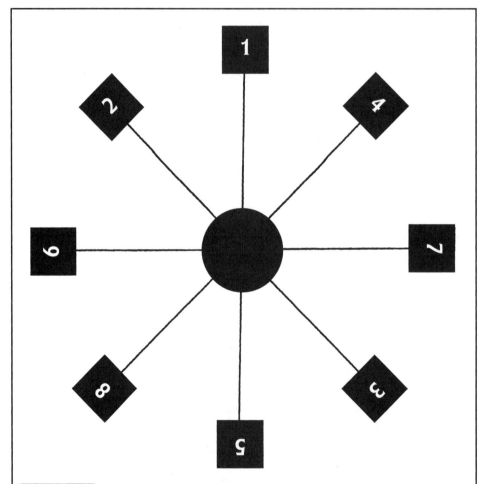

Source: "*Comfortable Interpersonal Distance Scale,*" from *Teaching Your Child the Language of Social Success* (p. 26), by M. P. Duke, S. Nowicki, Jr., and E. A. Martin (Atlanta: Peachtree Publishers). Copyright © 1996 by Marshall P. Duke, Stephen Nowicki, Jr., and Elisabeth A. Martin. Reprinted by permission of Peachtree Publishers.

**FIGURE 2.3** ▶ Comfortable Interpersonal Distance Scale

To assess receptive nonverbal skills:

▶ Turn off the sound on the TV and have the child tell you what's going on.
▶ Have the child just listen to the TV and tell you what's going on.
▶ Have the child observe people in public places such as malls, stores, and at sporting events, and describe the interactions and relationships.

To assess expressive nonverbal skills:

▶ Observe the child interacting with others and responding to social situations to determine if his or her feelings are being expressed appropriately. If parents and teachers have difficulty reading the child's emotions, others probably do, too.
▶ Ask the child to show different emotions, and take pictures with an instant, digital, or video camera.

In Chapter Three we describe additional activities that can be used to assess and teach emotional understanding.

## ▶ Sociometric Techniques

# David

*During their first meeting to discuss David, everyone agreed that Hal, the social studies teacher, would have the boys in his class complete a peer-nomination sociometric to gain a better understanding of his status in the group. Jan, the school counselor, commented, "Not only will we have a better idea of how David is perceived by his classmates, we will also be able to identify some boys who might be able to help David have better relationships."*

*When the sociometric was complete, members of the teacher assistance team were anxious to see the results. Hal distributed copies of what he called a sociogram, which showed a bunch of circles, each with a child's name. There were arrows going to and from some of the circles. "Let me explain what we've got here," he said.*

Sociometric techniques may be useful when teachers and parents are interested in the social worlds of children and youth. Two types of sociometric approaches are peer nominations and peer rating scales. Both approaches are based on the initial work of Moreno (1934).

### Peer Nominations

The *peer-nomination method* asks children to suggest peers when they are asked questions such as, "Who would you most (or least) want to invite to your birthday party?" "Who would you most (least) want to work with on a science fair project?"

"Who would you most (least) want to sit next to during lunch?" Positive and negative nominations enable us to determine if children are strongly liked (i.e., popular), strongly disliked (i.e., rejected), liked by most and disliked by some (i.e., accepted/average), both liked and disliked (i.e., controversial), or ignored (i.e., neglected). David's peer-nomination sociogram is shown as Figure 2.4. Each of the 11 boys in Hal's social studies class was asked to nominate one boy he would definitely like to play with and one boy he would definitely not like to play with. (Only boys were asked to make nominations because children of David's age tend to not have cross-gender friendships.) Types of nominations include positive nominations, reciprocal positive nominations (i.e., boys nominated each other as someone they would want to play with), negative nominations, and reciprocal negative nominations (i.e., boys nominated each other as someone they wouldn't want to play with).

## Peer Rating Scales

*Peer rating scales* ratings require that every child in the group is rated by peers (Yugar & Shapiro, 2001). A peer rating form appears as Figure 2.5. The form is designed to obtain information about how much students want to work or play with their classmates. The teacher lists the name of each member of the class or group and, when asked how much he or she would like to work or play with a classmate, the student circles 1 for "not at all," 2 for "not very much," 3 for "don't care," 4 for "sort of," and 5 for "very much." Scales may be simplified for younger children by using pictures.

Another example of a peer rating scale is the *Peer Acceptance Scale* (Bruininks, Rynders, & Gross, 1974). When given a list of every classmate, the child is asked to rate each as "wouldn't like," "all right," or "friend." Each child's score is determined by computing the average of all ratings. Advantages of peer ratings scales are that they provide information for every student in the group and allow comparisons among ratings.

When using sociometric techniques, five categories of children and youth emerge (Coie, Dodge, & Coppotelli, 1982; Thompson, Grace, & Cohen, 2001):

1. *Popular children.* Approximately 15% of children and adolescents fall within this category. They are nominated or rated highly by just about everyone. Popular children tend to be highly sociable.
2. *Accepted or average children.* Approximately 45% of children and adolescents fall within this group. These children share many of the characteristics of their more popular counterparts and tend to be nominated or highly rated by many peers. A few children may dislike them. Thompson et al. describe this group as "normal, healthy children" (p. 111).
3. *Rejected children.* Peers actively dislike about 12% of children and adolescents. Rejected children receive large numbers of negative nominations. Thompson et al. further categorize these children as either rejected–submissive or as rejected–aggressive. *Rejected–submissive* children and youth respond positively

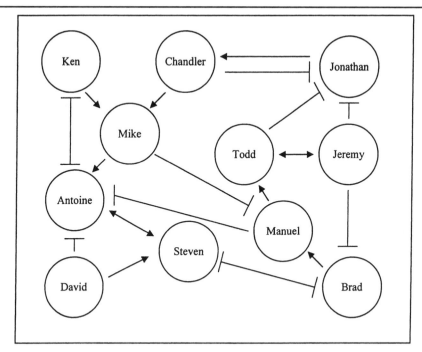

Key: ──────▶ Positive Nomination ─────┤ Negative Nomination

◀──────▶ Reciprocal Positive Nomination ├─────┤ Reciprocal Negative Nomination

[1] Each boy in Hal's class was asked to select one boy he definitely would like to play with and one boy he definitely would not like to play with:

| Name | Positive Nominations | Negative Nominations |
|---|---|---|
| Ken | 0 | 1 |
| Chandler | 1 | 0 |
| Jonathan | 0 | 3 |
| Mike | 3 | 0 |
| Todd | 2 | 0 |
| Jeremy | 1 | 0 |
| Antoine | 2 | 3 |
| David | 0 | 0 |
| Steven | 2 | 1 |
| Manuel | 1 | 1 |
| Brad | 0 | 2 |

**FIGURE 2.4** ▶ David's Peer Nomination Sociogram[1]

Please list the name of your teacher: _____

What grade are you in? _____

*Directions:* We are interested in finding out how much the students in your class would like to work with each other or play with each other. For each student on this list, circle one of the numbers to show how much you would like to play with them and circle one of the numbers to show how much you would like to work with them.

This is what the numbers mean:

1 = NOT AT ALL (I definitely would not want to work or play with this person)
2 = NOT VERY MUCH (I don't think I would want to work or play with this person)
3 = DON'T CARE (It really wouldn't matter to me if I played with this person or not)
4 = SORT OF (I think I would like to work or play with this person)
5 = VERY MUCH (I definitely would like to work or play with this person)

| NAME | WORK WITH? | | | | | PLAY WITH? | | | | |
|---|---|---|---|---|---|---|---|---|---|---|
| 1. _____ | 1 | 2 | 3 | 4 | 5 | 1 | 2 | 3 | 4 | 5 |
| 2. _____ | 1 | 2 | 3 | 4 | 5 | 1 | 2 | 3 | 4 | 5 |
| 3. _____ | 1 | 2 | 3 | 4 | 5 | 1 | 2 | 3 | 4 | 5 |
| 4. _____ | 1 | 2 | 3 | 4 | 5 | 1 | 2 | 3 | 4 | 5 |
| 5. _____ | 1 | 2 | 3 | 4 | 5 | 1 | 2 | 3 | 4 | 5 |
| 6. _____ | 1 | 2 | 3 | 4 | 5 | 1 | 2 | 3 | 4 | 5 |
| 7. _____ | 1 | 2 | 3 | 4 | 5 | 1 | 2 | 3 | 4 | 5 |
| 8. _____ | 1 | 2 | 3 | 4 | 5 | 1 | 2 | 3 | 4 | 5 |
| 9. _____ | 1 | 2 | 3 | 4 | 5 | 1 | 2 | 3 | 4 | 5 |
| 10. _____ | 1 | 2 | 3 | 4 | 5 | 1 | 2 | 3 | 4 | 5 |

Source: *"A Sample Peer Rating Assessment Form,"* from *Behavioral, Social, and Emotional Assessment of Children and Adolescents* (p. 147), by K. W. Merrell (Mahwah, NJ: Erlbaum). Copyright © 2003 by Erlbaum. Reprinted by permission.

**FIGURE 2.5** ▶ Peer Rating Form

to social–emotional skills interventions, whereas *rejected–aggressive children* resist intervention and are at risk for future mental health difficulties. Rejected–aggressive children have frequent altercations with their classmates and often disrupt the classroom. Thompson et al. stress that "rejected–submissive and rejected–aggressive children don't just 'grow out of it.' It takes intelligent, purposeful intervention on the part of educators and parents to reroute these children's lives" (p. 119).

4. *Neglected children.* Four percent of children and youth fall within this category. They are neither strongly liked nor actively disliked by their peers and are rarely nominated by peers. In teachers' and parents' eyes these children look the same as accepted children. Thus, adults regard them as "good kids" who are compliant, academically focused, and adult oriented. Although they usually have at least one friend, they remain invisible to their peers.

5. *Controversial children.* Approximately 4% of children and youth fall within this category. They are extremely well liked by some peers and extremely disliked by others, collecting both positive and negative nominations. This category often includes "class clowns," "queen bees," "bullies," and "rebels" (Thompson et al., 2001). These children understand how they affect others and use this knowledge to their advantage.

About 20% of children and adolescents fail to fall in any of these five categories. David's sociogram (shown as Figure 2.4) gives us information about the dynamics in Hal's social studies class. Mike and Todd are popular boys; they each received two or more positive nominations and no negative nominations. Most of the nominations Chandler, Jeremy, Steven, and Manuel received were positive. These students are considered average; they are accepted by their classmates. Jonathan and Brad (two negative nominations) are rejected by their classmates. Neither student received any positive nominations. David is neglected by his classmates; he is neither strongly liked nor strongly disliked by the boys in Hal's social studies class. Antoine is controversial; he is both strongly liked and strongly disliked by different classmates. Todd and Jeremy and Antoine and Steven have reciprocal positive relationships; each boy in each pair nominated the other as someone they definitely would like to play with. Steven and Brad and Ken and Antoine have reciprocal negative relationships; each boy in each pair nominated the other as someone they definitely would not like to play with.

Sociograms offer useful information for planning social–emotional skills interventions. For example, David would like to play with Stephen, so Hal could create situations for David and Stephen to interact.

## Advantages and Disadvantages of Sociometric Techniques

Sociometric techniques are useful for determining social status. These approaches can efficiently screen groups of children to identify individuals who may be at risk for social–emotional difficulties. Sociometric assessment also is useful for identifying children and youth to serve as positive social role models or as sources of social–emotional support for peers with social–emotional challenges (Merrell, 2003).

Despite their advantages, sociometric techniques also have several disadvantages. These measures can identify only children and youth who are not accepted by their peers; they do not identify the factors that contribute to this lack of acceptance (Foster, Inderbitzen, & Nangle, 1993). In addition, it cannot be assumed that children who do not receive positive nominations or those who receive negative nominations will benefit from social–emotional intervention. Other within-child characteristics, such as physical appearance or cultural differences, could cause peers to reject or ignore classmates. In such instances, teachers and parents would do better to focus on changing the perceptions and attitudes of peers, rather than focus on the child.

Another potential disadvantage of sociometric approaches is that the ratings are resistant to change. Once the peer group determines that a child is undesirable, the group's social perceptions of the child tend to remain fixed. Thompson et al. (2001) found when popular and unpopular children acted the same way, classmates cut the popular children slack but attributed negative motivations to unpopular children. Classmates even made excuses for popular children. Therefore, if teachers and parents want to assess the effects of social–emotional intervention, a sociometric technique is a poor choice because of the rating intractability.

Some teachers and parents are concerned that involving children in making negative nominations or ratings may encourage them to dislike their peers. But results of studies to date indicate that children are unlikely to be harmed by participating in sociometric assessment (L. K. Elksnin & N. Elksnin, 1995; Merrell, 2003). Adults must take care, however, to use these approaches in an ethical manner. Linda recalls a teacher who conducted a sociometric assessment of her eighth-grade class and subsequently posted the results on the bulletin board! To this day, she vividly remembers how one girl in the class despaired that "no one likes me" because she received no positive nominations. This child likely endured long-term negative effects from this experience.

To prevent such instances, Foster et al. (1993) make these recommendations when using sociometric techniques:

► Obtain parent permission (some parents may wish that their children not participate).
► Avoid administering sociometric measures immediately before unstructured activities such as recess to minimize discussion and negative comments about classmates.
► Avoid administering sociometric measures to polarized groups.
► Emphasize that nominations and ratings must remain confidential.

## ► Interviews

## Sarah

*After letting Sarah know the results of her BarOn, Melissa interviewed her about her social life at Vista Park. In preparation, Melissa planned to ask Sarah these questions:*

• *Do you have any close friends at school? How about in your neighborhood?*

- *Who were your closest friends in Mount Airy? What did you like most about each? How did you get to know each friend?*
- *What do you think your friends like about you?*
- *Are there girls (or boys) you want to be friends with in any of your classes at Vista Park? What do you like most about each?*
- *Do you have some ideas about how you might make friends with these girls (or boys)?*

*Melissa planned to use Sarah's responses to the questions to help her develop strategies to make friends at her new school.*

Interviews with children, teachers, parents, and others provide useful information about social–emotional skills. We will discuss how interviews with children and adults can assist in planning social–emotional skills interventions.

## Interviews with Children and Youth

Teachers and parents can interview children to

- ▶ determine how knowledgeable the child is about his or her own social–emotional competence and social–emotional skills;
- ▶ determine how motivated the child is to learn social–emotional skills;
- ▶ determine how social–emotional skills instruction fits with the child's academic, vocational, and interpersonal goals;
- ▶ observe the child's social skills during the interview, paying particular attention to level of communication, eye contact, affect, anxiety, inattention, nervousness, and so forth. (Merrell, 2003)

Interviews also can be used to assess children's social–emotional problem-solving ability (Leffert, Siperstein, & Millikan, 2000). Bryan, Sullivan-Burstein, and Mathur (1998) presented children with this scenario:

> One free period, Bill has nothing to do. He walks outside and sees two of his classmates playing a game. Bill really wants to play with them. He walks up to them, but they just keep on playing. (p. 421)

They then asked these questions:

- ▶ What do you remember about the story? Tell me everything you remember.
- ▶ What do you think the problem is?
- ▶ Why do you think that Bill's classmates won't stop and play?
- ▶ What are some ways that Bill could deal with this situation?
- ▶ Do you think it would be an okay, good, or bad idea for Bill to _____?
- ▶ Which of the solutions you thought of would you try first?

Figure 2.6 is an interview with a 10-year-old boy that was used to assess his social problem-solving ability. After determining the social–emotional problem-solving ability, the teacher or parent can provide a potential solution and ask the child to role play. Chapter Four presents strategies that may be used to improve social–emotional problem solving.

| | |
|---|---|
| I(nterviewer): | Sometimes best friends stop being best friends. What could happen to cause best friends to break up? |
| B(en): | You can accidentally run and fall and trip, and then they fall over you and think you tripped them, and that's why you lose a friend. |
| I: | So, you have misunderstandings about why you did something. Has that happened to you? |
| B: | Last weekend I had a new double wing boat and I told my friend Chris not to throw it because I said the missiles and bombs would come off. He goes, "Okay, I'll just take them off." I told him not to but he went ahead. It was already in mid-air by then: It hit the concrete because I couldn't catch it. It scattered all over the place. He won't buy me a new one so . . . (*pause*) |
| I: | It was your boat with missiles on it. He got ready to throw it. You said not to and he threw it anyway. |
| B: | Uh huh. So I told him how he threw it. He said he threw it underhanded so I could catch it. He didn't. He threw it overhanded as hard as he could. |
| I: | Why do you think he did that? |
| B: | I don't know. So while I was showing him how he did it, I used one of his guys this time because he had tore that boat up and it wasn't even mine. It was my friend Jeff's, and he [Jeff] told me I could use it and now he's [Chris] broken it. There are two things missing on it, and I think the reason he threw it was just to be mean. And he stole a little G.I. Joe man and gun and if he doesn't give it . . . He left over the G.I. Joe backpack and it holds three boomerangs, and if he doesn't give me my gun and man back, I won't give him the backpack. That's what my Dad says. |
| I: | So you think he threw the boat overhand like that against the wall [be]cause he just wanted to be mean? |
| B: | Yea[h]. |

**FIGURE 2.6** ▶ Assessing Social Problem Solving Using the Clinical Child Interview

Interviewing children and youth yields information that cannot be obtained through rating scales or observation. Data from rating scales do not tell us *why* a student behaves a certain way; cognitive processes cannot be observed. But, we also must recognize the limitations of interviews (Merrell & Gimpel, 1998). First, interviews are time-consuming to conduct. Thus, school district personnel may opt for

| | |
|---|---|
| I: | What makes you think he did it to be mean? |
| B: | When he gets with other kids he gets mean like some friends do. They think—you see, these other kids he plays with are mean and they don't like me and they tell him and he might not like me then. |
| I: | What did you want to happen when you threw his guy . . . what outcome did you hope for? |
| B: | I wanted to punish him so he wouldn't do that again. |
| I: | What could you do when something like that happens—like his throwing your boat against the wall? |
| B: | Nothing really. I showed him how to do it. I used his guy and when it hit the concrete, it broke and I said, "Okay, now we're even," and he said, "Okay, we're even." |
| I: | So you each broke something and were even. That's one thing you can do when a friend breaks something. What else could you do? |
| B: | Tell them not to do it, and if he does, make him buy you another one or tell their parents. |
| I: | Anything else? |
| B: | No. |
| I: | What do you think is the best thing to do if someone breaks one of your toys? |
| B: | Don't let them play with your toys. Like he always wants me to get out all my toys, and once I got them all out—I set up all my G.I. Joe[s] and he says, "Let's go play hide and seek" or something. Then I'll say "Okay. Now you made me bring it out now help me put it up." And he says "Okay and puts one thing up and then runs off and won't help me and makes me put it up. |

Source: "Assessing Social Problem Solving Using the Child Interview," from *The Clinical Child Interview* (pp. 146–148), by J. N. Hughes and D. B. Baker (New York: Guilford). Copyright © 1991 by Guilford. Used with permission.

**FIGURE 2.6** ▶(Continued)

more efficient social–emotional assessment approaches. Second, interview results are only as reliable as the person providing the information. Third, developmental issues may interfere with the interview process. During early childhood, for example, children often lack the verbal ability to describe their thoughts, feelings, and experiences. Young children also have difficulty understanding others' points of view. Further, elementary-aged children have difficulty dealing with abstractions, which make them poor interview candidates.

Although typically developing adolescents have the intellectual and social ability to fully participate in interviews, many youths who are referred for social–emotional skills intervention lack these skills (Merrell & Gimpel, 1998). Role play (discussed later in this chapter) may more accurately assess the social–emotional performance of children who are unable to participate fully in clinical interviews.

### Interviews with Adults

Useful information about a child or youth's social–emotional skills also can be obtained by interviewing parents, teachers, and employers, if appropriate. Such interviews can be used to identify essential social–emotional skills, as well as to determine the discrepancy between the child's social-emotional skills and those required in various environments such as the classroom, home, community, or employment setting. When planning an interview, teachers and parents should consider the following suggestions:

1. Establish your goal for the interview. Is the primary goal to obtain information, to establish rapport, or to gain cooperation?
2. Consider the information you want to obtain.
3. Develop a list of potential questions to ask.
4. Identify ways in which the interviewee's perspective may differ from your own perspective.
5. Identify potentially sensitive subjects.

## ▶ Behavioral Observation

## Thad

*Several months after Rita met with Thad's speech and language pathologist, Thad qualified for special education services because of his significant language delay. He started to attend an inclusive preschool that served eight children ages 2 through 4. Four of the children had developmental delays in language, cognition, motor, or social–emotional skills; four of them had typical development and acted as role models for the developmentally delayed preschoolers.*

*Thad seemed to enjoy his new class and his teacher, Sonja. His language skills began to improve, thanks to continued speech and language therapy, but he was still physically aggressive toward his classmates. Sonja placed Thad in time-out when he was aggressive. Although his aggression was not as frequent as when he first joined the class two weeks ago, Sonja was still concerned about the number of times Thad hit and pinched other children during unstructured activities.*

*She decided to observe Thad closely to better understand what events occurred before and after his physical outbursts, as well as to get an accurate estimate of how often Thad was physical with his classmates. Maybe she could come up with an effective way to teach Thad to play appropriately. Time-out wasn't getting rid of the problem and Thad didn't seem to be learning better ways to interact with his classmates.*

Observational data are extremely useful when teachers and parents want to

▶ determine if a child needs social–emotional skills instruction,
▶ understand the reason(s) behind a child's behavior,
▶ compare a child's social–emotional skills with those of other children his or her age,
▶ evaluate the effectiveness of instruction,
▶ communicate clearly with others.

Behavioral observation is an essential part of any social-emotional assessment (Gresham, 2001). In the sections that follow we describe the three steps of conducting behavioral observation when assessing social-emotional skills.

## Step 1: Define the Behavior to Be Observed

The first step before conducting behavioral observation is to define the social–emotional skill or interfering behavior in observable, measurable, and specific terms. The skill must be defined clearly enough to lead to high levels of agreement across observers. When the skill is defined precisely, teachers, parents, and others are able to develop and implement an appropriate assessment plan and evaluate the effectiveness of intervention (Hartshorne & Johnston, 1982). Several social–emotional skills are defined in Table 2.4.

*Sonja decided to observe two behaviors: sharing and physical aggression. She defined "sharing" as "offering a toy or other object to another child." She defined "physical aggression" as "hitting, pinching, punching, or inappropriately touching a classmate."*

## Step 2: Select a Recording System

The recording system that is selected is dependent upon the characteristics of the social–emotional skill of interest. *Rate* is an index of how frequently a behavior

**TABLE 2.4 ▶** Selected Social–Emotional Behaviors, Interfering Behaviors, and Their Definitions

| Social–Emotional Behavior | Definition |
| --- | --- |
| Asking for help | The child raises his/her hand and waits for the teacher to call on him/her before asking for help. |
| Sharing | The child offers a toy or other object to another child. |
| Listening | The child's eyes are on the speaker, and he/she does not talk while the other person is speaking. |
| Joining in | The child approaches a group, waits for an appropriate opening, then asks to join in a game or other activity. |
| Accepting a compliment | The child says "thank you" when another person says something positive about him/her. |
| Introducing yourself | The child waits until an appropriate time, greets the person, tells the person his/her name, shakes hands, if appropriate, asks the other person for his/her name, and tells the other person something to get the conversation going. |
| Appropriate social interaction | While on the playground, the child talks or plays with classmates without displaying verbal or physical aggression. |

| Interfering Behavior | Definition |
| --- | --- |
| Social isolation | While on the playground, the child is 10 or more feet away from classmates, who actively ignore him. |
| Physical aggression | The child hits, tugs at, or inappropriately touches a classmate. |
| Verbal aggression | The child verbally insults classmates or yells in their faces. |

occurs, such as the number of times the child initiates conversation within a given period of time. *Intensity*, or force, is the strength of the behavior. Intensity may be of interest when observing a child's verbal aggression toward others. A couple of

verbal insults lobbed at a classmate are of lower intensity than screaming obsceni-
ties at the classmate with a red, enraged face. *Temporal* characteristics include how
long the behavior lasts and how long before a behavior occurs. Several types of
recording systems are described next.

### Anecdotal Recording

When teachers and parents want to identify patterns of behavior, select behavior for
further observation, or determine how surrounding events influence behavior, anecdotal recording is useful, although it is time-consuming. Anecdotal recording
involves writing down everything that occurs during a specific time period. Figure
2.7 is an A–B–C recording sheet that Sonja's teaching assistant, Helen, used to

| Child's Name: | Thad Norwood |
|---|---|
| Teacher: | Sonja Abbott |
| Recorder: | Helen Oplinger, Assistant |
| Setting: | Free-play period, inclusive preschool class |
| Target Behavior: | Sharing: Thad offers a toy or other object to another child. |

| Time | Antecedent | Behavior | Consequence |
|---|---|---|---|
| 10:20 a.m. | Brian reaches for Thad's blocks | T hits B | SA gives verbal reprimand |
| 10:24 a.m. | SA asks T to share blocks with B | T knocks blocks off table | SA tells T that he has "one more chance to be good" or he'll go to time-out |
| 10:25 a.m. | T offers block to B; B ignores T and walks away | T walks over to center and quietly colors | SA tells T, "I told you for the last time to play nice. Now go to the time-out area" |
| 10:30 a.m. | — | T cries and stamps his feet | |
| 10:45 a.m. | SA announces that play time is over and T can leave the time-out area | T leaves time-out area and joins the circle for story | SA begins to read story |

**FIGURE 2.7** ▶ A–B–C Recording Sheet

record Thad's "sharing" behavior. The column headings designate Antecedents (events that precede the target behavior), Behavior (events occurring during the sequential conditions), and Consequences (events following the behavior). When assessing social–emotional or interfering behaviors, teachers and parents must act as good detectives who actively look for clues that help explain behavior.

*Sonja looked over the A–B–C recording sheet and determined that her behavior actually prevented Thad from sharing appropriately with his preschool classmates. When Thad offered a block to Brian, she sent him to time-out. Rather than "catching" Thad sharing and reinforcing that behavior with verbal praise, she focused on Thad knocking the blocks off the table.*

A *chronolog* also may be used for anecdotal recording. In using a chronolog, teachers and parents record events as accurately as possible to understand the dynamics of a social interaction, as seen in the following example:

> Jeffrey and his friends are getting equipment together to play soccer in the field behind Jeffrey's house. Sam (Jeff's younger brother) joins the group, dressed in his soccer clothes.
>
> "Oh no, you don't," says Jeff. "You're not coming with us. I'm tired of you always wanting to play with my friends and me. Go play with kids your own age!"
>
> "Ah, Jeff, Sam's not so bad," interjects Mike (Jeff's best friend). "We can get him to chase out-of-bounds balls."
>
> "That's not a bad idea, Mike. Come on, midget, let's get going," says Mike as he walks out the back door.

After watching and recording the above interaction, Jeff's dad has a much better understanding of how Mike influenced Jeff's behavior. He now has a couple of strategies he can use when he sits down with Jeff to develop a plan for Jeff to spend time alone with his friends while allowing Sam the occasional opportunity to play with the older boys.

When a numerical dimension (i.e., we can count the number of times a behavior occurs) of a behavior is of primary interest, teachers and parents can choose permanent product recording, event recording, interval recording, or time sampling.

### Permanent Product Recording

Permanent product recording involves using tangible items or environmental effects to assess social–emotional behavior. This is the method classroom teachers use when they assess student performance by grading tests or papers. When used to assess social–emotional skills, examples of this method include counting the number of performance citations an employer gives an adolescent, evaluating a thank-you note written by a child, or determining level of cooperation by grading a group project. This method is convenient because it does not involve observations. Many social–emotional skills, however, do not result in a permanent product.

## Event Recording

Event recording involves counting the number of times a given behavior occurs. This method is particularly useful when observing behavior that is discrete (has a discernible beginning and end). It should not be used when observing behavior that lasts a long time or that occurs frequently, because the actual occurrence of the behavior will be underestimated in the first case and in the second case the observer will be unable to discern the beginning and ending of the behavior. Event recording can be conducted easily while the observer is doing other things. Each time the behavior is observed, the teacher or parent can make a tally mark, click a golf wrist counter, or move a paperclip from one pocket to another.

## Interval and Time Sampling Recording

Whereas event recording yields the actual number of times a behavior occurs, interval recording and time sampling provide an estimate of behavior frequency. When using interval recording, the observer divides the observation period into equal intervals (usually not to exceed 30 seconds per interval).

*Partial-interval recording* involves noting whether a behavior occurred at any time during the designated interval. For example, the child may raise her hand three times during the interval, but hand raising would be recorded as having occurred only one time. With *whole-interval recording*, the observer records behaviors as having occurred *throughout the entire interval*. Interval recording can be used when observing discrete behaviors or when observing continuous or high-frequency behaviors.

*Time sampling* is similar to interval recording, except that observation periods are divided into minute intervals rather than second intervals. Using this method, the teacher or parent records the behavior as having occurred if it was observed at the end of the interval. Time sampling can be used when observing discrete behaviors or behaviors that occur at a moderate frequency. Unlike interval recording, which requires the full attention of the observer, time sampling allows the teacher or parent to do other things during the period of observation. Figure 2.8 is the time-sampling recording sheet that Sonja used to record Thad's behavior.

*Sonja decided to use time sampling to determine how frequently Thad was physically aggressive toward his classmates. To do so she observed for 30 minutes during free play for 10 days. She divided each 30-minute observation session into six 5-minute intervals. She began each session by setting a timer on her watch for 5 minutes. When the timer beeped, Sonya looked to see if Thad was physically aggressive toward his classmates. She marked the interval with an "X" if he was hitting, pinching, punching, or touching another child in an inappropriate way.*

*At the end of the 10th session, Sonja calculated the percentage of intervals that Thad had been aggressive toward classmates. The percentages ranged from 16% to 50%, with an average percentage for the 10 sessions of about*

| Student: | Thad Norwood |
|---|---|
| Target Behavior: | Physical aggression (i.e., hitting, pinching, punching, or inappropriately touching a classmate) |
| Recorder: | Sonja Abbott, Inclusive Preschool Teacher |
| Dates: | March 7-11, March 14-18 |

Observation Number 1                              % Intervals Occurred: 33%

| X | | X | | | |
|---|---|---|---|---|---|
| 5 | 5 | 5 | 5 | 5 | 5 |

Observation Number 2                              % Intervals Occurred: 50%

| X | | X | | X | |
|---|---|---|---|---|---|
| 5 | 5 | 5 | 5 | 5 | 5 |

Observation Number 3                              % Intervals Occurred: 16%

| X | | | | | |
|---|---|---|---|---|---|
| 5 | 5 | 5 | 5 | 5 | 5 |

Observation Number 4                              % Intervals Occurred: 50%

| X | | X | | X | |
|---|---|---|---|---|---|
| 5 | 5 | 5 | 5 | 5 | 5 |

Observation Number 5                              % Intervals Occurred: 33%

| | X | X | | | |
|---|---|---|---|---|---|
| 5 | 5 | 5 | 5 | 5 | 5 |

Observation Number 6                              % Intervals Occurred: 50%

| | X | | | X | X |
|---|---|---|---|---|---|
| 5 | 5 | 5 | 5 | 5 | 5 |

Observation Number 7                              % Intervals Occurred: 33%

| X | | | X | | |
|---|---|---|---|---|---|
| 5 | 5 | 5 | 5 | 5 | 5 |

Observation Number 8                              % Intervals Occurred: 16%

| | X | | | | |
|---|---|---|---|---|---|
| 5 | 5 | 5 | 5 | 5 | 5 |

Observation Number 9                              % Intervals Occurred: 50%

| | | X | | X | X |
|---|---|---|---|---|---|
| 5 | 5 | 5 | 5 | 5 | 5 |

Observation Number 10                            % Intervals Occurred: 33%

| X | | X | | | |
|---|---|---|---|---|---|
| 5 | 5 | 5 | 5 | 5 | 5 |

**FIGURE 2.8** ▶Time-Sampling Recording Sheet

*36%. Sonja's observational data confirmed her concern about Thad's aggressive behavior. If anything, the data indicated that his behavior was occurring at an even higher rate than Sonja initially thought.*

Interval and time sampling recording allows teachers and parents to observe more than one student or more than one behavior at the same time. For example, Figure 2.9 presents observational data for Justin, a fourth grader, on the playground. The observer noted if any of the four behaviors of interest occurred at any time during each interval. The behaviors recorded were physical aggression, verbal aggression, appropriate social interaction, and social isolation. (See Table 2.4 for definitions of these behaviors.)

### Duration and Latency Recording

When the temporal dimension of a behavior is of interest, teachers and parents should use duration or latency recording. *Duration recording* can be used when you are interested in how long a behavior occurs. For example, a teacher may be interested in knowing how long a child plays with another child, how long cooperative groups discuss a problem, or how long a child pays attention during a spelling lesson. A parent may be interested in how long a child converses during dinner. Duration recording is simple to do: Just start a stopwatch or timer when the behavior begins, and click the watch or timer off when the behavior ends. Then record the total amount of time.

If the observer is interested in the amount of time that elapses before a child engages in a target behavior, *latency recording* is the method of choice. For example, a teacher may be interested in learning the amount of elapsed time between the criticism by an employer of an adolescent's job performance and the adolescent's acknowledgment of the negative feedback. Similarly, a parent may be interested in finding out how long it takes her child to share a toy with his brother after being asked to share.

### Choosing an Observational Recording System

The choice of an observation system depends upon the characteristics of the behavior of interest and the observer's time constraints.

*The teacher, Sue, is concerned that Brian, a student in her third-grade class, does not play cooperatively with classmates on the playground. She first considers whether the behavior, "playing cooperatively," is numerical or temporal. Because she is interested in how long rather than how many times Brian plays with his classmates during the 30-minute recess period, she determines that the behavior is temporal rather than numerical. She then considers if she is interested primarily in the time lapsed before Brian begins to play or the total time elapsed from the beginning to the end of cooperative play. Because she is interested in the latter, Sue selects duration recording as the procedure to use when observing Brian and his classmates during recess.*

Name and Grade: Justin T., Grade 4    Date: October 17
Location: Central School Playground    Activity: Morning Recess
Observer: Chris Thompson    Start/Stop Time: 10:05–10:18 a.m.
Interval Length/Type: 20 seconds, partial interval

| INTERVAL | PA | VA | INT | ISO | INTERVAL | PA | VA | INT | ISO |
|---|---|---|---|---|---|---|---|---|---|
| 1 | | | | X | 21 | | | | X |
| 2 | | | | X | 22 | | | | X |
| 3 | | | | X | 23 | | | | X |
| 4 | | | X | | 24 | | | | X |
| 5 | | X | | | 25 | | | | X |
| 6 | | X | | | 26 | | | X | |
| 7 | | | | X | 27 | | | X | |
| 8 | | | | X | 28 | | | X | |
| 9 | | | | X | 29 | | | X | |
| 10 | | | | X | 30 | | | X | |
| 11 | | | | X | 31 | | | X | |
| 12 | | | X | | 32 | | | | X |
| 13 | | | X | | 33 | | | | X |
| 14 | | | X | | 34 | | | | X |
| 15 | | X | | | 35 | | | X | |
| 16 | X | | | | 36 | | | | X |
| 17 | | | X | | 37 | | | | X |
| 18 | X | | | | 38 | | X | | |
| 19 | | | | X | 39 | | X | | |
| 20 | | | | X | 40 | | X | | |

**CODING KEY:**
PA = physically aggressive    VA = verbally aggressive
INT = appropriate social interaction    ISO = socially isolated

Source: "An Example of Behavioral Observation Data That Were Collected Using a Partial Interval Coding Procedure for Social Behavior in a School Playground Setting," adapted from *Behavioral, Social, and Emotional Assessment of Children and Adolescents* (2d ed., p. 60), by K. W. Merrell (Mahwah, NJ: Erlbaum). Copyright © 2003 by Erlbaum. Reprinted by permission.

**FIGURE 2.9** ►Form for Playground Social Behavior

In addition to selecting a recording system, teachers and parents must consider when and where observation will occur, to ensure that they obtain a representative sampling of behavior across time, settings, and groups.

## Step 3: Graph Observational Data

Figure 2.10 is the graph that Sonja created from the time-sampling data she collected when observing Thad. The observation sessions always appear at the bottom of the graph. The behavior observed always is represented by the heading at the left side— in Thad's case, the percentage of time he was aggressive toward his peers. It could be the number of times a preschooler shares a toy, or the amount of time an adolescent spends paying attention, as examples. When graphing observational data, the guidelines are as follows:

▶ When using event recording, graph the number of behavior occurrences for each observation session. If the student raised his hand five times, graph the behavior as having occurred five times during that observation session.

▶ When using time sampling and interval recording, graph the percentage of intervals during which the behavior occurred. For example, if the behavior occurred during 8 of 10 intervals, record the behavior as having occurred 80% of the time.

▶ When using duration recording, graph the total amount of time the behavior occurred.

▶ When using latency recording, graph the total amount of time before the behavior began.

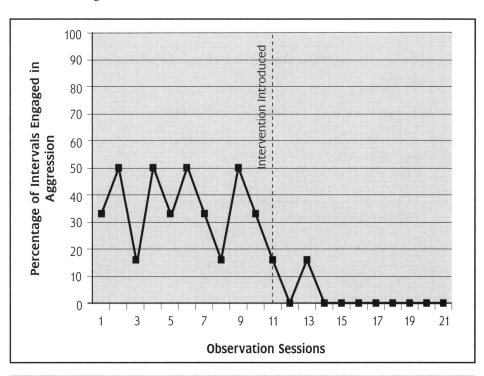

**FIGURE 2.10** ▶ Sonja's Graph of Thad's Behavior

Observation data should be graphed daily. These data can be used as a baseline (i.e., pretest) that can be used later to determine the effects of social–emotional skills instruction. Baseline data also can be used to compare the child's behavior with the behavior of other children. Determining that the child's behavior is significantly different from that of the peer group provides compelling evidence that social–emotional skills instruction is needed.

Once instruction begins, observers should continue to collect and graph data to determine if the intervention is having its desired effect. Sonja decided to teach Thad how to share and to give him plenty of praise and hugs when he shared. When Thad was aggressive, she asked him to go back to his work area. She then gave the "victim" plenty of attention. As shown by the graph in Figure 2.10, Sonja's efforts paid off. At the last observations, Thad was rarely physically aggressive. If the graphed data had indicated that Sonja's intervention was not producing positive changes in Thad's behavior, she could modify or adjust her instructional strategy.

### Advantages and Disadvantages of Behavioral Observation

Behavioral observation enables teachers and parents to answer many important questions. Its advantages are that

1. the data collected during observation help determine if the child's social–emotional skills are similar to those of other children of the same age;
2. the data allow teachers and parents to see if their intervention efforts are working, as the graphed data clearly communicate to others the frequency, duration, or latency of the child's behavior;
3. teachers and parents can use information from anecdotal records and chronologs to pinpoint causes of behavior.

For these reasons, behavioral observation should be part of any comprehensive social–emotional skills evaluation.

Behavioral observation also has several disadvantages. Some recording systems, such as anecdotal and interval recording, are time-consuming and difficult to use at school or at home. In addition, threats to validity must be taken into consideration (Merrell, 2003). The validity of observational data is threatened when behaviors are poorly defined or observers are unreliable; behavior is not validly represented when inappropriate recording systems are used (e.g., using event recording when observing a continuous behavior); the presence of an observer may influence the child's behavior, leading to invalid conclusions; and by focusing on specific behaviors, teachers and parents may overlook the big picture.

## ▶ Role-Play Assessment

Another way to identify children and youth in need of social–emotional skills instruction is to use role-play to help determine if a child can perform a specific social–emotional skill (Foster et al., 1993; Frisch, 1988). The three steps of role-play assessment are as follows.

## Step 1: Identify Skill Steps

First, we have to identify the steps that make up the social–emotional skill. Commercial curricula such as the *Skillstreaming* series (Goldstein & McGinnis, 1997; McGinnis & Goldstein, 1997, 2003) are excellent resources for identifying skill steps. For example, "Introducing yourself" includes these steps:

1. Decide if you want to meet the person.
2. Decide if it's a good time.
3. Walk up to the person.
4. Introduce yourself.
5. Wait for the person to tell you his/her name. If he/she doesn't tell you, ask. (McGinnis & Goldstein, 1997, p. 104)

Figure 2.11 is a role-play evaluation sheet we developed to assess an older student's ability to "Ask a co-worker or supervisor for help." The nine steps unique to this skill are clearly described, along with behaviors that occur throughout the skill, such as facing the person and having a relaxed body posture. Chapter Six offers additional strategies for task-analyzing social–emotional skills.

## Step 2: Create Role-Play Situations

Once the steps of the social–emotional skill are identified, the teacher or parent creates a role-play scenario, or situation, that requires use of the skill. For example, McGinnis and Goldstein (1997) created the following role-play situations for "introducing yourself": "There is a new student in your classroom. A friend of your parents is visiting your home. A new boy or girl moves into your neighborhood" (p. 104). Or the child may be asked to come up with a real-life situation in which he or she needs to use the skill. When constructing role plays, it is important to create situations across school, home, community, and employment settings. The example in Figure 2.11 shows a role-play scenario that required the young employee to ask the boss how to refill the drink machine.

## Step 3: Observe the Child Role-Playing the Skill

As the child performs the skill, the teacher or parent checks off each skill step that is performed correctly. For example, in Figure 2.11, the observer determines if each step is performed (competently or needing improvement) or not performed. Sometimes skill steps involve covert, cognitive behavior, such as steps 1 and 2 of "Asking a co-worker or supervisor for help" (i.e., determine if you need to ask for help, wait until a good time). Ask children what they are thinking before they

**Student:** John Rossi

**Social–Emotional Skill:** Asking a Co-worker or Supervisor for Help

**Role-Play Scenario:** It is your responsibility to refill the drink machine at Hamburger Haven. You were shown how to do it when you first started the job, but you forgot how to take the machine apart. There's a manual, but it doesn't make sense. You ask your boss, Mr. Case, for help.

**Skill Steps**
\+ = step performed competently
– = step performed, but needs improvement
0 = step not performed

- ☐ 1. Determine if you need to ask for help
- ☐ 2. Wait until a good time. Continue to work on something you can do while you are waiting.
- ☐ 3. Approach the person.
- ☐ 4. Explain what your problem is, or ask your question.
- ☐ 5. Listen when the person is talking to you.
- ☐ 6. Ask for more explanation or help if needed, and listen again.
- ☐ 7. Write down some notes if you're afraid you'll forget.
- ☐ 8. Thank the person for his or her help.
- ☐ 9. Continue working, using the information the person gave you.

**Behaviors that should occur throughout the skill:**
- ☐ The student was close to the person.
- ☐ The student faced the person.
- ☐ The student had a relaxed but serious body posture.
- ☐ The student engaged in eye contact with the person.
- ☐ The student used a pleasant tone of voice.

**Evaluator Comments:**

**Student Interview:**
How do you think you did?
What could you do better?
Name other situations in which you could use this skill.

Source: "Sample Role-Play Evaluation Sheet," from *Teaching Occupational Social Skills* (p. 22), by N. Elksnin and L. K. Elksnin (Austin, TX: Pro–Ed). Copyright © 1998 by Pro–Ed Inc. Reprinted with permission.

**FIGURE 2.11** ▶ Role-Play Evaluation Sheet

perform these covert steps. The interview strategies described earlier in this chapter are useful when assessing a child's problem-solving behavior during role play.

Role-play assessment is useful when (a) time does not allow observation in the natural setting, (b) the skill is unlikely to be observed because it rarely occurs, or (c) we want to observe the skill being performed rather than rely on a rater's perception (L. K. Elksnin & N. Elksnin, 1998).

# ▷ **Functional Behavioral Assessment**

We conclude this chapter with a review of functional behavioral assessment because this type of assessment relies on many of the approaches described earlier. Functional behavioral assessment (FBA) is a multimethod approach that uses data from interviews, rating scales, archival reviews, and behavioral observation to understand problem behavior and to develop *behavior intervention plans* (*BIPs*) (Barnhill, 2001–2002; Gresham, Watson, & Skinner, 2001; Sugai, Lewis-Palmer, & Hagan-Burke, 1999–2000; Sugai & Lewis-Palmer, 2004). FBA focuses on identifying the function or purpose of the behavior and the antecedents and consequences that maintain the behavior.

Behavior serves one of two functions for children and youth (Gresham, 2001):

1. To get something they want, such as material goods, social attention, or valued activities
2. To avoid or delay an undesirable situation, such as difficult tasks, social activities, or interruption of a valued activities

We should keep in mind that what is positively reinforcing for one child may be negatively reinforcing for another (Sprague, Sugai, & Walker, 1998). A problem behavior (or a class of problem behaviors) also may serve more than one function. For example, an introverted child may avoid social situations because she finds interacting with peers stressful *and* she enjoys solitary activities such as reading and painting.

The goal of FBA is to collect information that can be used to develop BIPs. Effective FBA enables teachers and parents to identify

1. the problem behavior,
2. antecedents that are apt to trigger the behavior,
3. consequences that are apt to maintain the behavior,
4. settings/events that are apt to exacerbate the behavior.

Although conducting FBA and developing BIPs are mandated by the Individuals with Disabilities Education Improvement Act (U.S. Congress, 2004) when identifying and serving students with disabilities, these approaches are useful for understanding and addressing the problem behavior of *all* children and youth.

Sugai et al. (1999–2000) has described two levels of FBA. Level I assessment involves collecting a small amount of data by observing the child, reviewing the child's permanent records, and conducting interviews. Teachers and parents move on to Level II if the information collected during Level I is insufficient to identify the behavior, the antecedents and consequences surrounding it, and settings and events that increase its severity. Assessment at Level II is more intensive and involves reviewing records and conducting multiple interviews and multiple observations across settings. Although these assessment methods are explained earlier in the chapter, we briefly describe each approach within the context of FBA.

## Interviews

Interviews are an integral component of FBA (Barnhill, 2001–2002; O'Neill et al., 1997). The types of questions that may be asked of teachers, parents, and others include:

▶ Can you describe the behaviors that are causing concern?
▶ What happens before the problem behavior occurs? Can you describe the circumstances (i.e., when, where, with whom) under which the behavior typically occurs?
▶ How would you characterize the function of the behavior? Do you think the child/adolescent uses the behavior to obtain reinforcement or to avoid an undesirable situation?
▶ What alternative behaviors does the child/adolescent have in his/her repertoire?
▶ What are some activities, events, and people the child/adolescent finds reinforcing?
▶ What are some activities, events, and people the child/adolescent regards as not being reinforcing?
▶ What types of interventions have you implemented? Which approaches have been most/least successful?

Gresham expanded the interview protocol to concentrate social–emotional skills within a consultation framework, in which two professionals collaboratively solve behavior problems. The following questions relate to problem identification, problem analysis, and problem evaluation. These questions enable teachers and parents to

▶ identify and define social skills difficulties;
▶ differentiate social skill acquisition, performance, and fluency deficits;
▶ identify competing problem behaviors that interfere with acquisition, performance, and/or fluency;
▶ obtain preliminary information regarding a possible functional analysis of behavior. (Gresham, 1998a, pp. 479, 480)

### Questions for Problem Identification

1. What social skills deficits are of most concern to you?
2. Please provide a clear, specific definition of each of the behaviors that concerns you.

3. Do you see these behaviors as being primarily acquisition deficits (can't do), performance deficits (won't do), or fluency deficits?
4. Approximately how often does this behavior occur? How frequently would you like to see these behaviors occur?
5. What, if any, interfering problem behaviors compete with the acquisition, performance, or fluency of the desired social skill? Provide a definition of each of these behaviors.
6. About how often do these behaviors occur?
7. Are there activities or times of day when the desired social skill is more likely? Less likely?
8. Are there activities or times of day when the interfering problem behaviors are more likely? Less likely?
9. Is the desired social skill more likely to occur with some peers than others? Describe these typical social interactions.
10. How does the child's failure to perform the desired social skill affect other children? You?

## Questions for Problem Analysis

11. When the child performs the social skill(s), what happens? What do you do? What do peers do?
12. When the child performs the competing problem behavior(s), what happens? What do you do? What do peers do?
13. What function do you think the interfering behavior serves for the child (social attention, task avoidance/escape, access to preferred activities)?
14. Does the child engage in undesirable behaviors that achieve the same results as the socially skilled target behavior? Are the undesirable behaviors equally or more functional in obtaining reinforcement?
15. If undesirable behaviors are equally or more functional, are they *more efficient* and *reliable* in achieving that function? Do the undesirable behaviors achieve the same reinforcement *more quickly* and *more consistently* than the socially skilled alternative behavior?
16. Are the competing undesirable behaviors associated with the presence of a specific stimulus (person, place, thing, time of day) or are they associated with the presence of many stimuli and situations?
17. What are some situations or activities in which the desired social skill could be taught using incidental teaching?
18. Describe how you might teach or prompt the social skill in these situations or activities.
19. Are there peers in the classroom who might be recruited to assist in teaching or prompting the desired social skill?
20. Do you think the desired social skill(s) would be best taught in a small group outside of the classroom? Why or why not?
21. What types of strategies could you implement to decrease the interfering or competing behaviors? Describe how you might use these.

22. What aspects of the proposed intervention do you like the most? Why? Which do you like the least? Why?
23. Which aspects of the proposed intervention would be easiest to implement? Why? Which aspects of the proposed intervention would be most difficult to implement? Why?
24. Here are some ways in which we could change the intervention. Do these changes make the intervention easier to implement? What additional changes would you recommend?
25. Do you think this intervention is likely to be effective? Why or why not?

### Questions for Problem Evaluation

26. Describe how you think the intervention worked.
27. What behavior changes did you observe? Did these changes make a difference in the child's behavior in your classroom? How? In other settings? How?
28. Is the child's behavior now similar to that of average or typical peers? If not, do you think the continued use of the intervention would accomplish this goal? Why or why not? How long do you think this might take if we continued the intervention?
29. How satisfied are you with the outcomes of this intervention? Why?
30. Would you recommend this intervention to others? Why or why not? What aspects of the intervention would you change before recommending this intervention to others?

Source: "Semistructured Functional Assessment Interview," from "Social Skills Training with Children: Social Learning and Applied Behavioral Analytic Approaches" (p. 480), by F. M. Gresham, 1998, in *Handbook of Child Behavior Therapy* (pp. 475–497), by T. S. Watson and F. M. Gresham (Eds.) (New York: Plenum Press). Copyright © 1998 by Plenum Press. Reprinted with permission.

## Archival Reviews

During Level I FBA, it is helpful to review a child's records. The following information is available in the permanent/cumulative records of all students:

- ▶ attendance records
- ▶ discipline referrals
- ▶ health/development history
- ▶ screening results (vision, hearing, speech and language screening, etc.)
- ▶ grades
- ▶ test scores for group-administered districtwide and statewide assessments
- ▶ response-to-intervention data
- ▶ teacher comments

In addition, children and youth with disabilities have a confidential record. This file contains the following:

- ▶ special education screening results (teacher ratings, behavior checklists, etc.)

- ▶ teacher assistance/child study team data
- ▶ special education evaluation results (e.g., psychological evaluations, educational evaluations)
- ▶ IEP
- ▶ 504 accommodation plan
- ▶ record of related services received
- ▶ types of accommodations/modifications provided in general education program
- ▶ observational data

### Rating Scales and Checklists

If a review of existing records fails to provide sufficient information, teachers, parents, peers, and the target student may be asked to complete a rating scale or a checklist from among those described earlier. Again, ratings will provide information about how frequently problematic behaviors occur, but they will do little to identify antecedents and consequences surrounding the behavior.

### Behavioral Observation

Direct observation, the "hallmark of FBA" (Barnhill, 2001–2002, p. 50), may be used at Level I or Level II. Observation should be conducted by following the guidelines described in this chapter. Using an A–B–C recording sheet like that presented as Figure 2.7 is particularly useful when conducting FBA. Once a problem behavior has been identified, a recording method may be selected to ensure that data collection yields valid indicators of the child's performance.

### The Goal of FBA

Teachers and parents must keep in mind that the primary goal of conducting an FBA is to develop a BIP for

- ▶ minimizing, preventing, or neutralizing the impact of setting events;
- ▶ removing antecedent events that trigger problem behavior and adding prompts that occasion appropriate behaviors;
- ▶ teaching appropriate replacement behaviors (e.g., self-management, social skills, adaptive responses); and
- ▶ removing consequent events that maintain problem behavior and adding reinforcers that encourage appropriate behavior. (Sugai, Lewis-Palmer, & Hagan-Burke, 1999-2000, p. 152)

## ▶ Chapter Summary

Effective assessment helps us determine the type of social–emotional skills problem a child/adolescent demonstrates, which is prerequisite for choosing an appropriate intervention. For example, acquisition, performance, and fluency problems each requires different interventions. Identifying problem behaviors is also critical because these behaviors interfere with learning and using social–emotional skills.

Because no one assessment approach provides all the information we need about a child's or an adolescent's social–emotional skills and problem behaviors, teachers and parents must use multiple assessment approaches, including rating scales, tests of emotional intelligence and nonverbal communication abilities, sociometric techniques, interviews, behavioral observation, role-play assessment, and functional behavioral assessment.

# CHAPTER 3

# Teaching Children and Youth to Understand and Regulate Emotions

## Goals of This Chapter

In this chapter you will learn

- the six nonverbal communication domains
- how to teach children expressive and receptive nonverbal communication skills
- the four emotional capacities children must have to be able to understand emotions
- strategies to increase emotional literacy
- the types of tasks used to assess children's role-taking abilities
- the five stages of role taking
- how to teach children and youth to be more empathetic
- how to help children and youth manage and control anger

# Terms to Know

anger control

dyssemic/dyssemia

empathy

eusemic/eusemia

feelings vocabulary

flooding

horizontal zoning

interpersonal space

nonverbal communication skills

objectics

opening moves

paralanguage

resting face

role taking

spatial zones for communication

synchronicity

*Four-year-old Robert Capaldi sat with his dad on a bench in the mall waiting for Mrs. Capaldi to finish her shopping. Mr. Capaldi enjoyed his son, and they both enjoyed watching other people. Robert tugged on his dad's arm. "Dad! See those people over there? They must be really mad at each other!"*

*"How can you tell, Robert?"*

*"Look at their mad faces, and they're throwing their arms around."*

*"I think you're right. Do you see those boys over there? How do you think they're feeling?"*

*Robert thought a minute. "They're happy 'cause they're with their friends. They're smiling and laughing—they have happy faces!"*

C hildren like Robert have an innate ability to understand how others feel. Robert is becoming an even better "reader of people" because his parents recognize that understanding emotions is an important life skill. Many children, however, must be taught this skill because they lack understanding of their own feelings and the feelings of others.

Understanding emotions is prerequisite to developing the social–emotional skills needed to build relationships and form friendships. Children begin by developing self-awareness, then move on to understanding how others feel. Understanding others' emotions is essential if children are to develop empathy.

The ability to perceive and identify emotions is tied to age and begins early. By age 3, typically developing children can identify the emotions of happiness, sadness, and fear; understand that events and situations cause these feelings; and are able to identify emotional states based on expressions, gestures, and vocal quality (Nabuzoka & Smith, 1995). Children and youth with disabilities such as learning disabilities (LD), mental retardation (MR), and autism are less able to perceive and recognize emotions than their typically developing peers (Gumpel & Wilson, 1996). In some cases, delayed emotional development extends through adolescence and adulthood. For example, several researchers have found that adolescents with LD were less able than their peers without LD to identify emotions such as happiness, anger, surprise, sadness, disgust, and fear (Most & Greenbank, 2000; Nabuzoka & Smith, 1995).

We begin this chapter by stressing the importance of nonverbal communication skills—that is, understanding what is being communicated through facial expressions, gestures, tone of voice, and so forth. We also offer strategies for how to improve children's receptive and expressive nonverbal communication skills. We then direct our attention to ways to increase children's emotional literacy, or understanding of their own feelings and the feelings of others. Understanding others' feelings enables children to assume the perspectives of other people and to develop empathy for others. The chapter concludes with strategies and activities to help children and youth manage and control angry feelings.

## ► Nonverbal Communication Skills

Only 7% emotional meaning is expressed through words! Facial expression, posture, and gesture communicate 55% and tone of voice 38% of emotional meaning (Mehrabian, 1968). When verbal and nonverbal messages conflict, listeners are more apt to believe the nonverbal message (Duke et al., 1996). Thus, nonverbal communication is integral to emotional understanding.

As Nowicki and Duke (1992) acknowledge, "You cannot *not* communicate nonverbally" (p. 12). They term individuals who have difficulty with nonverbal communication *dyssemic* (Duke et al., 1996; Nowicki & Duke, 1992). *Dyssemia,* they contend, is caused by the lack of opportunity to learn nonverbal language, emotional problems (e.g., anxiety, depression) that interfere with learning nonverbal language, or a brain dysfunction that causes a social-perception learning disability.

In contrast to dyssemic children and youth, *eusemic* children and youth are gifted in understanding nonverbal language and therefore enjoy social success.

Although dyssemia is rare, many children and youth benefit from being directly taught nonverbal skills. We will set forth strategies that can be used to teach skills in six nonverbal communication domains: paralanguage, facial expressions, postures and gestures, interpersonal distance (space) and touch, rhythm and time, and objectics (Duke et al., 1996; Nowicki & Duke).

## Paralanguage

*Bob and Sarah sat at the traffic light.*

*"What's the matter, Sarah?" Bob asked for the second time.*

*"Nothing. I'm glad we're going to see your parents," Sarah responded softly, then sighed.*

*Bob said, "I know something's up. Ever since you got off the phone with your boss, you've shut down. Did she say something to upset you?"*

Bob is relying on Sarah's *paralanguage*—her tone, loudness and intensity of voice, her sighs—to understand how she is feeling. Nearly one third of emotion is communicated through paralanguage. When we're on the phone, paralanguage becomes even more important because we can't rely on visual cues. Nowicki and his colleagues identified four aspects of paralanguage: tone of voice, nonverbal sound patterns, speech rate, and emphasis and variation in speech.

### Tone of Voice

Some teachers and parents masterfully use *tone of voice* as a management tool. One kindergarten teacher we know uses her "quiet voice" to get the attention of her students. We've observed a social studies teacher hold the interest of middle-school students by effectively varying his tone of voice during lectures. And our friends are uncanny at using excited voice tones to generate their toddler's enthusiasm for tasks such as cleaning up after an art project or putting away toys at the end of the day.

*Expressive ability* to use tone of voice effectively is an important skill. If you doubt that tone of voice supersedes the content of words, remember the late comedian Gilda Radner as one of the "whiners" on early *Saturday Night Live* television shows. Even when the "whiners" had something positive to say, their whiny tone of voice got in the way.

*Receptive ability* is equally important. Linda taught a 17-year-old with severe LD, who got into trouble because he lacked the ability to understand that spoken words and tone of voice may not match. One day he arrived late to English class. Dripping with sarcasm, his teacher said, "Why, Tim, isn't it wonderful you're here!" Tim promptly thanked the teacher, who attributed his thank-you as sarcasm answering sarcasm, a behavior that teachers (and parents) usually find intolerable.

### Nonverbal Sound Patterns

We can all recall comforting someone and using comforting sounds such as cooing, tut-tutting, "mmmmmmm"ing, and so forth. We also have been with friends, colleagues, and significant others who convey their boredom or impatience by sighing. In short, nonverbal sound patterns communicate an array of emotions.

### Rate of Speech

Are you a "fast talker" or a "slow talker"? While *rate of speech* is highly personal, it is affected by geography that promotes stereotypes such as the "fast-talking New Yorker" and the "slow-talking Southerner." Although we each have our preferred rate of speech, we must be flexible to adjust this rate to the needs of our listeners. When a teacher notices that she is speaking too rapidly for students to take notes in biology class, she slows down. A stranger speeds up while giving directions when she notices that the driver looks concerned because he is blocking traffic. The match between the speaker's rate of speech and the requirements of the listener is called *synchronicity.*

### Emphasis and Variation in Speech

Imagine if Dr. Martin Luther King had delivered his "I Have a Dream" speech in a monotone! However stirring his words, the speech would have fallen flat. In addition to conveying emotion and holding our attention, *emphasis and variation of speech* affects meaning. Read each of the following sentences, emphasizing the italicized word:

> *I* didn't say you stole the car.
> I didn't *say* you stole the car.
> I didn't say *you* stole the car.
> I didn't say you *stole* the car.
> I didn't say you stole the *car.*

## Facial Expressions

*Jamie got a last-minute invitation to go to the mall Saturday afternoon with the most popular girls in her fifth-grade class. The only problem was that she and her best friend, Dana, had planned to go to the movies together that day. Jamie really didn't want to miss out on the opportunity to be with the cool girls, so she asked Dana if she minded if they would go to the movies on Sunday afternoon instead. Dana said "okay," but the look on her face let Jamie know that she had hurt her best friend's feelings.*

*"No, let's go to the movies like we planned. We've been talking about it all week," Jamie said.*

*Dana's face lit up, and she said, "That's great! I really want to see the Olsens' new movie with you!"*

Socially–emotionally skilled children and youth understand what is being communicated through their own facial expressions and the expressions of others (Duke et al., 1996). But many children and youth are not adept at reading the facial expressions of peers and adults. To help these children, we first must teach them to recognize the "resting face," the expression people wear when they are not conscious of their expression. Then, we should teach the three *horizontal facial zones* that convey emotional states: (a) forehead and eyes, (b) nose and cheeks, and (c) mouth.

Children and youth also need to recognize and convey appropriate *intensity* in facial expressions. For example, looking intently serious while someone tells a joke looks inappropriate. Understanding horizontal zoning and intensity of expression is prerequisite to recognizing facial expressions.

Children need to smile and make eye contact during conversation. We are expected to look at a speaker's face 30% to 60% of the time to indicate interest (Duke et al., 1996). Engaging in eye contact does not mean gazing directly into another person's eyes, however, unless it is an intimate moment. Researchers at Kansas University's Institute for Research on Learning Disabilities found that adolescents with LD had to be taught to look at the person's "third eye" during conversation (Schumaker, 1992).

## Postures and Gestures

*Jamal and Elliott stood outside of their fourth-grade classroom. "Come on, Jamal—let's ask Mr. Moore if we can have more time to finish our science project."*

*They could see their teacher and a classmate near the lockers down the hall.*

*Waving his arms wildly, Mr. Moore was using his finger like a dagger to point at Steven. Steven slumped over and his head hung down.*

*"No way!" exclaimed Elliott. "Mr. Moore is really ticked off. I feel sorry for Steven."*

Elliott used postures and gestures to figure out how his teacher and his classmate were feeling. Understanding postures and gestures and using them appropriately are essential nonverbal skills. Children and youth who know how to use *gestures* appropriately tend to be accepted by their peers. Fingers, hands, and arms often are used as batons, "which emphasize, complement, or specify the meanings of words" (Nowicki & Duke, 1992, p. 68).

As illustrated in the above example, *posture* is a powerful communicator of an individual's mood, feelings, level of engagement, and the like. When we walk in to teach our graduate classes for the first time, we size up students' level of interest and commitment to learning by how they sit and look. Many children do not realize that they are conveying a negative impression through their posture and, thus, teachers, parents, and employers may assume incorrectly that they are not interested in what the other person is saying. Even if they aren't interested, they need to learn that it may be in their best interest to *look* interested!

Researchers at the University of Kansas taught students with learning disabilities to communicate interest in class by using the SLANT strategy (Ellis, 1991), which includes these steps:

1. **S**it up and have an upright, but relaxed posture.
2. **L**ean forward slightly.
3. **A**ctivate your thinking by asking yourself questions like, "What is this about?" and, "What do I need to remember?"
4. **N**ame key information by answering the teacher's questions, sharing your ideas or comments, and adding to others' comments.
5. **T**rack the talker by keeping your eyes on the teacher and students as they speak. (Ellis, 1991, p. 4)

Children and youth must learn that people have resting postures just as they have resting facial expressions. Then they must learn how to express (or hide) their feelings through posture, as well as understand how posture conveys the feelings of others.

## Interpersonal Distance (Space) and Touch

*Carla arrived early for the staff development session, so she had a choice of seats in the auditorium. She chose an aisle seat in the second row. Two minutes later a man she didn't know arrived and sat down next to her. The man didn't start a conversation. He just sat next to Carla and read a paperback. Carla felt uncomfortable, "Why would this man sit next to me when there are 200 other empty seats?" She didn't wait to find out but left the auditorium and waited in the lobby until several other teaching colleagues arrived.*

*Marcy wanted to crawl under the table. She had enjoyed the dinner party. Her hosts, Tom and Trish, and Marcy and her husband, Evan, were lingering over coffee and dessert.*
    *"Your new home is so lovely," Marcy said.*
    *"Yeah," added Evan. "How much did this castle cost you?"*

*Andrea was at her wits' end. She enjoyed having Michael in her fourth-grade class, but she was unable to teach him not to touch the other students inappropriately. Michael, who had Down syndrome, indiscriminately hugged and kissed boys and girls during cooperative groups, on the playground, and even when Andrea was instructing the class! Once he even licked Tameka, and her mother complained to the principal. In every other way, Michael was a welcome addition to the classroom, but his touching and kissing upset and even frightened the other students. Something had to be done—and soon.*

These examples illustrate the importance of not violating the physical and mental space of others. To be effective communicators, children and youth must understand the rules of personal space and touching.

The two types of interpersonal space are physical and mental. We carry our physical space with us, in our own personal space bubble. Violation of this personal physical space is one of the least tolerated communication errors. Thus, "space invaders" often cause problems in the classroom and tend to be actively disliked by peers.

Space zones vary among cultures. For example, Anglo-Americans tend to value more physical space between speakers than do Hispanic Americans and African Americans (L. K. Elksnin & N. Elksnin, 2000). Further, although both groups prefer 2 to 3 feet between speakers, Native American speakers converse side-by-side rather than standing face-to-face as do Anglo-Americans (Lee & Cartledge, 1996). Despite these differences, all children must recognize four "American" space zones (Hall, 1966, in Nowicki & Duke, 1992):

1. *Intimate zone:* extends from nearly touching to 18 inches from the other person. We rely on it when we are with family and friends, and when we are discussing personal/intimate subjects. (You may remember the "close talkers" on the television situation comedy *Seinfeld.* These characters inappropriately entered the intimate zone.)
2. *Personal zone:* extends from 18 inches to 4 feet. We use it with friends and acquaintances during everyday conversations.
3. *Social zone:* extends from 4 to 12 feet. It is used when we need to talk loudly so people we're about to meet or have just met can hear us. This zone is not appropriate for discussing personal or intimate topics, as others could overhear what is said.
4. *Public zone:* extends from 2 feet to infinity, to communicate using postures and gestures.

Some children and youth need to be taught these physical space zones directly. A teacher we know helped her second graders place masking tape around their desks to define each student's personal space zone. Permission was required to enter the zone, which prevented a lot of discipline problems. Students can physically practice matching behavior to appropriate zones using a full-scale picture like that shown as Figure 3.1. For example, teachers or parents can ask children to go to the zone that fits each of the following situations:

▶ You want to tell your best friend a secret—your family is going move out-of-state. *(intimate zone)*
▶ You wave so your sister's friends across the street will notice you. *(public zone)*
▶ You have a conversation in the cafeteria line. *(social zone)*
▶ You are discussing the results of last night's baseball game at the dinner table. *(personal zone)*
▶ Your classmate is completing an assignment at his desk. *(personal zone)*
▶ You tell your boyfriend that you really care about him. *(intimate zone)*

In addition to zones of physical space, we have zones of *mental space,* defined by Duke and colleagues (1996) as "things we consider to be private, things like

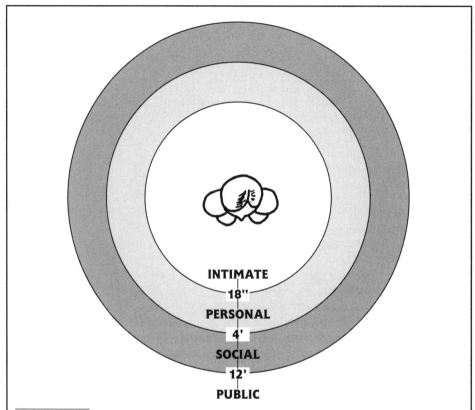

INTIMATE
18"
PERSONAL
4'
SOCIAL
12'
PUBLIC

Source: "Spatial Zones for Communication," in *Helping the Child Who Doesn't Fit In* (p. 45), by S. Nowicki, Jr. and M. P. Duke (Atlanta: Peachtree Publishers). Copyright © 1992. Reprinted by permission of Peachtree Publishers.

**FIGURE 3.1 ▶**Spatial Zones for Communication

personal thoughts or topics of conversation which, if made public, might cause us embarrassment" (p. 76). Some of these "off-limit" topics include finance (which Evan, in the earlier scenario, violated), health, and personal appearance. Many children and youth do not know they have crossed the line and entered a person's mental space because they don't pick up on nonverbal cues (e.g., looks of embarrassment, surprise, indignation). They have to be taught to recognize these warning signs. In addition, they must learn strategies for dealing with violations of their own mental space.

Many commercial social-skills curricula teach the skill "touching the right way." Programs designed to prevent child sexual abuse emphasize the importance of "okay touches" and "not-okay touches." Touching in the wrong place such as sexual areas or the upper chest, and touching with the wrong intensity such as poking, is viewed as frightening or weird.

Children and youth must learn what kind of *touching* is appropriate under which circumstances. They need to know how touching expresses emotions so they can understand the touches of others and touch others in an appropriate manner. For example, the ACCEPTS social skills curriculum (Walker et al., 1988) teaches elementary-aged children "touching the right way" by first defining the skill:

> Touching the right way means not touching too long or too hard. Touching too long makes people feel uncomfortable and touching too hard hurts. (p. 74)

Children are taught when it is okay to touch (e.g., to help someone up who has fallen, to get someone's attention, to pat someone on the back for doing a good job). The teacher (or parent) models positive and negative examples of touching the right way. Children then take turns role playing touching the right way.

## Rhythm and Time

*The three women had become friends through their professional organization. Kate, Rachel, and Emma enjoyed each other's company and decided to get together for strictly social reasons. They planned a "fly in" for a 3-day weekend in Santa Fe. By Day 3, Kate and Emma were discussing how they could have a "girlfriends weekend" next year, but without Rachel. Both women had run out of patience. Rachel got up 2 hours later than they did, and then it took her three times as long to get ready to go sightseeing. Actually, their trip began by waiting at the airport because Rachel missed her first flight out of New York.*

As Rachel would soon find out, it is important to be in sync with others. The nonverbal communication skills of rhythm and time include speech speed and rhythm, and time management (including arriving on time). Children and youth need to understand what they communicate through their use of time (i.e., expressive time usage), as well as what others communicate through their utilization of time (i.e., receptive time usage).

What we *do* with our time may contradict what we *say* we do with it. For example, a politician repeatedly states that she values family time. But her words do little to convince voters when she is observed spending little time with her spouse and children. For some, time is related to status, and high-status individuals (e.g., physician, principal, judge) are permitted to make lower-status individuals (e.g., patient, student, defendant/plaintiff) wait. By contrast, arriving on time sends a message that the individual values others' time.

Finally, children and youth must understand that interruptions are expected during public time but should be avoided during private time. During private time, people choose to be alone with their own thoughts. For example, it is okay to interrupt dad when he is reading the paper surrounded by family in the living room, but not appropriate to disturb mom when she says she needs some time to herself.

Children and youth may need instruction in time management that focuses on estimating time to complete tasks, strategies to prioritize tasks, and the like. Teaching older children to use day planners and assignment notebooks helps them manage time more effectively and efficiently.

## Objectics

*Irma was an older student in the special education graduate program. She had long, stringy, gray hair, and her clothes and glasses might have been in style 20 years ago. Other students avoided her. Several students arrived before class began at 4 p.m. to open the windows because, truth-be-told, Irma smelled. Her body odor was literally creating an aversive classroom environment. Recently, three students approached Dr. Wilton and explained they did not want to be in Irma's case group.*

### Expressive Objectics

Expressive objectics include style of dress, use of cosmetics, jewelry, hairstyle, personal hygiene, and body shape, which allow individuals to fit in with the group (Nowicki & Duke, 1992). Clearly, Irma's objectics were working against her ability to form relationships with her graduate-student peers.

In the film *Clueless,* Cher, played by Alicia Silverstone, takes on Tai, a fashion victim played by Brittany Murphy, as a personal project. Cher spends hours of her time transforming Tai's tough-girl image by having Tai wear her hair and clothes according to Beverly Hills standards. Understanding and following the rules of fashion are extremely important during early adolescence. Following fashion rules enables young people to join the peer group, where they find acceptance and security.

As Nowicki and Duke (1992) have aptly noted, "Young adolescents need to follow somewhat rigid rules of fashion" (p. 114). As teachers and parents, we must not rely on our own sense of adolescent fashion, because we're hopelessly out of date about what drives today's teen fashion scene. It's much safer to observe how "with-it" young people dress at school, in the mall, and on television.

Children and youth also need to understand the difference between *fashion* and *image.* Fashion trends come and go, but a person's image is of a more permanent nature. For example, at the time this book is being written, Britney Spears is the fashion icon for preteens. As you are reading this, others likely have replaced Britney. An individual's clothing conveys an image, as well as her fashion sense. Showing pictures of yourself and others looking conservative, rebellious, casual, formal, or projecting some other image drives home this point. A child also has to understand that image creates an impression, or an idea of a person in the minds of others.

Therefore, children and youth should be steered into discussions of the impressions they want to convey and to select appropriate attire for situations such as school, sports, church, synagogue, informal dances, proms, and so forth. Teachers and parents can have children discuss images being conveyed by people in magazines, on television, and at the mall.

Mannix (1993) developed the following questions to encourage children to think about dressing appropriately:

> ▶ Why do people make a fuss about wearing the right clothes?
> ▶ How does your appearance affect what people think of you?
> ▶ Do you ever have to get "dressed up" for something? What?
> ▶ Why do you think it's important to look as nice as you can on some occasions?
> ▶ What are some occasions when you can wear anything you want?
> ▶ Why do you think your parents would care if you went for a walk in the mud wearing your best clothes and shoes?
> ▶ Would you wear a suit (boys) or nice dress (girls) to ride your bike? Why/why not?
> ▶ If someone didn't have a lot of money or a lot of clothes, how could they still look nice in most situations? (pp. 397, 398)

### Receptive Objectics

In addition to expressive objectics, children and youth must have adequate receptive objectics. Receptive objectic ability involves "reading" other people based upon how they present themselves. For example, children must be able to identify a "safe" stranger if they need help, so that they approach a woman dressed like a mom as opposed to a man who is wearing Hells Angels' colors!

## ▶ Teaching Nonverbal Communication Skills

Table 3.1 outlines additional activities that teachers and parents can use to teach children and youth to understand and effectively use nonverbal communication skills. Teaching nonverbal communication skills is similar to teaching academic skills. For example, children learn to read (i.e., recognition/receptive skill) before they learn to write (i.e., production/expressive skill). Nowicki and Duke (1992) recommend that children and youth be taught nonverbal communication skills in four stages. In the sections that follow, we discuss each stage, using facial expressions as an example.

### Teaching Discrimination of Nonverbal Cues

Teachers and parents can teach children and youth to tell the difference between various facial expressions by using drawings, photographs, television images, or real people. Begin by pointing out resting versus non-resting faces. Move on to having children and youth focus on the three facial zones (forehead and eyes; nose and cheeks; mouth). Ask probing questions such as, "Are the expressions the same or

**TABLE 3.1** ►Activities for Teaching Nonverbal Communication Skills

| Area of Nonverbal Communication | Activity |
| --- | --- |
| *Paralanguage* | |
| Tone of voice | Identify emotions when teacher reads sentence using different voice tones. |
| | Read a script when given different situations surrounding different emotions. |
| Nonverbal sound patterns | Use different types of paralanguage to express feelings. |
| Rate of speech | Match rate with emotions such as happy, angry, sad. |
| | Tape voice and count number of words spoken per minute; compare with others. |
| *Facial expressions* | Demonstrate "resting face." |
| | Make facial expressions to convey different emotions. |
| | Identify emotions conveyed by people in public, on TV, and in magazines. |
| *Postures and gestures* | Assemble a dictionary of gestures/postures conveying specific emotions. |
| | Demonstrate postures under formal/informal situations. |
| *Interpersonal distance and touch* | Identify types of conversations that should/should not occur in each spatial zone. |
| | Discuss feelings when personal space is invaded. |
| | Demonstrate a touch for an emotion when role-playing. |
| *Rhythm and time* | Estimate length of time to complete activities. |
| | Keep track of number of times late or on time. |
| | Describe examples of public and private time. |
| *Objectics* | Develop dress codes for specific situations and use magazine pictures to illustrate. |
| | Describe image conveyed by dress when observing people in public. |
| | Develop dictionary of 'in" styles. |

Source: From "Fostering Social-Emotional Learning in the Classroom," by L. K. Elksnin and N. Elksnin, 2003, *Education, 124*, pp. 66, 67. Copyright © 2003. Reprinted by permission.

different?" "Do the two people have the same expression or different expressions?" Finally, ask these questions when children and youth examine entire faces rather than just facial zones.

## Teaching the Meaning of Nonverbal Cues

After children and youth are able to discriminate among various nonverbal cues, they must comprehend what each cue means. In the case of facial expressions, teach them to understand emotions conveyed by various facial expressions. Again, using pictures, drawings, and so forth, have children and youth learn how expressions in each of the three facial zones convey emotions such as anger, sadness, and happiness. Move on to more subtle emotions (confusion, disappointment, boredom, etc.).

After working on facial zones, have the children and youth identify emotions conveyed by the entire face. When opportunities present themselves, such as watching characters on television or observing people on the street, ask questions such as, "How do you think he/she is feeling?" "What makes you think so?" "How does the person's face tell you how he (or she) feels?"

Use the same strategies to teach children and youth how to recognize intensity of expression, beginning with facial zones and moving on to the entire face. Ask questions such as, "Do you think she is really, really mad, or just a little mad?" "Why do you think so?" "How does her face tell you how mad she is?" Show photographs of people's faces representing different intensity of emotions, and have children rate the level of emotional intensity on a scale of 1–5 and tell you why they assigned those ratings.

## Teaching Nonverbal Expressions

Once children and youth have developed nonverbal receptive skills, they are ready to learn to express themselves nonverbally. Begin by having the child show you (and himself/herself in the mirror) the "resting face." (Take a picture of the child's resting face for future reference.) Then have the child imitate facial expressions depicted in various photographs of people. Provide an emotion, and have the child make a corresponding facial expression. Begin with more obvious emotions, and move on to more subtle ones.

## Teaching Application of Nonverbal Cues to Social Situations

Begin by having children and youth role play social scenarios using appropriate nonverbal skills. For example, provide a situation and ask them to tell you how they would feel in the given circumstances. Then ask them to assume the appropriate facial expression. Prompt and cue children and youth to use appropriate nonverbal skills in actual social situations. (See Chapters Four, Eight, and Nine for more information about incidental teaching, or capitalizing on teaching opportunities.)

After a social situation has resulted in a positive (or negative) outcome, ask the child to tell you how he or she acted nonverbally, by asking questions, "How do you think your face looked?" "How were you feeling?" "How did her face look?" "How did you think he felt?"

# ▶ Increasing Emotional Literacy

Mastering the nonverbal communication skills described earlier is prerequisite for understanding emotions and developing empathy. *Emotional literacy* is "the ability to recognize, label, and understand feelings in one's self and others" (Joseph & Strain, 2003, p. 21). Children must be emotionally literate before they can regulate their emotions, solve social–emotional problems, and interact effectively with others. In the following discussion, we focus on ways to increase children's understanding of their own feelings and the feelings of others.

Mugno and Rosenblitt (2001) described four capacities that children and youth need so they can understand emotions: recognition capacity, container capacity, gross discrimination capacity, and fine discrimination capacity.

## Recognition Capacity

*When students came into Todd's seventh-grade class, they noticed that these words were written across the board:*

*angry     upset     sad/calm     indifferent     bored     happy     excited*

*After the class settled down, Todd asked his students to write down the word that best described how they felt at that exact moment. Then he asked the students to write down how they knew they felt a certain way. The class continued to discuss each word. "Think of a time when you were upset. How do you think your face looked? How did you feel inside? How did your voice sound? What did you do? Were you able to think clearly?"*

*Susan was sitting at the science center working on her report on coral reefs. When Angela pulled out a chair at the center, it knocked Susan's papers and books all over the floor.*

*"You knocked my stuff on the floor!" she exclaimed.*

*"I'm really sorry, Susan," said Angela, looking both embarrassed and dumbfounded.*

*Susan angrily pushed Angela out of the way as she crouched down to pick up her papers and books.*

*Angela thought to herself, "Why am I always so clumsy?"*

Recognition capacity is the ability to identify the presence of an emotion. The ability to perceive and identify emotions accurately is positively associated with peer acceptance, emotional adjustment, and social competence (Baum & Nowicki, 1998).

Children and youth can use the nonverbal skills discussed earlier in this chapter to relate their own facial expressions, body postures, and voice tones to how they are feeling. They also can be taught to be sensitive to internal cues such as feeling warm, sick, shaky, and so forth.

The PATHS (Promoting Alternative Thinking Strategies) curriculum (Kusche & Greenberg, 1994) teaches elementary-aged children to understand their feelings as well as the feelings of others. Teachers and parents teach children to use the following clues to determine their own feelings:

> ▶ How do I look? (Use of facial expressions and body postures) Point out that to see our facial expressions, we would have to use a mirror. However, we can feel our own facial expressions, and we usually use this to tell us how we think we look.
> ▶ What am I doing? (Use of bodily actions; e.g., throwing a tantrum, breaking something on purpose, helping someone)
> ▶ What's going on? (Use of situational and environmental clues)
> ▶ What am I saying? (Use of verbalizations)
> ▶ How do I sound? (Use of intonation)
> ▶ Has this happened to me before? (Past experiences with similar situations) (p. 561)

Todd helped his seventh graders focus on these clues through his guided discussion of the emotions on the board.

In addition to recognizing and understanding their own feelings, children and youth must understand others' feelings. Teachers and parents teach children to use these clues to determine the feelings of others:

> ▶ How does the person look? (Use of facial expressions and body postures)
> ▶ What are they doing? (Use of bodily actions)
> ▶ What's going on? (Use of situational and environmental cues)
> ▶ What is the person saying? (Use of verbalizations)
> ▶ How does the person sound? (Use of intonation)
> ▶ Has this happened to me before? (Past experiences with similar situations)
> ▶ How would I feel in this situation? (Projecting one's own feelings onto another person) (Kusche & Greenberg, 1994, p. 561)

Accurately interpreting the emotions of other people is an important social perception skill. *Social perception* is the ability to accurately interpret another's social message (Leffert et al., 2000). In our example, Susan misread Angela's behavior; she perceived that Angela deliberately knocked her papers and books on the floor. She failed to see Angela's looks of embarrassment and surprise, and she didn't hear the sincerity in Angela's voice when she apologized. Susan would have responded in a more socially appropriate way had she paid attention to Angela's nonverbal and verbal cues.

Many children and youth who have interpersonal problems misinterpret others' intentions by failing to accurately read nonverbal cues such as facial expressions and body postures, and verbal cues such as tone of voice. Teachers and parents must help them determine if what a peer did was accidental or deliberate (even if the end result is the same) (Leffert et al., 2000). Encouraging children to look for nonverbal and verbal behavior that confirms or disconfirms an event will help them more accurately interpret behavioral intent.

For example, Susan's teacher might ask her to describe how Angela looked and sounded. By having Susan focus on classmates' nonverbal and verbal cues, she can learn to respond in more socially appropriate ways.

## Container Capacity

*Deanna, 2½ years old, watched the two girls at the kitchen center in her pre-school. They had seated stuffed animals at the table and were serving tea and fruit to the panda, elephant, and bear. Deanna drew closer to the table, hoping the girls would let her join the party. But Amy and Becca, totally engrossed in their hostess roles, paid little attention to Deanna.*

*Deanna continued to watch the party, thinking about how much she would like to hold an animal. After about a minute, she whimpered, then started to cry loudly. Eventually she was crying so hard that she struggled to catch her breath. Rebuffing the assistant's attempts to comfort her, Deanna launched into a tantrum that lasted 10 minutes.*

The ability to organize and process emotion is called *container capacity.* Children and youth who don't have container capacity "hold their body rigid and shake, literally creating a bodily container" (Mugno & Rosenblitt, 2001, p. 69). Some children and youth allow the visceral, bodily response to a situation or event to cloud their thinking. Thus, Deanna was so overcome with emotion that she was not able to think of a solution to her problem (i.e., getting a stuffed animal and joining the group).

*Flooding* is the term used to describe the surge of neurons from the limbic system that can overwhelm the thinking part of the brain called the neo-cortex. Flooding results in the emotional part of the brain taking over the thinking part, which may lead to doing or saying something one may later regret (Kerr, 1999). Teaching children anger-control strategies helps them contain emotions. These strategies are discussed later in the chapter.

## Gross Discrimination Capacity

*Ann Balduchi watched her 8-year-old daughter, Samantha, struggle to put a puzzle together. The puzzle of more than 1,000 pieces was a photograph of a sailboat, and much of the puzzle was sky and ocean of almost the same color blue. The puzzle was much too difficult for a young child, but Samantha liked to take on challenges.*

*"How do you feel, Samantha?" her mom asked.*

*"Frustrated," Samantha responded.*

*Her mother prompted, "Is that a good feeling or a bad feeling?"*

*"It's more of a bad feeling than a good feeling," Samantha replied.*

*"How does your body let you know it's a bad feeling, Samantha?"*

*Samantha thought for a moment. "I feel fidgety inside, and my stomach feels funny."*

*Her mom suggested, "Maybe we can come up with a way to put the puzzle together. I always start with the frame of the puzzle. Let's sort all of the pieces that have a straight edge."*

*Samantha agreed. "You're right that could work—and then we could sort the sky pieces and the water pieces!"*

*Gross discrimination capacity* refers to the ability to determine if an emotion feels bad or good. Children and youth can be taught to recognize bodily cues that indicate good and bad feelings. The following are lists of pleasant and unpleasant feeling words, from Goldstein's (1999) PREPARE curriculum (pp. 680, 681). Teachers and parents can ask children to come up with their own lists of good and bad feeling words and the physical feelings that accompany each feeling.

| *Unpleasant Feeling Words* | *Pleasant Feeling Words* |
|---|---|
| Abandoned | Adequate |
| Angry | Affectionate |
| Betrayed | Bold |
| Bitter | Calm |
| Bored | Capable |
| Cheated | Challenged |
| Confused | Cheerful |
| Defeated | Comforting |
| Despair | Confident |
| Diminished | Content |
| Empty | Determined |
| Envious | Eager |
| Fearful | Ecstatic |
| Frightened | Energetic |
| Frustrated | Excited |
| Intimidated | Fascinated |
| Isolated | Fearless |
| Jealous | Free |
| Lonely | Fulfilled |
| Mean | Generous |
| Overwhelmed | Happy |
| Panicked | Helpful |
| Pressured | Important |

| | |
|---|---|
| Rejected | Inspired |
| Restless | Joyful |
| Sad | Kind |
| Scared | Loved |
| Strained | Loving |
| Skeptical | Peaceful |
| Tenuous | Proud |
| Threatened | Relaxed |
| Uneasy | Relieved |
| Vulnerable | Safe |
| Weepy | Satisfied |
| Worried | Secure |

Source: From *Feeling Word Vocabulary*, adapted from *The Prepare Curriculum* (pp. 680, 681) by A. P. Goldstein, 1999, Champaign, IL: Research Press. Copyright 1999 by Arnold P. Goldstein. Reprinted by permission.

## Fine Discrimination Capacity

The ability to differentiate and label emotions from the most overt to the most subtle is called *fine discrimination capacity*. Children and youth do not develop this capacity evenly. For example, they learn to make subtle discriminations (i.e., jealousy from anger, shame from guilt) between positive emotions before discriminating between negative emotions.

## Activities to Assess and Teach Emotional Vocabulary

To understand and differentiate feelings, children must have the vocabulary to describe them. Teachers and parents can teach children feeling words to expand their *feelings vocabulary*. We suggest, as a beginning, to introduce feelings words such as happy, sad, and angry, then move on to more subtle feelings such as those listed below, from Joseph and Strain (2003, p. 23).

Affectionate, agreeable, annoyed awful
Calm, capable, caring, cheerful, clumsy, confused, cooperative, creative, cruel, curious
Depressed, disappointed, disgusted
Ecstatic, embarrassed, enjoying, excited
Fantastic, fearful, fed-up, free, friendly, frustrated
Gentle, generous, gloomy, guilty
Ignored, impatient, important, interested
Jealous, joyful
Lonely, lost, loving
Overwhelmed
Peaceful, pleasant, proud
Relaxed, relieved

Safe, satisfied, sensitive, serious, shy, stressed, strong, stubborn
Tense, thoughtful, thrilled, troubled
Unafraid, uncomfortable
Weary, worried

When teaching children to make discriminations among feelings within a "feelings family," a *feelings meter* like the one pictured as Figure 3.2 is helpful. Ask the children to place a chip or other object on the feeling word that best describes how they feel about musical artists, sports, school subjects, and so forth. Then have them use the meter during the day to describe how they feel at a given moment.

Teachers and parents can foster emotional understanding by

> ▶ displaying pictures of people showing different expressions of emotion;
> ▶ reading, and encouraging children to read, books about feelings;
> ▶ labeling their own feelings;
> ▶ observing and labeling children's feelings;
> ▶ drawing attention to how a child is feeling;
> ▶ reinforcing children for labeling their feelings;
> ▶ promoting emotional literacy throughout the day. (Joseph & Strain, 2003)

Other strategies that can be used to each children and youth about their feelings appear below. Social–emotional skills programs that teach children and youth about feelings are listed in Table 3.2. Chapter Eight presents strategies that parents (and teachers) can adopt to become "emotion coaches."

### Changing Faces (Joseph & Strain, 2003)

Have young children make paper plate faces. Attach face parts (mouths, eyebrows, etc.) to the plate with brads. Have the children change facial expressions on their plates—from smile to frown, from eyebrows facing in (angry, frustrated, etc.) to facing out (worried, scared, surprised, etc.). Then read a story and have the children show how the characters feel by changing the expression on their plate faces.

### Mirrors (Joseph & Strain, 2003)

1. Give the child an unbreakable mirror.
2. Say feeling words or read a story with a lot of feeling words in it.
3. Have the child make a facial expression that corresponds to the feeling word.

### TV Show or Story Quiz

Watch a TV show or read a story. Then ask questions such as:

▶ How did the characters feel? How did you know?
▶ What were the characters thinking?
▶ How do you feel about how the characters felt?

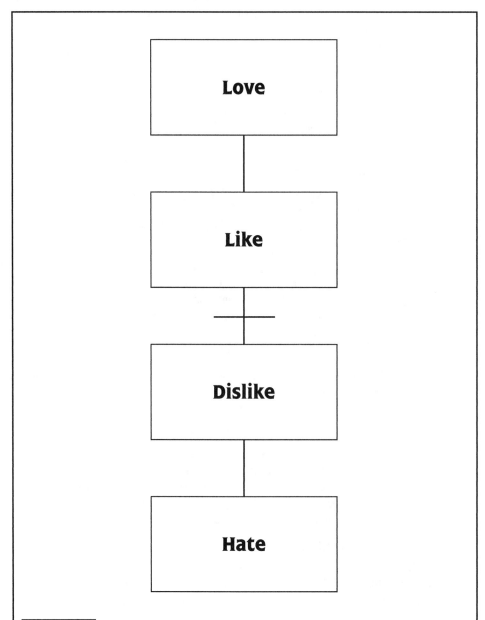

**FIGURE 3.2** ▶Feelings Meter

**TABLE 3.2** ▶Programs That Teach About Feelings

| Program | Author(s)/Date | Age/Grade |
| --- | --- | --- |
| Connecting with Others Program | Richardson (1996a; 1996b), Richardson & Evans (1997), Richardson & Meisgeier (2001) | Grades K–12 |
| Fostering Emotional Intelligence in K–8 Students | Doty (2001) | Grades K–8 |
| Passport Programs | Vernon (1998a, 1998b, 1998c) | Grades 1–2 |
| PATHS Curriculum | Kusche & Greenberg (1994) | Elementary |
| PREPARE Curriculum | Goldstein (1999) | Adolescents |
| Promoting Social Success | Siperstein & Rickards (2004) | Grades PreK-12 |
| Self-Science: The Subject Is Me | Stone & Dilleunt (1978) | Grades 2–8 |
| Skillstreaming Programs | Goldstein & McGinnis (1997), McGinnis & Goldstein (1997, 2003) | Grades PreK–12 |
| Social Skills Development | Antonello (1996) | Adolescents |
| The Stop & Think Social Skills Programs | Knopf (2001a, 2001b,2001c, 2001d) | Grades PreK–8 |
| Taking Part | Cartledge & Kleefeld (1991) | Grades PreK–3 |
| Think Aloud Small Group Program | Camp & Bash (1981) | Ages 6–8 |
| Think Aloud Classroom Programs | Camp & Bash (1985a, 1985b,985c) | Grades 1–6 |
| Thinking, Feeling, Behaving Programs | Vernon (1989a; 1989b) | Grades 1–12 |
| Working Together | Cartledge & Kleefeld (1994) | Grades 3–6 |

▶ Did the characters have the same goals?
▶ How did the characters handle the situations? Do you think individual characters handled the situation well? What are some ways the situation could be handled better?

### Feelings Charades (Elias, Tobias, & Friedlander, 1999)

1. Pick a picture of a facial expression or feeling word.
2. Have the child act out the feeling.

### Feelings Flashback (Elias, Tobias, & Friedlander, 1999)

1. Pick a "feelings" word or picture.
2. Share, and have the child share, a time when that feeling was experienced.
3. Expand by asking questions (Where were you? When did it happen? Who were you with? Where did it happen? Why did you feel that way?).

### Feeling Dictionary (Shapiro, 1997)

▶ Have child write down feeling words.
▶ Have child alphabetize words.
▶ Have child draw or select magazine pictures to illustrate each word.

---

## ▶ Role Taking

The ability to place oneself in another's "emotional shoes" is related to the developmental construct of role taking. *Role taking* (the opposite of Piaget's construct of egocentrism) is taking the perspective of another person (Shantz, 1975). Role taking begins when a child perceives another individual as a distinct entity and culminates when the child decenters, or simultaneously considers others' points of view. Role taking is related to social–emotional functioning, interpersonal problem-solving ability, and social acceptance. Developmental psychologists use several tasks to assess the perceptual, cognitive, and affective role-taking ability of children.

### Perceptual Role-Taking Tasks

Perceptual role-taking tasks assess the child's ability to assume another's physical viewpoint. Kurdek and Rodgon (1975) used two identical revolving trays on which were glued figures of Disney characters. The adult rotated her tray 90°, 120°, and 180°, and then directed the children to "turn your tray so you see Mickey Mouse, Goofy, and Pinocchio just the way I'm seeing them now." Children who were able to position their trays as the adult perceived her tray were regarded as demonstrating perceptual role-taking ability.

### Cognitive Role-Taking Tasks

Cognitive role-taking tasks measure the child's ability to infer another's thinking or knowledge. Kurdek and Rodgon (1975) showed a child seven picture cards that illustrated a story about a boy and his dog, and asked the child to describe the events presented by each picture. The adults removed three cards, then asked the child to predict the story a friend would tell if he were to sit down and look at the remaining four picture cards. The child with cognitive role-taking ability was able to perceive the friend's cognitive perspective and tell the story without including information available in the original seven cards.

## Affective Role-Taking Tasks

Affective role-taking tasks are designed to assess a child's ability to understand another's feelings and the reason for those feelings. Deutsch (1974) showed pre-schoolers videos that depicted congruous (e.g., a child looking happy when given a birthday gift) and incongruous (e.g., a child looking sad while eating an ice cream cone) emotional situations and asked them to identify feelings that were appropriate or inappropriate to each situation. The children who were able to assess the video characters' emotions were regarded as having affective role-taking ability.

## Stages of Role Taking

Children go through five stages of role taking. Each stage is discussed within the context of Holly's social dilemma.

*Holly is an 8-year-old girl who likes to climb trees. She is the best tree climber in the neighborhood. One day while climbing down from a tall tree, she falls off the bottom branch but doesn't hurt herself. Her father sees her fall. He is upset and asks her to promise not to climb trees anymore. Holly promises.*

  *Later that day, Holly and her friends meet Sean, whose kitten is caught up in a tree and cannot get down. Something has to be done right away or the kitten may fall. Holly is the only one who climbs trees well enough to reach the kitten and get it down, but she remembers her promise to her father. (Selman & Byrne, 1974, p. 805)*

### Level 1: Undifferentiated and Egocentric Role Taking (3–6 years)

At Level 1, children differentiate themselves from others but are unable to differentiate points of view. Children have difficulty understanding that another person may interpret the situation differently. Children at Level 1 predict that Holly will climb the tree to save the kitten, but they also predict that Holly's father will feel the same way she does about climbing the tree.

### Level 2: Differentiated and Subjective Role Taking (5–9 years)

At Level 2, children realize that their perspective and those of others may differ, but they cannot maintain their own perspective and simultaneously put themselves in the other's place to interpret the other person's actions. Children at this level of role taking predict that Holly's father may or may not be angry, depending on the information available. They recognize that Holly's perspective and those of her father may or may not be different.

### Level 3: Self-reflective or Reciprocal Role Taking (7–12 years)

At Level 3, children are able to reflect on their behavior and motivation from another's point of view. They also recognize that others can take their perspective. These reflections, however, occur sequentially rather than simultaneously. Children at this level of role taking predict that Holly won't be punished because Holly's father will understand that she had to climb the tree to save the kitten.

### Level 4: Third-party or Mutual Role Taking (10–15 years)

At Level 4, children understand that they and others can simultaneously reflect on each other's point of view. They can assume a disinterested point of view and consider a situation from the perspective of a third party, and thus are credited with the ability to assume the points of view of the observed parties. Children at this level predict that Holly will not be punished if she can convince her father that it was important for her to climb the tree.

### Level 5: In-depth and Societal Perspective Taking (about 14 years–adulthood)

According to Berk (1989), adolescents and adults have "an appreciation that mutual coordination of perspectives can take place on multiple or progressively deeper levels of understanding, including the levels of superficial information, shared interests, common expectations, or at a deeper level of unverbalized feelings and values" (p. 486). At Level 5, the individual considers Holly's dilemma within a societal context and may conclude that Holly's father will appreciate her desire to be kind to animals and therefore will forgive her for climbing the tree to save the kitten.

## Role-Taking Activity

Children's role-taking ability affects social–emotional skills instruction. For example, preschoolers cannot be expected to understand how others feel, because they are unable to assume others' perspectives. Although elementary-aged children are less egocentric and understand that others may see things or feel differently than they do, they are still unable to simultaneously hold their own and others' perspectives.

Children and youth who have limited role-taking ability may need practice and prompts to become more sensitive to how others perceive, think, and feel about various situations. The following activity (Kerr, 1999) can be used to help adolescents become more skilled at seeing another's point of view:

1. Discuss why it may be difficult to see another person's perspective.
2. Present situations in which characters have differing points of view. Example: Seventeen-year-old Chad wants to borrow the family car to pick up his friend at the airport. The airport is 50 miles away, and his friend's plane doesn't arrive until 9:30 p.m. Chad's dad will not let him take the car.

3. Have children role play in pairs, each child taking the point of view of one of the characters.
4. Create a chart for each situation. The chart should have two columns—one for each character.
5. Have members of the group list the concerns, feelings, and thoughts of each character.

---

## ▶ Empathy

*Rachel, age 13, looked out of the car window as her dad drove through an economically depressed part of the city. As the car came to a stop at a light, Rachel saw a woman and her two young children huddled over a heating grate. A nearby shopping cart appeared to hold all of the family's worldly possessions. The woman wore a light sweater and the children were dressed in layers of clothing. The outside temperature was 28°, and snow was expected.*

*Rachel opened the car door and jumped out.*

*"Rachel, what are you doing!" her dad yelled. He watched open-mouthed as his daughter gave her heavy winter coat to the woman and ran back to the car. For the next hour, Rachel and her father talked about the homeless family.*

*The next day, Rachel announced that she was going to start a "Coat Co-op." She would begin to help homeless families by asking students at her school to donate winter jackets and coats they no longer needed.*

Schonert-Reichi defined *empathy* as "a person's emotional responsiveness to the emotional experiences of another" (1993, p. 189). Children and youth must understand others' emotions and take their perspectives before they can feel empathy for others. Like role taking, the development of empathy is age-related, although some children, like Rachel, seem to be innately more empathetic than others.

Shapiro (1997) describes how empathy develops. *Global empathy* develops during infancy. Although a baby cannot differentiate between self and the world, he or she inevitably cries when another infant cries. From 1 to 2 years of age, children begin to understand that another's feelings of distress are not their own feelings. At about age 6, *cognitive empathy* develops, in which children see things from others' perspectives. Between the ages of 10 and 12, children develop *abstract empathy,* understanding the perspectives of people whom they have never met. During this period the children may begin to engage in charitable and altruistic acts.

Children and youth should be expected to be empathetic. Further, they should be encouraged to become involved in community service. As Shapiro (1997) aptly states, "In teaching children to care for others, there is no substitute for experience; talking is simply not enough" (p. 59). Barry Brazleton (2001), the eminent pediatrician, recommends the following strategies for nurturing compassion and empathy:

> ▶ Talk together about ways your family can help those less fortunate.
> ▶ Compliment your child on anything thoughtful he does for someone else.
> ▶ Encourage your child to help with household chores.
> ▶ Give your child some (but not too much) responsibility for a younger sibling.
> ▶ Help your child understand someone else's feelings. ("Did you see how sad Mary looked when she was not chosen for the team?")
> ▶ Encourage your child to seek neighborhood jobs . . . he'll feel he has contributed to the community.
> ▶ Take your child on outings to nursing homes and children's hospital wards so he can spend time with those who may be lonely or sad. As he gets older, suggest a volunteer job, but leave the choice of it to him.
> ▶ When your child is unkind to another child, don't scold. Instead, tell him you know how bad he must feel and help him apologize. (p. 30)

## ▶ Managing and Controlling Anger

*Rick and Paula were concerned about their 14-year-old son Jeremy, who "blew up" at the slightest provocation. His uncontrollable anger had gotten him in trouble both at home and at school. In the latest incident, Jeremy got into a shouting match with his science teacher. After Jeremy told the teacher to "get f_ _ _ ed," he was suspended for 3 days.*

*Rick and Paula frequently felt the brunt of Jeremy's anger, and their son had a real gift for saying the most hurtful things imaginable. And it wasn't just authority figures either. Friends and acquaintances felt Jeremy's wrath as well. His friendship circle was narrowing because kids didn't want to put up with his rages. He no longer was on the baseball team because he got into a fight with a teammate who struck out. Jeremy was next at bat, but his teammate made the third out. Jeremy yelled, "You stupid _ _ _ h o l e. You're about the most useless member on this team. Why don't you stay home?"*

According to Shapiro (1997), half of children referred for mental health services have anger-control problems. Their inability to contain themselves has serious implications not only for themselves, but also for society at large. Some children and youth with anger-control problems engage in violent behavior. Bodine and Crawford (1999) listed the following examples.

> ▶ *February 2, 1996:* At Frontier Junior High School in Moses Lake, Washington, the teacher and two students are killed

and a third student wounded when a 14-year-old enters an algebra class and opens fire with a hunting rifle he concealed in a trench coat.

▶ *February 19, 1997*: The principal and a student are killed and two students wounded when a 16-year-old opens fire with a shotgun in a common area at the Bethel, Alaska, high school.

▶ *October 1, 1997*: A 16-year-old in Pearl, Mississippi, is accused of killing his mother, then going to Pearl High School and shooting nine students. Two die, including the suspect's ex-girlfriend.

▶ *December 1, 1997*: Three students are killed and five others wounded in a prayer circle in a hallway before classes were scheduled to begin at Heath High School in West Paducah, Kentucky. A 14-year-old student of the school is arrested.

▶ *March 24, 1998*: Four girls and a teacher are shot to death and 10 others wounded during a false fire alarm at Westside Middle School in Jonesboro, Arkansas. Two boys, ages 11 and 13, are accused of setting the alarm and then opening fire from a nearby woods.

▶ *April 24, 1998*: A science teacher is shot to death in front of students at a graduation dance in Edinboro, Pennsylvania. A 14-year-old student of James W. Parker Middle School is charged.

▶ *May 19, 1998*: Three days before his graduation, an 18-year-old honor student opens fire in a parking lot at Lincoln County High School in Fayetteville, Tennessee, killing a classmate who allegedly was dating his ex-girlfriend.

▶ *May 21, 1998*: A 17-year-old student is killed and more than 20 other people wounded after a 15-year-old boy opens fire at Thurston High School in Springfield, Oregon. Following his apprehension at the school, the bodies of his parents are found at home.

▶ *June 15, 1998*: A teacher/coach and an adult volunteer aide are both wounded in Richmond, Virginia, when a 14-year-old opens fire in a crowded hallway outside Armstrong High School's main office during final exams week. Neither adult is wounded fatally; allegedly neither was the shooter's intended target.

▶ *April 20, 1999*: Two students, ages 17 and 18, in a prolonged siege of Columbine High School in Littleton, Colorado, kill a teacher and 12 students before killing themselves. Several others inside the school were wounded during the shooting and bombing rampage.

▶ *May 20, 1999*: A 15-year-old student opens fire in a commons area just before classes were scheduled to begin at Heritage

High School in Conyers, Georgia. Six students were injured in this shooting spree.

Source: From *Developing Emotional Intelligence* (p. 19, 20), by R. J. Bodine and K. K. Crawford, 1999, Champaign, IL: Research Press. Copyright © 1999 by R. J. Bodine and K. K. Crawford. Reprinted with permission.

Contrary to popular belief, violence is not confined to schools in inner-city neighborhoods. In fact, in each of the above cases the perpetrators were white students attending schools in small towns, rural communities, or suburban areas. Of those 973,000 students who reported carrying a gun to school during the 1997–98 school year, 59% were white, 18% black, 12% Hispanic, 3% Asian, and 3% Native American (Bodine & Crawford, 1999). Further, violent acts are not confined to older children. The American Psychological Association (1993) reported that children are committing violent acts at younger ages than ever before. Clearly, teaching children and youth to control and manage their anger is a major challenge for teachers and parents.

Anger-control programs teach children and youth to recognize how they feel when they get angry, to recognize events and situations that trigger their angry feelings, and to stop (count to 10, take a deep breath, etc.) before they do or say something they may later regret. Many programs also teach children how to relax so they can get their angry feelings under control. Ten points critical to anger management are (Kellner, 2001):

1. Anger is a normal and natural human feeling.
2. An anger trigger is a situation or event that sets us off.
3. An anger setting is a place where we tend to get angry.
4. An anger log helps us reflect on how we handled our anger this time and decide how we might handle it better next time.
5. Anger management helps us recognize our anger, interrupt ourselves before we behave inappropriately, and then substitute an anger management tool.
6. Anger shows itself in our physiology (our bodies). Deep breathing, counting, and muscle relaxation are examples of physiological tools for anger management.
7. What we think to ourselves has an effect on how angry we get. Self-talk and self-statements are thinking tools for anger management.
8. What we choose to do can help us stay calm and in control. Walking away or talking things out with a friend are examples of behavioral tools for anger management.
9. When we manage anger well, we stay in control, respect people and property, and get positive results.
10. Anger management helps us make our anger work for us: We think ahead and make plans to stay calm and in control. (p. 121)

Schneider and Robin (1973) developed an anger-control program that combines relaxation and problem solving. Young children are introduced to "Turtle" through a story about a turtle that withdraws into his shell when he starts to feel angry. Teachers and parents model "doing Turtle" by pulling arms close to the body, putting heads down, and closing eyes. The word "turtle" is used to cue children to "do the Turtle" when they are angry with themselves or others, or when they are asked to do so by a teacher or parent. Children are taught relaxation exercises because relaxation and anger are incompatible feelings. While doing "Turtle," children engage in relaxation exercise such as the following.

Have the children tense, then suddenly relax, muscles in each part of the body. For each muscle group, tell the children in a calming voice with little inflection:

"I'd like you to *make fists with your hands.*"
"Hold *your fists* as tight as possible, count to 10, then let go."
"Let go and feel how good it is, how relaxed and good you feel."
"Now, let's do it again. *Make fists with your hands.*"
"Hold *your fists* as tight as possible while I count: 10-9-8-7-6-5-4-3-2-1."
"Release. Let go and feel how good it is, how relaxed and good you feel."

As children practice their exercises, feel their muscles to make sure they are tensing and releasing their muscles. Have them repeat the exercises until they reach a high degree of fluency.

Have children tense and relax muscles in each part of the body (Schneider & Robin, 1973):

▶ Make fists to tense your *hands.*
▶ Bend your arms back at the elbow towards the shoulder to tense your *arms.*
▶ Push your feet against the ground to tense your *feet.*
▶ Bend your legs back at the knees to tense your *legs.*
▶ Press your lips together firmly, close your eyes tightly, and wrinkle your forehead to tense your *face.*
▶ Pull your stomach in to tense your *stomach.*
▶ Take a deep breath and hold it to tense your *chest.*

After mastering "Turtle," children learn to solve problems to prevent situations leading to anger and aggression.

Elias and Tobias (1996) developed several strategies children and youth can use to control their anger. Children first learn to identify their "Feelings Footprints"—body feelings that send them a message that they are about to lose control. These feelings might include feeling warm, short of breath, tense, and so forth. Next they identify their "Trigger Situations" that cause them to lose control. Finally, they learn to use the "Keep Calm Strategy":

Keep Calm is something that will help you get ready to solve problems and handle your Trigger Situations [i.e., situations that cause you to lose control]. There are four simple steps to remember:

1. Tell yourself to "Stop and take a look around."
2. Tell yourself to "Keep calm."
3. Take a deep breath through your nose while you count to 5, hold it while you count to 2, then breathe out through your mouth while you count to 5.
4. Repeat these steps until you feel calm. (p. 47)

A list of social–emotional skills programs that teach anger-control appears as Table 3.3.

Many children and adolescents (and some adults) have difficulty understanding the difference between aggressive and assertive behavior. The Waksman Social Skills Curriculum (S. Waksman & D. D. Waksman, 1998) directly teaches the difference between passive, aggressive, and assertive behavior. Similarly, Elias and Tobias (1996) developed the BEST behavior strategy to teach children the difference between a passive (Shrinker), aggressive (Blaster), and assertive/effective (Me) person. BEST teaches children to act like "Me" by following these steps:

| | |
|---|---|
| B—Body posture: | Standing up straight, being confident in yourself, but not arrogant. |
| E—Eye contact: | Looking the person directly in the eye, communicating with them openly. |
| S—Saying appropriate things: | Using appropriate language and saying what you really feel. |
| T—Tone of voice: | Using a calm voice, not whispering or shouting. (p. 50) |

In addition to teaching children and youth to control their anger, it is important to address behaviors that begin the escalation to violence. Bodine and Crawford (1999) refer to these behaviors as *opening moves,* examples of which include, in order of frequency:

1. unprovoked offensive touching
2. interference with someone's possession or object being used
3. interference with a request to do something
4. backbiting
5. playful verbal teasing
6. put-downs
7. rough physical play
8. insults

Children and youth who are emotionally intelligent are unlikely to make opening moves like these. In the chapters that follow we offer some specific strategies that teachers and parents can use to replace opening moves with more appropriate

**TABLE 3.3** ▶Programs That Teach Anger Control

| Program | Author(s)/Date | Age/Grade |
|---|---|---|
| ACCESS | Walker, Todis, Holmes, & Horton (1988) | Adolescents |
| EQUIP | Gibbs, Potter, & Goldstein (1995) | Grades K–12 |
| In Control | Kellner (2001) | Adolescents |
| Passport programs | Vernon (1998a, 1998b, 1998c) | Grades 1–12 |
| PATHS curriculum | Kusche & Greenberg (1994) | Elementary |
| The Power of Social Skills in Character Development | Scully (2000) | Adolescents |
| PREPARE curriculum | Goldstein (1999) | Adolescents |
| Ready-to-Use Social Skills Lessons and Activities | Begun (1995, 1996a, 1996b, 1996c) | Grades PreK–12 |
| Skillstreaming programs | Goldstein & McGinnis (1997), McGinnis & Goldstein (1997, 2003) | Grades PreK–12 |
| Social Skills Activities for Secondary Students with Special Needs | Mannix (1998) | Grades 6–12 |
| Social Skills in the Classroom | Stephens (1992) | Children & adolescents |
| Social Skills Intervention Guide | Elliott & Gresham (1991) | Grades 1–10 |
| Stop & Think Social Skills programs | Knopf (2001a, 2001b, 2001c, 2001d) | Grades PreK–8 |
| Teaching Social Competence to Youth & Adults with Developmental Disabilities | D. A. Jackson, N. F. Jackson, & Bennett (1998) | Adolescents & adults |
| Teaching Social Skills to Youth | Down & Tierney (1992) | Children & adolescents |
| Tough Kids Social Skills Book | Sheridan (1995–1996) | Grades K–8 |
| The Transitions Curriculum | Fulton & Silva (1998) | Grades 8–12 |
| A Volcano in My Tummy | Whitehouse & Pudney (1996) | Ages 6–10 |
| The Waksman Social Skills Curriculum | S. Waksman & D. D. Waksman (1998) | Middle school |
| Working Together | Cartledge & Kleefeld (1994) | Grades 3–6 |

social–emotional behavior. To resolve conflicts, children and adolescents are taught the skills of negotiation, mediation, and consensus building.

## ▶ Chapter Summary

Skills necessary to become emotionally literate include the ability to read and send nonverbal communication through tone of voice, rate of speech, facial expression, gesture, and posture. An understanding of physical and mental space, time, and objectics is also required to develop effective receptive and expressive nonverbal communication abilities. Recognizing and labeling emotions of self and others is prerequisite to understanding feelings. Understanding feelings of others enables children and youth to assume another person's perspective and to develop empathy for other people.

Many children and youth need direct instruction to become skilled in nonverbal communication, emotional understanding, perspective taking, and empathy. It also is important for children and youth to control and manage angry feelings. Anger-control strategies will prevent feelings from getting in the way of solving social–emotional problems—the topic of Chapter Four.

# Teaching Children and Youth Social–Emotional Problem-Solving Strategies

## Goals of This Chapter

In reading this chapter you will learn

- how social–emotional problem-solving ability is related to social competence
- how child development influences social–emotional problem solving
- the importance of modeling social–emotional problem solving for children and youth
- how to teach children problem-solving strategies
- how to conduct a social skills autopsy
- which programs focus on social–emotional problem-solving skills
- how to use children's literature to teach social–emotional problem-solving skills

# Terms to Know

alternative solutions

bibliotherapy

cognitive modeling

consequences

dynamic orientation

means–end thinking

positive alternative communication

power assertion communication

social–causal–recognition

social–emotional problem solving

social information processing

social skill autopsy

thought-structuring sequence

*Amy, a 12-year-old, moved from Kansas City to Charlotte, North Carolina. She was learning about her new community, her new neighborhood, and her new school. In Kansas she would have started junior high as a seventh grader. In North Carolina she was in her second year of middle school. There were other differences as well. In Kansas City, Amy walked to school. In Charlotte, she took the bus.*

*The first day Amy walked to her bus stop and noticed a group of girls about her age. It turned out that two of the girls were in her class at school. Amy wanted to get to know these girls, so she stood near the girls at the bus stop and during recess, hoping they would approach her. The girls didn't bother to say hello, but they didn't look unfriendly.*

*Amy thought about her situation. "My problem is that I want to make friends with these girls. I've tried to smile and look friendly, but they ignore me. I've tried to wait for them to come up to me, and that hasn't worked. One of the girls lives near me. I could walk with her to the bus stop and introduce myself. Then maybe she would introduce me to her friends." Amy tried her strategy the next day, and it worked!*

*The girl's name was Ashley, just like her best friend in Kansas City. Amy and she both liked horses and soccer. The best part was that Ashley introduced Amy to her two friends, Sara and Jenna.*

Children and youth must be able to solve social problems if they are to get along with others (Healey & Masterpasqua, 1992; Rahill & Teglasi, 2003; Wehmeyer & Kelchner, 1994). *Social–emotional problem solving* involves identifying the problem, generating potential solutions, selecting a solution, implementing a plan, and finally, evaluating the effectiveness of the plan. Problem-solving strategies are generic—they can be used to solve a wide array of social–emotional problems. These strategies require children to be actively involved in the instructional process as decision makers and as regulators of their own behavior (L. K. Elksnin & N. Elksnin, 1995; Elliott, Sheridan, & Gresham, 1989; Matson & Ollendick, 1988).

Berk (1989) defined social problem solving as "efforts to resolve conflict effectively—in ways that are socially acceptable but at the same time achieve results that are beneficial to self" (p. 498). Dodge (1986) conceptualized social problem solving as a five-step model of social information processing. When confronted with a social problem, the child must (a) encode social cues, (b) accurately interpret social cues, (c) search for an appropriate response, (d) select a response after evaluating the consequences of all responses generated, and (e) respond while monitoring how the response affects self and others.

In our opening example, Amy demonstrated good social information-processing ability. Had she misinterpreted the girls' feelings toward her (i.e., active dislike), she might not have tried to get to know them. She defined her problem/goal clearly. She recognized that her strategy of smiling and being in close proximity to the girls was not working, so she tried another solution, which helped her reach her goal. Finally, she evaluated the outcome of her plan and decided that it worked well. She'll probably try the same solution in similar situations.

Many of the skills that children need before engaging in social problem solving were described in Chapter Three, including (Shure & Glaser, 2001)

- ▶ language skills—concepts, emotions;
- ▶ perceptual skills—body language, facial expressions, tone of voice;
- ▶ cognitive skills—generating solutions and consequential thinking;
- ▶ motor skills—to demonstrate concepts, vocabulary words, and so forth.

We begin this chapter by discussing how social–emotional problem solving is a developmental skill that is essential for social competence. We stress the importance of modeling social–emotional problem-solving skills and present a thought-structuring sequence that can be used to lead children and youth through the problem-solving process. We describe several problem-solving strategies that teachers and parents can teach children, including the PATHS problem-solving strategy, FIG TESPN, and the social skill autopsy. We review several commercial curricula that are directed primarily to social–emotional problem solving. We then offer ways in which children's literature may be used to teach problem solving and end the chapter with problem-solving activities that can be used in school and at home.

# ▶ Developmental Aspects of Social Problem Solving

*It was Maggie Spenser's fourth week on the job at Burger King. Maggie's mom was the divorced mother of three children, ranging in age from 5 to 17-year-old Maggie. Mrs. Spenser worked long hours as a caterer, but after paying the rent, the utilities, and buying groceries, there was little extra cash.*

*Without her Burger King job, Maggie would be unable to buy new clothes and occasionally go out with her friends. She wanted to keep this job. The problem was that her manager, Mr. Zaremba, had asked her to work late tonight because another kitchen worker had called in sick, but Maggie had promised her mom that she'd leave 2 hours early so she could help her bake cookies for a catering job. The cookies had to be delivered early the next morning, and Mrs. Spenser would be up all night if Maggie didn't help out. Her mom worked so hard and was tired all the time, so Maggie didn't want to let her down. But Mr. Zaremba was a good boss, and he depended on Maggie, too.*

Much of what we know about children's interpersonal problem solving is based on the work of Spivack and Shure (1974, 1983), who identified six interpersonal cognitive problem-solving (ICPS) skills:

1. Generation of *alternate solutions*
2. Consideration of *consequences* of social acts
3. Development of *means–end thinking,* or the ability to articulate steps needed to solve a social problem
4. Development of *social–causal–recognition* that one's feelings and actions are reciprocally related to those of others
5. *Sensitivity to problems,* including awareness of social problems generally as well as problems relevant to a specific situation
6. *Dynamic orientation,* which recognizes that behavior may be the consequence of motives or antecedents that are difficult to identify

As would be expected, the number and quality of social–emotional problem-solving skills we use increase with age. In addition, certain skills are more essential for social–emotional competence at certain ages (Bierman & Montminy, 1993; Eisenberg & Harris, 1984). For example, the ability to generate alternative solutions and understand social consequences is extremely important for preschoolers. Means–end thinking is an essential skill for adolescents, and develops in earnest during preadolescence. However, there are variations in social–emotional problem-solving abilities among same-aged children. Brion-Meisels and Selman (1984) reported that young adolescents ranged across four levels of interpersonal negotiation ability:

*Level 0:*   *Impulsive egocentric negotiations,* which result in a "fight or flight" response from others. At this level, children are unable to coordinate their own perspectives and those of others. Although younger children may resort to a *physical* fight-or-flight response, typically developing adolescents rarely do so.

*Level 1:*　　*Command or one-way negotiations,* which result in a "command or give-in" response. At this level, children recognize that other individuals may have different perspectives but they are unable to coordinate the perspective of self and others. They rely on verbal commands and may negotiate differently with peers than with adults.

*Level 2:*　　*Reciprocal, exchange-oriented negotiations,* which result in an "influence or accommodating" response. Many younger adolescents negotiate at this level. They can consider how another individual perceives their needs and understand how to negotiate fairly, making deals, trades, or exchanges. They also understand how outcomes will affect the future. Adolescents who lack effective negotiation strategies at this stage often have difficulty establishing long-term friendships and developing good working relationships.

*Level 3:*　　*Mutual, collaborative negotiations,* which result in "meeting mutual needs." At this level, adolescents are able to compromise, collaborate, and set goals cooperatively. They adjust their negotiation strategies depending upon others' situations and feelings (e.g., a boss who is in a bad mood, a parent who is in a hurry to leave for work). They also assume the perspective of a third party, who in turn assumes multiple perspectives, leading to the development of mutually acceptable solutions. The skills that develop at this level support intimate, stable friendships and enable adolescents to negotiate effectively with parents and employers. Adolescents who fail to reach this level of negotiating often are frustrated and may respond by acting out or withdrawing.

Notice how closely each of the levels is tied to role-taking ability, which we described in Chapter Three. Interpersonal negotiation abilities affect children's ability to identify problems, generate alternatives, anticipate consequences, and evaluate outcomes. This point is illustrated by Table 4.1, which suggests how Maggie might solve her social–emotional problem at different levels of negotiation strategy.

Children and youth with disabilities often lag behind their typically developing peers in problem-solving ability. For example, children with mental retardation generate fewer solutions to problems (Gomez & Hazeldine, 1996; Healey & Masterpasqua, 1992; Wehmeyer & Kelchner, 1994). Children with learning disabilities have difficulty identifying problems and anticipating consequences (Bryan et al., 1998; Shondrick, Serafica, Clark, & Miller, 1992). Indeed, poor social–emotional problem-solving ability is a defining characteristic of children with emotional and behavioral disorders (Coleman, Wheeler, & Webber, 1993).

The good news is that children and youth with and without disabilities can be taught to be more effective social–emotional problem solvers (O'Reilly & Glynn,

**TABLE 4.1** ▶How Level of Negotiation Influences Social–Emotional Problem-Solving Skills

**Social–Emotional Problem-Solving Skills**

| Negotiation Level | Identification of Problem | Generation of of Solutions | Anticipation of Consequences | Evaluation of Results |
|---|---|---|---|---|
| **Level 0 Fight or Flight** | I'm leaving (intent and action are identical). | Walk out. | I won't have to work. | Did I leave? |
| | The boss won't let me leave. | Stay. | The boss will make me stay. | Did he make me stay? |
| **Level 1 Command or Give In** | I don't want to stay at work. | I'll quit if he makes me stay. He won't miss me. I'll say I'm sick. | I'll get fired. I'll help my mom. The boss won't mess with me. | Did I get the boss to let me go? |
| | The boss wants me to stay at work. | I'll just stay. | He'll keep giving me the worst jobs. He'll like me better. | Did the boss make me stay? |
| **Level 2 Reciprocal Exchange** | How can I leave and still help the boss? | I'll give reasons why I can't stay. I'll offer to stay next time. I'll offer to stay this time only. | He'll understand if I give him reasons. He may be willing to trade hours. I can't help my mom, so I need to find someone to help her. | Did each of us get what we wanted? |
| **Level 3 Mutual Collaboration** | How can we decide on a way to work out this problem and others like it? | I'll ask if I can leave this time and work out a schedule next time. | He may be disappointed. My mom may be disappointed. | Has communication between us improved? If not, what is the next step? |
| | Can I communicate my problem to the boss in a way he will understand? | I'll offer to stay this time but make up a schedule for the future. | Maybe he'll work out a schedule to deal with the problem in the future. | |

Source: Adapted from "Early Adolescent Development of New Interpersonal Strategies: Understanding Intervention," by S. Brion-Meisels and R. L. Selman, in *School Psychology Review, 13,* p. 285. Copyright © 1984 by the National Association of School Psychologists, Bethesda, MD. Reprinted with permission of the publisher.

1995; Rosenthal-Malek & Yoshida, 1994). For example, O'Reilly and Glynn (1995) found that adolescents with mild cognitive disabilities learned to use a problem-solving approach and were able to generalize the skills across settings and contexts. In the discussion that follows we describe several strategies that can be used to help children solve social–emotional problems.

## ► Teachers and Parents as Problem-Solving Role Models

*Sam, age 6, and his sister Maureen, 8, were doing their homework at the kitchen table when they heard their mom say, "I have a problem. I promised Mrs. Hernandez that I would work for her next Saturday afternoon so she could take her sister to the airport. I forgot about my promise and told your dad I would go to see him play in the golf tournament that same day. I really want to see your dad play, and I know he's counting on the whole family being there for the tournament. But Mrs. Hernandez is my friend and co-worker, and I don't want to let her down."*

*"What are you going to do?" Maureen asked.*

*"Well, I could tell Mrs. Hernandez to find someone else to work for her, but I'm sure she'd wonder what kind of friend I am to cancel at the last minute. I could tell your dad I forgot about my promise to Mrs. Hernandez and I had to keep it, but he'd be disappointed and he might think her friendship is more important to me than he is. Finally, I could try to find someone else to work for Mrs. Hernandez. That way, I wouldn't let her or your dad down. I think that's what I'll do."*

*Mom made a couple of calls before she found someone who could work Saturday. Then she called Mrs. Hernandez and told her she had found someone to work for her on Saturday because she had promised to watch the golf tournament. She told Sam and Maureen, "You know what? Mrs. Hernandez thanked me for getting someone to work for her when I wasn't able to work Saturday. She said she totally understood that I needed to be at the tournament. I guess my plan worked pretty well!"*

By modeling problem solving, teachers and parents can help children and youth acquire problem-solving skills. When situations present themselves, "think out loud" while working through this sequence:

1. What is my problem?
2. How can I solve it?
3. Am I using my plan?
4. How is my plan working?

Sam and Maureen's mother did a good job of working through each of these steps, and the kids saw that their mom's plan worked. Children also need to observe teachers and parents trying alternative solutions when the first plan doesn't work. By modeling social–emotional problem-solving steps throughout the day, we can help children use problem-solving routines independently.

Most children need more than a skilled model to learn social–emotional problem-solving skills. Teachers and parents will have to guide them through problem-solving steps. The thought-structuring sequence shown below begins with the adult "talking out loud" while solving a problem and culminates with children using "self-talk" to guide themselves through the problem-solving process. (Meichenbaum & Goodman, 1971).

**Step One—Cognitive Modeling:** The adult models the problem-solving strategy by talking out loud, asking questions like these generated by Camp and Bash (1981, 1985a, 1985b, 1985c):

What is my problem?
How can I do it?
Am I using my plan?
How did I do?

**Step Two—Overt, External Guidance:** The adult talks out loud, describing each step in the strategy sequence as the child performs the step.

**Step Three—Faded, Overt, Self-Guidance:** The child whispers each step in the strategy sequence while performing the step.

**Step Four—Covert, Self-Instruction:** The child uses "private speech" while performing each step of the strategy.

We must recognize that our communication styles may either encourage or discourage problem solving. Shure and Glaser (2001) identified four levels of adult-to-child communication:

*Level I:*   *Power assertion communication* is characterized by negative commands, demands, and time-outs.

*Level II:*   *Positive alternative communication* involves telling children what to do rather than what not to do.

*Level III:*   The *explanations and reasons* level is illustrated by these examples:

"If you don't share your room when your cousin comes to visit, he'll think that you don't like him."
"If you ask the girls if you can play, they probably will say yes."

Adults often use "I" messages to let children know how their behavior makes the adult feel.

"I feel really sad when you say you hate your baby brother."

"I am really proud of you when you share your toys with Evan."

*Level IV:* *Problem-solving communication* involves the use of open-ended questions that help children identify and solve problems:

"What happened before he said you couldn't play with him anymore?"
"How did you feel when you found out you weren't invited to the party?"

Although Levels II and III are more positive forms of communication than Level I, both still focus on telling children what to do. Level IV, however, promotes independent problem solving by allowing children to form their own hypotheses.

## Problem-Solving Strategies

Next we describe several problem-solving strategies that help children and youth become better social–emotional problem solvers.

### PATHS Problem-Solving Strategy

PATHS (Promoting Alternative Thinking Strategies; Kusche & Greenberg, 1994), a comprehensive social–emotional skills curriculum, includes a problem-solving unit designed to help elementary-aged children identify and solve problems. When identifying problems, children consider the following questions:

- ▶ Is there a problem?
- ▶ Who owns the problem?
- ▶ What is the problem? (p. 924)

Children determine who owns a problem by using clues. Clues indicating that the child himself or herself owns the problem are

- ▶ when we feel upset or confused,
- ▶ when something is bothering or troubling us,
- ▶ when we are in a difficult situation,
- ▶ when we feel like something is wrong,
- ▶ when we feel like we need help or advice about something. (p. 924)

Clues indicating that other people have a problem include

- ▶ when they look upset or confused,
- ▶ when they look like something is bothering or troubling them,
- ▶ when they are in a difficult situation,
- ▶ when they look like something is wrong,
- ▶ when they ask us for help or advice about something,
- ▶ when they tell us they have a problem. (p. 925)

The PATHS problem-solving strategy will help children identify problems, set goals, think of solutions and consequences of each, choose the best solution for the situation, and plan, implement, and evaluate the solution. The PATHS strategy underscores that not all plans are effective and that children may have to try another solution if their first solution doesn't work. The steps in the PATHS problem-solving strategy are as follows (Kusche & Greenberg, 1994):

Step 1:  STOP and CALM down.
Step 2:  Identify the PROBLEMS (collect lots of information).
Step 3:  Identify the FEELINGS (your own and other people's).
Step 4:  Decide on a GOAL.
Step 5:  Think of lots of SOLUTIONS.
Step 6:  Think about the CONSEQUENCES (what might happen).
Step 7:  Choose the BEST solution (evaluate all of the alternatives).
Step 8:  Make a good PLAN (think about the possible obstacles).
Step 9:  TRY MY plan.
Step 10:  EVALUATE—How did I do?
Step 11:  If you need to, TRY AGAIN. (p. 915)

## FIG TESPN

FIG TESPN is a component of *Improving Social Awareness–Social Problem Solving (ISA–SPS),* a program developed by Elias and Clabby (1989, 1992). Designed to be used on a systemwide basis to prevent social problems such as suicide, substance abuse, pregnancy, AIDS, and delinquency, the program focuses on three skill areas:

*Self-Control Skills*

1. Listen carefully and accurately
2. Remember and follow directions
3. Concentrate and follow through on tasks
4. Calm oneself down
5. Carry on a conversation without upsetting or provoking others

*Social Awareness and Group Participation Skills*

6. Accept praise or approval
7. Choose praiseworthy and caring friends
8. Know when help is needed
9. Ask for help when needed
10. Work as part of a problem-solving team

*Social Decision-Making and Problem-Solving Skills*

11. Recognize signs of feelings in self
12. Recognize signs of feelings in others
13. Describe accurately a range of feelings
14. Put problems clearly into words
15. State realistic interpersonal goals
16. Think of several ways to solve a problem or reach a goal
17. Think of different types of solutions
18. Do skills 6 and 7 for different types of solutions
19. Differentiate short- and long-term consequences
20. Look at effects of choices on self and others
21. Keep positive and negative possibilities in mind
22. Select solutions that can reach goals
23. Make choices that do not harm self or others
24. Consider details before carrying out a solution (who, when, where, with whom, and so on)
25. Anticipate obstacles to plans
26. Respond appropriately when plans are thwarted
27. Try out one's own ideas
28. Learn from experiences or from seeking out input from adults, friends
29. Use previous experience to help "next time." (Elias & Clabby, 1992, p. 17)

FIG TESPN is used throughout ISA–SPS (Elias & Clabby, 1992). FIG TESPN stands for the eight problem-solving steps shown below. Each of these steps is described in the following discussion.

**F**    **F**eelings cue me to problem-solve.
**I**    **I** have a problem.
**G**    **G**oal gives me a guide.
**T**    **T**hink of things I can do.
**E**    **E**nvision outcomes, both short and long term, for the children and for others.
**S**    **S**elect my best solution.
**P**    **P**lan the procedure, anticipate pitfalls, practice, and pursue it.
**N**    **N**otice what happened, and consider what I will do next.

Source: From *Emotionally Intelligent Parenting* by Maurice J. Elias, Steven E. Tobias, and Brian S. Friedlander, copyright © 1999 by Maurice J. Elias, Steven E. Tobias, and Brian S. Friedlander. Used by permission of Harmony Books, a division of Random House, Inc.

Elias et al. (1999, pp. 156, 157) developed the guiding questions for each step.

*Step One: Feelings cue me to thoughtful action.* Children and youth learn that bad feelings signal a problem that has to be solved. It is critical that the child correctly label the emotion he or she is experiencing in order to effectively solve the social problem (e.g., not labeling disappointment as anger). By using strategies such as those described in Chapter Three, we can help children develop a feelings vocabulary to label a full range of emotions. Guiding questions include:

▶ How are you feeling?
▶ How else are you feeling?
▶ I notice that you seem _____. How do you think _____ is feeling?

*Step Two: I have a problem.* The child learns that, although the problem may not be his or her fault, the child has the ultimate responsibility to solve it. He or she also learns that actions, not feelings, solve problems. The following questions may be used to help the child identify the problem:

▶ What exactly happened?
▶ What happened before this?
▶ What were you doing?
▶ What was _____ doing?
▶ What happened after?
▶ What did you do then?

*Step Three: Goals give me a guide.* Most children and youth need to be taught how to set goals. A major benefit of goal setting is that it reduces stress. By setting goals, children can go about meeting them rather than ruminating about problems. Parents and teachers can teach goal setting by having children work through the following steps (Raskind, Goldberg, Higgins, & Herman, 2002):

▶ Define what a goal is (i.e., objective, aim, desired outcome, etc.).
▶ Understand the benefits of goal setting and the downside of not setting goals.
▶ Develop strategies for setting and prioritizing goals.
▶ Determine whether goals are realistic and attainable.
▶ Understand the difference between short- and long-term goals.
▶ Develop action plans/steps for reaching goals.
▶ Anticipate and overcome obstacles.
▶ Reevaluate and re-adjust goals.
▶ Realize the benefits of working with others to reach goals.

*Step Four: Think of things I can do.* During this step the child is taught to think of as many solutions as possible without evaluating them. Younger children may need help coming up with multiple solutions. Questions that can be asked at this step include:

▶ What did you try to do?
▶ What have you thought of doing?
▶ What else can you think of doing?

As children become better at generating solutions, parents and teachers can help them assess the quality, as well as the quantity, of solutions (Coleman et al., 1993).

*Step Five: Envision outcomes.* Children must come to understand that every action has a consequence and that several consequences may result. Outcomes will not always be positive, and sometimes they will be both positive and negative. Some questions that will help children predict outcomes are:

- ▶ What would happen if you _____?
- ▶ Close your eyes. Can you imagine doing what you said you would do?
- ▶ What do you see happening?
- ▶ When do you see it happening?
- ▶ What might happen later?
- ▶ How might it affect you?
- ▶ What about other people. How might it affect them?
- ▶ What else could happen?
- ▶ What might happen if you ____?
- ▶ You thought about ____ and ____ as possibilities. What about ____ and ____?

*Step Six: Select my best solution.* Before the child selects a solution, he or she needs to review the original problem as well as the desired outcome. The best solution will be the one that will most likely solve the problem and help the child realize his or her goal. Good guiding questions include:

- ▶ Of the things you thought about, which one seems like the best thing to try first?
- ▶ Which one will get you to your goal?

*Step Seven: Plan the procedure, anticipate pitfalls, practice, and pursue it.* During this step, teachers and parents help children anticipate problems that might occur when they implement the plan. Being prepared for pitfalls helps the child to persevere and to avoid being impulsive. At this point, the child needs to make a commitment regarding when he or she will implement the plan. Going "public," that is, telling others about his plan, increases the probability that the child will follow through. These questions will help guide the child through this step:

- ▶ How would you do it?
- ▶ What is your plan?
- ▶ Can you show me what you're going to do?
- ▶ Can we practice together before you try it?
- ▶ What if things don't work out the way you want? What would you do then?
- ▶ What else could you try?
- ▶ What if ____ happened?
- ▶ How would you handle it?

*Step Eight: Notice what happened, and now what?* We must help children realize that plans meet with varying degrees of success and that not all plans will succeed. During this step, children learn self-evaluation strategies. A good guiding question to ask at this step might be:

▶ Okay, think about it and try it. When will we talk about what happened?

We recommend that children be taught to use the checklist shown as Figure 4.1 so they can practice their social–emotional problem-solving skills.

## The Social Skill Autopsy

*Lisa came home sobbing, "Tamika says we're not best friends any more because she can't trust me!" Lisa and Tamika had been close friends ever since they met in pre-school. Although Lisa's mom, Michele, knew that 8-year-old girls sometimes were fickle about friendships, the bond between Lisa and Tamika was strong.*

*Michele asked Lisa, "Did you do anything to make Tamika feel that way?" After Lisa's resounding "No!" Michele began to ask her daughter questions to get to the bottom of Tamika's change of heart toward Lisa. "Lisa, are you sure you didn't do or say something to make Tamika not trust you?"*

*Lisa thought for a while and said, "I think I know what I did to make Tamika not trust me. She asked me not to tell anyone that she liked Christopher, a boy in our class. I told Emily, who I sit with on the bus, when we were talking about boys we liked. I bet Emily said something to Tamika."*

*Michele asked her daughter, "How do you think Tamika felt when Emily knew she liked Christopher. How do you think you would feel if you were Tamika?"*

*Lisa thought she might be embarrassed in Tamika's situation, and she might be angry that a friend didn't keep her secret.*

*Then Michele asked her daughter, "Was what happened between you and Tamika a good thing or a bad thing?"*

*"Not so good," replied Lisa.*

*They ended the conversation by discussing what Lisa could do to keep her friend-ship with Tamika, and what she could do in the future to avoid a similar situation.*

*James had to cut the conversation short with his next-door neighbor, Roberta, a feisty 75-year-old, because he was due to pick up his 15-year-old son, Chandler, from soccer practice. He left with a smile on his face, though.*

*"How'd practice go?"*

*"Not so great," said Chandler. "I missed three goals!"*

*"Well, Roberta thinks you're great. She said you were one of the nicest and most considerate boys she knows. Any idea why she said that?"*

*Chandler replied, "Well, I mowed her lawn Wednesday, and I bring her trash out to the street on pick-up day."*

*"How do you think that makes her feel?" his dad asked.*

*Chandler thought a moment and said, "Like someone cares about her. Her children live far away, and she doesn't get to see her grandchildren very often. And Mr.*

Name_____ Date _____

1. My problem is _____

_____

_____

2. Possible solutions to the problem are

a. _____

b. _____

c. _____

d. _____

e. _____

3. The solution I'd like to try is _____

_____

4. Possible consequences if I implement the solution are

a. _____

b. _____

c. _____

5. I tried my solution in this situation: _____

_____

_____

6. The word that best describes how I feel about the outcome after
I implemented my solution is
[  ] pleased     [  ] indifferent     [  ] disappointed

7. When I have a similar problem in the future, I will _____

_____

_____

Source: "Social Problem-Solving Checklist," in *Teaching Occupational Social Skills* (p. 40), by N. Elksnin & L. K. Elksnin (Austin, TX: Pro-Ed). Copyright © 1998 by Pro-Ed Inc. Reprinted with permission.

**FIGURE 4.1** ▶Social Problem-Solving Checklist

*Thomason just died last year. She's probably lonely, and she also has to do every-thing herself."*

*"Well, you really made a positive impression on her. Do you think you will con-tinue to help her out?"*

*"Probably," said Chandler, "I like Mrs. Thomason, and I feel good when I help."*

In the above vignettes, Michele and James both conducted a *social skill autopsy,* a term coined by Richard Lavoie (1994) to describe a problem-solving strategy that teachers and parents can use to help children identify and solve social–emotional problems. An autopsy is generally known to be an examination of a body to deter-mine the cause of death. A social skill autopsy is the examination of a social outcome to determine its cause. The word *autopsy* comes from the Greek word *autopsia,* which literally means "to see with one's own eyes." When teachers and parents con-duct a social skill autopsy, they help children see with their own eyes how what they did or said caused a positive or negative social outcome.

Social skill autopsies may be conducted by following these steps:

What did you say or do?
What happened when you did or said it?
Was what happened positive, negative, or neutral?
In the future, what will you do in a similar situation?

The advantages of social skill autopsies are that they can be conducted as soon as opportunities present themselves. By immediately focusing on problems as they occur, children and youth are in a better position to analyze events. Autopsies also can be conducted by any and all of the important individuals in the child's life, including parents, teachers, employers, and peers. For example, teaching all person-nel in a school, including bus drivers, secretaries, cafeteria workers, and janitors, to perform social skill autopsies is an excellent way to promote generalization of prob-lem-solving and social–emotional skills. Keep in mind, however, that autopsies should be conducted privately.

## ▶ Social–Emotional Problem-Solving Programs

Table 4.2 is a list of programs that include a social–emotional problem-solving skills component. Following is a description of several programs that are devoted exclu-sively to teaching social–emotional problem solving.

### I Can Problem Solve

The goal of the I Can Problem Solve (ICPS) programs (Shure 1992a, 1992b, 1992c) is to teach children how to think so they can solve or prevent interpersonal problems. The programs are based upon the seminal work of Shure and Spivack (1971, 1978a, 1978b, 1980).

**TABLE 4.2** ►Programs That Teach Social–Emotional Problem Solving

| Program | Author(s)/Date | Age/Grade |
|---|---|---|
| Assessing and Teaching Job-Related Social Skills | Baumgart & Anderson (1987) | Adolescents |
| ASSET | Hazel, Schumaker, Sherman, & Sheldon (1996) | Adolescents |
| CLASSIC | Dygdon (1993) | Middle School |
| Connecting with Others programs | Richardson (1996a, 1996b), Richardson & Evans (1997), Richardson & Meisgeier (2001) | Grades K–12 |
| Getting Along With Others | N. F. Jackson, D. A. Jackson, & Monroe (1983) | Adolescents & Adults |
| I Can Problem Solve programs | Shure (1992a, 1992b, 1992c) | Grade K–6 |
| Learning to Get Along | D. A. Jackson, N. F. Jackson, Bennett, Bynum, & Faryna (1991) | Grades K-12 |
| Life Skills Activities for Secondary Students with Special Needs | Mannix (1995) | Adolescents |
| Passport programs | Vernon (1998a, 1998b, 1998c) | Grades 1–12 |
| PATHS curriculum | Kusche & Greenberg (1994) | Elementary |
| PREPARE curriculum | Goldstein (1999) | Adolescents |
| Problem Solving Skills for Children Ages 3–9 | Youngs (1995) | Ages 3–9 |
| Promoting Social Success | Siperstein & Rickards (2004) | Grades PreK–12 |
| Raising a Thinking Child workbook | Shure (2000a) | Preschool/ Elementary |
| Ready-to-Use Social Skills lessons & activities | Begun (1995, 1996a, 1996b, 1996c) | Grades PreK–12 |
| Skillstreaming programs | Goldstein & McGinnis (1997), McGinnis & Goldstein (1997, 2003) | Grades PreK–12 |
| Social Skills Activities for Special Children | Mannix (1993) | Elementary |
| Social Skills Development | Antonello (1996) | Adolescents & Adults |
| Social Skills for Daily Living | Schumaker, Hazel, & Pederson (1988) | Adolescents |

**TABLE 4.2** ▶(Continued)

| Program | Author(s)/Date | Age/Grade |
|---|---|---|
| Social Skills Intervention Guide | Elliott & Gresham (1991) | Grades 1–10 |
| Stop & Think Social Skills programs | Knopf (2001a, 2001b, 2001c, 2001d) | Grades PreK–8 |
| Teaching Social Competence to Youth & Adults with Developmental Disabilities | D. A. Jackson, N. F. Jackson, & Bennett (1998) | Adolescents & Adults |
| Technical-Related and Academic Career Competencies | Minskoff (1994) | Adolescents & Adults |
| Think Aloud small-group program | Camp & Bash (1981) | Ages 6–8 |
| Think Aloud classroom programs | Camp & Bash (1985a, 1985b, 1985c) | Grades 1–6 |
| Thinking, Feeling, Behaving programs | Vernon (1989a, 1989b) | Grades 1–12 |
| The Tough Kids Social Skills Book | Sheridan (1995–1996) | Grades K–8 |

### I Can Problem Solve—Preschool (ICPS–P; Shure, 1992a)

ICPS–P is designed to teach children ages 3 and 4 to solve problems they have with other people. The program consists of 59 lessons focusing on pre-problem-solving skills and problem-solving skills, a list of suggested materials, and a teacher script. Pre-problem-solving skills include vocabulary and concepts needed for problem solving, such as some–all, not, or–and, same–different, why–because, might–maybe, fair–not fair. Children are taught listening and paying-attention skills and ways to recognize individual differences. Problem-solving skills include alternative solutions (i.e., problem identification and generation of solutions), consequences (i.e., sequential thinking and understanding cause and effect relationships), and solution–consequence pairs (i.e., linking solutions with possible consequences).

Lessons can be taught to groups of from six to eight children, and teachers are encouraged to present each lesson as a "game." A critical component of the program is the process of problem-solving dialoguing. During dialoguing, the teacher guides the child in applying interpersonal cognitive problem-solving principles to real-life problems. Parent pages are included in the program to enable families to assist their children in applying these principles to problems at home.

### ICPS for Kindergarten and Primary Grades (ICPS-KP; Shure, 1992b)

The ICPS–KP consists of 83 lessons listed as either pre-problem-solving skills or problem-solving skills. Pre-problem-solving skills include essential vocabulary/concepts (i.e., is–not, or–and, some–all, if–then, same–different, before–after, now–later, might–maybe, why–because, fair–not fair, worried–relieved, happy, sad, angry, afraid, proud, frustrated, impatient), identification of own and others' feelings, listening and paying attention, sequencing and timing of events, and coping with frustration and waiting. Problem-solving skills include generating alternative solutions, predicting consequences, and linking solutions with consequences.

Instructors use scripts as guidelines for teaching each lesson using games, stories, puppets, and role playing. An essential component of the program is helping children apply ICPS principles to real-life situations. The ICPS gives suggestions for integrating problem solving into the curriculum and across classroom activities. For example, when teaching the construct of *some–all,* the instructor can ask children to identify some or all of the children involved in lunchtime, lining up, free play, and transition activities. Suggestions for integrating the construct within the curriculum include using *some–all* vocabulary during current events, reading, and mathematics instruction. ICPS–KP can be presented to either large or small groups.

### ICPS: Intermediate Elementary Grades (ICPS–E) (Shure, 1992c)

The ICPS–E consists of 77 lessons and is similar in format to the program for kindergarten and the primary grades. Pre-problem-solving skills include vocabulary/concepts such as is–not, or–and, same time, happy, angry, sad, afraid, jealous, frustrated, impatient, lonely, sympathetic, ashamed, embarrassed, surprised, disappointed, proud, worried, and relieved. Children learn to become more sensitive toward others, to recognize that others' feelings may differ from their own, to pay attention, to remember better, and to avoid false assumptions. Throughout the program, children learn that there's more than one way of thinking. Problem-solving skills include alternative solutions, consequences, solution–consequence pairs, and means–end thinking.

### Raising a Thinking Child Workbook (Shure, 2000a)

This workbook is designed to teach parents to teach their young children how to resolve conflicts and get along with others. The workbook complements the I Can Problem Solve programs.

## Think Aloud

Think Aloud (Camp & Bash, 1981, 1985a, 1985b, 1985c) is a set of social problem-solving curricula that uses the thought-structuring sequence to teach elementary-aged children to ask themselves questions such as:

- ▶ What is my problem?
- ▶ How can I do it?
- ▶ Am I using my plan?
- ▶ How did I do?

The curricula are designed to teach children to solve academic as well as social problems. For example, in Lesson Two of the Think Aloud small-group program, children are introduced to the *think aloud process* when the teacher asks the children to repeat what the instructor says while solving a coloring problem:

▶ What is my problem? Mrs. _____ wanted me to color a shape without going outside the lines.

▶ How can I do it? My plan is to go slowly and carefully.

▶ Am I using my plan? My answer is "yes" because I made a frame inside the circle. Was I using my plan when I went outside the line?

▶ How did I do? My answer to that question is: I was good at thinking out loud. I tried hard to stay inside the line. (Camp & Bash, 1981, p. 39)

The Think Aloud programs have been used with entire general education classes as well as in special education programs with students who have LD and ADHD. Teachers should be prepared for noisy classrooms as their students learn to "think out loud." Children are expected to eventually think to themselves.

# ▶ Using Children's Literature to Teach Problem Solving

*"Do you know what the word* criticism *means," Rebecca Knowles asked her second-grade class. "Yes, Danny, you have your hand up. What do you think criticism means?"*

*"It means that you did something bad and that somebody didn't like what you did."*

*"What do you think, class—is criticism doing something bad that someone doesn't like? Anna, do you agree with Danny?"*

*"I think it's when someone tells you about something you did that they didn't like."*

*"Class, raise your hand if you agree with Anna's definition of criticism: Criticism is when someone tells you about something you did that they didn't like."*

*After seeing that most students raised their hands, Rebecca told her class, "I think this is a good definition of criticism. I'm going to read a story about a boy named Justin. Justin feels really badly when someone criticizes him. He feels so badly that the name of this story is 'The Hurt.' But Justin finds some ways to deal with his problem of feeling really hurt when someone criticizes him. Let's see how he solves his problem." Rebecca began to read the story.*

When used effectively by teachers and parents, books can help children and youth develop strategies to solve social–emotional problems (Forgan & Gonzalez-DeHass, 2004). Through books children and youth learn about human behavior, that others have similar problems, and that a problem may have more than one solution.

## Forgan's Bibliotherapy Framework

*Bibliotherapy* is "the use of books to help people to solve problems" (Alex, 1982, p. 1). Forgan (2002) developed a four-step process for using bibliography to teach social–emotional problem solving through literature. We describe each step in the sections that follow.

### Prereading

After books are selected, children preview them by looking at the illustrations and discussing the title. Adults share information about the general plot and the characters and encourage children to relate the book to their own lives and experiences. During this step, it is helpful to use Forgan's KWL chart, which asks:

- ► What do you want to **K**now about the topic?
- ► What do you **W**ant to learn about the topic?
- ► What have you **L**earned about the topic?

### Guided Reading

During this step the adult reads the story aloud. Afterward, the children are given a few minutes to reflect on the story. They also may be given time to write down their thoughts in journals, if appropriate.

### Postreading Discussion

The primary goal during this step is for children to identify the primary problem the characters in the book confront, and to realize that others face similar problems. The children are asked to retell the plot, identify the feelings of the characters, and describe the situations that occur. The teacher and the parents guide the discussion by using probing questions.

### Problem-Solving/Reinforcement Activity

During this step children identify the problem presented in the story and come up with potential solutions. Forgan (2002) recommends using the I SOLVE routine:

| | |
|---|---|
| **I** | **I** dentify the problem. |
| **S** | **S**olutions to the problem? |
| **O** | **O**bstacles to the solutions? |
| **L** | **L**ook at the solutions again—choose one. |
| **V** | **V**ery good! Try it! |
| **E** | **E**valuate the outcome. (p. 78) |

## Teglasi and Rothman's STORIES Program

Teglasi and Rothman (2001) developed the STORIES program with a questioning format that children can use to link story components with social–emotional problem solving. Before reading the story, teachers and parents ask children to examine illustrations to interpret the facial expressions and postures of characters. While reading the story, the adult then asks these questions:

▶ *What is happening?* Have children identify the problem after considering the perspectives of the characteristics (e.g., bully, victim, bystander).

▶ *What are the characters thinking, and how are they feeling?* Have children identify the feelings of each character and ways in which feelings, intentions, and perceptions among characters influence the characters' thoughts and feelings.

▶ *What are the characters' intentions and goals?* Have children identify the characters' short- and long-term goals based upon how they think each character thinks and feels. Have them identify what their own goals would be in a similar situation.

▶ *What do the characters accomplish by their actions?* Have children predict outcomes based on the characters' actions, plans, and goals. Coach them to identify instances in which a character succumbs to emotion rather than reason, and settles for a solution in the short term rather than the long term (i.e., encourage cause-and-effect and means–end thinking).

▶ *How do the characters execute and monitor their behaviors?* Have children determine if the characters' actions were effective or ineffective and why (i.e., encourage them to identify sufficient or insufficient planning, controlled or uncontrolled emotions, effective or ineffective strategies).

▶ *What lessons are learned?* Have children identify life lessons that they and the characters learned based upon the situation.

### Book Talks

Book Talks, ilustrated as Figure 4.2, offers another way to guide children to analyze stories and engage in problem solving while reading. Children also can use the PATHS problem-solving strategy or FIG TESPN, described earlier.

## ▶ Applying Problem-Solving Strategies to Academic Subjects

The problem-solving strategies discussed earlier in this chapter are easily applied to academic subjects. For example, Book Talks formats lend themselves particularly well to analysis of literature in language arts classes. Questions that can be used to promote problem solving in social studies and history classes are as follows (Elias & Tobias, 1996, pp. 110, 111).

### Framework for Thinking about Important Events in History

1. What is the event you are thinking about? When and where did it happen? Put the event into words as a problem, choice, or decision.
2. What people or groups were involved in the problem? What were their different feelings? What were their points of view about the problem?

## Format for Older Children

1. Think of an event in the section of the book assigned. When and where did it happen? Put the event into words as a problem.
2. Who were the people involved in the problem? What were their different feelings and points of view about the problem? Why did they feel as they did? Try to put their goals into words.
3. For each person or group of people, what are some different decisions or solutions to the problem that he, she, or they thought of that might help in reaching their goals?
4. For each of these ideas or options, what are all of the things that might happen next? Envision and write down short- and long-term consequences.
5. What were the final decisions? How were they made? By whom? What? Do you agree or disagree? Why?
6. How was the solution carried out? What was the plan? What obstacles were met? How well was the problem solved? What did you read that supports your point of view?
7. Notice what happened and rethink it. What would you have chosen to do? Why?
8. What questions do you have, based on what you read? What questions would you like to be able to ask one or more of the characters? The author? Why are these questions important to you?

## Format for Younger Children

I will write about this character: _____

My character's problem is:

_____

_____

How did your character get into this problem?

_____

_____

How does the character feel?

_____

_____

What does the character want to happen?

_____

_____

Which questions would you like to ask the character you picked, one of the other characters, or the author?

_____

_____

---

Source: "Questions Assigned to Students in Problem Solving Applied to Literature Analysis/Book Talks," in *Social Problem Solving: Interventions in the Schools* (p. 109), by M. J. Elias and S. E. Tobias (New York: Guilford Press). Copyright © 1996 by Guilford Press. Reprinted by permission.

**FIGURE 4.2** ▶Book Talks

3. What did each of these people or groups want to happen? Try to put their goals into words.
4. For each person or group, name some different options or solutions to the problem that they thought might help them reach their goals.
5. For each option or solution, picture all the things that might have happened next. Envision both long- and short-term consequences.
6. What were the final decisions? How were they made? By whom? Why? Do you agree or disagree? Why?
7. How was the solution carried out? What was the plan? What obstacles or roadblocks were met? How well was the problem solved? Why?
8. Rethink it. What would you have chosen to do? Why?

**Framework for Thinking About Current Events**

1. What is the event you are thinking about? When and where is it happening? Put the event into words as a problem, choice, or decision.
2. What people or groups were involved in the problem? What are their different feelings? What are their points of view about the problem?
3. What do each of these people or groups want to happen? Try to put their goals into words.
4. For each person or group, name some different opinions or solutions to the problem that they think might help them reach their goals. Add any ideas that you think might help them that they might not have thought of.
5. For each option or solution you listed, picture all the things that might happen next. Envision long- and short-term consequences.
6. What do you think the final decision should be? How should it be made? By whom? Why?
7. Imagine a plan to help you carry out your solution. What could you do or think of to make your solution work? What obstacles or roadblocks might keep your solution from working? Who might disagree with your ideas? Why? What else could you do?
8. Rethink it. Is there another way of looking at the problem that might be better? Do other groups, goals, or plans come to mind?

Source: "Thinking about Important Events in History, Thinking about Current Events," from *Social Problem Solving: Interventions in the Schools* (pp. 100, 111), by M. J. Elias and S. E. Tobias, 1996, New York: the Guilford Press. Copyright © 1996 by The Guilford Press. Reprinted by permission.

# ▶ Principles for Teaching Problem Solving

When teaching children and youth social–emotional problem solving, teachers and parents must keep in mind the following principles (Elias & Tobias, 1996):

▶ *Assume the role of facilitator.* To be effective, teachers and parents must ask students questions and guide them through the problem-solving process. Some teachers and parents find it difficult to relinquish the authoritarian role.

▶ *Remind children to use previously mastered skills.* For example, children may have to be cued to use the PATHS problem-solving strategy or FIG TESPN when they experience a negative emotion. They may need reminders to label emotions and to use some of the anger-control strategies described in Chapter Three.

▶ *Model social-problem solving as often as possible.* Teachers and parents need to model social–emotional problem solving as they solve their own problems. By "thinking out loud," they help children and youth to see the benefit of using these strategies.

▶ *Ask open-ended questions.* We reviewed four levels of communication earlier. When teachers and parents use the first three levels, they tell children what to do. To promote independent problem solving, we must ask children open-ended questions. Young children often find it particularly difficult to answer "why" questions, such as "Why did you take your brother's toy?" and "Why did you call him names?" Try replacing "why" questions with questions such as the following (Elias & Tobias, 1996):

> What happened?
> What did you want to happen?
> How are you feeling?
> What was the other person doing?
> What happened before this? (p. 72)

▶ *Follow a question with a question.* This strategy promotes discussion and sends children a message that you are interested in what they have to say.

▶ *Assume a nonconfrontational demeanor.* Elias and Tobias call this the "Columbo technique," named after the TV detective played by actor Peter Falk. Detective Columbo obtained useful information by asking questions in a non-threatening manner. This technique helps children and youth identify inconsistencies in their thinking.

▶ *Paraphrase what the child says.* Paraphrasing is a tried-and-true counseling and therapeutic technique in which the teacher or parent restates the child's words. Paraphrasing validates children's feelings and lets them know that you are actively listening.

▶ *Be patient and persistent.* The development of social–emotional problem-solving skills may be a slow process, particularly for children and youth with disabilities. By integrating problem solving within all aspects of life in the classroom and at home, children and youth *will* master these skills eventually.

▶ *Be creative and flexible.* Activities that can be used to teach social–emotional problem solving are presented next. Parents and teachers can modify and adapt these approaches to meet their needs and the needs of children.

# ▶ Activities for Teaching Social–Emotional Problem-Solving Skills

### Family or Class Meeting (Shapiro, 1997)

1. Establish ground rules: Let others finish talking, respect others' opinions and feelings, give everyone a chance to participate, begin and end on time (usually a 30-minute meeting).
2. Let each person discuss and "think out" a problem by identifying the problem, thinking of alternative solutions, comparing each solution, picking the best solution.
3. Follow up at the next meeting by finding out if the solution worked.

### TV Show/Movie (Elias & Tobias, 1996)

1. Select a television show or a movie that features children confronting interpersonal problems.
2. Watch the show together.
3. Apply problem-solving steps using PATHS or FIG TESPN.

### Solution Brainstorming (Shapiro, 1997)

1. Have the children come up with as many solutions to a problem as they can.
2. Have the children pick the "best" solution.
3. Divide children into groups and award points for each solution.
4. Go back and cross out "silly" solutions and circle "good" ones.

### Solutions Tic-Tac-Toe (Shure, 1996)

1. Create 3 × 5 cards with real-life problems encountered by the group.
2. Have each child draw a card.
3. If the child comes up with a "good" (i.e., reasonable) solution, he or she gets to make an "X" or "O" on the tic-tac-toe board.

### Finding Exceptions (Shapiro, 1997)

Sometimes the solution is that a problem doesn't exist. For example, a girl says "everyone" in class is teasing her. By using probing, open-ended questions, the parent or teacher narrows the problem to just one girl. This activity enables children to come up with positive and possible solutions rather than being overwhelmed by the problem.

## ▶ Chapter Summary

Problem solving involves identifying the problem, generating potential solutions, selecting a solution, implementing a plan, and evaluating the plan's effectiveness. Problem-solving skills enable children to solve a wide array of social–emotional problems, which may lead them to use these skills in many situations and settings (Elias & Clabby, 1992; L. K. Elksnin & N. Elksnin, 1995; Gumpel & Golan, 2000; Soto, Toro-Zambrana, & Belfiore, 1994). By teaching problem-solving routines like FIG TESPN or the PATHS strategy, and by conducting social skill autopsies, teachers and parents can help children become more adept at identifying and solving social–emotional problems. In addition to acquiring social–emotional problem-solving skills, children must learn how to perform specific social skills such as sharing, beginning and ending a conversation, and apologizing (Coleman et al., 1993; L. K. Elksnin & N. Elksnin, 1995; Elliott et al., 1989; Jones, Sheridan, & Binns, 1993). Teaching children specific social–emotional skills is the topic of subsequent chapters.

# CHAPTER 5

# Teaching Children and Youth Peer-Pleasing Social–Emotional Skills

## Goals of This Chapter

In this chapter you will learn

▶ why having friends is essential for social–emotional and academic growth

▶ how friendship develops during early childhood, middle childhood, and adolescence

▶ the social–emotional skills that are important at different ages

▶ how to help children and youth make and keep friends

▶ how to help children and youth develop conversational skills

▶ peer-mediated interventions that promote friendship

# Terms to Know

autorepresentational play

buddy systems

constructive play

correspondence training

naturalistic teaching strategies

peer-mediated interventions

peer-pleasing social–emotional skills

peer tutoring

positive peer reporting (PPR)

pretend play

representational play

self-mediated interventions

sensorimotor play

symbolic play

teacher-pleasing social-emotional skills

tootling

*When my daughter Kelsey was in kindergarten, my husband and I met with her teacher for the year-end conference. She had nice things to say about our child, but do I remember the specifics? Nope. What I recall vividly is being told that Kelsey didn't seem to feel that she belonged and would sit apart from the group during meeting time. And I'll never forget my reaction. I started to cry. Right there in front of the teacher. Would those tears have welled up if I'd just learned that Kelsey didn't have an aptitude for math? I really don't think so. There's something about fitting in with other kids that strikes deep into every parent's heart.* (Larson, 2001, p. 94)

Friends make your kids happy. Psychologists say that it's not popularity that parents should wish for their child, but that he or she have one or two very close friends. It's through these quality-over-quantity friendships that a child feels secure and grows. (Spencer, 2003, p. 108)

*L*ike Kelsey's mom, most parents want their children to get along with other children and to have friends. And, Spencer (2003) points out, it's not how many friends a child has that matters but, instead, that the child has a couple of *good* friends. Parents of children with disabilities have particularly strong feelings about their children's social lives. For example, when Wiener and Sunohara (1998) interviewed mothers of children with learning disabilities, they found that the mothers were more concerned with their children's social relationships than they were with their children's academic achievement. Further, there is a strong, positive relationship between having friends and succeeding in school, based on study results:

▶ Young children who are rejected and neglected are more likely to underachieve in kindergarten (Kim, 2003; Pellegrini, 1992).
▶ Sixth graders who had a friend achieved at a higher level than sixth graders who did not have a friend (Wentzel et al., 2004).
▶ Adolescents who had friends had better grades and higher test scores than youth without friends (Berndt & Keefe, 1995; Berndt et al., 1990; Wentzel & Caldwell, 1997).

Social–emotional skills are important, yet insufficient for children to form friendships. Still, lack of social–emotional skills hinders the ability to make friends. Friendship helps children develop social–emotional skills such as cooperation and handling conflict (Thompson et al., 2001).

Stanovich (1986) first described the *Matthew effect* in reading: Early development of reading skills "results in reading/academic experiences that facilitate the development of other cognitive structures that lay the foundation for successful reading achievement at more advanced levels" (Stanovich, 1988). In other words, the rich get richer, and the poor get poorer. There is also a Matthew effect of friendship: Children who have friends become more socially skilled, and more socially skilled children tend to develop more friendships.

We must recognize that the social–emotional skills peers value are often different from those that teachers and other adults value. For example, Walker (1983) found that teachers regarded as important skills the ability to comply with teacher requests, follow established classroom rules, and sit quietly and attend to the teacher. But peers valued a child's willingness to join in and compliment others. Children and youth need both kinds of skills: *teacher-pleasing skills* to succeed academically, and *peer-pleasing skills* to develop and sustain friendships.

This chapter focuses on peer-pleasing skills and builds on skills described in Chapters Three and Four: Children who understand their own and others' emotions and who can identify and solve social–emotional problems are able to make and keep friends. We begin by reviewing how friendship develops during early childhood, middle childhood, and adolescence, pointing out that children value different skills at different ages. Then we offer specific strategies that teachers and parents can use to help children and youth make and keep friends. Because conversational skills are essential across ages, we devote a portion of the chapter to essential conversation skills and strategies to teach them. Given the importance of involving peers in interventions designed to promote social interaction, we close the chapter with a review of peer-mediated interventions during early childhood, middle childhood, and adolescence.

## ▶ What We Know About Friendship

Friendship is about quality, not quantity. Thompson et al. (2001), authors of *Best Friends, Worst Enemies*, report that school-aged children on average have five close friends. The importance of having friends cannot be overestimated. Friends help children make the transition from the safety of the family to the uncertain, larger world, giving them the courage to grow and experiment. Friends provide children with a bigger family and expose children to different social norms (Thompson et al., 2001). Friends protect children from negative events and help children withstand difficult times. Loyal friends are buffers against rejection by other children. If parents can help their child make one good friend, the positive effects are immeasurable.

Because many children with disabilities have developmental delays, their understanding of friendship may not be the same as that of their nondisabled peers (Kolb & Hanley-Maxwell, 2003). Interviews with mothers of children with LD, for example, indicated that these children's friends often were much younger (Wiener & Sunohara, 1998). Further, children with LD often confused friends and acquaintances, as revealed by mothers' comments (Wiener & Sunohara, 1998):

> He doesn't quite understand that a friend is someone that you talk to; well, to me anyhow, a friend is someone that you would talk to on a regular basis, go out with on a regular basis. He thinks because he knows 20 different kids, they're friends. (p. 245)

> He talks about people who are his friends, that he hasn't seen for 4 years, and I've also heard him talk about people who are his friends, that he's just met. . . . You don't call a person you've just met your friend. (p. 246)

## ▶ Developmental Aspects of Friendship

The friendships of children and youth and their expectations for friendship change over time (Eisenberg & Harris, 1984; L. K. Elksnin & N. Elksnin, 1995). Consequently, different social–emotional skills are needed at different ages. We will discuss children's friendships during early childhood, middle childhood, and adolescence.

## Friendship During Early Childhood (Ages 3 to 7)

*Jerri had been a preschool teacher for 14 years. She was continually amazed at how some children seemed to have a natural ability to get along and how others didn't seem to have a clue. She smiled as she watched the 4-year-olds in her preschool class interact during playtime. Natasha approached Brian and Christine, who were building with blocks.*

*"Can I help make the fire station?"*

*"It's not a fire station, it's a boat," Brian and Christine said in chorus.*

*"Okay, can I make a dock for the boat?" continued Natasha.*

*"Well, okay, as long as you don't use any of the blue blocks, 'cause they're for the boat," cautioned Christine.*

*The three children played happily for the next 10 minutes.*

*Adam wandered from center to center. He watched other children play from a distance, yet didn't attempt to join them. Jerri smiled as she watched Juanita offer Adam a plastic tumbler and ask, "Would you like some juice? We're serving snacks as soon as the cookies are done."*

*At the beginning of each year, Jerri paid careful attention to her students' interactions. Her observations helped her develop strategies to help children interact positively with one another. Today was only the third day of school, and already Jerri knew that Stephen was going to need plenty of support to get along with his classmates. She watched as he took the tumbler away from Adam. Stephen had a difficult time sharing with others. Already, children were avoiding him. If a child saw Stephen coming, he or she immediately moved to another center.*

Children establish friendships through play. For preschoolers, "play is the primary context in which children acquire and practice skills essential to developing social competence" (Craig-Unkefer & Kaiser, 2002, p. 3). Play enables children to resolve disputes, master the art of persuasion, and learn how to role play. Skills that young children need to engage in play include receptive and expressive language, initiation and maintenance of conversation, and taking turns. Children with developmental delays in motor, cognitive, and language ability may have difficulty interacting socially with their peers.

Sheridan, Foley, and Radlinski (1995) have described six stages of play, along with how each stage relates to social–emotional development:

1. *Sensorimotor play* involves simple visual-sensory-motor manipulation such as touching, grasping, and so forth. For example, a baby may reach out and touch a mobile that is hung over his or her crib. During this stage a baby is unable to differentiate between self and others.

2. *Constructive play,* which involves "action-oriented discovery, problem solving, and elaboration" (Sheridan et al., p. 4), usually develops during the latter months of the child's first year. During this stage babies use objects in purposeful ways such as pushing a toy car rather than banging it on a table.

3. *Representational play* begins during the child's second year. During this stage children begin to categorize shared and unique characteristics between and among objects. Examples of representational play include "serving dinner" using a variety of objects and materials, and building a city of blocks.

4. *Autorepresentational play,* which also begins during the child's second year, involves self-use of objects such as the child's pretending to use a toy telephone.

5. *Allorepresentational play,* which emerges at about 18 months, is marked by the child's ability to direct play toward other individuals or objects.

6. *Symbolic play* refers to the child's ability to move from play dependent on concrete objects to abstract thought. During this stage, children move from *parallel play* (i.e., playing alongside another child) to *coordinated play* (i.e., playing with another child). Because interactions are based on proximity and convenience, friendships of toddlers are extremely transitory (Merrell & Gimpel, 1998).

It is important to note that the earliest very young children can have a relationship is between 8 to 10 months, when they can move (i.e., crawl) toward another child.

*Pretend play,* or the ability to initiate, collaborate, and take others' perspectives, is essential for forming friendships. Some young children, especially those with disabilities, do not engage in pretend play without some support from adults. Strategies teachers and parents can use to support pretend play include (Bromer, 1999; Craig-Unkefer & Kaiser, 2002; Doctoroff, 1996):

▶ Providing and helping children identify props such as clothing and objects.

▶ Tailoring props to children's needs. For example, a child with a physical disability may need clothing with large openings and Velcro closures.

▶ Coaching and giving children suggestions to join a group or act out an activity such as "making dinner" or "taking care of the baby," or assuming a role such as teacher, parent, doctor, or firefighter.

▶ Modeling "pretend use" of toys and props.

▶ Organizing structured play groups with a theme (e.g., train, doctor's office, schoolroom) and appropriate props, and assigning children roles.

▶ Introducing an activity, asking leading questions, suggesting ways for children to be involved, and elaborating on a theme.

▶ Increasing children's understanding of themes and roles through stories, circle time, field trips, and discussion about roles and props.

▶ Teaching and letting children practice pretend play scripts that include roles, dialogue, and actions.

Especially good indicators of friendship include the number and length of reciprocal interactions and the number of turns taken (Strain, 2001). During early childhood, a friend is a child who is available to play. Play enables young children to form these "activity-based" friendships (Berk, 1989; Damon, 1977). At this age, children's friendships are governed by concrete characteristics, and children are appreciated for what they do (e.g., sharing, giving things, and the like). Friendships tend to be fleeting. They begin easily when a child shares and end just as abruptly when a child refuses to share, is physically aggressive, or is not in physical proximity. To maintain friendships, sharing is an essential, yet difficult, skill for toddlers to perform consistently.

### Important Social–Emotional Skills During Early Childhood

Critical social–emotional skills during early childhood include the following (Conroy, Langenbrunner, & Burleson, 1996; Lewis, 1994; Strain & Smith, 1996):

- ▶ Initiating and maintaining positive interactions with peers
- ▶ Responding positively to peer interactions
- ▶ Sharing materials and toys with peers
- ▶ Assisting peers
- ▶ Refusing peer interactions in an appropriate manner
- ▶ Taking turns
- ▶ Suggesting and organizing play activities
- ▶ Accepting the play suggestions of peers
- ▶ Communicating needs and wants appropriately
- ▶ Maintaining conversation
- ▶ Expressing anger appropriately
- ▶ Giving and receiving affection

McGinnis and Goldstein (2003) identified 40 skills that are critical for preschool and kindergarten students. The eight skills essential for making friends in early childhood are listed, along with skills for older children, in Table 5.1.

### Ways to Promote Friendship During Early Childhood

There are many strategies to help toddlers and preschoolers establish friendships, including the following:

- ▶ *Provide young children with a secure foundation.* "Good and loving social experiences with a parent, repeated hundreds and thousands of times, form the child's expectations of what social life will bring" (Thompson et al., 2001, p. 18). The primary caregiver, usually the mother, is the very young child's "first friend." The child and caregiver form a strong bond called *attachment.* Securely attached infants show a definite preference for the caregiver and seek contact on the caregiver's return. Securely attached children use the primary caregiver as a secure base from which to explore the environment. Consequently, they have more opportunities to develop interpersonal skills and initiate social interactions (Beckman & Lieber, 1992).
- ▶ *Directly teach social–emotional skills valued by peers.* These skills include those listed earlier and skills listed in Table 5.1. A five-step sequence for teaching specific social–emotional skills is presented in Chapter Six. Social skills programs that teach children peer-pleasing skills are listed in Table 5.2.

**TABLE 5.1** ▶Essential Friendship-Making Skills

| Early Childhood[1] | Middle Childhood[2] | Adolescence[3] |
|---|---|---|
| Greeting others | Introducing yourself | Listening |
| Reading others | Beginning a conversation | Starting a conversation |
| Joining in | Ending a conversation | Having a conversation |
| Waiting your turn | Joining in | Saying "thank you" |
| Sharing | Playing a game | Introducing yourself |
| Offering help | Asking a favor | Introducing other people |
| Asking someone to play | Offering to help a classmate | Giving a compliment |
| Playing a game | Giving a compliment | Asking for help |
| | Suggesting an activity | Joining in |
| | Sharing | Apologizing |
| | Apologizing | Convincing others |
| | | Sharing something |
| | | Helping others |
| | | Standing up for a friend |

[1] Source: From *Skillstreaming in Early Childhood* (Rev. ed.) by E. McGinnis and A. P. Goldstein, 2003, Champaign, IL: Research Press. Copyright © 2003 by E. McGinnis and A. P. Goldstein. Reprinted by permission.
[2] Source: From *Skillstreaming the Elementary School Child* (Rev. ed.) by E. McGinnis and A. P. Goldstein, 1997, Champaign, IL: Research Press. Copyright © 1997 by E. McGinnis and A. P. Goldstein. Reprinted by permission.
[3] Source: From *Skillstreaming the Adolescent* (Rev. ed.) by A. P. Goldstein and E. McGinnis, 1997, Champaign, IL: Research Press. Copyright © 1997 by A. P. Goldstein and E. McGinnis. Reprinted by permission.

▶ *Give young children the opportunity to be with other children regularly.* If children are not with other children frequently, separation anxiety will interfere with the development of friendships. Arrange play dates in the home to provide opportunities for young children to interact (Thompson et al., 2001). Plan activities with children who share interests such as watching TV, playing games, and the like (Shapiro, 1997).

▶ *Make friendship an important topic of discussion and action.* Frequently discuss the importance of friendship, allow children to demonstrate it, and act as a good friendship role model (Cooper & McEvoy, 1996; Shapiro, 1997).

▶ *Arrange the environment to promote social interaction.* Use *affection strategies*, including games, songs, and activities, that encourage young children to show affection toward one another (Lowenthal, 1995, 1996). Begin activities by having children use a sign of friendship such as a smile or a hug. Familiar songs (e.g., "If You're Happy and You Know It") and similar activities make children feel comfortable and promote social interactions (Cooper & McEvoy, 1996).

▶ *Use correspondence training* with young children who have difficulty interacting, especially children with disabilities. When children are in a group, ask a

**TABLE 5.2** ▶Programs That Teach Peer-Pleasing Skills

| Program | Author(s)/Date | Age/Grade |
| --- | --- | --- |
| ACCEPTS | H. M. Walker, McConnell, Holmes, Todis, J. Walker, & Golden (1988) | Grades K–8 |
| ACCESS | Walker, Todis, Holmes, & Horton (1988) | Adolescents |
| CLASSIC | Dygdon (1993) | Middle School |
| A Collaborative Approach to Teaching Social Skills | Warger & Rutherford (1996) | Grades K–12 |
| Connecting with Others Programs | Richardson (1996a, 1996b) Richardson & Evans (1997) Richardson & Meisgelier (2001) | Grades K–12 |
| EQUIP | Gibbs, Potter, & Goldstein (1995) | Grades K–12 |
| Fostering Emotional Intelligence in K–8 Students | Doty (2001) | Grades K–8 |
| Getting Along with Others | N. F. Jackson, D. A. Jackson, & Monroe (1983) | Adolescents & Adults |
| I Can Problem Solve (ICPS) Programs | Shure (1992a, 1992b, 1992c) | Grades K–6 |
| Learning to Get Along | D. A. Jackson, N. F. Jackson, Bennett, Bynum, & Faryna (1991) | Grades K–12 |
| Let's Talk: Developing Pro-social Communication Skills | Wiig (1982) | Ages 9–21 |
| Let's Talk for Children | Wiig & Bray (1983) | Ages 4–9 |
| Let's Talk Intermediate Level | Wiig & Bray (1984) | Ages 10–Adult |
| Life Skills Activities for Secondary Students with Special Needs | Mannix (1995) | Grades 6–12 |
| Passport Programs | Vernon (1998a, 1998b, 1998c) | Grades 1–12 |
| PATHS Curriculum | Kusche & Greenberg (1994) | Elementary |
| Play Time Social Time | Odom & McConnell (1993) | Ages 3–5 |
| The Power of Social Skills in Character Development | Scully (2000) | Adolescents |
| PREPARE Curriculum | Goldstein (1999) | Adolescents |

**TABLE 5.2** ▶(Continued)

| Program | Author(s)/Date | Age/Grade |
|---|---|---|
| Promoting Social Success | Siperstein & Rickards (2004) | Grades PreK–12 |
| Raising a Thinking Child Workbook | Shure (2000a) | Preschool– Elementary |
| Ready-to-Use Social Skills Lessons & Activities | Begun (1995, 1996a, 1996b, 1996c) | Grades PreK–12 |
| Self-Science: The Subject Is Me | Stone & Dilleunt (1978) | Grades 2–8 |
| Skillstreaming Programs | Goldstein & McGinnis (1997) McGinnis & Goldstein (1997, 2003) | Grades PreK–12 |
| Social Skills Activities for Special Children | Mannix (1993) | Elementary |
| Social Skills Activities for Secondary Students with Special Needs | Mannix (1998) | Grades 6–12 |
| Social Skills Development | Antonello (1996) | Adolescents |
| Social Skills for Daily Living | Schumaker, Hazel, & Pederson (1988) | Adolescents |
| Social Skills for School and Community | Sargent (1991) | Grades K–12 |
| Social Skills in the Classroom | Stephens (1992) | Children & Adolescents |
| Social Skills Intervention Guide | Elliott & Gresham (1991) | Grades 1–10 |
| Social Standards at School | J. Kinney & T. Kinney (2003) | Grades 1–6 |
| Stacking the Deck | Foxx & McMorrow (1983) | Adults |
| The Stop & Think Social Skills Programs | Knopf (2001a, 2001b, 2001c, 2001d) | Grades PreK–8 |
| Systematic Instruction of Social Skills | Sargent (1988) | Grades 1–12 |
| Taking Part | Cartledge & Kleefeld (1991) | Grades PreK–3 |
| Teaching Friendship Skills | Huggins, Moen, & Manion (1993–1995) | Grades 1–6 |
| Teaching Social Competence to Youth & Adults with Developmental Disabilities | D. A. Jackson, N. F. Jackson, & Bennett (1998) | Adolescents & Adults |

**TABLE 5.2** ▶(Continued)

| Program | Author(s)/Date | Age/Grade |
|---|---|---|
| Teaching Social Skills: A Practical Instructional Approach | Rutherford, Chipman, DiGangi, & Anderson (1992) | Elementary |
| Teaching Social Skills to Youth | Down & Tierney (1992) | Children & Adolescents |
| Thinking, Feeling, Behaving | Vernon (1989a, 1989b) | Grades 1–12 |
| The Tough Kids Social Skills Book | Sheridan (1995–1996) | Grades K–8 |
| Waksman Social Skills Curriculum | S. Waksman & D. D. Waksman (1998) | Middle School |
| Working Together | Cartledge & Kleefeld (1994) | Grades 3–6 |

child what he or she will do (e.g., "I'm going to play with Janna," "I'm going to share my toy with Tony," and so forth). When the child follows through, provide reinforcement in the form of praise, food, or toys.

▶ *Have peers who are socially well adjusted interact and play with children who are less socially skilled* (Lowenthal, 1995, 1996). When grouping children, make sure that at least 30% of children in the group have well developed social skills (Cooper & McEvoy, 1996). (More information about peer-mediated interventions is presented later in this chapter.)

▶ *Use naturalistic teaching strategies.* Naturalistic teaching involves structuring the environment and capitalizing on the young child's interests (Kohler, Anthony, Steighner, & Hoyson, 2001). These strategies are presented as Table 5.3.

### Friendship During Middle Childhood (Ages 8 to 12)

Mary and Eleanor have the kind of friendship kids are supposed to have: They traipse back and forth between houses without my having to arrange a play date or get in the car. They ride bikes. They go to movies. They eat dinner together. They wear matching necklaces; one says "best" and the other says "friends." (Spencer, 2003, p. 108)

Paula Spencer, a frequent magazine contributor, described Mary and Eleanor's reaction when they learned that Eleanor's family would be moving. Eleanor and

**TABLE 5.3** ▶Description of Naturalistic Teaching Strategies

| Strategy | Description |
| --- | --- |
| *Use novel materials* | The teacher incorporates materials that are unique. These are items in which the child has shown a previous interest, such as Pooh characters, balloons, bubbles, and so forth. |
| *Join the activity* | The teacher joins the activity and engages with children in play-related actions and themes. |
| *Invite the child to make choices* | The teacher invites the child to choose desired actions and/or materials. This can be done through questions and nonverbal overtures (e.g., holding out a container of markers so the child can select one). |
| *Use incidental strategies* | The teacher places items out of reach, blocks the child's access to desired items, sabotages the materials, and acts in ways that violate the child's expectations (uses materials incorrectly or responds to child's overtures in the wrong way). |
| *Use comments or questions* | The teacher uses comments and asks questions to facilitate the child's interest and/or play-related talk (e.g., "I think I'll put my baby right next to yours"; "Why are you coloring your turtle purple?"). |
| *Require expansion of talk* | The teacher responds to the child's talk in a manner that generates elaboration. If the child requests a ball, the teacher might ask, "What color is the ball?" and "What are you going to do with it?" before giving the child the ball. |
| *Invite interactions with peers* | The teacher encourages interaction with other children by drawing the child's attention to peers or prompting peers to direct overtures to the focal child (e.g., "Maybe you could ask Sam if he will play with you"). |

*Source:* From "Teaching Social Interaction Skills in the Integrated Preschool: An Examination of Naturalistic Tactics," by F. W. Kohler, L. J. Anthony, S. A. Steighner, and M. Hoyson, in *Topics in Early Childhood Special Education, 21*, p. 95. Copyright © 2001 by Pro-Ed Inc. Reprinted with permission.

Mary, both third graders, "scrawled messages in chalk and on the driveway and in the dust on the van: 'don't buy our house! Mary + Eleanor = friends 4 ever!'"

Berk (1989) characterized this stage of play as one of mutual trust and assistance. Play soon becomes more complex and involves rule-based activities (Bierman & Montminy, 1993). Although children still value friends who share and give gifts, they also begin to value personality characteristics and like or dislike other children based on their disposition or personal qualities. The common denominator of children's friendship during this stage, however, is the ability to share activities rather than values. Children are concerned with "reciprocal trust," and the ability to trust is essential. If that trust is violated, or if a promise is broken, the friendship is compromised until the child apologizes or offers an explanation (Selman, 1980). The primary mode of communication is cooperation and collaboration.

During this age span, relationships with parents and other adults become less important and the peer group more important. The group sets the standards for behavior, and children rely on affirmation from one another (Thompson et al., 2001). "The use of humor, gossip, negative evaluation, and teasing increase[s]" at this stage (Merrell & Gimpel, 1998, p. 34). Adhering to gender-appropriate rules of behavior also becomes important. Friendships usually are formed with same-sex peers. Children try to figure out characteristics of popular kids, and they assess themselves to determine if they are "cool" and fit in (Thompson et al., 2001). The number of friends increases and friendships tend to remain stable (Bierman & Montminy, 1993).

Although friends during middle childhood are still playmates, these friendships are much deeper than those of younger children: "The important role friends play in providing mutual respect and admiration about their shared life is the reason children seek each other out with such intense longing" (Thompson et al., 2001, p. 51).

Because friendships are stable during middle childhood, children who are rejected at this age continue to be rejected during adolescence. Rejected children misinterpret peers' behavior as aggressive, and they often rely on aggression to solve problems. As friendships become more secure, children share different opinions and occasionally criticize their friends.

### Important Social–Emotional Skills During Middle Childhood

Compared to earlier and later stages, the following skills are characteristic of middle childhood:

- ▶ Cooperating
- ▶ Collaborating
- ▶ Respecting others
- ▶ Joining in
- ▶ Complimenting
- ▶ Interaction skills such as listening, answering, and taking turns
- ▶ Showing a sense of humor

McGinnis and Goldstein (1997) identified 60 essential social–emotional skills for children during middle childhood. Eleven of these skills related to forming friendships are listed in Table 5.1.

### Ways to Promote Friendship During Middle Childhood

We offer several strategies teachers and parents can use to help children make and keep friends during middle childhood:

▶ *Directly teach social–emotional skills valued by peers.* These skills include those listed above and those listed in Table 5.1. A five-step sequence for teaching specific social–emotional skills is presented in Chapter Six. Table 5.2 lists social skills programs that teach peer-pleasing skills.

▶ *Counteract negative self-statements that keep children from making friends.* Elias, Tobias, and Friedlander (1999) identified seven negative self-statements that discourage friendship formation. We list them, along with strategies teachers and parents can use to counteract them, in the box on pages 146 and 147.

▶ *Be sure that kids have time for friends.* Keep a log of how much time your child spends on certain activities during the week (e.g., lessons, sports, watching TV, homework). If at least 4 hours a week aren't devoted to developing close friendships, drop nonessential activities (Frankel, 1996).

▶ *Teach children to use group behaviors that allow them to cooperate and collaborate.* At home, allow children to learn group skills within the family group. Be a good role model by being active in adult groups (Shapiro, 1997). In school, give children the opportunity to use group skills in cooperative learning groups or by serving as peer tutors, as described in Chapter Nine. Another way to promote collaboration is to teach children to play cooperative games. Examples include Cooperative Robot and Cooperative Volleyball (Shapiro, 1997). Cooperative Robot involves having three children hold hands with each other. The middle player—the youngest of the three—is the "brain," and he or she directs the players on either side to complete an activity such as making a sandwich and feeding it to all three heads, making a bed, or picking up items off the floor. With Cooperative Volleyball, players must keep a balloon in the air as long as they can, but everyone must hit the balloon before a player can hit it a second time.

▶ *Assist children in recognizing things and activities they have in common.* Help children develop activity-based skills, encourage them to participate in extracurricular activities, and seek neighborhood and community activities that your child might enjoy. Activities could include classes, team sports, and groups such as Scouts. Encourage children to join groups of peers with similar interests, skills, and characteristics.

▶ *Help children to develop a sense of humor.* The ability to laugh puts people at ease. Parents can help children develop a sense of humor by looking for the funny aspects of things. Marano (1998b, pp. 103, 104) suggests these activities:

▷ *Cut out funny pictures from newspapers and magazines.* Share them with your kids.

Negative self-statements can prevent children and youth from making and keeping friends (Elias et al., 1999). Some examples of negative statements follow, along with strategies that can be used to counteract them.

### #1: I'm not like everyone else.

What child says:      *I'm different from them so they won't want to be with me.*

*They're better than me so they won't want to be with me.*

*I'm better than them so they won't want to be with me.*

### #2: It's a catastrophe.

What child says:      *They didn't call me, so they hate me.*

*I did something so bad and so embarrassing that no one will ever forget. I will never live this down. I might as well just move to another town.*

*I was the only one who didn't get the joke, and everyone thinks I'm the stupidest person in the class.*

### #3: It's not my fault. It's their fault.

What child says:      *They're just a bunch of creeps, and nobody would want to be friends with them.*

*I didn't do anything wrong. It's her problem.*

*Those girls are just a bunch of snobs and unfriendly to everybody, not just mean to me.*

### #4: I don't see why they got annoyed.

What child says:      *So what if I borrowed his glove without asking? I'd lend him my stuff. What's the big deal?*

*All I said was that she looked fat in that dress. I was just teasing. She's just too sensitive.*

*I took more food than anyone else because I was hungrier. I didn't think they would get upset.*

### #5: I don't know what to say.

What child says:      *Every time I'm around those kids, I just freeze up. I'm so scared I'll say something totally stupid.*

*I won't know anyone at the party. They're all rich kids, and we don't have anything in common.*

*That group of boys is really good at skateboarding. I don't know how to skateboard. What if they ask me to go skateboarding?*

### #6: I know what to do, but I just can't do it.

What the child says:  *I want to invite those girls to my party, but I'm afraid they think I'm not cool and they'll laugh at me.*

*I'd like to volunteer to work on the homecoming float, but whenever I talk to someone I don't know, I get so nervous I feel like I'm going to throw up.*

*I really want to join that club, but I can't ask her. I feel so intimidated. Every time I'm around her, I trip or knock something over.*

### #7 There's no way.

What the child says:  *It would be great if I could be friends with them, but it's never going to happen. They're just too different, and they won't like me.*

*In my dreams! Other kids can have really good friends they can share secrets with. Not me. I've always been by myself.*

*I'd like to start out on the right foot at this new school. But they will figure out that I'm a weirdo, just like at the last school.*

### Strategies to Change Negative Self-Statements

Sometimes negative self-statements are so deeply entrenched that it is difficult to get children to think differently. But, parents and teachers can use the following strategies to try to change the seven negative mindsets (Elias et al., 1999):

▶ Make statements that run counter to what you believe is the child's negative self-talk.

▶ Provide examples that are exceptions to the child's negative perceptions.

▶ Help the child practice skills (e.g., conversation skills, introducing self) he or she needs to overcome negative self-perceptions.

▶ Help the child understand his or her feelings through emotion coaching, as described in Chapter Eight.

▶ Teach the child problem-solving strategies like those described in Chapter Four.

▶ Be sure the child dresses to fit in with his or her peers. (See suggestions in Chapter Three.)

▶ Use literature as a way to discuss friendship, shyness, and so forth. (See ideas in this chapter about teaching friendship through literature.)

▷ Tell them about funny things that happened to you during the day.

▷ Tell (clean) jokes to your kids and listen to their jokes (be sure to laugh—or at least smile).

▷ Read funny stories, nonsense poems.

▷ Take your kids to humorous movies.

▷ Encourage and appreciate occasional bouts of silliness.

▷ Sometimes, when you are angry at your kids, make a silly face at them.

▷ Come up with a set of private signals within your family, to use in public when one of you has made a fool of himself or herself or stepped over some line. Choosing a funny but subtle expression takes the sting out of silent reprimands.

▷ Remember that little humorous acts often produce big changes in the climate of relationships.

► *Help children to select indoor and outdoor interactive toys.* To qualify as interactive, a toy must have these qualities (Frankel, 1996, p. 26):

▷ Requires two persons (indoor toys) or at least two persons (outdoor toys) to play.

▷ Does not encourage aggression.

▷ Is fun for you and your child to play.

▷ Has simple rules.

▷ Does not take too long (no more than 45 minutes) to play.

► *Use children's literature to teach friendship skills.* We offer some tips for teaching friendship skills in the box on pages 150 and 151.

► *Teach aggressive children self-control strategies.* Interfering behaviors such as inattention, hyperactivity, impulsivity, and verbal and physical aggression make it difficult for children to get along with others. Throughout this book we offer strategies for teachers and parents to use to help children control their behavior.

► *Point out friendship-making skills in videos and TV shows.* Ask questions like these:

▷ Why were _____ friends?

▷ What qualities did _____ have that would make him/her a good friend?

▷ Would you want to be friends with _____? Why or why not?

## Friendship During Adolescence (Ages 13–17)

*Susan and Monica were the best of friends. They met when Susan moved to Bradenton in the sixth grade. Now they were getting ready to graduate from high school and head off to college—Susan to the University of Virginia and Monica to Duke University. When asked why they were such good friends, they gave the following answers.*

*Susan: "We have a lot in common. Both of us enjoy tennis and running. We like the theater, and we're both members of the Thespian Society. We're pretty good students, but we like to have fun. But most important, we know everything about each other—the good and the bad—and we've been through good and bad times together."*

*Monica: "There's no one I trust more than Susan. I've shared my deepest, darkest secrets with her, and I know she keeps them to herself. I know we're friends for life."*

*Susan: "Even though we're going to different colleges, they're not that far apart. We'll see each other on weekends and during school breaks."*

*Monica: "Yeah—and there's always the phone and e-mail!"*

During adolescence the notion of friendship evolves from one of shared activities to one of shared values. Berk (1989) characterized adolescent friendship as having intimacy and mutual understanding. Adolescents regard themselves and others in abstract rather than in concrete terms (Sprinthall & Collins, 1988). Whereas younger children describe people and may select friends based solely on what they look like and/or what they do, adolescents are interested in individuals' personality traits, a perspective that influences selection and retention of friends (Bierman & Montminy, 1993). They are able to describe others, including their friends, in much more objective terms than are younger children (Sprinthall & Collins, 1988).

Adolescents value individuals who are accepting and understanding and with whom they can share their innermost thoughts. Friends are those who can help them get through hard times. Adolescents understand that becoming friends takes time as they get to know a person and determine their compatibility and potential for closeness. They understand the difference between a friend as someone to whom they can trust innermost secrets and an acquaintance to whom they do not disclose confidences (Thompson et al., 2001).

At this age, friendships are stable and only a serious event will terminate a friendship. Friendships are no longer formed strictly along gender lines. The romantic relationships of older adolescents allow them to further develop social–emotional skills learned during same-sex friendships (Thompson et al., 2001).

Building on the growing peer influence of middle childhood, the peer group exerts an even stronger influence during adolescence. Relationships with peers are critical for adolescents to (Christopher, Nangle, & Hansen, 1993)

▶ establish systems to support their social and emotional needs,
▶ develop social values and moral reasoning skills,
▶ improve/maintain self-esteem,
▶ promote adult-like behavior and interpersonal competence,
▶ establish independence,
▶ enhance social status,
▶ enjoy recreational activities,
▶ experiment with sexual roles and develop sexual attitudes.

# Teaching Friendship Skills Through Literature

## Selecting Books

When selecting books, consider the following:[1]

▶ Be sure the skill(s) in the book match the skills you want to teach.

▶ Avoid books with violent themes.

▶ Choose simple story lines that make the target skill explicit.

▶ Choose short stories in the interest of time.

▶ Make sure the books reflect cultural diversity and avoid gender stereotypes.

▶ Keep in mind that children find contemporary biographies of great interest.

Use these resources to find books:

▶ See Appendix B for a listing of children's books chosen by children that cover topics related to social–emotional competence.

▶ *Readers Guide to Books in Print*

▶ DeGeorge suggests these books:[2]

| | |
|---|---|
| *We Are Best Friends* | *That New Boy* |
| *A Friend Is Someone Who Likes You* | *A New Boy in Kindergarten* |
| *Are We Still Friends?* | *New Neighbors* |
| *Santiago* | *Wendy and the Bullies* |
| *The Trouble With Friends* | *Fast Friends* |
| *Angelina and Alice* | *Rosie and Michael* |
| *I Want to Play* | *Rock Finds a Friend* |
| *May I Bring a Friend?* | *New Friend* |
| *Will You Be My Friend?* | *Will I Have a Friend?* |

Adolescents who are most likely to be rejected are those who are either ostracized by their peers or who socially withdraw from the peer group (Bierman & Montminy, 1993).

Until about age 10, children demonstrate extreme family loyalty, rarely telling family secrets to "outsiders" (Thompson et al., 2001). When they reach adolescence, children begin to talk to friends about their families. In addition to establishing friendships with individuals with whom they identify and share secrets, adolescents are heavily influenced by clothing, which Thompson et al. describe as "the psyche worn on the outside" (p. 52).

## Teaching a Friendship Lesson

Use these steps:[3]

▶ *Anticipatory set.* "Pretest" (i.e., informally and orally) children to make sure they understand vocabulary, concepts, location of story, plot, main idea of the story, and so forth. Introduce the skill, and discuss why it is important.

▶ *Presentation of material.* Read the story. Ask guided questions during and after the story. Identify the steps for making friends. Make the connection between the skill and the story.

▶ *Guided practice.* Have children practice skills by themselves through role play. Have children role-play with other children, if possible.

▶ *Independent practice.* Have children identify situations where they can use the new friendship skill. Have them role-play using the skill in these situations. Have them write a summary of the story and their thoughts about making friends. (Younger children can draw pictures to illustrate the story and their ideas about friendship.) Read another story that targets the same skill and have children independently identify the steps in the friendship-making skill. Continue to reinforce use of the skill through other books and activities.

▶ *Closure.* Summarize the story and the steps in the friendship-making skill. "Posttest" children by asking them questions about the story and the skill to make sure they know why the skill is important, how to perform it, and where and when they can use it.

---

[1] "Learning Social Skills Through Literature for Children and Adolescents," by G. Cartledge & M. W. Kiarie, *Teaching Exceptional Children, 34,* 40–47.

[2] "Friendship and Stories: Using Children's Literature to Teach Friendship Skills to Children with Learning Disabilities," by K. L. DeGeorge, *Intervention in School and Clinic, 33*(3), 157–162.

[3] DeGeorge.

### Important Social-Emotional Skills During Adolescence

The following skills are critical for adolescents to make and keep friends (Mannix, 1998; Marano, 1998a, 1998b; Walker et al., 1988):

- ▶ Objectics (i.e., understand how to look in order to fit in)
- ▶ Being a good listener
- ▶ Entering and maintaining a conversation
- ▶ Negotiating

▶ Compromising
▶ Showing a sense of humor
▶ Complimenting
▶ Offering assistance
▶ Following through
▶ Making others feel comfortable
▶ Revealing oneself
▶ Keeping confidences

Goldstein and McGinnis (1997) identified 50 essential social–emotional skills for children during adolescence. Fourteen of these skills, listed in Table 5.1, are crucial for making friends. Social skills programs that teach adolescents peer-pleasing skills are given in Table 5.2.

### Ways to Promote Friendship During Adolescence

The following strategies may be used to help adolescents make and keep friends (L. K. Elksnin & N. Elksnin, 1995):

▶ *Help adolescents to understand their values and those of others.* Have them articulate their values and tell you the qualities they like to see in a friend. Have them discuss if their values and those of their friends are similar.
▶ *Help adolescents understand how similarities and differences both enrich relationships.* Have them complete the Same and Different activity sheet shown as Figure 5.1.
▶ *Help adolescents develop strategies to make new friends.* Once adolescents have a clear idea of their values and interests, help them identify groups and organizations that promote these values and interests. Discuss extracurricular activities that are available during and after school and that are likely to attract individuals with shared interests. Make adolescents aware of volunteer opportunities.
▶ *Counteract negative self-statements that keep adolescents from making friends.* Negative self-statements are common during adolescence, as well as during middle childhood. Use the strategies presented earlier in this chapter to counter common negative self-statements that prevent children from making friends.
▶ *Help adolescents develop skills and traits that their peers value.* We listed skills that adolescents highly value. Be sure that the adolescent can perform each of these skills fluently. Using the five-step sequence described in Chapter Six, directly teach skills that are deficient.
▶ *Consider the use of peer-mediated and self-mediated interventions.* The peer group exerts tremendous influence over adolescents. For this reason, the peer-mediated interventions described later in this chapter often are highly effective with this age group. Because adolescents have a high need for being independent, they respond well to monitoring, recording, and evaluating their interpersonal interactions.

## Same and Different

In Column 1, write down things you like to do (e.g., sports, shopping, church groups, volunteering and things that interest you (e.g., playing video games, dancing, singing, watching TV). Write the names of friends in Columns 2 and 3 along with things you think they like to do and things you think interest them.

| 1<br>Things I Like | 2<br>Things _____ likes<br>(name) | 3<br>Things _____ likes<br>(name) |
|---|---|---|
| _____ | _____ | _____ |
| _____ | _____ | _____ |
| _____ | _____ | _____ |
| _____ | _____ | _____ |
| _____ | _____ | _____ |
| _____ | _____ | _____ |
| _____ | _____ | _____ |

Highlight (with a highlighter pen) each friend's interests and activities that are on your list. List *shared* interests and activities here:

You and
Friend #1: _____

You and
Friend #2 _____

_____

_____

_____

_____

List your friends' interests and activities that are *different* from yours:

_____

_____

_____

_____

_____

_____

**FIGURE 5.1** ▶Same and Different Activity Sheet

## ► Developing Conversational Skills

Conversation skills such as entering, initiating, and maintaining conversation are important friendship skills for children of all ages. Critically important skills include the following (Shapiro, 1997, pp. 174–176):

- ► Sharing personal information about oneself
- ► Expressing one's needs and desires clearly
- ► Modulating one's responses to others' cues and words
- ► Questioning others about themselves
- ► Offering help and suggestions
- ► Extending invitations
- ► Providing positive feedback
- ► Staying with the conversation
- ► Showing that you are a good listener
- ► Showing that you understand the feelings of another person
- ► Expressing interest in another person
- ► Expressing acceptance
- ► Giving affection and approval
- ► Showing empathy
- ► Offering help and suggestions when they seem appropriate

Here are some strategies that teachers and parents can use to teach and promote the use of conversational skills:

- ► *Promote family conversation.* As parents, make a commitment to promote conversation at dinner, in the car, and so forth.
- ► *Have the children observe TV talk show hosts.* Begin by having children watch videotapes of talk show hosts (e.g., Oprah Winfrey, Jay Leno) as they interview guests (Guevremont, 1990). Follow this with discussion about the conversational strategies hosts use to make their guests comfortable. Emphasize that the host's primary goal is to make sure the guest feels comfortable during the interview. Assign children the roles of hosts and guests. Have the hosts interview the guests. Tape each interview (not to exceed 3 minutes). Play the tape and evaluate how well each host did.
- ► *Teach conversational give-and-take.* Marks and colleagues (1999) developed several strategies to teach conversational skills to children and youth with Asperger syndrome, who often monopolize conversations:
  - ▷ Provide *visual, concrete examples* of reciprocal conversations using metaphors such as playing tennis and putting a puzzle together.
  - ▷ Teach *questioning skills* by having children write down potential questions. Introduce them to the *two-question rule*, which involves asking a question and following up with another question to prevent one-sided conversations.

▷ Teach *passive listening skills* by encouraging responses such as "Hmm," "I understand what you mean," and "Cool," and help children understand that they don't always have to be the ones to do the talking.

▷ Help children and youth develop *social scripts* such as "meeting someone for the first time," "entering a conversation," "talking in a small group," and so forth, and allow them to role-play each script in a safe environment.

▷ Teach *survival strategies* to use when things go wrong. Examples include ending a conversation by saying "I have to go now" and changing the subject if the child invaded somebody's mental space (see Chapter Three).

▶ *Teach conversational skills in a highly structured way.* For some children and youth, especially those with communication disorders and learning disabilities, conversational skills have to be taught in an explicit, structured manner. Wiig and colleagues designed several curricula designed to teach language skills critical for social success: *Let's Talk: Developing Prosocial Communication Skills* (1982), *Let's Talk for Children* (1983), and *Let's Talk Intermediate Level* (1984). Other useful programs include *Social Communication Skills for Children* (McGann & Werven, 1999) and *Talkabout, A Social Communication Skills Package* (Kelly, 1996).

▶ *Have the speech and language pathologist address the child's social–emotional communication skills.* Many children receiving speech and language services have difficulty communicating in a socially appropriate manner. Where appropriate, be sure children's IEPs include objectives that focus on social communication skills.

# ▶ Recruiting the Support of Peers

Because peers are critical in the development of interpersonal skills, often peers are involved in teaching and supporting less socially skilled children and youth (Ang & Hughes, 2001; Arnold & Hughes, 1999; Moroz & Jones, 2002). Efforts to use peers are referred to as *peer training* or *peer-mediated intervention*. We will describe peer-mediated interventions that can be used during early childhood, middle childhood, and adolescence.

## Peer-Mediated Interventions During Early Childhood

Many social–emotional skills interventions for preschoolers are aimed at increasing and enhancing peer interactions (Odom, McConnell, & McEvoy, 1992). Peer-mediated interventions have proven effective in increasing the level of social interaction of young children (Kamps et al., 1998; Kamps et al., 2002; Gonzalez-Lopez & Kamps, 1997; Mathur & Rutherford, 1991; Pierce & Schreibman, 1997; Storey, Danko, Strain, & Smith, 1992; Strain, 2001). The use of peers with young children, particularly those with disabilities, includes the strategies of

▶ *peer proximity* (placing target children with socially competent peers),

▶ *peer prompting and reinforcing* (having socially competent peers ask target children to use social skills or reinforce use of these skills),

▶ *peer initiation* (having socially competent peers invite target children to play).

A primary advantage of peers is that they are more available and more effective than adults because target children often are more motivated to respond to peers than to adults. Peer interventions also encourage target children to learn clusters of related skills and to use these skills across multiple settings and peers.

### Buddy Systems

In this strategy, socially adept *buddies* are enlisted to interact with less proficient peers. Buddies are selected based upon gender and shared interests, among other characteristics. Buddies are taught skills such as staying close to the target child, talking with the target child, and playing with the target child (English, Goldstein, Kaczmarek, & Shafer, 1996). Parents and teachers praise buddies and target children for staying, playing, and talking together. Odom and Watts (1991) taught preschoolers to initiate activities with peers with autism. Buddies were asked to share, assist, and compliment target children. Peer interactions increased, but only when teachers prompted, or reminded, the buddies to interact.

### Puppet Script Training

Young children can learn friendship-making skills such as greeting, and initiating and maintaining conversation, by using puppets (Gronna, Serna, Kennedy, & Prater, 1999). Cartledge and Kleefeld (1991) developed a social–emotional skills training program called Taking Part, in which social skills are introduced in vignettes acted out by animal stick puppets.

## Peer-Mediated Interventions During Middle Childhood

In large classrooms it may be difficult to carry out social–emotional skills interventions. Using peers to deliver interventions frees up teachers' time. It is essential, however, that teachers carefully select peers who are willing to participate, comply with teacher requests, demonstrate positive behavior toward others, and respond to the social initiations of less well accepted children (Gable, Strain, & Hendrickson, 1979). When training peers, Gable and his colleagues offered these guidelines:

▶ Recruit peers who meet the above criteria.
▶ Describe the social–emotional skills intervention.
▶ Teach peers how to intervene by prompting, modeling, rehearsing, practicing, and reinforcing appropriate intervention efforts.
▶ Prepare peers for rejection when they first begin to work with children who are withdrawn.
▶ Following training, give peers frequent, specific, informative feedback.

### Buddy Systems

To increase social interactions, elementary-aged children can benefit from the buddy system and learn skills such as initiating a conversation and keeping it going, complimenting, and cooperating. This strategy is effective in increasing and improving social interactions of children with disabilities such as autism (Gonzalez-Lopez & Kamps, 1997; Kamps et al., 2002).

### Positive Peer Reporting

Teachers and parents are all too familiar with children "tattling" on classmates and siblings. *Positive peer reporting* (PPR) turns the notion of tattling on its head by having children publicly praise peers' appropriate behavior (Bowers, Woods, Carylon, & Friman, 2000). C. H. Skinner, Cashwell, and A. L. Skinner (2000) call PPR "tootling" (telling the teacher or parent when a child did something socially appropriate), as opposed to "tattling" (telling the teacher or parent when a child did something inappropriate). Teachers and parents may introduce PPR, or tootling, as follows:

> For the next few weeks, we'll be working on peer relations. Everyone will take turns being the "star." Each day, everyone will have a chance to praise the star's good behavior. How do we praise good behavior? (Moroz & Jones, 2002, p. 239)

Next, teachers and parents teach children the steps of PPR (Jones, Young, & Friman, 2000, p. 34):

1. Look at the person.
2. Smile.
3. Report something positive the person did or said during the day.
4. Say something positive like "good job" or "way to go."

After teaching the steps in PPR, teachers and parents provide examples, and have children provide examples, of situations in which to use PPR. Teachers and parents model praise statements and have children come up with their own praise statements. In a study conducted by Moroz and Jones (2002), the teacher announced the "star for the day." During 7- to 10-minute PPR sessions, the teacher asked the group to praise the star, and then evaluated the praise statements and rewarded the students with praise and rewards. PPR has effectively increased positive social interactions in general and special education classrooms (Ervin, Johnston, & Friman, 1998; Ervin, Miller, & Friman, 1996; Jones et al., 2000; Skinner et al., 2000), and at home (Bowers, McGinnis, Ervin, & Friman, 1999).

### Shared Activities

Teaching elementary-aged children shared activites promotes social interaction and may lead to friendship. For example, when children with and without mental retardation were taught a board game, interactions increased and the children with mental retardation used their social skills in other situations as well (McMahon, Wacker, Sasso, Berg, & Newton, 1996).

### Peer Tutoring

Peer tutoring can increase the level of acceptance of children by their peers. For example, children with LD tend to be less well accepted by their peers. D. Fuchs, L. S. Fuchs, Mathes, and Martinez (2002) reported that students with LD who were in a same-age tutoring program called Peer-Assisted Learning Strategies (PALS) enjoyed the same social status as their nondisabled peers. By comparison, children with LD who were not in the PALS program had lower social standing.

## Peer-Mediated Interventions During Adolescence

Peer-mediated interventions are used less frequently with adolescents than with younger children. This is surprising considering the great influence of the peer group at this age (L. K. Elksnin & N. Elksnin, 1995). We will briefly describe several peer-mediated interventions.

### Positive Peer Reporting

As with elementary-aged children, positive peer reporting (PPR) has been used successfully with adolescents. In one study, PPR led to enhanced social status of socially rejected, delinquent adolescents (Jones et al., 2000).

### Peer Tutoring

Teaching peers tutoring skills and having them teach their friends these skills is an efficient, effective way to increase the quantity and quality of social interactions between students with and without disabilities (Duan & O'Brien, 1998; Romer, Haring, & White, 1996). An advantage of this approach is that target children often generalize their use of social skills across settings, situations, and peers.

### Clubs

Because after-school clubs are an integral part of high school, friendship clubs are an appropriate way to promote social–emotional skill development. Sodac (1997) started an AMICUS club for students with and without disabilities in which students were selected for membership through teacher- and self-nomination. Adolescents who reported that they "didn't do anything over the weekend" or that they "just watched TV" were considered good candidates for membership. Goals of the club were to

- ▶ promote appropriate social relationships,
- ▶ foster out-of-school contacts,
- ▶ encourage open communication and effective social interaction skills,
- ▶ enhance self-esteem through fellowship and membership in an after-school activity club,
- ▶ promote school spirit through scheduled involvement in school activities. (p. 64)

Weekly meetings were held to plan weekend activities (e.g., movies, athletic events, parties, picnics), community-service activities (e.g., visiting nursing homes, serving food at the homeless shelter), and overnight/extended trips (e.g., campouts, visiting an amusement park), and fundraisers.

## Is Inclusion Enough?

As we have discussed throughout, many children and youth with disabilities have social–emotional problems, and they are often rejected by their nondisabled peers. Inclusion, or placing children with disabilities in general education classrooms, is often insufficient in itself to promote social–emotional competence. Still, the access it affords to typically developing peers is valuable in forming friendships. For example, Buysse, Goldman, and Skinner (2002) found that young children with disabilities who were in child-care programs with nondisabled peers in the majority were almost twice as likely to have at least one friend than were young children with disabilities in special education programs with children with disabilities in the majority. Panacek and Dunlap (2003) reported that children who were in segregated classrooms for students with emotional and behavioral disorders had limited social networks. Further, whereas children in general education classrooms counted their classmates as their friends, children in E/BD self-contained special education classes did not identify classmates as friends; they identified children near their homes as friends.

Inclusion offers the advantage of giving children with disabilities access to larger social networks. Coupled with direct instruction of social–emotional skills and peer-mediated interventions such as those described here, access will help children with disabilities acquire the skills needed to make and keep friends. Strategies teachers can use to encourage friendship among children with and without disabilities are as follows (Calloway, 1999):

1. Be open and honest about disabilities.
2. Let children share about their own disability.
3. Keep your curricula barrier-free.
4. Utilize all your resources. (Have kids brainstorm ways to adapt activities.)
5. Make disability a comfortable concept.
6. Create social opportunities.
7. Use "friendship activities" to help establish good peer relationships.
8. Provide equal access for typically achieving peers.
9. Be a good model.
10. Teach social skills in your classroom.
11. Believe in the uniqueness of each child.
12. Include therapists in your daily routine.
13. Promote independence and autonomy in all children.
14. Intervene proactively. Respond immediately to any rejection of one child by another. Limits should be clearly set, stressing that all children must be treated with respect.
15. Encourage collaboration.

16. Provide opportunities for children to learn about specific disabilities.
17. Counteract stereotypic ideas about disabilities.
18. Explore a variety of both differences and similarities among people.
19. Teach communication.
20. Provide social praise and/or reinforcers. (pp. 176–177)

## ▶ Chapter Summary

Children's expectations and definitions concerning friendship evolve from a concrete, behavioral orientation to an abstract, psychological orientation. They progress from forming self-centered, egocentric relationships to reciprocal friendships. Very young children regard momentary acts as "friendship," whereas the friendships of older children endure over time.

More specifically, friendships during early childhood are based upon proximity and shared activities, and they are often fleeting. As children become less egocentric, they start to develop reciprocal friendships during middle childhood. Although friendships at this age are still activity-based, children begin to like or dislike other children based upon their personality characteristics. During adolescence, youth are more interested in children who share their values and who accept and understand them. At this age, friendships are relatively stable and relationships with friends become more important than those with parents and other adults.

Different social–emotional skills are essential at different ages. Among these, conversational skills are essential when making and keeping friends. The skills that peers value often are quite different from the skills that teachers value.

# CHAPTER 6

# Teaching Children and Youth Teacher-Pleasing Social–Emotional Skills

## Goals of This Chapter

In reading this chapter, you will learn

▶ the difference between teacher-pleasing social–emotional skills and peer-pleasing social–emotional skills

▶ which teacher-pleasing skills are important during early childhood, middle childhood, and adolescence

▶ how to teach older students school survival skills

▶ how to teach teacher-pleasing social–emotional skills using a five-step instructional sequence

▶ the importance of the hidden curriculum

▶ how to develop school scripts

# Terms to Know

academic enablers

cognitive steps

cultural curriculum

de facto curriculum

general situations

hidden curriculum

model behavioral profile

nonverbal skill steps

official curriculum

rationale statements

role-play situations

school cultural curriculum

scripts

social rules

underground curriculum

verbal skill steps

*Dan, a resource teacher for more than 20 years, wasn't surprised when sixth-grade teacher Roy requested that Paul be removed from his social studies class. Paul had learning disabilities in reading and written expression and had worked hard to improve his skills in these areas. Dan knew that Paul could handle the work in Roy's class. Paul was extremely bright and really liked most social studies subject matter. He got a lot of information from watching shows on the Discovery, Animal Planet, and National Geographic cable channels, though he'd struggle through difficult reading material if the subject interested him. All Paul needed was a couple of minor accommodations—mainly a little more time to complete reading assignments and the option of using a computer to write essays.*

*What ticked off Roy was that Paul arrived late to his class an average of twice a week. As if that wasn't bad enough, he didn't come prepared for class and he had a real attitude when he was criticized or when his teacher asked him to make corrections to his essays. Come to think of it, his attitude could use some readjusting when it came to working cooperatively in a group, too.*

*"No," Roy thought, "I have too many students who really want to learn to waste my time on a kid with an attitude like Paul. Like, for example, Megan. Her academic problems were more serious than Paul's, but she was grateful for anything her teacher did to help her understand her assignments."*

*Dan had observed the same outcome for years: Teachers would move mountains for students who had "good student behaviors" but had little patience for those like Paul who lacked them.*

Many children and youth with poorly developed social–emotional skills have difficulty in the classroom. Thus, about 15% of elementary teachers' referrals for assistance relate to problems with social–emotional skills (L. K. Elksnin & N. Elksnin, 1995). Social–emotional skills are highly related to academic achievement as measured by grades and standardized test performance (Elliott, Malecki, & Demaray, 2001; Porath, 2003; Wentzel, 1993). And, as discussed in Chapter One, children and youth with social–emotional skill deficits are more likely to drop out of school and/or to become delinquent.

Elliott et al. (2001) characterize social–emotional skills as *academic enablers:*

> We conceptualize the effect of social skills on achievement as analogous to the impact of medications on the learning of students with attention difficulties. That is, like medications, social skills do not make students smarter or more knowledgeable, but they help prepare students to use the learning skills and knowledge they have to demonstrate achievement. (p. 22)

Porath (2003) emphasized that social development and academic achievement are intertwined, observing that children who get along with teachers and classmates are able to follow school rules and routines and do better academically than children who lack social–emotional skills.

The social–emotional skills essential for school success, or *teacher-pleasing social–emotional skills,* often differ from the skills needed for peer acceptance. Teachers tend to value academically related skills, such as following directions, volunteering answers, and completing work, over peer-to-peer skills. Individualized education programs (IEPs) of students with disabilities frequently target school-related skills such as following verbal and written directions and staying on task (Pray, Hall, & Marksley, 1992). Gresham (1998a) suggested that teacher-pleasing behaviors such as these form the model behavioral profile, which promotes academic achievement. Behaviors forming this profile have little to do with the skills needed for interpersonal adjustment as described in Chapter Four.

Figure 6.1 presents items of a rating scale designed to assess the social competence and school adjustment of elementary-aged children (Walker & McConnell, 1995b). Notice the types of behaviors that peers value (subscale II) compared to behaviors that teachers value (subscales I and III).

That teachers value skills different from skills valued by peers is not surprising: Teacher-pleasing social–emotional skills are those that make managing the classroom easier and teachers' lives less difficult. Indeed, some teachers discourage the development of successful peer interaction skills because they perceive these behaviors as potentially disruptive in the classroom (Gresham, 1990). As the resource teacher, Dan, observed repeatedly, and as his student, Paul, was to learn, teacher-pleasing behaviors affect academic outcomes.

In this chapter we examine the types of social–emotional skills that teachers value most highly. Teachers perceive children and youth who master these skills positively and, when teachers have positive impressions of students, the teachers are

**I: Teacher-Preferred Social Behavior Subscale (16 items)**

Shows sympathy for others.

Compromises with peers when situation calls for it.

Responds to teasing or name calling by ignoring, changing the subject, or some other constructive means.

Accepts constructive criticism from peers without becoming angry.

Is sensitive to the needs of others.

Expresses anger appropriately (e.g., reacts to situation without becoming violent or destructive).

Appropriately copes with aggression from others (e.g., tries to avoid a fight, walks away, seeks assistance, defends self).

Cooperates with peers in group activities or situations.

Uses physical contact with peers appropriately.

Listens while others are speaking (e.g., as in circle or sharing time).

Controls temper.

Can accept not getting her/his own way.

Finds another way to play when requests to join others are refused.

Is considerate of the feelings of others.

Gains peers' attention in an appropriate manner.

Accepts suggestions and assistance from peers.

**II: Peer-Preferred Social Behavior Subscale (17 items)**

Other children seek child out to involve her/him in activities.

Changes activities with peers to permit continued interaction.

Shares laughter with peers.

Makes friends easily with other children.

Asks questions that request information about someone or something.

Spends recess and free time interacting with peers.

Plays or talks with peers for extended periods of time.

Voluntarily provides assistance to peers who require it.

Assumes leadership role in peer activities.

**FIGURE 6.1** ▶ Subscale Items of the Walker–McConnell Scale of Social Competence and School Adjustment—Elementary Version

Initiates conversation(s) with peers in informal situations.

Interacts with a number of different peers.

Compliments others regarding personal attributes (appearance, special skills, etc.).

Is socially perceptive (e.g., "reads" social situations accurately).

Plays games and activities at recess skillfully.

Keeps conversation going.

Maintains eye contact when speaking or being spoken to.

Invites peers to play or share activities.

### III: School Adjustment Subscale (10 items)

Uses free time appropriately.

Has good work habits (e.g., is organized, makes efficient use of class time).

Listens carefully to teacher instructions and directions for assignments.

Answers or attempts to answer a question when called on by the teacher.

Displays independent study skills (e.g., can work adequately with minimum teacher support).

Responds to conventional behavior management techniques (e.g., praise, reprimands, time-out).

Responds to requests promptly.

Attends to assigned tasks.

Does seatwork assignments as directed.

Produces work of acceptable quality given her/his skill level.

Source: "Profile/Rating Form," adapted from the *Walker-McConnell Scale of Social Competence and School Adjustment—Elementary Version, User's Manual* (p. 32), by H. M. Walker & S. R. McConnell (San Diego, CA: Singular Publishing Group). Copyright © 1995 by Singular Publishing Group. Reprinted by permission.

**FIGURE 6.1** ▶(Continued)

more likely to work with them to help improve their academic performance. We begin by discussing teacher-pleasing skills that are critical during early childhood, middle childhood, and adolescence. Then we introduce a five-step sequence for teaching specific social–emotional skills. We close the chapter by emphasizing the importance of children and youth learning to follow school routines.

## ▶ Social–Emotional Skills That Teachers Value During Early Childhood

*Ann, who taught 4-year-olds at the Little Tykes Preschool, sat next to Julia's mom, Brenda, and said, "Julia is causing a lot of problems in class. She doesn't listen during group activities and interrupts me and the other children during discussion. I'm also concerned that she doesn't tackle new things. If anything is the least bit new or difficult, she lies down on the floor and refuses to try. I'm spending a lot of time trying to get Julia's behavior under control."*

*Brenda wasn't surprised by the teacher's observations because she encountered many of the same behaviors at home. But she was troubled by Ann's attitude toward her daughter. She clearly didn't like Julia.*

*After thinking for a moment, Brenda said, "I'm concerned about the same behaviors at home. Is there some way the two of us could come up with a plan to help Julia improve her behavior at home and school?" Relieved that Brenda acknowledged her daughter's problems and was willing to work to solve them, Ann replied pleasantly, "I'm sure we can put our heads together and come up with a plan."*

As we pointed out in Chapter Four, many social skills that are critical during early childhood relate to establishing relationships with peers. For example, McGinnis and Goldstein (2003) identified the following friendship-making skills as essential for young children: greeting others, reading others, joining in, waiting one's turn, sharing, offering help, asking someone to play, and playing a game. Nevertheless, young children attending day-care and preschool encounter structured settings for the first time, and early-childhood teachers value certain behaviors that help them manage groups of children and establish environments conducive for learning.

Teacher-pleasing skills that are important during early childhood are as follows (McGinnis & Goldstein, 2003):

- ▶ Listening
- ▶ Saying thank you
- ▶ Asking for help
- ▶ Ignoring
- ▶ Asking a question
- ▶ Following directions
- ▶ Trying when it's hard
- ▶ Interrupting (p. v)

These skills provide a foundation for children as they make the transition into elementary classrooms, which place greater demands on them. Mastering these foundation skills enables young children to establish positive relationships with teachers and avoid becoming discipline problems. These skills should be taught directly to many young children, using the five-step instructional strategy discussed in this chapter.

## Social–Emotional Skills That Teachers Value During Middle Childhood

*Cynthia thought, "Most teachers are in denial. They say they don't have favorite students, but they do." She certainly did. She'd been teaching elementary-aged students for almost 27 years and she knew which type of student she liked to teach. Being bright and able to learn wasn't as important to Cynthia as having a good attitude toward teachers and learning. Kids who looked interested, who asked questions, who accepted feedback, and who appreciated her attention were the ones she enjoyed teaching. If the truth were told, Cynthia would go out of her way to work with a student who possessed these traits.*

*That's why Cynthia enjoyed working with Anna, who was what some would call a "slow learner." But Anna was anxious to please, and tenacious.*

*Contrast Anna with Sydney, a bright child but with few endearing qualities. He was argumentative and constantly disturbed his classmates. Sydney had a short fuse and showed little emotional self-control. To top it off, he sauntered into class, then sat slumped in his desk, looking like he'd rather be anywhere but in Cynthia's sixth-grade classroom.*

*"I guess you could say that Sydney's best quality is that he's absent a lot," Cynthia confided to her colleague during lunch.*

Teacher-pleasing skills are extremely important at this age for several reasons:

▶ *Increased environmental demands and teacher expectations.* When children leave preschool and enter elementary school, they encounter more highly structured environments and increased teacher expectations. Children are expected to sit and listen to the teacher for extended periods. They must take more responsibility for learning by bringing materials to class, asking for assistance, and following verbal and written directions. Teachers expect children during middle childhood to exert some self-control, handle frustration, and express anger appropriately.

▶ *Introduction of academic skills that form the foundation for future learning.* From first through fourth grades, children learn the language and mathematical skills that provide the basis for all future learning. Children who lack teacher-pleasing skills have two strikes against them: (a) Teacher-displeasing behavior makes it difficult for them to learn, and (b) these behaviors make teachers less willing to work with them.

▶ *Middle childhood as setting the stage for continued achievement and school success.* Children who are successful during the elementary years are less likely to have social and academic problems during adolescence. Consequently, they are less likely to drop out of school and/or to become delinquent (Marcus & Sanders-Reio, 2001; Merrell & Gimpel, 1998; Shapiro, 1997).

The most important teacher-pleasing behaviors during the elementary years are (Alsopp, Santos, & Linn, 2000; Lane, Givner, & Pierson, 2004; McGinnis & Goldstein, 1997, 2003; Mannix, 1986; Walker & McConnell, 1995b):

| | |
|---|---|
| Listening | Asking questions |
| Asking for help | Answering questions |
| Waiting for help | Ignoring distractions |
| Saying "thank you" | Not disturbing others |
| Bringing materials to class | Accepting criticism |
| Following instructions | Making corrections |
| Completing assignments | Showing self-control |
| Working independently | Expressing anger appropriately |
| Working in a group | Handling classroom frustrations |
| Contributing to discussions | Deciding on something to do |
| Offering to help | Setting goals |

As shown in the vignette, Anna possesses many of these behaviors, whereas Sydney lacks most of them. We recommend that, using the assessment procedures discussed in Chapter Two, teachers and parents determine which of the skills a child lacks and teach the needed skills using the instructional routine discussed later in this chapter.

---

## ▶ Social–Emotional Skills That Teachers Value During Adolescence

*"Okay, people," said Eli, "let's talk about what teachers like." His class was for students in danger of failing ninth grade, chosen to participate in "School 101" because they lacked basic understanding of the nonacademic require-ments of high school, such as coming to class, being on time, looking inter-ested, and so forth. Some of the students also had poorly developed reading and writing skills. School 101 was designed to teach these students the behav-iors valued by teachers, in response to research showing that even kids with minimal academic skills could navigate high school successfully if they were to adopt what teachers regard as good student behavior.*

*"Think about each of your six teachers and their pet peeves. Besides being good students academically, what are some things they like to see students do? We'll make a list on the board. Remember, no names please. . . . Joey?"*

*"Ms. Lassiter gets real upset if you're late to class."*

*"Okay, that's a good example, Joey. But remember—no names please."*

*After 10 minutes, Eli's students had generated a list of 20 nonacademic behaviors valued by their teachers.*

School presents unique challenges for adolescents. When students enter middle, junior, and high school, they are expected to demonstrate a higher level of independence than they do in elementary school. The stakes are high, with course grades and test scores determining whether they will or will not graduate. Adolescents who fail to acquire the academic foundation skills during middle childhood are particularly vulnerable. To make matters worse, environmental demands are complex. Students are expected to adjust to the styles and requirements of many teachers and to adopt work habits to cope with the increased academic pressures and expectations. Many students are ill equipped to meet these demands.

Exactly what kinds of skills are critical for school success during adolescence? Referring to Figure 6.2, Walker and McConnell (1995a) identified 53 behaviors that relate to social competence and school adjustment. Many of the behaviors that form the self-control and school adjustment subscales are teacher-pleasing behaviors, or behaviors that teachers report as being important for school success. Similarly, Zigmond and Kerr (1985) identified 26 behaviors that form six factors related to high school success:

1. Taking an interest in school
2. Organization skills
3. Task completion
4. Independence
5. Interpersonal skills
6. Following school rules

The behaviors of each of the six factors that make up Zigmond and Kerr's School Survival Skills Scale (1985) are presented as Figure 6.3. The School Survival Skills Curriculum designed to teach these behaviors is reviewed next.

## ▶ School Survival Skills Curriculum

The School Survival Skills (SSS) Curriculum (Silverman, Zigmond, & Sansone, 1981; University of Pittsburgh, 1986) is designed to enable students with disabilities to be successful in general education classrooms. It is also appropriate for adolescents who are at risk for school failure. The curriculum focuses on three important areas:

1. Behavior control
2. Teacher-pleasing behaviors
3. Study skills

**I: Self-Control (13 items)**

Displays self-control in difficult situations.

Compromises with peers when situation calls for it.

Responds to teasing or name-calling by ignoring, changing the subject, or some other constructive means.

Accepts constructive criticism from peers without becoming angry.

Accepts the consequences of his/her actions.

Expresses anger appropriately (e.g., reacts to situation without becoming violent or destructive).

Copes effectively with being upset or depressed.

Appropriately copes with aggression from others (e.g., tries to avoid a fight, walks away, seeks assistance, defends self).

Uses physical contact with peers appropriately.

Can accept not getting her/his own way.

Gains peers' attention in an appropriate manner.

Accepts suggestions and assistance from peers.

Is sensitive to the needs of others.

**II: Peer Relations (16 items)**

Relates well to the opposite sex.

Changes activities with peers to permit continued interaction.

Shares laughter with peers.

Takes pride in her/his appearance.

Makes friends easily with others.

Participates or talks with peers for extended periods of time.

Has a sense of humor.

Initiates conversation(s) with peers in informal situations.

Cooperates with peers in group activities or situations.

Interacts with a number of different peers.

Participates in games and activities skillfully.

Keeps conversation(s) with peers going.

Invites peers to interact or share activities.

Assumes leadership role in peer activities.

Spends free time interacting with peers.

Others seek student out to involve her/him in activities.

**FIGURE 6.2** ▶Subscale Items of the Walker–McConnell Scale of
Social Competence and School Adjustment—Adolescent Version

## III: School Adjustment (15 items)

Has good work habits (e.g., is organized, makes efficient use of class time, etc.).

Asks questions that request information about someone or something.

Does what he/she agrees to do.

Listens carefully to teacher instructions and directions for assignments.

Displays independent study skills (e.g., can work adequately with minimum teacher support).

Responds to conventional behavior management techniques (e.g., praise, reprimands, time-out).

Responds to requests promptly.

Listens while others are speaking.

Attends to assigned tasks.

Maintains eye contact when speaking or being spoken to.

Does seatwork assignments as directed.

Produces work of acceptable quality given her/his skill level.

Uses free time appropriately.

Answers or attempts to answer a question when called on by the teacher.

Is personally well organized.

## IV: Empathy (6 items)

Compliments others regarding personal attributes (e.g., appearance, special skills, etc.).

Selects another activity when requests to join others are refused.

Is considerate of the feelings of others.

Shows sympathy for others.

Is sensitive to the needs of others.

Appropriately stands up for his/her rights.

## Items not assigned to scales:

Voluntarily provides assistance to peers who require it. (Item 14)

Feels good about herself/himself. (Item 29)

Is socially perceptive (e.g., reads social situations accurately). (Item 32)

---

Source: "Profile/Rating Form," adapted from the *Walker–McConnell Scale of Social Competence and School Adjustment—Adolescent Version, User's Manual* (p. 36), by H. M. Walker & S. R. McConnell (San Diego, CA: Singular Publishing Group). Copyright © 1995 by Singular Publishing Group. Reprinted with permission.

**FIGURE 6.2** ▶(Continued)

## Factor I: Taking an Interest in School
Exhibits interest in improving academic performance
Uses time productively while waiting for teacher
Is persistent even when faced with a difficult task

## Factor II: Organization
Organizes study time well
Identifies central theme of lecture (demonstrates by stating or writing the main ideas and supporting facts)
Is good at taking tests

## Factor III: Task Completion
Brings necessary materials to class
Completes assigned work
Asks for help with schoolwork when necessary
Follows written directions
Appropriately handles corrections on class work
Turns in assignments when they are due

## Factor IV: Independence
Can concentrate on work without being distracted by peers
Works well independently

## Factor V: Interpersonal Skills
Talks calmly to an adult when perceived to be unjustly accused
Speaks appropriately to teachers
Complies with requests of adults in authority
Accepts punishment if caught doing something wrong
Manages conflict through non-aggressive means
Behaves appropriately in a variety of settings
Stays calm and in control of emotions

## Factor VI: Following School Rules
Responds to others when they speak
Stays awake in class
Attends class
Gets to class on time
Arrives at school on time

Source: *"Managing the mainstream: A contrast of the behaviors of learning disabled students who pass their assigned mainstream courses and those who fail,"* by N. Zigmond & M. M. Kerr, April 1985, paper presented at meeting of American Educational Research Association, Chicago, IL. Reprinted with permission.

**FIGURE 6.3** ▶ Selected Items From the School Survival Skills Scale

The Teacher-Pleasing Behaviors strand consists of six components, each of which is discussed here.

## Step 1: Identifying and Following Explicit and Implicit Classroom Rules

*"What if we didn't have any rules or laws in the United States?" asked the teacher, Greta. "Give me some examples of what might happen?"*

*Angela volunteered, "If we didn't have traffic rules like stopping at a red light, we'd have a lot of accidents and people could get hurt or killed."*

*"That's a good example, Angela. Any other ideas?"*

*Pete offered, "If we didn't have laws against things like robbery or murder, people might be afraid to leave their houses."*

*"Okay—another good example. Let's make a list of rules for this school."*

*After her ninth-grade class came up with a list, Greta asked the students to decide whether each rule was essential or nonessential. Then she began to discuss classroom rules. "Do teachers have rules for their classrooms? How do you know what the rules are? Are some rules obvious—posted in class, announced by the teacher? Are other rules the kind you just know about even though they're not written down or discussed by the teacher?"*

Adolescents need to understand that rules may be explicit (i.e., those posted or announced by the teacher) or implicit (i.e., those required or desired by the teacher, but not posted or announced). In addition, they must recognize that explicit and implicit rules vary from teacher to teacher. The rules may even be contradictory across classrooms. Greta taught her students about rules by asking them to

▸ identify rules that are essential and those that are not,
▸ list rules they must follow outside of school and determine which rules are essential and which are not,
▸ discuss the consequences of not following school rules,
▸ identify explicit and implicit rules for each class.

Figure 6.4 gives rules for three high school teachers. The variance is obvious, making it especially important that students learn to identify behaviors that violate rules and the consequences for violating the rules. Upon completing this component of the SSS, the student is to identify the explicit and implicit rules in each class.

## Step 2: Identifying and Meeting Classroom Requirements

*Michael, teacher of English 10, was determining the final grades for the quarter. He used a point system for grading. For example, if students' scores were above 90%, they earned an "A." Students' scores in the 80% to 89% range earned them a "B," and so forth. Michael, however, didn't rigidly adhere to the*

**Mrs. Barnes, Spanish I Teacher**

*Explicit rules:*   Complete homework.
Participate in small-group activities.

*Implicit rules:*   Don't talk to friends.
Do best work—review and correct work before turning in.
Don't waste time.

**Mr. Lehr, Information Technology Teacher**

*Explicit rules:*   Come to class on time.
Bring book to class.
Don't ask to go to the bathroom during class.
Raise hand to speak.
Stay in assigned seat.

*Implicit rules:*   Look interested during lecture.
Ask for help after you try to solve the problem yourself.
Try hard.
Use time wisely.

**Mr. Richert, English 10 Teacher**

*Explicit rules:*   Turn in homework.
Complete work on time.
Bring materials to class.

*Implicit rules:*   Follow directions.
Ask intelligent questions during discussion.
Answer questions during discussion.

**FIGURE 6.4** ▶Explicit and Implicit Rules of Three High School Teachers

point system. For example, Timothy earned 89% of the possible points for the quarter. An extremely conscientious student, he consistently came to class prepared and on time. He wasn't a behavior problem, and he seemed genuinely interested in the subject matter. Michael assigned a grade of "A" to Timothy.

By contrast, Leanne, who also earned an 89% received a grade of "B." Unlike Timothy, she often was late to class. She talked to her classmates constantly and looked like she'd rather be anywhere than in class.

To be successful in the classroom, students must understand the teacher's requirements in each class and whether they meet or fail to meet expectations. To teach this concept, the teacher might have students begin by listing behaviors on which the grades are based. Behaviors might include (Zigmond & Kerr, 1981):

| | |
|---|---|
| Turning in homework | Having the textbook |
| Coming to class on time | Grades on tests |
| Not cutting class | Answering questions |
| Staying in your seat | Working quietly |
| Not talking to your friends | Not going to the bathroom |
| Not swearing | Raising your hand to talk. |
| Having a pencil and notebook | |

This exercise helps students realize that many of these behaviors do not depend on academic ability, so even if they have poor reading and writing skills, they can adopt behaviors that will help them succeed in class. For example, in Michael's class, punctuality, preparation, and interest are highly valued behaviors—so highly valued, actually, that grades rise and fall based upon students' meeting these expectations.

From a generic list of behaviors, each adolescent identifies a class in which he or she is having difficulty. She then develops a list of grade-based behaviors and identifies the behaviors she is and is not exhibiting in that class. The student selects several behaviors to exhibit and monitors their use over several weeks. After completing this component, the student will be able to recognize requirements in each class and determine if they are met.

## Step 3: Identifying and Using Appropriate Classroom Behaviors

*Susanna was a delight to have in class. Carol had taught U.S. history for 18 years, and Susanna ranked right up there as one of her all-time favorite students. She always came prepared for class, often arriving several minutes early so she could ask her teacher to clarify a concept. She always went the "extra mile" on her homework assignments. In class, Susanna participated but never dominated or sought attention. Her comments and questions were thoughtful. Even though she was an outstanding student, Susanna was modest and got along beautifully with her peers.*

Susanna exhibited all of the "good student behaviors" that teachers value. Many other students do not demonstrate these behaviors and must be taught directly to identify and use them.

Teachers introduce the concept of appropriate classroom behaviors by discussing observable, nonacademic behaviors that good students use in the classroom. Usually students have little difficulty coming up with a list of behavior standards such as coming to class regularly, arriving on time, and being prepared. They may need some prompting to identify subtle verbal and nonverbal behaviors that convey interest, including those addressed by the SLANT strategy, described in Chapter Three.

After discussing good student behaviors in general, students are asked to identify appropriate behaviors for each class. Students must understand that behavioral expectations often differ from teacher to teacher. For example, the student's English teacher might expect students to raise a hand before speaking, whereas the U.S. history teacher might not require this behavior during discussion. Videotaping students in class and having them role play good student behaviors will help them see any potential gaps between teacher expectations and student performance.

A small number of students (i.e., some students with disabilities) may never be able to figure out behaviors that individual teachers highly value. In this case, teachers and parents have to help them understand the "hidden curriculum." (Strategies for identifying the hidden curriculum are discussed elsewhere in this chapter.) After completing this component of the SSS curriculum, the student identifies nonacademic behaviors that each of her teachers considers appropriate.

## Step 4: Exhibit Appropriate Behaviors in Controlled Settings

*Jorge gave his SSS students a minute to settle in, then said, "I want each of you to review the 'good student behaviors' you listed as those you need to master for each of your academic classes."*

*After 5 minutes, he asked the students to get out a sheet of paper and said, "Put the behaviors in order—listing the behaviors you want to master first at the top of your paper. One way to prioritize is to identify behaviors required by all your teachers as those you want to focus on first."*

*After the students developed their lists, Jorge led a discussion about the behaviors the students identified and the ways in which they developed their priority lists. Then he said, "Each of you is going to give all of your attention to your top-priority behavior. I want you to think about when you need to use the behavior during the day. I'll be looking for times during the day for you to use that behavior, too. If you forget to use it, I'll remind you. We'll also come up with a reward system so when you use appropriate behavior, you can earn free time and points toward your grade."*

Jorge is creating a supportive environment for students to practice "good student behaviors." During this component, the SSS teacher creates opportunities for students to choose and practice "good student behaviors." The teacher reminds the students to exhibit behaviors at appropriate times and reinforces students when they demonstrate them. Students select one behavior to focus on, then, after mastering this behavior, move on to other behaviors. The goal during this component is for the student to substitute appropriate behavior for problematic behavior within a supportive instructional setting. After the student is successful in this controlled setting, he or she is ready to use "good student behaviors" in all high school classes.

## Steps 5 and 6: Using Teacher-Pleasing Behaviors and Improving Teaching-Pleasing Behaviors

The goal of the last two components of the SSS is for the student to use the "good student behaviors" in actual classes. The student begins by focusing on using "good student behaviors" in one class. After he or she is successful in a single class, the student selects another class, and yet another, until he or she has adopted behavior that each teacher regards as appropriate. After students master "teacher-pleasing behaviors," the SSS teacher can help them identify "employer-pleasing behaviors" (see Chapter Seven) and "parent-pleasing behaviors." Having students create a chart like the one in Figure 6.5 is helpful. Students list behaviors valued by a teacher. They then give the chart to the teacher, who notes if the student demonstrated the behaviors in class that day.

| **Student:** *James Ellis* | **Teacher:** *Mr. Richert* | | | | |
|---|---|---|---|---|---|
| **Behavior** | **Mon.** | **Tues.** | **Wed.** | **Thurs.** | **Fri.** |
| Come to class on time. | | | | | |
| Ask questions during discussion. | | | | | |
| Turn in homework on time. | | | | | |
| Bring materials to class. | | | | | |
| Follow directions. | | | | | |
| Ask intelligent questions during discussion. | | | | | |

Source: Adapted from "Teaching Coping Skills to Adolescents with Learning Disabilities," by R. Silverman, N. Zigmond, and J. Sansone, *Focus on Exceptional Children, 13* (6), p. 15. Copyright © 1981 by Love Publishing.

**FIGURE 6.5** ▶ Chart for Teacher-Pleasing Behaviors

## ▶ Teaching Teacher-Pleasing Behaviors

We often expect children and youth to learn social–emotional skills on their own, but some children require direct instruction to learn these skills. Teachers can help their students, and make their job of classroom managers easier, by teaching "teacher-pleasing" skills. We recommend using a five-step sequence, which we adapted (L. K. Elksnin & N. Elksnin, 1995; N. Elksnin & L. K. Elksnin, 1998) based on the work of Hazel and colleagues (1995). Each step is described next, using the teacher-pleasing skill *Following Verbal Directions.* Readers can use the social–emotional skills planning and teaching sheet shown as Figure 6.6 to create lessons for teaching other skills. We recommend that teachers complete this sheet to plan the lesson, and use it to guide student discussion during the lesson. It is much more effective for students to generate definitions, skill steps, rationale statements, general and specific examples, and social rules than for teachers to provide this information in a lock-step fashion.

### Step One: Define/Describe the Skill

Students first should have a clear and concise *definition of the skill.* Teachers should not assume that students understand what it means to "work independently," "wait for help," or "accept criticism." The definition must be clear enough for students to recognize the skill behavior when they see and don't see it. After giving students a definition of the skill, the teacher describes the steps they are to follow to perform it.

*Skill steps* include *verbal* (what students *say*), *nonverbal* (what students *do*), and *cognitive* (what students *think*). In addition to the sequential skill steps, provide the student with the behaviors that occur throughout the skill. Examples of these *body basics* (Hazel et al., 1995) include facing the person, maintaining eye contact, assuming an appropriate facial expression, maintaining appropriate body posture, using an appropriate voice tone, and so forth.

### Example: Following Verbal Directions

Definition:    Following verbal directions means that you say or do what someone tells you to say or do.

Skill Steps:
1. Listen carefully to what the person says.
2. Think about what the person says.
3. Ask the person questions about what you don't understand.
4. Repeat the directions to yourself or to the other person.
5. Follow the directions.

Body basics (in no particular order):
- ▶ Look at the person.
- ▶ Have a serious facial expression.
- ▶ Have a serious, but relaxed, posture.
- ▶ Use a serious tone of voice.

Skill: _____

**Step One: Definition of Skill:** _____

_____

_____

Skill Steps:

   1. _____

   2. _____

   3. _____

   4. _____

   5. _____

   6. _____

   7. _____

   8. _____

Body Basics:

   1. _____

   2. _____

   3. _____

   4. _____

**Step Two: Rationale Statements**

Positive Statements:

   If _____

   Then _____

   If _____

   Then _____

Negative Statements:

   If _____

   Then _____

   If _____

   Then _____

**FIGURE 6.6 ▶**Social–Emotional Skills Instructional Planning Sheet

## Step Three: General Situations in Which to Use Skill:

1. _____
2. _____
3. _____

## Step Four: Role-Play Situations:

1. _____
   _____
2. _____
   _____
3. _____
   _____
4. _____
   _____
5. _____
   _____
6. _____
   _____

## Step Five: Social Rules:

1. _____
   _____
2. _____
   _____
3. _____
   _____

**FIGURE 6.6** ▶(Continued)

## Step Two: Give Students a Reason to Learn the Skill

Students must understand *why* they are learning a skill. They need to know how they will benefit by learning and using the skill. In addition, they need to understand that there may be negative consequences if they do not learn and use the skill. The teacher provides the students with *positive and negative rationale statements* informing them of the consequences of using or failing to use a skill. This step is essential to motivate students to use the skills in the classroom.

When developing rationale statements, the teacher must be sure that they address short-term outcomes and that they are specific, believable, and personalized. An easy way to construct statements is to use an "If . . . then" format, as shown in the following examples.

### Example: Rationale Statements for "Following Verbal Directions"

Positive statements:
- ▶ If you learn to follow verbal directions, then you will be able to complete your classroom assignments correctly.
- ▶ If you learn to follow verbal directions, then you will be able to finish your work more quickly and easily.

Negative statements:
- ▶ If you don't learn to follow verbal directions, then you may have to redo your classroom assignments.
- ▶ If you don't learn to follow verbal directions, then your teacher may get angry and you will get in trouble.

## Step Three: Describe General Situations in Which to Use the Skill

The purpose of this step is to give students parameters for using the skills. Describing *general situations* to use the skill increases the likelihood of the student's generalizing the skill (discussed in greater detail in Chapter Nine). As teachers and parents, our ultimate goal is to ensure that children and youth use social–emotional skills when and where they count. General situations may be used to cue students (and for students to cue themselves) to use a given skill. These statements send the message that "now is an appropriate time/situation to use the skill."

### Example: General Situations in Which to Use the Skill "Following Verbal Directions"

- ▶ A good time to follow directions is when the teacher tells you to say or do something.
- ▶ A good time to follow directions is when the teacher tells you to listen carefully and to do exactly what she says.
- ▶ A good time to follow directions is when the teacher says it's important to do exactly what he tells you to do.

## Step Four: Teach the Skill Using Role-Play Scenarios

General situations provide students with general instances in which to use the skill; and *role-play* scenarios describe specific situations in which to use the skill.

Teachers should help students generate role-play situations. When role-play situations are based on students' life experiences (rather than generated by the teacher or taken from a commercial curriculum), students are more apt to use social–emotional skills when and where they count, as they feel they are more relevant and meaningful.

When using role-play situations to teach the skill, we recommend that teachers adopt role-play guidelines as developed by Goldstein and McGinnis (1997):

▶ Let students know that each person will role-play the skill.

▶ Set up the role play by having the students describe a real-life situation, assigning a main actor (the student who will perform the skill) and a supporting actor (the student who plays the other person—teacher, peer, parent—involved in the situation). Have students describe the actor and the setting characteristics in detail to enhance the realism of the role-play situation.

▶ Conduct the role play by reviewing the roles of each participant: The main actor performs the skill steps; the supporting actor assumes the role of the other person; the rest of the class observes to determine if the main actor performs the skill steps. At the conclusion of the role play, observers are asked to evaluate the main actor's performance. It is helpful to begin by assigning observers a specific step to watch for when introducing a skill. During the role play the teacher coaches the main and supporting actors. If students need to be reminded of skill steps and/or role responsibilities, stop the role play. Continue the role play until every student has assumed the role of main actor.

▶ Provide the main actor with specific, informative feedback. Ask the supporting actor to evaluate the main actor's performance. Did he or she follow each of the skill steps? How well did he or she perform each of the steps? Ask the observers to comment on the main actor's performance. Ask the main actor to assess his or her performance and to respond to the comments of others. Finally, provide feedback to the actors and observers and summarize the main actor's performance. Consider videotaping or audiotaping role plays so the main actors can observe and evaluate their performance of steps.

### Example: Role-Play Situations for Following Verbal Directions

▶ Your teacher explains the steps to follow to complete your social studies assignment.

▶ Your mom tells you how to cook a frozen pizza in the microwave.

▶ Your friend gives you directions to her house.

## Step Five: Help Students Identify Social Rules

Social rules guide students in using a skill. The rules govern what is regarded as generally acceptable social behavior. For example, the social rules relating to the skill "accepting criticism" include avoiding arguments, arguing with authority figures, and interrupting the person.

### Example: Social Rules for Following Verbal Directions

▶ Ask the person for help if the task is too difficult.

▶ Ask the person to repeat the directions if you didn't hear them the first time.

By applying these five steps, teachers can effectively teach students "teacher-pleasing behaviors" and other important social–emotional skills. Table 6.1 lists

**TABLE 6.1** ▶Programs That Teach Teacher-Pleasing Skills

| Program | Author(s)/Date | Age/Grade |
|---|---|---|
| ACCEPTS | Walker, McConnell, Holmes, Todis, Walker, & Golden (1988) | Grades K–8 |
| ACCESS | Walker, Todis, Holmes, & Horton (1988) | Adolescents |
| ASSET | Hazel, Schumaker, Sherman, & Sheldon (1995) | Adolescents |
| Basic Social Skills for Youth | Boys Town Press (1992) | Grades 6–12 |
| A Collaborative Approach to Teaching Social Skills | Warger & Rutherford (1996) | Grades K–12 |
| Fostering Emotional Intelligence in K–8 Students | Doty (2001) | Grades K–8 |
| Getting Along with Others | N. F. Jackson, D. A. Jackson, & Monroe (1983) | Adolescents & Adults |
| I Can Behave | Mannix (1986) | Grades K–6 |
| Learning to Get Along | D. A. Jackson, N. F. Jackson, Bennett, Bynum, & Faryna (1991) | Grades K–12 |
| Life Skill Activities for Secondary Students with Special Needs | Mannix (1995) | Grades 6–12 |
| The Power of Social Skills in Character Development | Scully (2000) | Adolescents |
| PREPARE Curriculum | Goldstein (1999) | Adolescents |
| Ready-to-Use Social Skills Lessons & Activities | Begun (1995, 1996a, 1996b, 1996c) | Grades PreK–12 |
| The SCORE Skills | Vernon, Schumaker, Deshler (1996) | Grades 4–12 |
| Skillstreaming Program | Goldstein & McGinnis (1997), McGinnis & Goldstein (1997, 2003) | Grades PreK–12 |

**TABLE 6.1** ▶(Continued)

| Program | Author(s)/Date | Age/Grade |
|---------|----------------|-----------|
| Social Skills Activities for Special Children | Mannix (1993) | Elementary |
| Social Skills Activities for Secondary Students with Special Needs | Mannis (1998) | Grades 6–12 |
| Social Skills for Daily Living | Schumaker, Hazel, & Pederson (1988) | Adolescents |
| Social Skills for School and Community | Sargent (1991) | Grades K–12 |
| Social Skills in the Classroom | Stephens (1992) | Children & Adolescents |
| Social Skills Intervention Guide | Elliott & Gresham (1991) | Grades 1–10 |
| Social Standards at School | Kinney & Kinney (2003) | Grades 1–6 |
| The Stop & Think Social Skills programs | Knopf (2001a, 2001b, 2001c, 2001d) | Grades PreK–8 |
| Systematic Instruction of Social Skills | Sargent (1988) | Grades 1–12 |
| Taking Part | Cartledge & Kleefeld (1991) | Grades PreK–3 |
| Teaching Cooperation Skills | Huggins (1990-1994) | Grades K–6 |
| Teaching Social Competence | Knapczyk & Rodes (2001) | Grades K–12 |
| Teaching Social Competence to Youth & Adults with Developmental Disabilities | D. A. Jackson, N. F. Jackson, & Bennett (1998) | Adolescents & Adults |
| Teaching Social Skills: A Practical Approach | Rutherford, Chipman, DiGangi, & Anderson (1992) | Elementary |
| Teaching Social Skills to Youth | Down & Tierney (1992) | Children & Adolescents |
| Technical-Related and Academic Career Competencies (TRACC) | Minskoff (1994) | Adolescents & Adults |
| Think Aloud Small-Group Program | Camp & Bash (1981) | Ages 6–8 |
| Think Aloud programs | Camp & Bash (1985a, 1985b, 1985c) | Grades 1–6 |
| Working Together | Cartledge & Kleefeld (1994) | Grades 3–6 |

social skills programs that focus on teacher-pleasing skills. Teachers and parents can select skills from these programs and use the five-step teaching sequence to teach each skill.

# ► Teaching Students Scripts

*At the end of October, almost all of Adrienne's first graders were into the routine of school. They could follow the schedule and knew that whole-group writing followed reading groups, and that story time followed recess. They knew what materials to take out of their cubbies for different activities during the day. They knew that they had to be quiet before they could line up for lunch or leave at the end of the day.*

*But Adrienne was at the end of her patience with three of her students, who didn't seem to "get it." Tamika, Michael, and Antonio seemed to be clueless with respect to understanding the day-to-day classroom routines. Each day seemed like a novelty to them. They were not prepared, didn't seem to understand what was expected, and generally seemed "out of sync" with their classmates. Worst of all, their inability to get with the group persisted despite constant reminders and gentle disciplinary measures.*

*"Come to think of it," mulled Adrienne, "a few students every year never seem to fall into the routine, even by the end of the year."*

Schools house six curricula (Nelson, 1989, 1990):

1. The *official curriculum,* endorsed by state and local education agencies. For example, states and school districts require that certain skills be mastered at specified grade levels.
2. The *de facto curriculum,* dictated by state-adopted textbooks. For example, the reading curriculum is determined by the basal reading series (e.g., Ginn, Scott Foresman, Houghton Mifflin) used by a district.
3. The *cultural curriculum,* giving a context for understanding the official curriculum. Children and adolescents whose parents convey to them messages such as "School is your job" and "Education is important" are more likely to be successful in school.
4. The *school cultural curriculum,* including the explicit and implicit rules that govern behavior and communication during formal classroom interactions. We discussed classroom rules earlier in this chapter. Explicit classroom rules are those posted on the board. An implicit classroom rule is the way an individual teacher wants students to request assistance.
5. The *hidden curriculum,* "conveyed largely through such mechanisms as tone of voice, nonverbal messages about personal value, the attention paid to a child's contributions in formal and informal discussions, and opportunities that children have to participate in the varied activities of school" (Nelson, 1990, p. 20).

The rules of this curriculum may be hidden from both teachers and students, neither being aware of the rules governing classroom behavior.

6. The *underground curriculum,* governed by the rules of the peer group. Cazden (1988) described the underground curriculum as the "official talk of the peer culture." The teacher models the official curriculum; peer interactions reflect an entirely different culture (Nelson, 1989, 1990).

Tamika, Michael, and Antonio are having difficulty understanding many of these curricula. Certainly they have not mastered the school culture and hidden curricula. Adrienne is frustrated that these three students are not in sync with the rest of the class but admits that she has a few students each year with similar difficulties. These students need explicit instruction to understand. Their teacher has to make explicit what is implicit. One way to do this is to help students develop *school scripts.*

Most of us have little difficulty navigating an unfamiliar airport. We have a basic understanding of where the check-in kiosk, baggage claim, and ground transportation areas are located. We know the post-911 check-in routine. We know that whether we fly in or out of O'Hare, LaGuardia, Reagan National, or LAX airports, certain things are predictable, including long lines, frequent delays, and so on. In short, we understand the hidden (and not-so-hidden) aspects of airports. We have mastered the "airport script."

Scripts are outlines of how to behave in certain situations. Younger students (like those in Adrienne's class) use scripts for reading groups, lunch, recess, and assemblies. Older students develop scripts for changing classes, asking for information about an upcoming test, leaving school prepared to complete homework assignments, and so forth. Scripts allow students to

▶ spend energy acquiring new information as opposed to figuring out what to do,
▶ assess what they do not know so they can acquire needed information,
▶ stay in the teacher's good graces because they know what they are supposed to do in the classroom. (L. K. Elksnin, 1997)

If students do not know how to develop their own scripts, teachers need to teach them directly how to follow classroom routines by following these steps (Craighead, 1990):

1. Outline the routine with the child.
2. Brainstorm variations on the routine.
3. Specify the cues for activation of the script.
4. Role-play the script.
5. Cue the child in the natural environment.
6. Provide strategies for coping with weaknesses. (p. 114)

Knapczyk and Rodes (2001) developed an extensive list of school tasks and activities that teachers identified as essential. Activities, along with behaviors

**TABLE 6.2 ▶**Suggested Classroom Activities

*Preschool to Kindergarten*

▶ Morning arrival
▶ Language lessons with stimulus cards
▶ Story time
▶ Free play time in the classroom
▶ Cleanup time
▶ Transition to playground
▶ Free play during recess

*Primary Level: Grades 1 to 3*

▶ Presentation of day's lesson
▶ Transition to reading groups
▶ Reading out loud
▶ Vocabulary game (two teams)
▶ Lining up to go outside
▶ Unorganized activities on playground
▶ Playing on playground equipment
▶ Talking in small groups on playground
▶ Lining up to leave school that day

*Intermediate Level: Grades 4 to 6*

▶ Presentation of lesson
▶ Homework review and boardwork activity
▶ Worksheet activity
▶ Grading worksheets
▶ Small-group activity

*Intermediate Level: Continued*

▶ Entering cafeteria, getting in line
▶ Eating with friends
▶ Playing organized games on playground

*Middle School/Junior High School Level: Grades 7 and 8*

▶ Class start-up and preview
▶ Small group discussion
▶ Review of homework assignments
▶ Class dismissal
▶ Entering building at start of day
▶ After lunch conversation.

*High School Level: Grades 9 to 12*

▶ Getting ready for class
▶ Large group discussion
▶ Working on projects with partners
▶ End of lab activities and cleanup
▶ Independent work activity
▶ Watching a video
▶ Passing time before lunch
▶ Going through the food line
▶ Eating at lunch tables
▶ Socializing after lunch

Source: "School Tasks and Activities," from *Teaching Social Competence: Social Skills and Academic Success* (pp. 173–196), by D. Knapczyk and P. Rodes (Verona, WI: IEP Resources). Copyright © 2001 by IEP Resources. Reprinted by permission.

required for each, are grouped by grade level. The listing of activities is presented as Table 6.2. This list serves as a starting point for developing school scripts. Of course, activities vary across teachers and settings. Teachers can list the essential activities in their classes to determine which scripts to teach. In the long term, teachers will save a substantial amount of time by explicitly teaching *all* students the essential scripts for the class. Knowing how to follow classroom routines prevents many classroom behavior problems. Because not all teachers are acquainted with scripts and their importance, parents may wish to ask teachers if their child has difficulty following classroom routines.

## ▶ Chapter Summary

Children and youth need social–emotional skills that teachers value. Otherwise, they run the risk of academic failure. Teachers are much more willing to work with students, even those with academic problems, when they have social–emotional skills considered essential in the classroom. These skills aren't the same as the skills valued by peers, as discussed in Chapter Five.

A five-step instructional sequence that can be used to teach these skills is:

1. Define/describe the skill.
2. Give students a reason to learn th skill.
3. Describe general situations in which to use the skill.
4. Teach the skill using role-play scenarios.
5. Help students identify social rules.

Finally, children and youth can be taught scripts, or outlines of how to behave in certain situations.

# CHAPTER 7

# Teaching Occupational Social–Emotional Skills

## Goals of This Chapter

In reading this chapter, you will learn

▶ the social–emotional skills that are considered essential by employers and other employment experts

▶ some social–emotional skills are more important than others for specific jobs

▶ how to assess social–emotional skills using a variety of approaches

▶ how to teach problem solving within an occupational context

▶ how to teach specific occupational social–emotional skills

▶ the curricular options available for teaching occupational social–emotional skills

# Terms to Know

career and technical education (CTE)

ecological assessment

employment competencies

occupational social–emotional skills

Secretary's Commission on
     Achieving Necessary Skills (SCANS)

social awareness

soft skills

*Having been in the fast-food business for more than 20 years, Jim Harvey had many teenagers work for him. By and large, the kids did a good job, although their reading and math skills hadn't exactly improved during the last two decades. Jim could deal with teaching kids the correct way to give customers change—counting it out instead of just dumping the bills and coins in the person's hand or, worse yet, tossing the money on the counter. Some of the kids had a tough time reading company manuals. In most cases, though, Jim showed them how to set up the coffee or French fry machines just one time and things worked out fine.*

*What Jim couldn't deal with were kids that couldn't get along on the job— the kind of kid who had an attitude problem with customers, co-workers, and supervisors. Jim could live with having to help kids with basic math and reading tasks, but he was darned if he was going to teach them how to treat customers decently.*

*B*efore teachers and parents know it, children reach adolescence and approach high school graduation. Unfortunately, many students do not have adequate social–emotional skills when they leave school. Adolescents with disabilities are particularly vulnerable, with parents and teachers rating from 11% to 18% of them as having low overall social skills (U.S. Department of Education, 2002). Therefore, the need to teach social–emotional skills to adolescents with disabilities is widely acknowledged (Clement-Heist, Siegel, & Gaylord-Ross, 1992; Eckert, 2000; O'Reilly & Glynn, 1995; Post, Storey, & Karabin, 2002; Sarkees-Wircenski & Scott, 2003; Storey, Lengyel, & Pruszynski, 1997; U.S. Department of Education, 1996).

We know that social–emotional inadequacies have far-reaching consequences when students join the workforce. As illustrated by Jim Harvey's attitude toward some of his young workers, social–emotional skills are reported as even more important than academic or technical skills for successful employment (M. Cohen & Besharov, 2002; N. Elksnin & L. K. Elksnin, 1998; Rosenbaum, 2001). Thus, D. W. Johnson and R. T. Johnson (1990) reported that 90% of job loss is related to social–emotional problems rather than employees' ability to perform the job! Rosenbaum (2001) conducted a longitudinal study of high school students and reported that social–emotional skills were correlated with grades, educational attainment (i.e., post-high school education), and later earnings.

In previous chapters we discussed ways in which teachers and parents can help children and youth become more socially skilled at school and home. In this chapter we focus on how teachers and parents can teach young people social–emotional skills that are essential for employment and career success. We call these skills *occupational social–emotional skills*. We begin by identifying essential occupational social–emotional skills, and we then describe approaches that can be used to assess these skills. We conclude the chapter by offering several curricular options for teaching young people the skills they need so they can gain and maintain employment.

## ▶ What Employers Want

Employers like Jim Harvey resoundingly place high value on their employees' social–emotional skills. Results of surveys repeatedly indicate that employers are less concerned with technical skills than social–emotional skills. For example, results of a U.S. Department of Labor survey showed that the qualities most desired by employers when they looked for entry-level employees were social–emotional competencies (Carnevale, Gainer, & Meltzer, 1990).

Carnevale et al. (1990) reported that employers considered the following social–emotional skills essential for employment success:

▶ *Communication skills:* oral communication, listening
▶ *Adaptability skills:* problem solving, creative thinking
▶ *Developmental skills:* self-esteem, motivation/goal setting
▶ *Group effectiveness skills:* interpersonal skills, teamwork, negotiation

Similarly, Goleman (1998, pp. 12, 13) noted that employers most desire these skills:

- ▶ Listening and oral communication
- ▶ Adaptability and creative responses to setbacks and obstacles
- ▶ Personal management, confidence, motivation to work toward goals, a sense of wanting to develop one's career and take pride in accomplishments
- ▶ Group and interpersonal effectiveness, cooperativeness and teamwork, skills at negotiating disagreements
- ▶ Effectiveness in the organization, wanting to make a contribution, leadership potential

When Goleman (1998) analyzed the competencies for 181 positions from 121 companies, he found that two-thirds of the competencies involved social–emotional skills rather than cognitive or technical skills. Likewise, Cherniss (2000) reported that two thirds of competencies related to superior performance on the job were social–emotional skills such as "self-confidence, flexibility, persistence, empathy, and the ability to get along with others" (p. 434).

After surveying 51 employers Rosenbaum (2001) found that they valued three types of social–emotional skills:

1. Normative compliance: attendance, dependability, positive attitude, avoiding rule infractions, and handling social conflict
2. General work procedures: effort, persistence, problem solving, attention to quality, and preparing for next tasks
3. Social skills: communicating about work tasks with coworkers, leadership, and participating in activities beyond job tasks, such as maintaining operations and organizing the work group (p. 174)

Employers consider social–emotional competencies essential for all employees, whether entry-level or mid- to upper-management. For example, when recruiters identified and assessed the relative importance of competencies of business candidates, attributes such as communication skills, interpersonal skills, and the ability to work in teams were ranked most highly (Alsop, 2002).

Further, employers report that many employees lack the social–emotional competence that is so valued on the job (Cherniss, 2000). For example, results of a Harris Education Research Council employer survey in 1991 indicated that

- ▶ only half of employees were motivated to learn new skills and improve their job performance,
- ▶ four in 10 employees were unable to cooperate with co-workers and supervisors,
- ▶ 80% of entry-level job applicants were described as lacking in self-discipline.

When Rosenbaum (2001) interviewed employers about the work habits of new employees, he found that many new workers missed work or were late to work during the first week on the job! These same employees did poor-quality work and often talked back to supervisors. Because of some employees' poor social–emotional skills, it should come as no surprise that many employers offer training programs to improve these skills. Cherniss (2000) reported that "American industry [including *Fortune 500* companies] currently spends over $50 billion each year on training, and much of this training focuses on social and emotional abilities" (p. 433).

The American Society for Training and Development (1997) noted that 80% of 50 leading companies provided social–emotional training to their employees. Recognition by mid- to upper-level management employees of the importance of social–emotional skills, or *soft skills,* has led to publication of "do-it-yourself" emotional intelligence guides to enable employees to get ahead in the workplace and have an edge over their co-workers (Weisinger, 1998).

The relationship between social–emotional competence and success in employment provides a strong incentive for teachers and parents to teach social–emotional skills to help youth become employed, remain employed, and advance in the workplace. Helping young people acquire essential occupational social–emotional skills enables them to be successful at work and in life.

## ► Essential Occupational Social–Emotional Skills

In 1990, the U.S. Secretary of Labor created SCANS (Secretary's Commission on Achieving Necessary Skills Commission) to identify essential workplace skills and competencies in order to develop a foundation curriculum for secondary and post-secondary Career and Technical Education (CTE). The goal of SCANS was to promote "a high-performance economy characterized by high-skill, high-wage employment" (Packer & Brainard, 2003, p. 1).

A national panel of experts in business, labor, and education began by identifying skills that were universally important for all occupations. These competencies were reported in *What Work Requires of Schools: A SCANS Report for America 2000* (Secretary's Commission, 1992). As seen in Table 7.1, interpersonal skills and personal qualities were identified as workplace domains and foundation skills.

As shown in Table 7.2, interviews with CTE teachers, employers, and employment experts, and reviews of relevant literature, also led to identification of occupational social–emotional skills required in all employment settings.

We introduced the construct of emotional intelligence (EI) in Chapter One. EI pioneers first focused on its relationship with school success. More recently, researchers have explored how EI affects employment success (Goleman, Boyatzis, & McKee, 2002). Daniel Goleman, whose book, *Emotional Intelligence: Why It Can Matter More Than IQ* (1995), captured the attention of the public, developed a framework of emotional competencies for the workplace. As seen in Figure 7.1, Goleman (2001) identified 20 competencies that form four clusters. Personal competencies involve self-awareness and self-management. Social competencies related

**TABLE 7.1** ▶SCANS Five Problem Domains and Three-Part Foundation Learning

| Workplace Problems Domains | Foundation Skills |
|---|---|
| **Planning for Resources**<br>Time—sets relevant, goal-related activities; ranks and allocates time<br>Money—uses or prepares budgets; keeps detailed records<br>Material—acquires, stores, and distributes materials, supplies, etc.<br>Human resources—assesses skills and distributes work | **Basic Skills**<br>Reading—locates, understands, and interprets written information<br>Writing—communicates thoughts, ideas, information in writing<br>Arithmetic—performs basic computations<br><br>Listening—receives, interprets, and responds to verbal messages<br>Speaking—organizes ideas and communicates orally |
| **Information**<br>Acquires—identifies need for data; obtains and evaluates<br>Organizes—organizes, processes, and maintains information<br>Interprets—selects, analyzes information, and communicates results<br>Uses computers—to acquire, organize, analyze, and communicate information | **Thinking Skills**<br>Creative thinking—generates new ideas<br><br>Decision making—specifies goals and constraints; chooses best alternatives<br>Problem solving—recognizes problem and devises/implements a solution<br>Mental visualization—thinks about what something will be<br>Knowing how to learn—uses efficient learning techniques<br>Reasoning—discovers and applies underlying rules or principles |
| **Interpersonal Skills**<br>Participates as a member of a team—contributes to group effort<br>Serves clients/customers—works to satisfy client/customer expectations<br>Exercises leadership—communicates ideas to justify position and lead others<br>Negotiates—works toward agreements involving an exchange of resources<br>Works with diversity—works well with people from diverse backgrounds | **Personal Qualities**<br>Responsibility—exerts a high level of effort and perseveres toward goal<br>Self-esteem—believes in self and maintains a positive view of self<br>Sociability—demonstrates to others that he/she cares about them<br>Self-management—assesses self accurately; sets goals; exhibits self-control<br>Integrity/honesty—chooses ethical courses of action |
| **Systems**<br>Understands systems—social, organizational, and technological systems<br>Monitors—distinguishes trends; predicts impact<br>Improves/designs—modifies existing systems and designs new ones | |
| **Technology**<br>Selects—judges which technology will produce desired results<br>Applies—understands procedure for setup and use of machines<br>Maintains—prevents, identifies or solves technological problems | |

Source: From "Implementing SCANS," by A. C. Packer and S. Brainard, 2003, *The Highlight Zone No. 10*, page 10. Copyright © 2003 by the Highlight Zone. Reprinted with permission: National Dissemination Center for Career and Technical Education, The Ohio State University, Columbus, OH.

|  | Self<br>(Personal Competence) | Other<br>(Social Competence) |
|---|---|---|
| Recognition | **Self-Awareness**<br><br>▶ Emotional self-awareness<br>▶ Accurate self-assessment<br>▶ Self-confidence | **Social Awareness**<br><br>▶ Empathy<br>▶ Service orientation<br>▶ Organizational awareness |
| Regulation | **Self-Management**<br><br>▶ Emotional self-control<br>▶ Trustworthiness<br>▶ Conscientiousness<br>▶ Adaptability<br>▶ Achievement drive<br>▶ Initiative | **Relationship Management**<br><br>▶ Developing others<br>▶ Influence<br>▶ Communication<br>▶ Conflict management<br>▶ Visionary leadership<br>▶ Catalyzing change<br>▶ Building bonds<br>▶ Teamwork and collaboration |

Source: "A Framework of Emotional Competencies," *An EI-Based Theory of Performance* (p. 28), by D. Goleman, in *The Emotionally Intelligent Workplace*, by G. Cherniss and D. Goleman (Eds.) (San Francisco: Jossey–Bass). Copyright © 2001 by Jossey-Bass. This material is used by permission of John Wiley & Sons, Inc..

**FIGURE 7.1** ▶A Framework of Emotional Competencies

to other people include social awareness and management of relationships. Recognition of one's own and others' emotions are prerequisite to regulating self and others.

The skills presented in Tables 7.1 and 7.2 and Figure 7.1 are generic occupational social–emotional skills that transcend specific occupations. The list offers a place to start when planning instruction. Some occupational social–emotional skills, however, are more important for certain jobs than for others. For example, Evenson (1999) identified the following "soft skills" as essential for individuals in the customer service industry:

▶ Being positive
▶ Being honest
▶ Being committed
▶ Being aware
▶ Being interested
▶ Being helpful
▶ Being respectful

**TABLE 7.2** ▶ Critical Occupational Social–Emotional Skills

| Author (Year) | Occupational Social–Emotional Skills Identified | Source of Information |
|---|---|---|
| Bullis, Nishioka–Evans, Fredericks, & Davis (1992) | *Job-Related Social Problem Domains:*<br>Accepting criticism or correction from a work supervisor<br>Requesting help from a work supervisor<br>Following instructions from a work supervisor<br>Quitting a job<br>Taking time off<br>Social problems created by not working as fast as a co-worker<br>Talking to a work supervisor about personal problems<br>Social problems created by working with a co-worker to complete a job<br>Dealing with teasing or provocation from co-workers<br>Managing personal concerns in the workplace<br>Making friends with co-workers<br>Talking with a co-worker about his or her behavior<br>Accepting criticism or correction from a co-worker<br>Job-related fighting<br>Stealing and lying<br>Job-related dating | Review of E/BD literature |
| Carnevale, Gainer, & Meltzer (1990) | *Communication Skills:*<br>Oral communication<br>Listening<br>*Adaptability Skills:*<br>Problem solving<br>Creative thinking<br>*Developmental Skills:*<br>Self-esteem<br>Motivation/goal setting<br>*Group Effectiveness Skills:*<br>Interpersonal skills<br>Teamwork<br>Negotiation | Survey of employers |
| Elrod (1987) | Gets along with others<br>Takes criticism constructively<br>Follows directions<br>Works as a member of a team | Survey of CTE teachers |

**TABLE 7.2 ▶**(Continued)

| Author (Year) | Occupational Social–Emotional Skills Identified | Source of Information |
|---|---|---|
| | Has a positive attitude<br>Is dependable<br>Accepts responsibility<br>Works independently<br>Is honest<br>Obeys safety rules | |
| Goleman (1998) | Listening and oral communication<br>Adaptability and creative responses to setbacks and obstacles<br>Personal management, confidence, motivation to work toward goals; a sense of wanting to develop in one's career and take pride in accomplishments<br>Group and interpersonal effectiveness, cooperativeness and teamwork; skills at negotiating disagreements<br>Effectiveness in the organization, wanting to make a contribution, leadership potential | Survey of employers |
| Greenan (1983), Greenan & Smith (1981) | *Generalizable Social Skills*<br><br>*Work Behaviors:*<br> Work effectively under supervision<br> Work without need for close supervision<br> Work cooperatively as a member of a team<br> Get along and work effectively with people<br> Show up regularly and on time<br> Work effectively under pressure<br> See things from another's point of view<br> Engage appropriately in social interactions<br> Take responsibility for one's own judgments, decisions, and actions<br> Plan, carry out, and complete activities at one's own initiation<br><br>*Instructor/Supervisor Conversation Skills:*<br> Instruct or direct someone in performance of task<br> Follow instructions or directions<br> Demonstrate how to perform a task<br> Assign others to carry out specific tasks<br> Speak in a relaxed, confident manner | Survey of CTE teachers |

**TABLE 7.2** ▶(Continued)

| Author (Year) | Occupational Social–Emotional Skills Identified | Source of Information |
|---|---|---|
| | Compliment or provide constructive feedback<br>Handle criticism, disagreement, and disappointment<br>Initiate and maintain conversations<br>Initiate, maintain, and draw others into conversations<br>Join in group conversations | |
| Mathews, Whang, & Fawcett (1980, 1981, 1982) | Getting a job lead from a friend<br>Telephoning a potential employer to arrange a job interview (when there is a job opening)<br>Telephoning a potential employer to arrange a job interview (when there is no job opening)<br>Participating in a job interview<br>Accepting a suggestion from an employer<br>Accepting criticism from an employer<br>Providing constructive criticism to a co-worker<br>Explaining a problem to a supervisor<br>Complimenting a co-worker on a job well done<br>Accepting a compliment from a co-worker | Review of literature; surveys of CTE counselors, university placement counselors, employers, and personnel managers |
| Minskoff (1994) | *Domains:*<br>Verbal communication (13 skills)<br>Nonverbal communication (4 skills)<br>Social problem solving (6 skills)<br>Social awareness (2 skills)<br>Compliance (3 skills)<br>Cooperation (3 skills)<br>Civility (2 skills) | Survey of CTE teachers, employers, employees |
| Montague (1988) | Ordering job responsibilities<br>Understanding instructions<br>Asking a question<br>Asking for help<br>Asking for assistance<br>Offering assistance<br>Giving instructions<br>Convincing others<br>Apologizing<br>Accepting criticism | Review of literature; survey of employers |

**TABLE 7.2 ►**(Continued)

| Author (Year) | Occupational Social–Emotional Skills Identified | Source of Information |
|---|---|---|
| Rosenbaum (2001) | *Normative Compliance:*<br>  Attendance<br>  Dependability<br>  Positive attitude<br>  Avoiding rule infractions<br>  Handling social conflict<br>*General Work Procedures:*<br>  Effort<br>  Persistence<br>  Problem solving<br>  Attention to quality<br>  Preparing for next tasks<br>*Social Skills:*<br>  Communicating with co-workers about<br>    work tasks<br>  Participating in activities beyond job tasks,<br>    such as maintaining and organizing the<br>    work group | Survey of employers |
| SCANS<br>(U.S. Department<br>of Labor, 1992) | *Interpersonal Skills:*<br>  Participates as member of a team—<br>    contributes to group effort<br>  Serves clients/customers—works to satisfy<br>    client/customer expectations<br>  Exercises leadership—communicates ideas<br>    to justify position and lead others<br>  Negotiates—works toward agreements<br>    involving exchange of resources<br>  Works with diversity—works well with<br>    people from diverse backgrounds<br><br>*Personal Qualities:*<br>  Responsibility—exerts a high level of effort<br>    and perseveres towards goal<br>  Self-esteem—believes in self and maintains<br>    a positive view of self<br>  Sociability—demonstrates to others that<br>    he/she cares about them<br>  Self-management—assesses self accurately,<br>    sets goals, exhibits self-control<br>  Integrity/honesty—chooses ethical courses of action | CEOs,<br>presidents in<br>business, labor,<br>and industry |

- ▶ Being appreciative
- ▶ Being compassionate
- ▶ Being humble

The assessment strategies described next will help teachers identify skills specific to career and technical education settings, as well as current and anticipated job settings.

## ▶ Assessment Issues Related to Occupational Social–Emotional Skills

*Connie coordinated the career and technical education program for students with disabilities at Wachovia High School. Nearly 2,300 students attended WHS, about 250 of whom had special needs. Connie was concerned about one of the students with emotional–behavioral disorders, Joe. A junior, Joe spent half of the day in a self-contained E/BD class and the rest of the day working at Home Depot with the support of a job coach, Maria.*

*Last week, Maria met with Connie to talk about Joe.*

*"Connie, Joe is dangerously close to losing this job placement. He is great at stocking the shelves but has had several run-ins with Toby, his supervisor. Toby had some suggestions about how Joe could stock the shelves more efficiently and arrange the pallets so they wouldn't block the aisles but Joe would have none of it. His constant refrain is, 'Don't treat me like I'm stupid.'*

*"Joe's inappropriate response to feedback is the major problem I've observed, but Toby pretty much has said that Joe's behavior just doesn't cut it, whether with him or Joe's co-workers. He even mentioned that Joe isn't 'good for business' because of the way he treats customers.*

*"I've asked Toby to give me some specifics, but I'm at a loss about what specific behaviors are creating problems. All I know is that Joe has made great strides in managing his behavior, and I really thought this placement would work out great for all concerned."*

*Connie and Maria spent the next half hour talking about Joe's situation and decided that they had to collect some information. Because Joe had no problem performing his job duties, they developed an assessment plan that would focus on his social–emotional skills.*

Chapter Two provided an overview of social–emotional skills assessment. Many of the approaches described in that chapter may be used when planning occupational social–emotional skills instruction. For example, rating scales, interviews, behavioral observation, and functional behavioral assessment can be used to identify

▶ who may benefit from occupational social–emotional skills instruction,
▶ essential occupational social–emotional skills,
▶ the disparity between occupational social–emotional skills needed by the adolescent and the skills he or she actually has,
▶ reason(s) for occupational social–emotional skills problems,
▶ skills the adolescent must be taught.

In the following discussion, we apply these approaches to the assessment of social–emotional occupational skills.

## Rating Scales and Checklists

*In the assessment plan that Connie and Maria developed, Toby was to complete the Scale of Job-Related Social Skill Performance (SSSP) for Joe. Using the SSSP, Toby would read a description of a positive social behavior, then decide if Joe was "proficient," "somewhat proficient," "fair," "somewhat inept," or "inept." Toby also would rate how frequently Joe exhibited certain negative behaviors. Connie and Maria both hoped that Toby, after completing the rating scale, would be better able to describe Joe's problem behaviors.*

Rating scales and checklists are particularly useful when we want to obtain information from many individuals (e.g., peers, employers) across a variety of settings (e.g., school, work, community). We will review the rating scales and checklists designed specifically to assess occupational social–emotional skills, listed in Table 7.3.

### Community-Based Social Skill Performance (CBSP) Assessment Tool (Bullis, 1998)

The CBSP is designed to assess the social performance of adolescents with emotional and behavioral disorders (EBD) in home and community settings. It also may be administered to adolescents with learning disabilities or mental retardation who have secondary behavior problems. The 78 items comprise four factors. Two of these, Positive Social Behavior and Social Skill Mechanics, address positive social behaviors. The Antisocial Behavior and Self-Control factors focus on negative social behavior.

For each positive behavior item, students are rated as "proficient," "somewhat proficient," "fair," "somewhat inept," or "inept." Negative behavior items are rated according to frequency scenarios. The evaluator reads each social scenario and the adolescent reports that the behavior occurs "never," "yearly," "monthly," "weekly," or "daily." The CBSP also includes the Test of Community-Based Social Skill Knowledge, composed of 39 social scenarios for females and 41 scenarios for males. The evaluator reads each social scenario and the student chooses from among four multiple-choice alternatives.

**TABLE 7.3** ▶Rating Scales and Checklists Designed to Assess Occupational Social–Emotional Skills

| Scale | Author(s)/Year |
| --- | --- |
| Community-Based Social Skill Performance Assessment Tool | Bullis (1998) |
| Scale of Job-Related Social Skill Performance | Bullis, Nishioka, Fredericks, & Davis (1997) |
| Social Competence for Workers with Developmental Disabilities | Calkins & Walker (1990) |
| Test of Interpersonal Competence for Employment | Foss, Cheney, & Bullis (1986) |

### Scale of Job-Related Social Skill Performance (SSSP) (Bullis, Nishioka, Fredericks, & Davis, 1998)

The SSSP is designed to assess the job-related social skills of adolescents and young adults with EBD. It also may be administered to students who have learning disabilities, speech and language disorders, or mental retardation and secondary behavior problems. The scale contains 87 items in six sections. Items in the first five sections—Positive Social Behaviors, Self-Control, Personal Issues, Body Movements, and Personal Appearance—describe positive social behaviors in which the student is rated as "proficient," "somewhat proficient," "fair," "somewhat inept," or "inept" for each behavior. Negative Social Behaviors, the sixth section of the scale, requires raters to assess frequency of behavior (i.e., never, yearly, monthly, weekly, or daily). The SSSP also includes a Scale of Job-Related Social Skills Knowledge, with 40 "verbal role-play" items describing social situations in employment settings. For example:

> Charles was to work with a co-worker to clean out sawdust from a machine. They worked for 5 minutes, and then the co-worker took a long break, leaving Charles to do the work alone. Charles was mad because he got stuck doing the job. (p. 16)

The student is asked to think about what he or she would say or do and to pick the best response. Using a scoring rubric, student responses are evaluated as "effective," "fair," or "ineffective."

### Social Competence for Workers with Developmental Disabilities (SCWDD) (Calkins & Walker, 1990)

The SCWDD is an assessment and intervention-planning tool designed to help workers with developmental disabilities be successful in integrated employment settings. The evaluator first determines if the worker exhibits each of 16 behaviors that either enhance or impair employment. The evaluator then determines if the worker is expected to demonstrate or not to demonstrate the behavior in the work environment, or if the behavior is not required. A mismatch between worker and setting occurs when the worker lacks a behavior that is required or demonstrates a behavior that is not permitted in the setting. Interventions are developed to lead to a better match between the worker's behavior and the demands of the employment setting.

### Test of Interpersonal Competence for Employment (TICE)
### (Foss, Cheney, & Bullis, 1986)

The TICE is a 61-item test designed to assess the job-retention skills of adolescents and young adults with mild mental retardation. It may be administered orally to as many as 10 individuals at a time. The two sections of the TICE consist of multiple-choice items related to supervisor interaction and co-worker interaction. The items describe situations reported to be related to problematic interpersonal relations with supervisors, such as dealing with criticism, requesting assistance, and following instructions; and with co-workers, such as working cooperatively, handling teasing, and resolving personal concerns.

## Interviews

*With results from the SSSP in hand, Maria asked Toby to meet for a few minutes during his break to talk some more about Joe.*

*"Mr. Washington, from your ratings of Joe's behavior, it seems that his biggest problems are that he doesn't make eye contact with people, doesn't take suggestions from supervisors and co-workers, doesn't offer assistance, and doesn't apologize when he does or says something upsetting. It looks like his strengths are that he follows directions, works well independently, comes to work regularly and on time, and follows safety rules. Does this seem about right?"*

*"Well, yeah, that does pretty much sum up the good, the bad, and the ugly as far as Joe is concerned. Actually, I sort of forgot about Joe's good qualities. I've had a fair number of people show up late or not at all. And I've had some workers who had to have their hands held all day—couldn't make a judgment call if their lives depended on it. To tell you the truth, Joe's bad attitude covers up a lot of his good qualities. I'm just not sure I have the energy or the will to deal with his problems."*

Teachers may conduct interviews with CTE educators and employers to identify social–emotional skills required on the job. Interviews with adults also help teachers pinpoint the disparity between needed skills and skills in the adolescent's repertoire.

Further, teachers gain useful information from interviewing adolescents, including levels of social awareness and problem-solving ability. Interviews can be used, too, to assess the adolescent's level of motivation to acquire occupational social–emotional skills. Finally, through observations during the interview, teachers learn if adolescents convey appropriate affect, maintain eye contact, sustain attention, and communicate effectively. The guidelines described in Chapter Two will help focus the interview and increase the probability of obtaining useful information.

## Behavioral Observation

*As the interview drew to a close, Maria asked if she could shadow Joe for a few days. "One of the concerns I have is that you mentioned that Joe is 'bad for business,' based on how he interacts with customers. I didn't know he had much interaction with customers since he's a stocker."*

*"Well, you know, stockers are sometimes the first people customers see when they're stumbling around the aisles trying to find something. It's a big store and people are tired, want to find their item, check out, and go home. Before a stocker hits the floor, he's taught to be helpful to customers. But Joe, he's another story. When customers ask him a question, they get a look that would freeze hell over. I've asked him about it, and his favorite response is, 'It's not my job.'"*

*Maria spent the next week observing Joe for about 2 hours each day. She chose the busiest times of the day so there would be plenty of opportunities for Joe–customer interaction. Joe did have a look about him when a customer approached him. She asked Joe about it.*

*His response? "I don't know where crap is in this store. I'm not going to look dumb or get in trouble 'cause I send these people to the wrong aisle!"*

By observing the CTE or employment setting, the observer can determine the types of social–emotional skills required. For example, while observing students in the high school computer repair program, we determined that offering and accepting constructive criticism were important skills. When we observed co-workers in the Wal-Mart break room, we learned that conversational give-and-take, "getting the joke," and gently ribbing fellow workers were essential social–emotional skills in that setting.

Observing the student in the CTE or employment setting enables teachers and others to determine if critical occupational social–emotional skills are being used where and when they count. (See Chapter Two for specific steps to follow when conducting behavioral observation.) The evaluation form in Figure 7.2 may be used to identify occupational social–emotional skills through observing and interviewing in the training or employment setting.

## Role-Play Assessment

*Maria wanted to get a better idea about what Joe did when someone gave him suggestions. She designed a role-play scenario in which she'd be Toby and Joe*

Evaluator _____Date _____

Site: _____

**Occupational Social–Emotional Skills Identified During Observation**

1. _____

2. _____

3. _____

4. _____

5. _____

6. _____

**Occupational Social–Emotional Skills Identified During Interviews**
Circle Information Source:
> P = peers, CTET = career and technical education teacher,
> E = employer, CW = co-worker

Source of Information:

P   CTET   E   CW _____

_____

_____

P   CTET   E   CW _____

_____

_____

P   CTET   E   CW _____

_____

_____

P   CTET   E   CW _____

_____

_____

_____

Source: "Site Evaluation Form for Identifying Relevant Occupational Social Skills," adapted from *Teaching Occupational Social Skills* (p. 34), by N. Elksnin and L. K. Elksnin (Austin, TX: Pro-Ed). Copyright © 1998 Pro-Ed Inc. Reprinted with permission.

**FIGURE 7.2 ▶** Site Evaluation Form for Identifying Relevant Occupational Social–Emotional Skills

*would be himself. In the scenario, Joe would be busily stocking shelves in the Paint Department like he usually did. His boss would tell him that he was doing a good job but that he needed to work faster. He then would give Joe some pointers about faster ways to stock.*

*In setting the stage, Maria instructed Joe, "Joe, I want you to say and do what you would say and do if you really were with Mr. Washington. I also want you to tell me what you're thinking before you say or do something."*

When adolescents cannot be observed in training or employment settings, role-play assessment can be extremely helpful. Figure 7.3 is the role-play sheet that Maria used to assess Joe's ability in "accepting criticism from an employer or co-worker." The four steps unique to this skill are clearly described, along with behaviors that occur throughout the skill, such as staying close to the person and having a relaxed, but serious, body posture. While observing the student act out the role-play scenario, the teacher or parent records each skill step as "performed competently," "performed but needs improvement," or as "not performed." Maria determined that Joe needed to work on all four skill steps and most of the body basics. In particular, she decided to teach Joe strategies to stop and think before responding to suggestions or criticism.

Self-assessment of performance and self-awareness of similar situations in which to use the skill are obtained by interviewing the adolescent following the role play. Maria discovered that Joe's assessment of his ability to use the skill was inflated. Joe's remark that this was a good skill to use "to get my mother off my back" showed that Joe didn't understand that responding to criticism could lead to positive behavior changes that would benefit *him.*

The role-play evaluation sheet may be used to assess a variety of occupational social skills. Teachers and parents also can develop their own role-play scenarios or use scenarios included in the programs listed in Table 7.4.

### Functional Behavioral Assessment

As we pointed out in Chapter Two, functional behavioral assessment (FBA) combines many assessment approaches. FBA can help identify behaviors of concern in the training or employment setting, and the function served by these behaviors. Information obtained during FBA can be used to develop behavior intervention plans (BIPs) to reduce or eliminate problem behaviors and teach relevant occupational social–emotional skills. Chapter Two contains specifics for conducting FBA.

## ▶ Teaching Youth to Solve Occupational Social–Emotional Problems

*Stan sat at the table with his 17-year-old son, Jackson, who was ticked off because he had just found out that a co-worker, Samantha, received a raise.*

*Student:*    *Joe Morgan*

*Occupational Social–Emotional Skill:* *Accepting Criticism from an Employer or Coworker*

**Role-Play Scenario:**    *You are stocking shelves in the paint department at Home Depot. Your supervisor, Mr. Washington , spots you and tells you that you're doing a good job but that you need to work faster.*

*Skill Steps*

+ = step performed competently; – = step performed, but needs improvement;
0 = step not performed

\_\_\_\_**–**\_\_ 1. Listen to what the person has to say.    *Joe jumped in before Mr. W. finished.*

\_\_\_\_**–**\_\_ 2. Think about what the person said.    *Joe thought about it for about 30 seconds.*

\_\_\_\_**–**\_\_ 3. Give your side, if appropriate.    *He was quick to say why his way was better.*

\_\_\_\_**0**\_\_ 4. Say you will change if you think you should, and/or thank the person.

*Body basics that should occur throughout the skill:*

\_\_\_**+**\_\_\_       Stay close to the person.    *Mr. W. approached Joe and Joe didn't move.*

\_\_\_**0**\_\_\_       Face the person and maintain eye contact.    *Joe continued stocking—looking down at his box or at the shelves.*

\_\_\_**0**\_\_\_       Have a relaxed, but serious, body posture.    *Joe held his body rigidly as he put cans on the shelf.*

\_\_\_**–**\_\_\_       Use a serious tone of voice.    *Joe's voice tone was serious, but his volume escalated.*

*Evaluator comments:*

*Joe really needs to work on this skill. He needs to learn to stop and think and lose his defensive posture. I think that Joe lacks confidence and this has a lot to do with why he has trouble accepting criticism/suggestions.*

*Student Interview*

How do you think you did? *Joe thought he did pretty well.*

What could you do better? *Joe thought he could thank Mr. W.*

Name other situations in which you could use this skill. *Joe thought this skill would be good to use to "get my mother off my back."*

**FIGURE 7.3** ▶ Role-Play Evaluation Sheet

**TABLE 7.4** ▶Adolescent Programs With Occupationally Relevant Role-Play Scenarios

| Program | Author(s)/Date |
|---------|----------------|
| ACCESS | Walker, Todis, Holmes, & Horton (1988) |
| ASSET | Hazel, Schumaker, Sherman, & Sheldon (1996) |
| The PREPARE Curriculum | Goldstein (1999) |
| Skillstreaming the Adolescent | Goldstein & McGinnis (1997) |
| Social Skills Activities for Secondary Students with Special Needs | Mannix (1998) |
| Social Skills in the Classroom | Stephens (1992) |
| Social Skills for Daily Living | Schumaker, Hazel, & Pederson (1988) |
| Social Skills for School and Community | Sargent (1991) |
| Stacking the Deck | Foxx & McMorrow (1983) |
| Systematic Instruction of Social Skills | Sargent (1988) |

*Samantha had been working at Sunrise Computers for only 6 weeks! Jackson had worked for the company more than a year—full-time during the summer and part-time during the school year.*

*"It's not fair," Jackson said for about the fifth time. "Sam hasn't been with Sunrise for more than a couple of weeks. I know more about computers than she does—in both the hardware and the software departments. Now I find out she's pulling down nine dollars an hour and I'm still getting eight, the same pay as last summer."*

*"Jax, I can understand why you're upset. But is the problem that Sam got a raise or that you didn't get one?" his father probed.*

*Jackson mulled this over, "You're right, Dad. My problem is that I didn't get the raise."*

*"Okay, let's work together to set some goals and develop a plan to meet them."*

*After about 20 minutes, Stan and his son had come up with a plan. Jax would set up a time to meet with his boss, outline his contributions to Sunrise, summarize the skills he brought to the job, and emphasize his commitment to the company (he planned on working until he finished his associate's degree at the local technical college). Before he met with his boss he would try to find out how much other employees with similar skills and experience were paid. This information would help Jax come up with a salary figure.*

We teach occupationally related problem solving in the same ways we teach general social–emotional problem-solving skills. The strategies to teach problem-solving skills described in Chapter Four may be used to teach adolescents how to solve problems within an occupational context. As shown in the vignette, Jackson's dad helped him solve the problem of getting his employer to give him a raise by working through the FIG TESPN steps:

1. Feelings cue me to thoughtful action.
2. I have a problem.
3. Goals give me a guide.
4. Think of things I can do.
5. Envision outcomes.
6. Select my best solution.
7. Plan the procedure, anticipate pitfalls, practice, and pursue it.
8. Notice what happened, and now what?

Adolescents also can be taught to use the social problem-solving checklist introduced as Chapter Four, Figure 4.2 to identify problems, generate solutions, anticipate outcomes, try a solution, and valuate the actual outcomes.

In Chapter Four we described how to use social skill autopsies to solve social–emotional problems at school and home. Social skills autopsies are equally effective in helping adolescents identify and solve social–emotional problems that occur on the job. When CTE teachers, job coaches, employers, and others conduct autopsies, adolescents are given more opportunities to improve their performance in occupational social–emotional skills and to generalize their skills across people and settings.

Many programs teach adolescents social–emotional problem-solving strategies. For example, the ACCESS Program (Walker et al., 1988) includes the "Triple A Strategy" to help adolescents solve problems by

▶ Assessing the situation they are in,
▶ Amending or deciding on things to do to result in a more positive outcome,
▶ Acting by implementing the changes identified in step two.

Table 7.5 presents a list of adolescent programs that teach social–emotional problem solving.

---

## ▶ Teaching Occupational Social–Emotional Skills

The instructional model described in Chapter Six may be used to teach adolescents essential occupational social–emotional skills such as working cooperatively, requesting assistance, accepting criticism, displaying a positive attitude, and dealing with pressure. A social–emotional skills instructional planning sheet (first introduced in Chapter Six) for "Accepting Criticism" is presented as Figure 7.4. When

**TABLE 7.5** ▶Adolescent Programs That Teach Social–Emotional Problem Solving

| Program | Author(s)/Date |
| --- | --- |
| ACCESS | Walker, Todis, Holmes, & Horton (1988) |
| ASSET | Hazel, Schumaker, Sherman, & Sheldon (1996) |
| CLASSIC | Dygdon (1993) |
| Life Skills Activities for Secondary Students with Special Needs | Mannix (1998) |
| The PREPARE Curriculum | Goldstein (1999) |
| Ready-to-Use Social Skills Lessons & Activities for Grades 7–12 | Begun (1996a, 1996b, 1996c) |
| Skillstreaming the Adolescent | Goldstein & McGinnis (1997) |
| Social Skills for Daily Living | Schumaker, Hazel, & Pederson (1988) |
| Social Skills Development | Antonello (1996) |
| Teaching Social Competence | D. A. Jackson, N. F. Jackson, & Bennett (1998) |
| Technical-Related and Academic Career Competencies (TRACC) | Minskoff (1994) |
| Thinking, Feeling, Behaving: Adolescents in Grades 7–12 | Vernon (1989a, 1989b) |
| The Waksman Social Skills Curriculum | S. Waksman & D. D. Waksman (1998) |

teaching occupational social–emotional skills, the following instructional sequence has proven to be effective (Goldstein & McGinnis, 1997):

1. Teacher/parent models/role-plays the skill.
2. Teacher/parent asks adolescent to evaluate performance by considering the skill steps introduced in Step 1.
3. Adolescents role-play the skill.
4. *Every* student role-plays *every* skill.
5. Adolescents who are not role-playing the skill evaluate their peers' performance by considering the skill steps introduced in Step 1 as shown in Figure 7.4.
6. Teacher/parent gives each role player positive and negative feedback.

**Skill:** *Accepting Criticism From an Employer or Co-Worker*

1. **Definition of Skill:** *Accepting criticism means allowing an employer or co-worker to tell you that something you did or said bothered him or her.*

   **Skill Steps:**
   *1. Listen to what the person has to say.*
   *2. Think about what the person said.*
   *3. Give your side, if appropriate.*
   *4. Say you will change if you think you should, and/or thank the person.*

   **Body Basics (in no particular order):**
   - *Stay close to the person.*
   - *Face the person and maintain eye contact.*
   - *Have a serious facial expression.*
   - *Have a relaxed but serious body posture.*
   - *Use a serious tone of voice.*

2. **Rationale Statements**
   **Positive Statements:**
   *If you learn to accept criticism,*
   *Then you will be able to improve your job performance and perhaps get a raise.*
   *If you learn to accept criticism,*
   *Then you will avoid getting into fights with your boss and co-workers.*

   **Negative Statements:**
   *If you don't know how to accept criticism,*
   *Then your supervisor may get angry and think that you are not willing to change.*
   *If you don't know how to accept criticism,*
   *Then you may receive a poor performance evaluation and not get a pay increase.*

3. **General Situations in Which to Use Skill:**
   *A good time to accept criticism is when you have done or said something that made you not do your job as well as you could.*
   *Another time to accept criticism is when you've done something that upset your supervisor and you want to change your behavior.*

4. **Role-Play Situations:**
   *Your distributive education teacher tells you that you aren't paying attention in class and you are missing important information.*
   *At the fast food restaurant where you work, your co-worker tells you that she doesn't think you are doing your fair share when it comes to "setup" the first thing in the morning.*

5. **Social Rules:**
   *Social rules that apply to accepting criticism include:*
   - *Do not argue with authority figures.*
   - *Do not interrupt when the other person is talking.*
   - *Avoid getting into an argument.*

   ---
   Source: "Occupational Social Skills Instructional Planning Sheet," adapted from *Teaching Occupational Social Skills* (pp. 37, 38), by N. Elksnin & L. K. Elksnin (Austin, TX: Pro-Ed). Copyright © 1998 by Pro-Ed. Reprinted by permission.

**FIGURE 7.4** ▶ Social–Emotional Skills Instructional Planning Sheet for Accepting Criticism From an Employer or Co-Worker

Having adolescents complete the planning sheet prior to role-playing becomes the first part of the lesson. In our experience, it is better to have adolescents generate role-play scenarios based on their real-life experiences, as these scenarios are likely to be more motivating and facilitate generalization to real-world people and settings.

# ▶ Curricular Options

Four curricular options are available for teaching occupational social–emotional skills. We can

1. adopt/adapt general social–emotional skills curricula with occupational examples,
2. adopt occupational social–emotional skills curricula,
3. develop/select programs based on employment competencies,
4. develop programs based upon the results of ecological assessment.

## Adopt/Adapt General Social–Emotional Skills Curricula

Various commercial curricula for teaching adolescents social–emotional skills are available. Although these programs are not designed specifically to teach occupational social–emotional skills, teachers, parents, and adolescents can develop role-play scenarios relevant to CTE and employment settings. Many of the general social–emotional skills programs listed in Table 7.4 include occupational role-play scenarios.

## Adopt Occupational Social–Emotional Skills Curricula

A few curricular programs are designed specifically to teach occupational social–emotional skills. These programs focus on social–emotional skills regarded as important in all employment settings. Programs, along with targeted occupational social–emotional skills, are listed in Table 7.6.

## Develop/Select Programs Based on Employment Competencies

The SCANS interpersonal and personal qualities in Table 7.1 and the *employment competencies* identified by employers and CTE teachers in Table 7.2 discussed earlier in this chapter provide direction when developing or selecting occupational social–emotional skills programs. Teachers can develop a skills matrix like our example in Table 7.7 to identify skills addressed by specific curricula. The matrix helps us decide which program is the best match for the skills that should be taught or if programs should be used in combination to form our curriculum. For example, the PREPARE curriculum and Social Skills in the Classroom include all but three of the skills of interest.

**TABLE 7.6** ▶Curricula Designed to Teach Occupational Social–Emotional Skills

| Program/Author(s)/<br>Date of Publication | Occupational Social–Emotional Skills |
| --- | --- |
| *Assessing and Teaching*<br>*Job-Related Social Skills*<br>(Baumgart & Anderson, 1987) | demonstrating honesty, acknowledging and following instructions, maintaining good hygiene, controlling anger and stress, explaining a problem/asking for help, exhibiting enthusiasm for the job, working cooperatively with others, dressing appropriately for the job, accepting criticism, demonstrating flexibility when changes occur, not doing personal business at work |
| *Job-Related Social Skills*<br>(Montague & Lund, 1991) | prioritizing job responsibilities, understanding directions, giving instructions, asking questions, asking permission, asking for help, accepting help, offering help, requesting information, taking messages, engaging in conversation, giving directions, receiving complaints, giving compliments, convincing others, apologizing, accepting criticism, responding to complaints |
| *Playing a Role: Real Life*<br>*Vocational Rehearsals*<br>(Sigler & Fitzpatrick, 2000) | makes introductions, deals with angry people, admits mistakes, uses nonverbal behavior to convey sincerity and honesty, listens attentively |
| *Social Competence for Workers*<br>*with Developmental Disabilities*<br>(Calkins & Walker, 1990) | asks questions, follows instructions, accepts criticism, follows workplace rules and safety procedures, is neatly groomed, adapts to change, interacts with co-workers, shows courtesy toward co-workers and supervisors |
| *Social Skills on the Job*<br>(American Guidance<br>Service, 1989) | wears appropriate clothes, has good hygiene, calls in when sick, arrives on time, greets authority figures, acts appropriately during break, does own share of work, maintains work schedule, admits mistakes, responds to introductions, knows when to ask for help, knows who to ask for help, deals with heckling, deals with criticism |

**TABLE 7.6** ▶(Continued)

| Program/Author(s)/ Date of Publication | Occupational Social–Emotional Skills |
|---|---|
| *Technical-Related and Academic Career Competencies* (Minskoff, 1994) | 33 skills in 7 domains: verbal communication (e.g., begins and ends conversations); nonverbal communication (e.g., uses eye contact); social problem solving (e.g., evaluates solutions); social awareness (e.g., picks positive and negative environmental cues); compliance (e.g., uses appropriate nonverbal behavior with authority figures); cooperation (e.g., uses mediation strategies); civility (e.g., refrains from using profanity) |
| *The Transitions Curriculum: Volume I: Personal Management* (Fulton & Silva, 1998) | 80 lessons organized within 4 units: winning with personal power (e.g., self-esteem, decision making); using effective communication skills (e.g., being assertive, listening); choosing the best career for you (e.g., knowing your values, maximizing your options); opportunities (e.g., knowing about jobs, military training, college). Skills are correlated with SCANS Foundations Skills. |

### Develop Programs Based Upon Results of Ecological Assessment

Ecological assessment involves identifying essential occupational social–emotional skills by observing the CTE or employment setting, as well as interviewing employers and employees (N. Elksnin & L. K. Elksnin, 1998, 2001). We discussed interview and observation procedures earlier in this chapter, as well as in Chapter Two. Teaching relevant skills for the CTE increases the probability that adolescents will complete their preparation programs successfully. If adolescents are being prepared for specific occupations, they must visit prospective job sites to determine the social–emotional skills needed to be successful employees. We recommend using the site evaluation form in Figure 7.2 for this purpose.

## ▶ Chapter Summary

Employers value social–emotional skills even more highly than the ability to perform the job. Social–emotional skills highly valued by employers include communi-

**TABLE 7.7** ▶Matrix of Critical Occupational Social–Emotional Skills Identified by Employers and Skills Taught by Social Skills Programs

| Critical Skills | Social Skills Program | | | |
| --- | --- | --- | --- | --- |
| | ACCESS | ASSET | PREPARE | Social Skills in the Classroom |
| Listens | X | | X | X |
| Accepts criticism | | X | X | X |
| Apologizes | | | | X |
| Asks for help | | | X | X |
| Offers assistance | | | X | X |
| Follows directions | | | X | X |
| Deals with teasing | | | X | X |
| Works as member of a team | | | X | |
| Works independently | | | | X |
| Accepts consequences | X | | | X |
| Accepts compliments | X | | | |
| Gives compliments | X | | X | X |
| Negotiates | | | X | X |
| Convinces others | | | X | |

cation skills, cooperating with co-workers, persistence, and self-discipline. Successful employees have a high level of self-awareness that enables them to effectively regulate their emotions. In addition, they are aware of the feelings of others and are able to effectively manage relationships. Assessment approaches such as rating scales, interviews, and observation yield information that can be used to teach adolescents critical occupational social–emotional skills. In addition to learning specific skills, adolescents also must learn how to solve social–emotional problems on the job. By teaching occupational social–emotional skills, teachers and parents help adolescents acquire the skills to become employed, remain employed, and advance in the workplace.

# CHAPTER 8

# Parents as Teachers

## Goals of This Chapter

In reading this chapter, you will learn

▶ the principles of emotionally intelligent parenting and ways to improve emotional intelligence
▶ how to become an emotion coach
▶ how to teach social–emotional skills incidentally
▶ the importance of including social–emotional objectives in IEPs
▶ how to help children find, make, and keep friends

# Terms to Know

emotionally intelligent parenting

disapproving parents and teachers

dismissive parents and teachers

emotion coaches

incidental teaching

individualized education program (IEP)

laissez-faire parents and teachers

*As Dana observed her 8-year-old son Gus at his birthday party, she relived many painful memories. Since the time he was a toddler, Gus had difficulty fitting in with other children. He was a bright, thoughtful, sensitive child who was shy to the point of withdrawal when he was with groups of children. At this party, which Gus had not wanted, he stood off to the side as he watched his classmates and the neighborhood children play and act like kids.*

*Gus used to try to be part of the group, but his awkward attempts at conversation and his clumsy body language usually resulted in his being ignored at best, and being teased at worst. With each passing year, he made fewer attempts to make friends. Dana could see the pain on her son's face each time he was ignored or rejected, and it was breaking her heart. When the party was over, Gus softly asked, "Mom, why don't kids like me?"*

*P*arents will relate to Dana's pain about Gus's social circumstance, as they have experienced the same pain on some occasion with their own children. This pain may cut to the bone if a parent experienced social rejection as a child. This may make it even more difficult for parents to help their children find acceptance. The only times we have seen parents break down and cry during conferences is when they discuss the social rejection of their children. As a psychologist and a special educator, the two of us would be hard-pressed to think of one instance in which parents showed raw emotions because of a child's difficulties in reading or math. A child who cannot read can be provided with books on tape, or learn the material from a lecture. A child who cannot compute can learn to use a calculator. One reason for parents' despair is that *problems with social–emotional skills cannot be accommodated!*

One of the authors of *Best Friends, Worst Enemies: Understanding the Social Lives of Children* (Thompson, Grace, & Cohen, 2001), Michael Thompson, commented that "as both a parent and a psychologist, I believe that there is no area in which a parent feels more powerless to make a significant difference than in relation to a child's social life" (p. 7). One reason for feeling powerless is that, unlike in other aspects of children's lives, parents can't step in and fix the problem. They cannot make friends for their child. They can, however, teach their child important social–emotional skills and adopt strategies to support their children's friendships.

The importance of parent involvement in social–emotional skills instruction cannot be overstated (L. K. Elksnin & N. Elksnin, 2000; Haynes & Comer, 1996; Kolb & Hanley-Maxwell, 2003; Weare, 2004). While teachers can assume responsibility for teaching social–emotional skills at school, parents are the likely instructors at home and in the community. Because parents are with their children for more time than others during the day, social–emotional issues are a constant presence. Finally, because social–emotional problems have a devastating effect on the child and other family members, parents are often highly motivated to improve their child's social–emotional skills.

This text is written for teachers and parents alike. In this chapter we offer some particularly practical strategies for parents to use to help their children become more socially and emotionally competent. We recognize that teachers and parents are in different situations. Teachers typically provide highly structured learning experiences, whereas parents tend to rely on "teachable moments." In this chapter we offer strategies that parents can use when teaching opportunities present themselves. We begin by discussing the importance of becoming an emotionally intelligent parent. We then describe steps parents can take to become emotion coaches, and we offer incidental teaching as a way for parents to teach social–emotional skills throughout the day. We close the chapter by suggesting ways by which parents can support their child's friendships.

## ▶ Emotionally Intelligent Parenting

As defined in Chapter One, emotional intelligence is a person's ability to understand emotions and regulate them in a way that is socially satisfying. Emotionally intelligent individuals are more likely to be successful in life than those who are not. In addition to directly teaching children social–emotional skills, parents can adopt the five principles of *emotionally intelligent parenting* (Elias et al., 1999). These principles are as follows:

- ▶ Be aware of your feelings and those of others.
- ▶ Show empathy and understanding of others' points of view.
- ▶ Regulate and cope positively with your emotions.
- ▶ Be goal- and plan-oriented.
- ▶ Use positive social skills when handling your relationships.

Figure 8.1 lists questions parents can ask themselves in order to determine if they and their children demonstrate emotional intelligence. The underlying theme in emotionally intelligent parenting is that what parents *do* is much more important than what they *say*. Parents can remind their children to control their negative feelings ad nauseum, but children are much more apt to imitate how their parents handle their own negative feelings. If parents frequently get angry and express that anger inappropriately, they shouldn't be surprised if their children fail to regulate their own negative feelings.

## ▶ Emotion Coaches

*Sandi was into her third year of teaching fourth graders. She frequently used cooperative learning activities in her classroom with much success. Students seemed to enjoy working in groups on social studies and science projects, in particular. Sandi was amazed at how well the groups worked together. The only problem was Eddie. He couldn't get along with his classmates. Sandi tried static groups for a while because she thought Eddie and his group members might establish rapport. Boy, was she wrong! Then she tried to change groups fairly often so no one group would be stuck with Eddie for too long.*

*On Thursday, Sandi reached the end of her rope. Eddie jumped up from his group's table and grabbed the science project display board the group had worked on for 2 weeks. "I hate this f———- class, and I'm tired of being called stupid!" he screamed, as he proceeded to rip the poster board into pieces.*

*"I've had it with you, Eddie!" Sandi said in a loud voice. "You can't get angry toward your classmates like that. There is no reason you can give me*

To help you better understand how to apply *emotionally intelligent parenting* to your everyday family issues, take a moment to assess your emotional intelligence and that of your children. Ask yourself the following questions:

*My Emotional Intelligence:*

1. How well do I know my own feelings? How well do I know the feelings of my family? Think of a recent problem in the family. How were you feeling . . . your child(ren) feeling . . . others involved feeling?
2. How much empathy do I have for others? Do I express it to them? When was the last time I did this? Am I sure they are aware of what I am doing? Am I able to understand another's point of view even during an argument?
3. How do I cope with anger, anxiety, and other stresses? Am I able to maintain self-control when stressed? How do I behave after a hard day? How often do I yell at others? When are my best and worst times, and do these vary on different days?
4. What goals do I have for myself and my family? What plans do I have for achieving them?
5. How do I deal with everyday, interpersonal problem situations? Do I really listen to others? Do I reflect back to people what they are saying? Do I approach social conflicts in a thoughtful manner? Do I consider alternatives before deciding on a course of action?

*My Child's Emotional Intelligence:*

1. How well can my child verbalize feelings? If I ask him/her how he/she feels, can my child respond with a feeling word or does he/she tell me what happened? Can my child identify a range of feelings with gradations in between? Can my child identify feelings in others?
2. How does my child show empathy? When was the last time he/she seemed to relate to another's feelings? Does my child show interest in others' feelings? When I tell him/her stories about others' misfortunes, how does he/she react? Can my child understand different points of view? Can he/she see both sides of an argument? Can my child do this in a conflict situation?
3. Can my child wait to get what he/she wants, especially when it is something he/she really wants? Can my child wait to get something that is right there in front of him/her that he/she can't have? How well can my child tolerate frustration?
4. What goals does my child have? What goals would I like him/her to have? Does my child ever plan things out before doing something? Have I ever helped him/her develop a plan for achieving a goal?

**FIGURE 8.1** ▶An Informal Measure of Family Members' Emotional Intelligence

5. How does my child resolve conflicts? How independent is he/she in resolving conflicts? Does he/she listen, or turn others off? Can he/she think of different ways of resolving conflicts?

**Strengths:** For both yourself and your children, think about areas of strength, the areas you and they are really good at. Give yourself a pat on the back for having these—we mean it!—and praise your children for theirs as soon as you can. Also, think about areas you would like to focus on for change. Think of what times of day you are most likely to show these skills, and when you are less likely to show them. These patterns are important, because we help ourselves when we try to swim with the current, as opposed to going against it.

**Find the answers:** You may find you are not sure of some of the answers to the questions we pose. This is more common than not, because we are asking parents to think about things a little differently than they are used to doing. One way to get some answers is to videotape a (non-offensive) sitcom and then watch it with your child. Or read a story to your child. At various points in the tape or story, pause and discuss the following:

- ▶ How the main character is feeling
- ▶ How the other characters are feeling and what they are thinking
- ▶ How your child feels about the characters' feelings
- ▶ What the different characters' goals are and what they think the characters' plans might be
- ▶ How your child thinks the characters handled the situation
- ▶ What your child thinks was good about how the characters handled the problem and what the characters could have done better

Source: "How to Build Your Child's 'EQ:' A Guide for Emotionally Intelligent Parenting," by M. J. Elias, S. E. Tobias, and B. S. Friedlander, in *The Communiqué*, November, 1999, p. 2. Copyright © 1999 by the National Association of School Psychologists, Bethesda, MD. Reprinted with permission of the publisher.

**FIGURE 8.1** ▶(Continued)

*that makes it okay for you to be so angry that you're entitled to destroy someone's work! You can just leave the class and go tell Mr. Faircloth that you can't get along with your classmates and that you got in trouble again!"*

*Jill knew that all was not right with her daughter, Maggie, as soon as she got home from school. Maggie came in the kitchen door, threw her pack down on*

# Top Ten List of Ways to Be a More Emotionally Intelligent Parent

10. **Expect your children to do as you do, not as you say.** Modeling EQ skills is extremely important if you really want your children to use them. Show them how to regulate their feelings and express their anger appropriately by doing so yourself.

9. **Remind them, remind them, remind them.** How many times is a child exposed to the letter "A" before he/she is expected to read it? Self-control and problem-solving skills are a lot harder to learn, and children need a lot of prompts and cues before they will begin to use the skills independently.

8. **Use active listening.** Everyone wants to be heard and understood. Paraphrasing back to children what they are saying to you reinforces them for communicating to you. It also allows you to gently rephrase their statements into more appropriate or accurate language. For example, when you ask how a child feels and his/her reply is that his/her sister is an idiot, you can help him/her clarify his/her feelings by saying, "Gee, it sounds like you are really upset with her." This opens the door to communication rather than shutting it with criticism.

7. **Ask open-ended questions.** Avoid making accusations such as "Why did you hit him?" Ask what happened, what was he doing, what did he want to have happen? Open-ended questions encourage the child to talk openly.

6. **Ask a question, ask another question.** It is important to stay in a questioning mode. If you follow up a question with another question, you will get more information, encourage the child to think more, and avoid a lecture on your part (which will certainly end communication).

5. **Sometimes appear to know less than you do.** Ask questions as if you do not understand. Instead of "Why did you fail that test?" ask, "I don't understand how you got this grade. What happened?" When the child says he/she studied, say, "That doesn't seem fair. What could have happened so the studying didn't work?" This gets the child to think in a nondefensive manner.

4. **Be patient . . . be VERY patient.** Learning the skills necessary to get along in all kinds of social situations and to manage strong feelings is not easy, especially if the skills don't seem to come naturally to your child. It can take a long time, both when teaching it and when children are learning it. Fortunately, childhood lasts a long time. Be patient with them and with yourself. Look for small improvements, starting in certain situations or with certain people. Build on these improvements and you will find it easier than expecting miracles. Skills take time to learn but then last for a lifetime.

3. **If you bend, you won't break.** Be flexible in the way in which you try to build your child's EQ. Look for a variety of opportunities to teach and reinforce these skills. Above all, do not expect perfection in yourself or others.

2. **Know your child.** Some children learn quickly; others take more time. Generally, as children get older, they can handle more independence and responsibility but give only as much independence as the child can take responsibility for.

1. **Have fun!** Enjoy your children. Have a sense of humor. Situations usually aren't as bad as you think at first. Even when things are especially troubling, being depressed about it and angry at your child all the time will definitely not help. Children learn best when they have a close, loving relationship and when they are having fun. Make learning the skills of Emotional Intelligence fun. Your whole family will benefit.

Source: "How to Build Your Child's 'EQ': A Guide for Emotionally Intelligent Parenting," by M. J. Elias, S. E. Tobias, and B. S. Friedlander, in *The Communiqué,* November, 1999, p. 3. Copyright © 1999 by the National Association of School Psychologists, Bethesda, MD. Reprinted with permission of the publisher.

*the floor, and screamed, "I'm never going back to that school again. I hate Mrs. Hampton! She yelled at me in front of the whole class!" Tears ran down Maggie's face as her mother hugged her.*

*After the tears stopped, Jill asked her daughter what happened. Maggie told her that Mrs. Hampton asked her a question about the Aztecs during social studies class. Maggie was daydreaming so she didn't hear Mrs. Hampton ask her the question. When the teacher realized that Maggie wasn't paying attention, she disciplined her in front of the class by saying, "Maggie, this isn't the first time you weren't paying attention in class. How are you going to go to sixth grade next year when you can't keep your mind on your studies?"*

*What really mortified Maggie was that she heard a bunch of the boys at the back of the room laughing at her.*

*Jill listened to her daughter, then said, "It must have been so embarrassing for you to be singled out in front of the whole fifth grade."*

*Maggie agreed, "Mom, it was awful having everyone look at me when I felt so dumb. I was thinking about our camping trip this weekend, and I wasn't paying attention. I know a lot about the Aztecs, though. I read the assignment in the social studies book, and I saw a really neat show about the Aztecs on the History Channel last week."*

*As Maggie calmed down, Jill helped her describe her feelings, and Maggie decided that she was more embarrassed than angry, and that she liked her teacher most of the time. Then Jill and her daughter began to brainstorm some strategies to help Maggie pay better attention in class.*

According to Gottman (1997), parents and teachers are of two types: those who give guidance about emotions—emotional coaches like Jill—and those who do not—like Maggie's teacher. *Emotion coaches* help children and youth understand their feelings and the feelings of others (L. K. Elksnin & N. Elksnin, 2000). They look upon a child's expressions of negative emotions as teaching opportunities.

Gottman posits that parents and teachers fall within four categories:

1. *Dismissive parents and teachers* disregard, ignore, or trivialize negative emotions.

2. *Disapproving parents and teachers* criticize negative emotions and often punish emotional expression.

3. *Laissez-faire parents and teachers* accept negative emotions, but they do not guide behavior.

4. *Emotion coaches* use emotional moments as teaching opportunities, guiding children to understand their feelings and the feelings of others.

Gottman developed a list of characteristics for each type of parent (or teacher), as shown in the box on pages 228–229.

# Four Styles of Parenting

### The Dismissing Parent

- ▶ treats the child's feelings as unimportant, trivial
- ▶ disengages from or ignores the child's feelings
- ▶ wants the child's negative emotions to disappear quickly
- ▶ characteristically uses distraction to shut down the child's emotions
- ▶ may ridicule or make light of a child's emotions
- ▶ believes children's feelings are irrational, and therefore don't count
- ▶ shows little interest in what the child is trying to communicate
- ▶ may lack awareness of emotions in self and others
- ▶ feels uncomfortable, fearful, anxious, annoyed, hurt, or overwhelmed by the child's emotions
- ▶ fears being out-of-control emotionally
- ▶ focuses more on how to get over emotions than on the meaning of the emotion itself
- ▶ believes negative emotions are harmful or toxic
- ▶ believes focusing on negative emotions will "just make matters worse"
- ▶ feels uncertain about what to do with the child's emotions
- ▶ sees the child's emotions as a demand to fix things
- ▶ believes negative emotions mean the child is not well adjusted
- ▶ believes the child's negative emotions reflect badly on his/her parents
- ▶ minimizes the child's feelings, downplaying the events that led to the emotion
- ▶ does not problem-solve with the child; believes that the passage of time will resolve most problems

*Effects of this style on children:* They learn that their feelings are wrong, inappropriate, not valid. They may learn that there is something inherently wrong with them because of the way they feel. They may have difficulty regulating their own emotions.

### The Disapproving Parent

- ▶ displays many of the Dismissing Parent's behaviors, but in a more negative way
- ▶ judges and criticizes the child's emotional expression
- ▶ is overly aware of the need to set limits on his/her children
- ▶ emphasizes conformity to good standards or behavior
- ▶ reprimands, disciplines, or punishes the child for emotional expression, whether the child is misbehaving or not
- ▶ believes expression of negative emotions should be time-limited
- ▶ believes negative emotions have to be controlled
- ▶ believes negative emotions reflect bad character traits
- ▶ believes the child uses negative emotions to manipulate; this belief results in power struggles
- ▶ believes emotions make people weak; children must be emotionally tough to survive
- ▶ believes negative emotions are unproductive, a waste of time
- ▶ sees negative emotions (especially sadness) as a commodity that should not be squandered
- ▶ is concerned with the child's obedience to authority

*Effects of this style on children:* Same as the Disapproving Parent style.

## The Laissez-Faire Parent

▶ freely accepts all emotional expression from the child
▶ offers comfort to the child experiencing negative feelings
▶ offers little guidance on behavior
▶ does not teach the child about emotions
▶ is permissive; does not set limits
▶ does not help children solve problems
▶ does not teach problem-solving methods to the child
▶ believes there is little a person can do about negative emotions other than ride them out
▶ believes that managing negative emotions is a matter of hydraulics: Release the emotion, and the work is done

*Effects of this style on children:* They don't learn to regulate their emotions; they have trouble concentrating, forming friendships, getting along with other children.

## The Emotion Coach

▶ values the child's negative emotions as an opportunity for intimacy
▶ can tolerate spending time with a sad, angry, or fearful child; does not become impatient with the emotion
▶ is aware of and values his/her own emotions
▶ sees the world of negative emotions as an important arena for parenting
▶ is sensitive to the child's emotional states, even when they are subtle
▶ is not confused or anxious about the child's emotional expression; knows what has to be done
▶ respects the child's emotions
▶ does not poke fun at or make light of the child's negative feelings
▶ does not say how the child should feel
▶ does not think he/she has to fix every problem for the child
▶ uses emotional moments as a time to
  ▷ listen to the child
  ▷ empathize with soothing words and affection
  ▷ help the child label the emotion he/she is feeling
  ▷ offer guidance on regulating emotions
  ▷ set limits and teach acceptable expression of emotions
  ▷ teach problem-solving skills

*Effects of this style on children:* They learn to trust their feelings, regulate their own emotions, and solve problems. They have high self-esteem, learn well, get along well with others.

---

## ▶ Gottman's Steps for Emotion Coaching

Gottman's five steps for emotion coaching are described in the following pages.

### Step One: Be Aware of the Child's Emotions

For teachers and parents to understand what the child is feeling, they must move beyond their own agendas. Sandi's agenda is for the students to get along with each other and for classroom disruptions to be kept to a minimum. Eddie's agenda is to not look stupid in front of his classmates because, in truth, he finds many of the projects extremely difficult.

Sandi perceives Eddie as a student who cares little about getting along with his classmates and one who deliberately wants to challenge her authority in the classroom. Eddie's outbursts are not acceptable classroom behavior, but they are unlikely to lessen until he understands his feelings and develops some strategies for dealing with them in a more acceptable way. His teacher, however, is unlikely able to act as Eddie's emotion coach because she has assumed the role of disapproving teacher.

Many parents become concerned if their children are not able to establish good relationships with their teachers. As a mother, Jill wants her daughter to get along with her teachers. Still, she is able to move beyond her agenda to understand that Maggie felt mortified when she was reprimanded in front of her entire class. Jill acted as an emotion coach, guiding Maggie to better understand her feelings. Figure 8.2 includes other examples of conflicting parent/teacher agendas and children's feelings.

### Step Two: Consider Negative Emotions as Teaching Opportunities

Negative emotions, our own and those of others, tend to make us uncomfortable. We must not dismiss children's emotions by disregarding, ignoring, or trivializing negative feelings. In particular, adults often trivialize or dismiss a child's feelings while they would not even consider dismissing or trivializing the feelings of another adult. To avoid this, try placing the child's situation within an adult context. Practice by identifying how the child and you would feel in each of the examples shown in Figure 8.3.

We must be sure we don't resort to reprimands or punishment when children express themselves emotionally. (This is not to say that we don't work to help children and youth respond in more socially–emotionally appropriate ways.) Sandi missed a teaching opportunity. By punishing Eddie, she failed to help him learn to understand his feelings and develop appropriate ways of dealing with them. By contrast, Jill didn't dismiss or trivialize her daughter Maggie's feelings of anger toward her teacher and classmates. Instead, she acknowledged her daughter's feelings, then helped her to correctly label them.

### Step Three: Listen Empathetically to Validate the Emotion

Consider the example of Elise, who arrives home after a difficult day at work. During the weekly staff meeting, her boss criticized her performance on a project she

### Situation One

Your 10-year-old son comes into the house screaming about his 6-year-old brother: "I hate Alex. He always follows me and my friends around."

| | |
|---|---|
| *Your agenda:* | You want your children to get along and love each other. |
| *Child's feeling:* | Frustration |
| *Wrong response:* | "Ah, come on, Sam, you know you love Alex." |
| *Emotion coach response:* | "I bet it's frustrating sometimes when Alex trails after you. I think he follows you and your friends because he looks up to you guys. What do you think?" |

### Situation Two

You're busy checking in at the airport. You get boarding passes for you and your 4-year-old daughter Audrey. When you turn around, Audrey is not next to your carry-on bag. You are frantic. When you see a security guard with a crying Audrey in tow, you run to Audrey.

| | |
|---|---|
| *Your agenda:* | You were scared senseless when Audrey disappeared, and you never want this to happen again. |
| *Child's feeling:* | Fear |
| *Wrong response:* | "Audrey, why can't you stay where I tell you to stay!" |
| *Emotion coach response:* | "I was scared when I couldn't find you, and I bet you were scared when you couldn't find me. Let's hold each other, and then we can talk about what happened." |

### Situation Three

Your sixth-grade class is working in social studies groups. Each group is identifying similarities and differences between Argentina, Venezuela, and Chile with respect to demographics, imports, and exports. Michael, who has a learning disability, rockets out of his seat and yells, "You're all stupid, and I'm not staying in this group any more!" Then he runs back to his desk, sits, and puts his head down.

| | |
|---|---|
| *Your agenda:* | You want the students in your class to get along. You rely on cooperative learning groups to enable students to pool their strengths. Michael has a severe reading disability, but he loves social studies and knows a lot about South America because he and his family lived in Brazil for 3 years. |
| *Child's feelings:* | Frustrated and sad |
| *Wrong response:* | "Michael, no student in this class has a choice about which group he's in! Now you get out of your desk, go back to the group, and apologize to your classmates." |
| *Emotion coach response:* | You give Michael a couple of minutes. As the groups get ready to go to recess, you take Michael aside. "You seemed frustrated and kind of sad while you were in your group. What was going on?" |

**FIGURE 8.2** ▶When Parents' Agendas and Children's Feelings Conflict

| Child Example | Adult Example |
|---|---|
| Child is reprimanded by teacher in front of class. | Adult is criticized by boss during staff meeting. |
| *Child's Feeling:* | *Your Feeling:* |
| Child comes home with disciplinary note from teacher. Child's mother says, "What did you do?" | Adult tells spouse that she received a low performance evaluation from her supervisor. Her spouse says, "What did you do to make him do that?" |
| *Child's Feeling:* | *Your Feeling:* |
| Child comes home in tears. "The fifth-grade boys called me a dork." | Adult sees an old neighbor after a long absence. "You sure are a bigger person since last I saw you! I take it your wife is still a great cook!" |
| *Child's Feeling:* | *Your Feeling:* |
| Child says, "I hate those girls. They never invite me over." Her dad says, "You don't really hate those girls." | An adult finds out that everyone is going to a surprise party for a colleague except her. Her friend asks, "What did you do to offend everyone in your office?" |
| *Child's Feeling:* | *Your Feeling:* |

**FIGURE 8.3** ▶ Children's Situations Placed Within an Adult Context

had worked on for 2 months. Clearly upset, Elise tells her husband, "I was so angry I was shaking inside when my boss criticized my work on the Dixon project in front of the entire staff!"

Her husband, Stewart, replied, "You must have done *something* for your boss to criticize you publicly."

We know how we would feel in a similar situation—dismissed, misunderstood, and even angrier! Interactions like this one are true "relationship breakers."

When people experience negative emotions, often the best thing to do is simply listen and let them vent. Listening communicates that we care about the person's feelings, even though we may not approve of how he or she is feeling. Empathetic listening also gives the person an opportunity to calm down and reach a point of being willing and able to solve problems. We have all experienced situations similar to that of Elise. We wanted affirmation, not evaluation.

### Step Four: Help the Child Label the Emotion

As emotion coaches, we give children and youth the *language* of emotions. Being able to correctly label an emotion helps children and youth understand that others have similar feelings; it also makes some feelings less threatening and scary. In our example, Jill helped her daughter Maggie label her feeling as embarrassment.

In Chapter Three we discussed how children and youth develop the ability to make subtle discriminations among positive emotions before being able to differentiate subtle negative emotions. Teachers and parents may have to teach finer gradations within emotion clusters like these examples (Bodine & Crawford, 1999):

> ▶ *Anger:* Fury, outrage, resentment, wrath, exasperation, indignation, vexation, acrimony, animosity, annoyance, irritability, hostility
> ▶ *Sadness:* Grief, sorrow, cheerlessness, gloom, melancholy, self-pity, loneliness, dejection, despair
> ▶ *Fear:* Anxiety, apprehension, nervousness, concern, consternation, misgiving, wariness, qualm, edginess, dread, fright, terror, panic
> ▶ *Surprise:* Shock, astonishment, amazement, wonder, agape
> ▶ *Shame:* Guilt, embarrassment, chagrin, remorse, humiliation, regret, mortification, contrition (pp. 82, 83)

Examples of social–emotional skills curricula that include lessons designed to help children and youth become better able to use words for how they feel include the Connecting with Others Programs (Richardson, 1996a, 1996b; Richardson & Evans, 1997; Richardson & Meisgeier, 2001); Fostering Emotional Intelligence (Doty, 2001); the PATHS curriculum (Kusche & Greenberg, 1994); Self-Science: The Subject Is Me (Stone & Dilleunt, 1978); and the Thinking, Feeling, Behaving programs (Vernon 1989a, 1989b). Table 3.2 in Chapter Three gives a comprehensive listing of programs.

### Step Five: Establish Limits and Teach Problem-Solving Strategies

Emotion coaches help children and youth become better managers of their feelings. Although they validate feelings, they do not condone inappropriate behavior.

Teachers and parents who act as emotion coaches enable children and youth to behave in positive and productive ways by setting limits while considering three behavior zones (Gottman, 1997):

1. The *green zone* encompasses behaviors that are desired and sanctioned.
2. *Yellow-zone* behaviors are not sanctioned but are tolerated to give children and youth some "wiggle room" during exceptional or difficult times. Examples include when a child is extremely tired, when the child's routine changes dramatically, and during times of family crisis.
3. *Red-zone* behaviors are not tolerated under any circumstance. These behaviors are dangerous, immoral, unethical, illegal, or socially unacceptable.

After firmly and consistently establishing limits, emotion coaches teach children and youth problem-solving strategies. Chapter Four outlines ways to help children and youth become effective social–emotional problem solvers. Conducting social skill autopsies is a particularly effective way to teach and reinforce problem-solving skills. When children do or say something that leads to either negative or positive social outcomes, parents can ask questions like those in Table 8.1.

In addition to conducting social skill autopsies, parents can use the FIG TESPN strategy to promote social–emotional problem solving. (FIG TESPN is described in Chapter Four.) *The Raising a Thinking Child Workbook* (Shure, 2000) is another good problem-solving resource for parents. The workbook instructs parents in how to teach young children to resolve conflicts and get along with others.

Emotion coaching is an important skill for parents and teachers to master because coaching helps children understand and regulate their emotions and learn to

**TABLE 8.1** ►Questions to Ask During a Social Skill Autopsy

| Question | Example |
| --- | --- |
| ► What did you say or do? | I borrowed Tim's glove. |
| ► What happened when you said or did it? | He's mad at me and said never to touch his things again! |
| ► Was the outcome positive or negative? | Not very positive—Tim hates me, and I'll never get to use his equipment again. |
| ► Why do you think there was a positive or negative outcome? | Well, I've borrowed Tim's stuff before and he never got mad. This time, though, he wasn't around so I borrowed the glove without asking. I think not asking made him mad. |
| ► What will you do in a similar situation next time? | I should ask him or not borrow it. Or maybe if he's not around, at least leave him a note that I borrowed the glove. |

solve social problems. Some additional strategies parents and teachers can use when coaching are as follows (Gottman, 1997):

1. Avoid excessive criticism, humiliating comments, and mocking.
2. Use scaffolding and praise to coach your child.
3. Ignore your adult agenda.
4. Create a "mental map" of the child's daily life. Know about people in the child's world and how he/she feels about each person. Know the child's various environments (school, community, home, job, and so forth) and how the child feels about each place.
5. Do not side with the enemy.
6. Place the child's experiences within an adult context.
7. Empathize and don't impose your solutions on the child's problem.
8. Give the child choices and the opportunity to assume responsibility.
9. Be honest with the child.
10. Understand your power base as a teacher or parent.
11. Be patient!

We caution that at certain times, parents and teachers should *not* use emotion coaching. These include

- ▶ when you're pressed for time,
- ▶ in front of other people,
- ▶ when you're upset or tired,
- ▶ when a red-zone behavior occurs,
- ▶ when the child fakes an emotion to manipulate. (Gottman, 1997)

## ▶ Seize Social–Emotional Teaching Opportunities

*Jim and April sat at the dinner table and watched as their 16-old-daughter, Shannon, responded to questions with single words—no, yes, yeah. Their old friends from college, Kent and Christie, were trying to engage Shannon in conversation, but without success.*

*Christie tried again. "Shannon, your mom tells me that you're on the soccer team. Is that right?"*

*"Yeah," said Shannon, as she looked at her plate while twisting her hair. Shannon's face was the picture of boredom.*

*Her dad finally reached his limit. Raising his voice, he said, "Shannon, we've had just about enough of your rude behavior. Go up to your room until you learn to be polite to our friends."*

*Shannon got up abruptly, almost knocking over her chair, and ran upstairs to her room.*

*"Sometimes you have to let kids know you're not going to put up with their rude behavior," Jim said, as an uncomfortable silence settled around the table.*

*Nine-year-old David often got angry at his 5-year-old brother, Brian. Like many little brothers, Brian looked up to David and liked to follow him and his friends wherever they went. David considered Brian a pest and got angry when Brian tried to join in to play computer games or asked to play basketball.*

*David's mom and dad both thought David needed to control his anger toward Brian and to work on anger control in general. They thought of situations and times during the day when David was most likely to get angry. Then they came up with some strategies to teach David when he felt angry. They sat down with their son and told him that they used tricks like counting to 10 so they could calm down when they got angry at each other, people at work, or their children. After they calmed down, they could tell the person what he or she did to make them so upset. David's mom and dad told him that using these strategies helped them show self-control. If he would learn to use the strategies, he could show self-control, just like grown-ups do.*

*The next time David's mom saw him start to get angry at his brother, she gently reminded him, "What can you do when you feel angry?" To her surprise, David started to count to 10. After a while, he said, "Brian, I like you, but sometimes I want to play with my friends by myself. We're older, and we like to do older-kid things." David's mom and dad continued to remind or prompt him to use his new strategy. After several weeks, they noticed a real improvement in his self-control.*

Parents (and teachers) have no problem acknowledging that academic skills such as reading and mathematics must be taught; however, they often expect children to develop social–emotional skills spontaneously. Jim decided that Shannon made no effort to make conversation with his friends and labeled her behavior as rude. He responded by punishing his daughter by sending her to her room. (Of course, if Shannon wasn't enjoying the dinner conversation, she may not have considered leaving the table as punishment!)

We recognize that some children and adolescents may *choose* to behave in ways that we find socially unacceptable. Other children, however, don't have the social–emotional skills to make choices. Punishing Shannon by having her leave the dinner table will not teach her the conversational skills she needs to acquire to become a scintillating (or even adequate) dinner guest. Taking time to teach social–emotional skills can have a big payoff for children and their families.

An effective way to teach these skills is to seize teaching opportunities throughout the day by using a technique called incidental teaching (Brown, McEvoy, & Bishop, 1991; Schulze, Rule, & Innocenti, 1989). Table 8.2 provides examples of how social–emotional skills can be incidentally taught throughout the day in a classroom with preschool students with and without disabilities.

Incidental teaching has five steps, each of which is described below. The Incidental Teaching Planning Sheet shown as Figure 8.4 can help parents plan and evaluate incidental social–emotional skills instruction.

**TABLE 8.2** ▶Opportunities to Teach Incidentally in an Inclusive Preschool Classroom

| Activity | Incidental Teaching Direction by Teacher | Child Interactive Response | Anticipated Response from Peer(s) |
|---|---|---|---|
| **PLAY**<br>Billy is playing with blocks and Susie (TC*) is standing and watching. | "Susie, why don't you play with Billy?" "Billy, share the blocks with Susie." | Susie sits down next to Billy and says, "Me play, too." | Susie begins to build a fort of blocks with Billy. |
| **LUNCH**<br>David (TC*) needs help opening a milk carton. | "David, ask Dana to help you open your milk carton." | "Dana, help me, please." | Dana helps David open his milk, and David says, "Thanks, Dana." |
| **TRANSITION**<br>Bill (TC*) needs his chair moved from table to large group. | "Susie, will you be a good friend and help Bill move his chair to large group?" | Susie says, "Bill, I'll help you. Where do you want to sit today?" | Bill walks to the large group with his walker and points next to Susie's chair while Susie moves his chair next to hers. |
| **ARRIVAL**<br>Todd (TC*) has trouble with the buttons on his coat when he comes to school. | "David, remember Todd has trouble unbuttoning his coat. Why don't you show him how you unbutton *your* coat?" | David approaches Todd and says, "Todd, you want to unbutton your coat? Watch me." | Todd nods his head yes and approaches David. Todd watches David unbutton and tries to undo his own buttons the same way. David helps him if necessary. |
| **CLASSTIME**<br>Howard is walking from large group to the snack table | "Oh, Mary (TC*), look, Howard fell down. Let's give him a big hug and make sure he's okay." | Mary and the teacher walk over to Howard. Mary hugs Howard and asks if he's okay. | Howard hugs Mary and says, "Let's go eat." |
| **FINE-MOTOR ACTIVITY**<br>Paul (TC*), who is mute but can work complex puzzles, is working on a 20-piece puzzle. | "Look, Paul, Al needs help with his puzzle. Show him how to work it." | Paul shows Al where a piece of the puzzle goes and smiles. | Paul and Al take turns putting in pieces of the puzzle. After completing the puzzle, Al says, "We did it." |

*TC = Target Child

Source: "Incidental Teaching of Social Behavior: A Naturalistic Approach for Promoting Young Children's Peer Interactions," by W. H. Brown, M. A. McEvoy, and N. Bishop, in *Teaching Exceptional Children, 24*, 36. Copyright © 1991 by Council for Exceptional Children. Reprinted by permission.

Parent _____ Child _____

Step One: Select the social-emotional skill(s) to be taught:

_____
_____
_____

Step Two: Identify potential teaching times and situations:

_____
_____
_____

Step Three: Identify ways to prompt skill use:

_____
_____
_____

Step Four: Identify reinforcement strategies:

_____
_____
_____

Step Five: Evaluate the performance of you and your child

How did I prompt?

_____
_____

How did my child respond?

_____
_____

How did I reinforce my child?

_____
_____

What kind of feedback did I give my child?

_____
_____

Will I do anything differently next time?

_____
_____

**FIGURE 8.4** ►Incidental Teaching Planning Sheet for Parents

## Step One: Select the Social–Emotional Skill to Be Taught

Based upon personal observation, and the observations of others, parents can select specific social–emotional skills from which their children can benefit. These skills include those described in previous chapters as helping children and adolescents understand emotions, make friends, and get along with teachers and classmates. For example, Shannon clearly needs to learn how to make conversation. (Specific ways to teach conversational skills are presented in Chapter Five.) David's parents observed that he often succumbed to angry feelings rather than showing self-control. (Strategies to help children and youth control their anger are included in Chapter Three.)

Teaching skills that parents, teachers, and other children highly value have the greatest payoff because children will be positively regarded when they use these skills. Positive regard leads to using skills often, which in turn allows children to practice and become more proficient. Some of these skills are sharing, accepting criticism, giving and receiving compliments, understanding the feelings of others, controlling anger, listening, following directions, and taking conversational turns.

## Step Two: Identify Potential Teaching Times and Situations

After identifying the skill, try to anticipate situations and times during the day when you can teach it. Table 8.3 lists some critically important skills at home and school, along with situations and times during the day when they may best be taught. Parents and teachers also have to identify times during the day when it is difficult or impossible to teach social–emotional skills. Examples for parents include when family members are trying to get out of the door in the morning, at the end of the day when parents and children are tired, or when a parent is busy trying to get dinner on the table. Teachers will not be able to incidentally teach social–emotional skills when they are involved in whole-class instruction or when students are taking timed tests.

## Step Three: Identify Ways to Prompt Skill Use

Parents and teachers use prompts to remind children and adolescents to use a needed social–emotional skill. The three kinds of prompts are verbal, visual, and physical.

1. *Verbal prompts.* An example of a verbal prompt is when a parent reminds a child to say "thank you" by saying things like, "What do you say when someone pays you a compliment?" or "What do you say when someone gives you something?" Examples of other verbal prompts are:

    ▶ Now might be a good time to listen carefully so you can follow directions.
    ▶ What skill do you think will work in this situation?
    ▶ Don't you think it would be nice to share your toys with Dionne?

    Also, use of a code such as "Do Turtle" will remind young children to use their anger-control routine (see Chapter Three).

**TABLE 8.3** ▶Times and Situations in Which to Teach Skills

| Skills to Teach | Situations/Times in Which to Teach |
| --- | --- |
| *Sharing* | Playing a game as a family<br>Playing a game with brother/sister<br>Completing an art project<br>Playing with a visiting child<br>Receiving a new toy or game |
| *Accepting Criticism* | Soccer coach criticizes performance<br>Dad criticizes how chore is performed<br>Mom criticizes appearance<br>Employer criticizes job performance<br>Friend criticizes behavior during a game |
| *Taking Turns During Conversation* | In the car on the way to school<br>At the dinner table<br>When friends come to visit<br>When adults come to visit<br>When meeting a new person |
| *Listening* | When asked to do a chore<br>When asked to take a phone message<br>When family members talk with the child<br>When asked to get the weather report<br>When asked to help with food preparation |

2. *Visual prompts.* As an example of a visual prompt, a teacher might show Todd a picture of a yellow caution light to remind him that he is starting to lose control and should count to 10. We have a "Quiet Please" light that flashes when the noise level in the classroom gets too loud. Angie might point to her eyes to remind her child to engage in eye contact when having a conversation. Or parents could use a prearranged signal, such as pointing to their chest, to remind their child to think about another person's emotional state.

3. *Physical prompts.* Young children and children with disabilities sometimes do not respond to verbal or visual prompts. In these cases, parents and teachers can rely on *physical prompts* to guide the child to use the skill. For example, if Carla fails to share her stuffed animals with a visiting child, her parent might say, "Carla, wouldn't it be nice to share your bear with Stacy?" while holding Carla's arm to extend the bear to Stacy.

Prompts do not *cause* children and adolescents to use social–emotional skills, but when used effectively, they can dramatically increase the odds that a child will use them. Jotting down a couple of verbal, visual, or physical prompts on the planning sheet helps prompting to become much more automatic. Physical prompts should be used as a last resort because these prompts make children dependent upon adults. Ultimately, the goal is for children and adolescents to use social–emotional skills independently *without* being reminded. Only when they reach this level of independence will they use social–emotional skills appropriately throughout the day, irrespective of our presence.

## Step Four: Identify Reinforcement Strategies

*Reinforcement* means rewarding or responding to children positively after they use a social–emotional skill. For example, if we greet a neighbor each morning when we go out to get the paper, we will continue to greet the neighbor if she responds positively to our greeting (smiles, nods, greets, etc.). If we barely receive a grunt, however, we likely will stop saying "Good Morning!" before long because we did not receive positive reinforcement.

Although common types of reinforcement are food, money, toys, and other tangible items, we recommend relying on *praise* for several reasons. First, most children and youth respond positively to praise. Second, and even more important, praise is socially appropriate. What better reinforcement to use during social–emotional skills instruction than a *social reinforcer!* Finally, praise occurs naturally during social intercourse, whereas few friends or co-workers are apt to ply you with food following a good deed or a job well done!

At the same time, we need to recognize that some children and youth are resistant to praise, and that we may have to "up the reinforcement ante." In this case, *activity reinforcers* are often effective. Activity reinforcement means letting a child engage in a favorite activity such as playing Nintendo, going to the movies, getting extra playtime after school, and so forth, after he performs a social–emotional skill, usually for a specified number of times. For example, David and his parents agreed that he could take a friend to the movies on Saturday if he had two or fewer angry episodes with his brother Brian.

We like activity reinforcers because, unless they involve solitary activities such as playing computer games, they require children to engage in social interaction.

The Incidental Teaching Planning Sheet in Figure 8.4 can be used to come up with ways to reinforce the skill you are incidentally teaching. For example, Brian's parents could write down these praise statements:

▶ David, I'm really proud of you. You showed self-control and dealt with your anger well.
▶ You're really acting mature. By controlling your anger, you're acting like a grown-up!
▶ David, you did a great job of controlling yourself. I know that having Brian follow you around all of the time can be frustrating. But he looks up to you and by showing self-control you're a good role model.

The important thing is for parents to write down the words so they won't have to think too hard about what to say when the child or adolescent uses the targeted social–emotional skill. Of course, parents must remember to praise their child any time he or she uses any social–emotional skill appropriately!

### Step Five: Evaluate the Performance of You and Your Child

Finally, parents must evaluate how well they taught the child when they first begin to incidentally teach. Use the Incidental Teaching Planning Sheet (Figure 8.4) to focus on the following:

▶ *How did I prompt?* Did you use the prompts you prepared? Did you use verbal prompts? Nonverbal prompts? Did the prompts sound natural?

▶ *How did my child respond?* Did your child use the social–emotional skill when provided with a verbal or visual prompt? Did performance require that you physically prompt?

▶ *How did I reinforce my child?* Did you use the reinforcers you thought you would use? Did your child respond to praise? Did your praise sound natural? Did you use an activity reinforcer?

▶ *What kind of feedback did I give my child?* Feedback is a critique of the child's performance. For feedback to lead to improvements in skill performance, it must be specific and informative. The child must be given information about what he or she did correctly and what the child needs to improve. Think of how you learned a new skill, such as tennis, painting, or Thai cooking. The tennis instructor critiqued your serve so you could become a better server. The painting instructor gave you pointers about how, by using a variety of brushes, you could more effectively create an illusion of a tree. The cooking instructor told you that your use of herbs and spices in the Tom Yum Kung (Hot and Sour Shrimp) was just right.

▶ *Will I do anything differently next time?* Overall, how do you think you did? Are there areas in which you think you need improvement (e.g., use of praise, reinforcement, feedback)? How can you become a better incidental teacher?

## ▶ Include Social–Emotional Objectives in Your Child's IEP

In addition to addressing social–emotional skills at home, parents should ask schools to address their children's social lives. The individualized education program (IEP) is the obvious vehicle for addressing social–emotional issues facing children and youth with disabilities (Simpson, 1996). Although many of the suggestions that follow specifically address how parents can help schools address the social–emotional needs of their children with disabilities, many parents of children without disabilities will find these strategies equally appropriate.

Parents must communicate to school personnel that they regard their children's social emotional–development to be just as important as their academic progress. Siperstein and Bak (1988) offer these suggestions when developing IEPs:

▶ *Be sure that the child's IEP contains social–emotional objectives.* Often, IEP objectives focus on improving academic rather than social–emotional skills.

▶ *Be sure that the social–emotional objectives focus on improving peer interactions as well as developing teacher-pleasing behaviors.* When IEPs *do* include social– emotional objectives, they often are skills of value to teachers rather than children.

▶ *Be sure that the specific strategies that will be used to improve social–emotional skills are described.* For instance, approaches might include teaching social–emotional skills using a commercial curriculum such as Skillstreaming in Early Childhood (McGinnis & Goldstein, 2003), teaching the child to use the FIG TESPN problem-solving strategy (see Chapter Four), and conducting social skill autopsies throughout the day. Strategies should enable special and general education teachers to work together so the children learn to use social– emotional skills in each class.

▶ *Be sure that the social–emotional skills are actually being taught.* In addition to asking for updates regarding mastery of IEP objectives, request frequent updates through teacher-to-home notes, telephone calls, e-mail messages, and face-to-face meetings. IEPs must include procedures that will be used for evaluating the mastery of objectives. For example, if the goal for a socially withdrawn child is to increase conversational interactions with peers, an objective means of determining this increase must be outlined within the IEP.

▶ *Support staff-development opportunities that help teachers teach social–emotional skills appropriately and effectively.* With the increasing emphasis on academic instruction, many special and general education teachers are not trained to teach social–emotional skills. Let administrators know that you value social–emotional skills instruction, and expect teachers to be as well versed in the social curriculum as they are in the academic curriculum. Serve on school committees, advisory boards, and attend PTO meetings and parent–teacher conferences. Recommend some of the books included as Appendix A in this text.

▶ *Collaborate with teachers to teach social–emotional skills.* Using the same or compatible approaches at home and school will help children learn skills more rapidly.

▶ *Communicate frequently with teachers to inform them about social–emotional successes and failures at home and in the community.* Teachers must know if using the skill is generalizing from school to home. Parents also can inform teachers if their child needs certain social–emotional skills outside of school.

## ▶ Supporting Friendship

Friendships are extremely important to children because friends provide affection, companionship, a sense of intimacy, a dependable alliance, and self-validation (Thompson et al., 2001). Although parents cannot make friends for their children, there are many ways they can support and nurture friendships. As Thompson et al. (2001) note, "If parents can learn to recognize, support, and celebrate children's friends, they will give their sons and daughters a great social foundation" (p. 12). Before adopting support strategies, it is important for parents to put children's friendships in perspective. The box on pages 244–245 offers some pointers for parents to better understand children's friendships.

---

# Friendship Pointers for Parents

### Get to Know Your Child's World

▶ Observe your child. Listen to your child: Does he ever talk about other kids? Does she complain about the way other kids treat her? Aggressive kids are always complaining that social problems are someone else's fault.

▶ Talk to your child. In the most matter-of-fact voice you can summon, ask your child what he/she is doing, and with whom. Get a picture of your child's daily life. Some questions to ask:

> ▷ "How did things go today?" or "Tell me—what was your day like?"
> ▷ "Who do you like in your class?" and "What do you like about ___?"
> ▷ "Who is nice in your class?" and "Who is mean?"
> ▷ "Who are your friends?"
> ▷ "What kinds of things do you like to do together with your friends?"
> ▷ "Who in your class really likes you?" and "How do you know?"
> ▷ "Who do you think doesn't like you?" and "How do you know?" and "What kinds of things do you say to him/her?"
> ▷ "What do you do during breaks?"
> ▷ "Do you ever wish you had more friends?"

▶ Listen to your child. Smile at your child. Touch your child. Nod in response to your child's conversation. You are modeling the social skills you want your child to develop and also are constructing a base from which your child can feel safe to explore the world. You also will learn when social problems may require more support.

▶ Demonstrate that you have all the time in the world to hear what your child has to say. Turn off the phone, or at least turn on the answering machine. Or go for a walk in the woods. Then your child will feel comfortable enough to reveal his/her world. Children often do not bother talking about their life if they pick up a signal that their parents aren't paying full attention. And it's amazing what they will tell you if they think you won't punish them or be angry or disappointed in them for what they say. Have a conversation, rather than give a lecture.

## Ask Your Children How Peers Treat Them

▶ Children are often ashamed or afraid to bring up the subject, so parents must.
▶ Ask your child to tell you something good that happened that day. Then ask him/her to tell you something bad that happened.
▶ One way to get children to talk about hurtful social experiences they may be having is to talk about past experiences of your own: "Did I ever tell you about the time my best friends threw rocks at me—how terrible it felt?"
▶ Read books about friendship—the Frog and Toad series, the George and Martha series— or watch videos such as *Harriet the Spy* together. As you do, ask your child to think about how the character was feeling, and ask, "Has anything like that ever happened to you?" You can do this only when children are open to it, and not in a "teachy" way.
▶ When you suspect that something might be an issue and that your child's feelings were hurt but he/she isn't talking about it, describe a hypothetical situation. Explain the reasons for the social behavior, and ask, "What do you think a person should do?"

## What to Do When a Child Says, "No One Wants to Play With Me"

▶ Take it seriously, and be thankful your child trusts you enough to confide this distressing information.
▶ Don't try to persuade him/her that it couldn't possibly be true; that only convinces a child that you can't be trusted with such sensitive information.
▶ Tread gently. Children who are being picked on feel ashamed, and they blame themselves for their difficulties. They are reluctant to talk to parents in the first place, for fear of being reprimanded. Your child's feelings on this matter are not trivial.
▶ Engage your child in a conversation about any recent changes in his/her social milieu. Is your child being picked on? Has a bully joined the class?
▶ Talk to the teacher to find out what is going on in school. Ask the teacher for advice. But don't stop there.
▶ Find out from our child what social tasks she has the most trouble with, and together explore and rehearse steps your child can take.

## Don't Blame Your Child for Peer Problems

Social relationships are complex. Most people require a lifetime to master these. Sometimes even a lifetime is not enough!

Source: *Pointers for Parents.* From *"Why doesn't anybody like me?": A guide to raising socially confident kids* (pp. 13–15), by H. E. Marano, 1998, New York: William Morrow and Company. Copyright © 1998 by Hara Estroff Marano. Reprinted by permission of HarperCollins Publishers Inc.

## Enlisting Others' Help

Before becoming concerned about a child's peer relationships, parents should seek out opinions of teachers and other parents. They should consider if their expectations are reasonable, taking into account the child's personality and developmental level. There is a big difference between friendship and popularity. While only 15% of children fall into the popular group, having even one friend can provide all of the benefits of friendship (Thompson et al., 2001).

## Twenty-Five Ways Parents Can Help Their Children Make Friends

1. Be a friendship role model and friendship teacher.
2. Make friends with the parents of your children's friends and enemies.
3. Model a broad view of friendship and avoid friendship stereotypes such as limiting friendship based on age, gender, and ethnicity. Cross-generational and cross-cultural friendships help children develop a wide array of social–emotional skills.
4. Help kids not to engage in "turn-off" behavior (bragging, saying unkind things about friends, embarrassing friends in front of others) and engaging in "befriendably" behavior (keeping promises, letting people know they like them, listening, apologizing when wrong or when there are hurt feelings, helping friends, returning things, talking over problems with friends, sharing things, knowing friends' likes and dislikes).
5. Tell your child when he/she is being a good (or not-so-good) friend. Go with a child and a friend (or potential friend) to lunch, the mall, or another activity. Observe how the child relates. At an appropriate time at home, conduct a social skill autopsy: Review what happened, and give the child feedback.
6. Make sure the children's clothing and hairstyle "fit" with peers'.
7. Be a matchmaker. Help your child to identify other children he/she would like to be friends with, and provide opportunities for them to form friendships.
8. If you have just moved, invite neighborhood children over and introduce yourself to their parents.
9. Make your child's peers welcome in your home. Talk to them, compliment them, and invite them back!
10. Scout out what children do after school and on weekends by talking with other parents, teachers, recreation department personnel, and so forth.
11. Help your child connect by teaching him/her how to join a group.
12. Be a confidence-builder by finding out your child's interests and encouraging these and new interests.
13. Think before placing a child with social–emotional weaknesses in a potentially embarrassing situation. For example, if a child has a hard time in large groups, build up to this situation gradually by arranging situations that allow him/her to build relationships with one or two peers at first. Take the child to the place where the Cub Scout or Girl Scout troop meets and introduce him/her to the troop leader so your child will feel more comfortable and confident when he/she attends the first meeting.

Still, parents should know where their child stands in the group.

> Sixty percent of children are going to be in the popular or accepted categories at school; another 20 percent are classified as ambiguous but are not considered at risk. The 4 percent of neglected children who have made that one vital friend by the end of elementary school are considered to be out of harm's way. That leaves approximately 15 percent who are at risk. If your child is one of these kids, you have to face this painful fact and wade in to help before your child drowns. (Thompson et al., 2001, pp. 257, 258)

14. Provide friendship opportunities at school, church, and in the neighborhood. Let adult leaders know that the child has social weaknesses before the child participates in activities such as camp, Scouts, or clubs. Ask the leader to monitor the child's interactions to prevent rejection.
15. Allow children with social–emotional weaknesses, especially those who are shy and withdrawn, the option of solitude. For some children, entertaining themselves reduces stress.
16. Give kids opportunities to make friends through extracurricular activities and the development of lifelong interests. Sports, in particular, provide opportunities for kids to make friends. Learning to play a musical instrument such as an electric guitar may provide friendship opportunities. For younger children, parents can meet other parents to set up play dates.
17. Teach kids to play board games as a way to work on social skills, and the kids will have something they can do with other kids.
18. Encourage kids to invite friends on family outings.
19. Discourage kids from joining cliques; the happiest kids are those with one or two close friends.
20. Encourage kids to use e-mail to keep connected.
21. Ask teachers and other parents for feedback to find out how well your child gets along with other kids.
22. Work with your child's teachers to teach and support social–emotional skills at home and school.
23. If there are social–emotional problems, take action by teaching these skills yourself and making sure they are taught and reinforced in school.
24. In the case of serious problems, consider if the child should be enrolled in social skills groups or if the child and/or family needs counseling or therapy.
25. Recognize that when other skills, such as the ability to attend or to control anger, improve, social–emotional skills improve as well.

---

Sources: *Best Friends, Worst Enemies: Understanding the Social Lives of Children,* by M. Thompson, C. O. Grace, and L. J. Cohen (New York: Ballantine Books, 2001); *Emotionally Intelligent Parenting: How to Raise a Self-Disciplined, Responsible, Socially Skilled Child,* by M. J. Elias, S. E. Tobias, and B. S. Friedlander (New York: Harmony Books, 1999); "Learning to Be a Friend," by N. Parello, in *Working Mother, 19*(10), Oct. 1996, 75, 78–79; "Phenomena Related to Poor Adaptation" (pp. 211–241), by M. Levine, in *Educational Care: A System for Understanding and Helping Children with Learning Problems in Home and School,* by M. Levine (Cambridge, MA: Educators Publishing Service, 1994); "12 Secrets to Raising Popular Kids," by K. A. Larson, in *McCall's, 94,* pp. 100–101.

Chapter Five offers additional strategies for promoting and supporting friendships specific to the stages of early childhood, middle childhood, and adolescence. The book *Good Friends Are Hard to Find* (Frankel, 1996) contains excellent suggestions for helping children find, make, and keep friends, as well as how to deal with bullying and general meanness.

---

# ▶ Using Literature to Support Social–Emotional Learning

Literature offers an excellent way to support social–emotional learning (Gottman, 1997). When Linda taught adolescents with learning disabilities, she began to read to them to get them interested in literature and reading independently. She read stories by Edgar Allen Poe, including the *Telltale Heart* and the *Fall of the House of Usher,* and books such as *Alive,* which chronicled the ordeal of a Chilean soccer team whose plane crashed in the Andes. The subject matter is on the macabre side (e.g., the soccer team resorts to cannibalism in *Alive,* and family members are buried alive in *Fall of the House of Usher*), but was high on the interest scale of the mostly adolescent boys. At the end of the period after students had completed their assignments, the reading period became a reward.

Many parents and teachers stop reading to children when the children learn to read on their own. This is a shame, as many older children enjoy being read to when books address topics of interest. Parents can use books to help children and youth understand their emotions and the emotions of others, become better social problem solvers, and learn about friendship and how to be a friend. Films and television shows may be used in similar ways.

## Using Literature to Increase Emotional Understanding

Parents can select books from the list provided in Appendix B to help children and adolescents understand their emotions and the emotions of others. While reading, ask questions such as:

▶ How does the character feel?
▶ Have you ever felt that way? If so, when?
▶ How do you know the character feels that way?
▶ Why do you think he or she feels that way?
▶ How would you feel if you were in that character's situation?

Other strategies that parents can use to increase emotional understanding are described in Chapter Three.

## Using Literature to Improve Social–Emotional Problem Solving

In Chapter Four we discussed a process for using literature to teach social–emotional problem-solving skills. Parents are encouraged to use the Book Talks format introduced in that chapter to help children and adolescents analyze social–emotional problems confronted by the story characters. Chapter Four includes a process for using bibliotherapy to teach social–emotional problem solving. In addition, parents can ask these questions when reading to their children:

▶ What is the character's problem?
▶ Have you ever had a similar problem? Tell me about it. How did you solve it?
▶ How do you think the character might be able to solve his/her problem?
▶ How did he/she try to solve the problem? What do you think will happen? Did the solution work?
▶ What do you think the character will do next time he/she has a similar problem?

### Using Literature to Promote Friendship Skills

Books such as *We Are Best Friends, Are We Still Friends?, Will You Be My Friend?, New Neighbors,* and *Wendy and the Bullies* illustrate friendship-making and friendship-keeping skills, as well as how to make friends in a new neighborhood or school and how to deal with aggressive children who bully and intimidate. Older children will enjoy *Whose Side Are You On?* and *Fried Green Tomatoes at the Whistle Stop Café.* Parents can use the guidelines provided in Chapter Five to teach friendship skills. When reading, parents should ask these questions:

- ▶ How did the characters make friends/keep friends?
- ▶ What kind of friendship skills did the characters have?
- ▶ Can you describe these skills? Can you break them down into steps?
- ▶ Do you know how to perform that skill? Show me.
- ▶ Can you give me some examples of when you would use these skills?

## ▶ Chapter Summary

We cannot overemphasize the importance of parents being involved in their children's social–emotional development. For many children and youth, acquiring social–emotional skills is a slow and arduous process. If these children are to stand a chance of reaching competency, parents have to take on the role of social–emotional skills instructor. The underlying theme of emotionally intelligent parenting is that what parents *do* is much more important than what they *say.* By adopting the five principles of emotionally intelligent parenting—being aware of feelings, showing empathy, regulating emotions, setting goals, and using positive social–emotional skills—parents are in a strong position to help their children become more socially–emotionally skilled. Parents can use social skill autopsies and incidental teaching to fit in social–emotional skills instruction into their busy days. By reading to their children, parents can help children understand emotions and solve social problems.

# CHAPTER 9

# Getting Children and Youth to Use Social–Emotional Skills

## Goals of This Chapter

In reading this chapter, you will learn

▶ the factors that affect generalization of social–emotional skills

▶ how to link social–emotional and academic skills instruction

▶ the advantages of co-teaching social–emotional skills

▶ how cooperative learning, incidental teaching, self-management strategies, and homework help children and youth learn and use social–emotional skills

▶ how to implement social–emotional learning programs at school- and districtwide levels

# Terms to Know

behavior clusters

cooperative learning

co-teaching

curriculum matrix

generalization

infusion model

integration model

reinforcement

school constitution

self-management strategies

stimulus control

thematic learning

topography

*Bill and Rachel were making a real effort to teach and reward their son, 12-year-old Ben, for carrying on a conversation. They worked on Ben's conversational give-and-take during car trips and at the dinner table. They had begun to notice improvements in Ben's ability to listen, share information, express interest in others, and stay with a conversation. Therefore, his behavior at the picnic really had them stymied. The Hancocks, who just moved in next door, invited them to share a casual supper on their deck. The Hancock kids were the same age as Ben and his brother, Mark.*

*During the cookout Ben sat on the sidelines. Attempts by the Hancocks to engage him in conversation were met with grunts and yeahs and no's. Bill and Rachel met with similar responses. When they walked into their house, Bill could no longer contain his embarrassment and frustration with his son. "What's the matter with you? You acted like a jerk at the Hancocks. I'm sure they think you're really unfriendly. Why didn't you at least try to talk to the Hancock kids?"*

*"I don't know those people, Dad. I don't have anything to say to them," was Ben's honest reply.*

Although we have been successful in teaching many children and youth social–emotional skills, we have been far less successful at promoting *generalization,* or use of skills across people, settings, and situations (Brown & Odom, 1994; Forness & Kavale, 1996; Hundert & Houghton, 1992; Kavale & Forness, 1996; Kavale & Mostert, 2004; Quinn, Kavale, Mathur, Rutherford, & Forness, 1999; Rahill & Teglasi, 2003; Rosenthal-Malek & Yoshida, 1994; Scott & Nelson, 1998; Sheridan, Hungelmann, & Maughan, 1999; Smith & Gilles, 2003; Torrey, Vasa, Maag, & Kramer, 1992). One reason the generalization of social–emotional skills is so difficult is that these skills are complex and require extraordinary attention to detail when planning for generalization to the natural environment.

To illustrate, Scott and Nelson (1998) offer the example of the many nuances and subtleties of handshaking. The topography, or shape, of handshaking depends on the familiarity of the person to be greeted, whether the encounter occurs in a formal or an informal setting, time of day, type of setting, cultural environment (e.g., business/peer culture, majority/minority culture), and so forth. How do we account for all of these permutations when we plan and deliver social–emotional skills instruction? How do teachers and parents get children and youth to use social–emotional skills when and where they count?

As an example, most of us are able to generalize "clothes-washing behavior." Our washing machine may be a top loader with a dial that is pulled out to start the wash cycle. Other dials control the water level and the temperature. When using a Laundromat on vacation, we would have little difficulty figuring out how to operate a front-loading washing machine with a dial that is pushed in to start the wash cycle. Similarly, we have a good idea of how to navigate strange airports because of our knowledge of "airportness." We are able to generalize check-in, boarding, and baggage pick-up behaviors whether we are in an airport in New York City, Los Angeles, London, or Singapore. We know the airport *script.*

If individuals are unable to generalize, learning is difficult because each situation and setting is novel. Ben's being with people other than members of his family, and in a place other than his own home, made it difficult for him to use the conversational skills his parents had helped him develop. In addition to teaching Ben conversational skills, Bill and Rachel also should teach their son to use strategies to promote generalization of those skills.

In this chapter we describe ways to increase the chances that children and youth will use social–emotional skills when and where they are appropriate. We begin by discussing factors that affect children's use of social–emotional skills across individuals, situations, and settings. We go on to talk about the importance of linking social–emotional and academic skills instruction and offer specific ways to make this connection. We also discuss the advantages of teacher collaboration when delivering social–emotional skills instruction and recommend cooperative learning, incidental teaching, and self-management as powerful instructional strategies. We close the chapter by underscoring the importance of home–school–community collaboration and suggest ways to deliver social–emotional skills instruction on schoolwide and districtwide levels.

# ▶ Factors That Affect Generalization

Factors affecting generalization of social–emotional skills include instructional setting, skill selection, stimulus control, and reinforcement. Much of the information we present here is based upon the seminal work of Stokes and Baer (1977) and Stokes and Osnes (1986).

## Instructional Setting

If instruction of social–emotional skills is restricted to a single place such as the general education or the special education classroom, children will not likely use the skills in other settings. Ideally, we need to teach children and youth social–emotional skills in natural settings where prosocial behavior occurs. If this is not possible, teachers and parents can promote generalization by the following:

▶ *Arranging the physical environment to resemble the natural setting.* For example, a special education teacher could arrange the resource room to look like the student's general education classroom.

▶ *Assigning role-play situations that occur at school, at home, in the community, or on the job.* For example, when teaching conversational skills, Ben's parents could ask him to come up with different situations in which he would be expected to make conversation. Or they could suggest situations such as meeting a new classmate or talking to guests who come for dinner as times to use his newly acquired skill.

▶ *Using schedules of reinforcement similar to those in the natural setting.* Upon learning that reinforcement rarely occurs in an employment setting, a job placement coordinator, for example, could make a point of gradually reducing the amount of reinforcement students receive for using appropriate social–emotional skills in the classroom.

## Skill Selection

Social–emotional skills that are highly valued by peers and adults alike are more apt to be reinforced and to endure over time (Stokes & Osnes, 1986). Selecting skills presented in Chapters Five, Six, and Seven helps ensure that children and youth learn behaviors valued by others. As mentioned, teachers, parents, peers, employers, and co-workers also may be interviewed to identify relevant skills. Or teachers and parents might observe natural settings to determine which social–emotional skills are reinforced.

## Stimulus Control

A behavior is under stimulus control when it occurs in the presence of a certain stimulus or condition but not in the presence of other conditions. For example, a child's behavior is under stimulus control when the child speaks in a "quiet voice" in the library but not on the playground.

When teaching a new behavior, it must be brought under stimulus control by using standardized instructional procedures and requiring mastery before teaching new behaviors. *Teaching tightly*—or teaching each skill directly and repetitively— helps students learn new skills but does little to promote generalization of social–emotional skills to new people, settings, and situations. A child may use a "quiet voice" in the library but not when visiting a relative in the hospital.

Teachers and parents can overcome the negative effect of stimulus control by *teaching loosely* (Brown & Odom, 1994; Smith & Gilles, 2003), such as:

▶ *Using instructional language similar to language children and youth encounter in the natural setting.* If teachers use formal language when teaching peer-pleas- ing skills such as sharing or giving a compliment, children may have a hard time using these skills when they actually are with their peers.

▶ *Using a variety of models and role players.* When the same person models every skill or the same individuals enact all role plays, children begin to associate using certain skills with only those individuals. Having many different people model and role-play skills helps children and youth generalize those skills across a variety of individuals.

▶ *Teaching several skills at the same time.* Many social–emotional skills form *behavior clusters.* For example, conversational skills include body basics such as eye contact, appropriate tone of voice, and so forth; decision-making skills such as deciding who to speak with and what to talk about; knowing how to begin and end a conversation; and engaging in conversational give-and-take. By gradually introducing new skills as children approach mastery of earlier introduced skills, we encourage them to use a variety of skills at school and home. This also leads to more reinforcement opportunities, which in turn strengthen use of the skill.

▶ *Teaching social–emotional skills throughout the day.* If social–emotional skills are taught only during a prescribed class period, children and youth are unlikely to use them the rest of the day. Teachers and parents can promote use of skills by capitalizing on teachable moments. Approaches such as teaching incidentally and conducting social skill autopsies make social–emotional skills instruction an all-day affair.

▶ *Integrating social–emotional skills instruction within the curriculum.* When children learn to read, they use this skill across subject areas. The more they read, the better they read. When social–emotional skills instruction is incorpo- rated within subject areas such as social studies, science, and language arts, chil- dren and youth have more opportunities to acquire and use these skills.

## Reinforcement

Reinforcing a child each and every time he or she performs a social–emotional skill helps the child to continue to use the skill and become more proficient at using it.

Once a skill is mastered, however, generalization is promoted by using different reinforcement strategies. Rarely in life do we receive immediate and consistent reinforcement.

To prepare children and youth for a world of delayed, inconsistent, and sometimes nonexistent reinforcement, teachers and parents must adjust the schedule, source, amount, and nature of reinforcement. By using *intermittent schedules of reinforcement* (not reinforcing each and every time a social–emotional skill is performed), *delayed schedules of reinforcement* (not reinforcing immediately following skill performance), and *thin schedules of reinforcement* (not frequently reinforcing), teachers and parents will encourage generalization of social–emotional skills to school, home, and community settings. Because our goal is for children and adolescents to have positive social interactions, reinforcers must be of the natural variety, such as enjoying conversation, having fun playing a game, and the like (Scott & Nelson, 1998).

# ▶ Instructional Approaches That Promote Generalization

In the following, we describe instructional approaches that promote generalization. These approaches include integrating curricula, co-teaching and collaboration, cooperative learning, incidental teaching, teaching children and youth self-management strategies, and assigning homework.

### Integrating Curricula

*A fourth-grade teacher, Margaret, was struck by the difficulties her students had in getting along with one another. They teased each other unmercifully and zeroed in with laser precision on each other's shortcomings. From discussions with other teachers, Margaret learned that this group of kids, by and large, had been together since kindergarten and had plenty of time to hone their skills of making one another angry and upset.*

*"If things are this bad in September, this is going to be a long year," sighed Margaret. For what seemed the hundredth time, she had just sat down with two students to determine what precipitated an angry exchange of insults.*

*Margaret was a firm proponent of teaching students social–emotional skills. She also was a realist and knew that to be effective, she had to incorporate her instruction within the academic curriculum. Embedding social–emotional skill instruction within the social studies and language arts curricula would allow Margaret to meet her dual goals of establishing a positive class climate and teaching students skills they would need on the statewide accountability exam in March.*

As teachers, we recognize the importance of integrating academic instruction (writing, reading, mathematics) across the curriculum to avoid fragmentation. When teaching social–emotional skills, however, we sometimes make the mistake of not integrating these skills with academic skills. Curriculum integration serves two purposes:

1. *It enables teachers to fit social–emotional instruction into the school day.* We know that teachers are more likely to teach social–emotional skills if they are able to teach the skills within the context of academic subjects (Forgan & Gonzalez-DeHass, 2004; Forness & Kavale, 1996; Gresham et al., 2001).

2. *It helps children generalize social–emotional skills across settings and situations.* Stimulus control of social behavior is avoided when children and youth use social–emotional skills in language arts, social studies, and science classes (L. K. Elksnin, 1994; L. K. Elksnin & N. Elksnin, 1995).

Next we will describe some strategies that teachers can use to teach social–emotional skills in an interdisciplinary fashion. These strategies include adopting infusion and integration models and developing curriculum matrices.

### Infusion Model

Reisberg (1998) and Williams and Reisberg (2003) describe an infusion model that supports inclusion of students with disabilities in general education classes by teaching social–emotional skills through curriculum integration as shown by Figure 9.1. These authors suggest that teachers do the following:

1. *Determine the focus of the theme, unit, chapter, or subject to be taught.* Williams and Reisberg selected the American Civil War as the unit of instruction.

2. *Identify additional disciplines and topics to be included in the plan and record them on a curriculum matrix or semantic web.* The topics in Figure 9.1 include famous battles, political figures, slavery, important dates, political events, and economics.

3. *Identify the specific skills and knowledge that will be taught in each of the disciplines or topics included in Step 2.* Williams and Reisberg (2003) selected social–emotional skills that decreased reliance on violence and aggression. These skills included active listening, empathic listening and responding, sending "I" messages, anger management, and problem solving. Children learn anger management using the CALM strategy (p. 208):

   C  Can you tell when you're starting to get upset and angry?
   A  Are there any techniques you can use to help calm yourself down?
   L  Look at those, choose the best one, and try it!
   M  Monitor yourself. Is it working? If it is—great! If not, try it again or try another one.

| VIP Social Skill | Content Unit: Civil War | | | | | |
|---|---|---|---|---|---|---|
| | Famous Battles | Political Figures | Slavery | Important Dates | Political Events | Economics |
| Active Listening | 1 | | | 1 | | 1 |
| Empathic Listening & Responding | | | 2 | | | |
| "I" Messages | | | 2 | | | |
| Anger Management (CALM) | | | 2 | | | |
| Problem Solving (ICAN) | | 3 | | 4 | 5 | |

Instructional Arrangements:

1 = Large-group didactic  2 = Small groups with adult  3 = Independent in-seat
4 = Small groups without  5 = Pairs                    6 = Other
    adult

Source: "Successful Inclusion: Teaching Social Skills Through Curriculum Integration," by G. J. Williams and L. Reisberg, in *Intervention in School and Clinic, 36*, p. 208. Copyright © 2003 by Pro-Ed. Reprinted by permission.

**FIGURE 9.1** ►Social–Emotional Skills—Academic Skills Curriculum Matrix

Problem solving was taught using the ICAN strategy (p. 208):

**I**   Identify your problem.
**C**   Can you name some solutions?
**A**   Analyze those—how do you think they will work?
**N**   Now, pick one and use it! If it worked, great! If not, try it again or try another one.

4. *Gather resources and materials for the students.* Resources for the Civil War unit might include:

- ▶ high school textbook
- ▶ nonfiction books written by Bruce Catton (e.g., *Mr. Lincoln's Army of the Potomac, Glory Road*) and Shelby Foote (e.g., *The Civil War*)
- ▶ fiction books such as Stephen Crane's *The Red Badge of Courage*
- ▶ autobiographies such as *Narrative of the Life of Frederick Douglass, An American Slave,* an autobiography; and *Incidents in the Life of a Slave Girl* by Harriet A. Jacobs
- ▶ movies such as *Glory, Gettysburg, Gone with the Wind,* and *North and South*
- ▶ videos such as Ken Burns's *Civil War*
- ▶ speakers, including historians from local colleges and universities

5. *Develop learning activities and lessons that address the skills and information.* When planning lessons, teachers should think about instructional arrangements, ways for students to practice the skills, ways for students to demonstrate mastery, and methods that will be used to evaluate student learning (Reisberg, 1998). As shown by Figure 9.1, Williams and Reisberg (2003) identified topics and instructional arrangements (i.e., large-group didactic, small groups with adult, independent in-seat, small groups without adult, pairs) that would be used to teach each social–emotional skill. Developing a matrix allows teachers to logically match social skills with theme units and assignments.

Doty (2001) used a similar approach, *thematic learning,* to infuse emotional intelligence skills within the academic curriculum. She regards the characteristics of academic intelligence and emotional intelligence as separate, yet inextricably intertwined constructs. Academic intelligence includes knowledge and skills such as

- ▶ math facts and concepts,
- ▶ vocabulary words,
- ▶ global understanding,
- ▶ scientific processes,
- ▶ written and oral communication.

Emotional intelligence includes disposition and feelings such as

- ▶ cognizant awareness of self and others,
- ▶ approval of self and others,
- ▶ self-responsibility,
- ▶ personal meaning,
- ▶ honesty and ethics. (Doty, 2001, p. 12)

Thematic learning requires that all subject-area and emotional intelligence skills and objectives revolve around a theme such as the Revolutionary War. As shown in

Figure 9.2, critical emotional intelligence skills are integrated within lesson objectives in the areas of reading, mathematics, writing, and science.

### Integration Model

Rather than using a theme or a unit to determine which social–emotional skills are infused, teachers can begin by identifying social–emotional and general academic skills to be taught (Korinek & Popp, 1997), then match skills and integrate them within the general curriculum.

    Complementary academic and social skills include those listed in Table 9.1. For example, if working in cooperative groups is a general academic skill required in many classes, the teacher could teach social–emotional skills that facilitate group work, such as taking turns, sharing, accepting criticism, and offering feedback. Teachers can use a planning sheet like the one shown as Figure 9.3 to identify subject areas, lesson objectives, and ways to tie in emotional intelligence skills such as emotional problem solving and emotional understanding.

| Subject | Lesson Objective | Emotional Intelligence Integration |
|---|---|---|
| Reading/ Language Arts | Students compare and contrast colonist and British points of view with a Venn diagram. | Students share Venn diagram results orally and discuss what actions the colonists took based on their strong beliefs. |
| Math | Students chart battles and casualties. | Based on numbers of casualties, was freedom worth the price they paid? Students discuss this. |
| Writing/ Language Arts | Students write a letter to a relative in England. | Students explain their feelings and actions as colonists who want freedom from England. |
| Science | Students collect data to determine who actually fired the first shot at Lexington. | Students discuss the question: Were there alternatives to this issue other than war? |

Source: "Sample Theme: Revolutionary War," from *Fostering Emotional Intelligence in K–8 Students* (p. 15), by G. Doty (Thousand Oaks, CA: Corwin Press). Copyright © 2001 by Corwin Press. Reprinted by permission of Corwin Press, Inc.

**FIGURE 9.2** ▶Sample Theme: Revolutionary War

**TABLE 9.1** ▶Complementary Academic and Social–Emotional Skills

| Academic Skills | Social–Emotional Skills |
| --- | --- |
| Understanding of scientific method | Predicting social–emotional outcomes |
| Writing a persuasive argument | Negotiating with others |
| Participating in class discussions | Conversational skills |
| All academic skills | Social–emotional problem-solving skills |
| Working in cooperative groups | Taking turns, sharing, accepting criticism, offering feedback |

Source: "Collaborative Mainstream Integration of Social Skills with Academic Instruction, by L. Korinek and P. A. Popp, in *Preventing School Failure, 41*(4), 148–153.

Certain subject areas lend themselves naturally to teaching social–emotional skills, and literature offers an excellent means of teaching social–emotional skills such as problem solving and understanding emotions (Forgan & Gonzalez-DeHass, 2004).

The *social skill literature strategy* (SSLS) integrates social–emotional skills within the literature curriculum (Anderson, 2000). Using the SSLS worksheet shown as Figure 9.4, students

- ▶ identify main events;
- ▶ identify characters, characters' emotions, and emotional cues/signals;
- ▶ generate alternative outcomes for at least one event had characters behaved differently;
- ▶ have their work checked by the teacher, paraeducator, or peer.

### Curriculum Matrix

Another alternative that enables teachers to coordinate academic and social–emotional skills instruction is to develop a curriculum matrix. The teacher can start by listing, on the left side of the page, the social–emotional skills he or she wishes to teach. Across the top of the page the teacher lists subject areas or specific objectives for a subject area. He or she then determines if a specific social–emotional skill can be addressed within a subject area or a subject area objective. Figure 9.5 is a matrix that illustrates how anger-control lessons presented in the program *A Volcano in My Tummy* (Whitehouse & Pudney, 1996) may be integrated within speaking/listening, reading, spelling, writing, drama, and art.

More recently published programs often link social–emotional and academic skills. For example, Kellner (2001) includes activities to connect anger-management skills to subject areas such as science, math, health, civics, language arts, art, music,

| Subject | Lesson Objective | Emotional Intelligence Benefits |
|---|---|---|
| Reading | Cause and effect | The teacher reads various passages from well-known stories. Students determine the cause and effect. The class discusses how the characters could have solved their problems in more appropriate ways. |
| Writing | Personal narrative | During essay writing, students have the opportunity to share a time in their lives when they reacted appropriately in a bad situation. |
| Social Studies | Understanding the Confederate point of view in the Civil War | In cooperative groups, students discuss the feelings and emotions of the Confederate soldiers. |
| Health | Smoking cessation | A class discussion in which students are given the chance to discuss the loss of a loved one because of conditions resulting from tobacco use. |

Source: "Sample Planning Sheet," by G. Doty, in *Fostering Emotional Intelligence in K–8 Students* (p. 14). (Thousand Oaks, CA: Corwin Press). Copyright © 2001 by Corwin Press. Reprinted by permission of Corwin Press, Inc.

**FIGURE 9.3** ▶Sample Planning Sheet

and dance. Children learn about the physiology of anger by studying its effects on different body systems (e.g., circulatory system, respiratory system, skin). A connecting activity involves having the school nurse take each child's blood pressure (health/science) and chart and graph the results (math) to compare the effects of anger and stress on blood pressure.

## Co-Teaching and Collaboration

*Melissa and Jenny were ecstatic about their co-teaching arrangement. When their principal asked them to think about co-teaching in the fall, they were skeptical. Since becoming a special education teacher, Melissa had operated out of her resource room, where her students with learning disabilities came for direct instruction and help with their content-area classes. Melissa wasn't sure she wanted to give up her autonomy. Besides, she had heard horror*

| Play: *Romeo and Juliet* | Author: *Shakespeare* | Act *3* Scene *1* |
|---|---|---|

**Step #1: Interpreting Events**

| What were the main events? | Consequences? | Cross-Check |
|---|---|---|
| 1. *Tybalt fights Mercutio* | *Mercutio dies* | + |
| 2. *Romeo fights Tybalt* | *Tybalt dies* | + |
| 3. *Prince exiles Romeo* | *Romeo and Juliet separated* | + |

**Step # 2: Interpreting Feelings and Signals**

| Characters | Emotions Experienced | Signals | Cross-Check |
|---|---|---|---|
| *Tybalt* | *anger & revenge* | *drawing sword* | + |
| *Mercutio* | *anger* | *drawing sword* | + |
| *Romeo* | *love, anger, & revenge* | *words, pp. 100–105* | + |
| *Benvolio* | *fear* | *works, pp. 123–125* | + |

**Step #3: Developing Alternative Outcomes**

| Character's Actions or Events | Outcome | |
|---|---|---|
| *If Tybalt had not started the fight . . .* | *Romeo and Juliet would not have been separated.* | + |

Source: "Using Literature to Teach Social Skills to Adolescents with LD," by P. L. Anderson, in *Intervention in School and Clinic*, 35, 2000, p. 276. Copyright © 2000 by Pro-Ed. Reprinted by permission.

**FIGURE 9.4** ▶ Social Skill Literature Strategy Worksheet

stories of special education teachers becoming glorified teacher assistants during co-teaching.

    Jenny also had doubts about co-teaching. She wasn't sure she wanted another teacher in her seventh-grade language arts classroom. She had a good relationship with her students, and she didn't think another adult would add much to the class.

    What changed the minds of these two teachers were conversations they had with successful co-teachers who touted the advantages of sharing expertise, ideas, and management. Melissa saw an additional potential advantage: Year

| LESSON | Speaking/ Listening | Reading | Spelling | Writing | Drama | Art |
|---|---|---|---|---|---|---|
| 1 A Volcano in My Tummy (6 yrs. +) | ✓ | | | | | ✓ |
| 2 Bottling Anger (9 yrs. +) | ✓ | | | ✓ | | |
| 3 Are You a Volcano? (6 yrs. +) | ✓ | | | ✓ | | |
| 4 The Anger Rules (6 yrs +) | ✓ | | | | | ✓ |
| 5 Dirty Anger/Clean Anger (6 yrs. +) | ✓ | | | ✓ | | |
| 6 Craig's Angry Day (7 yrs. +) | ✓ | ✓ | | | | |
| 7 The Inside Story (7 yrs. +) | ✓ | ✓ | | | | ✓ |
| 8 Technoparent (8 yrs. +) | ✓ | ✓ | | ✓ | | |
| 9 Time Out (7 yrs. +) | ✓ | | | | | |
| 10 Safe Ways of Getting Angry (8 yrs. +) | ✓ | | | ✓ | | |
| 11 Creative Anger (6 yrs. +) | | | | | | ✓ |
| 12 Tension Scale (6 yrs. +) | ✓ | | | ✓ | | |
| 13 Magic (7 yrs. +) | | | | ✓ | ✓ | |
| 14 Role Playing (8 yrs. +) | | | | | ✓ | |
| 15 The Four Levels of Muscle (8 yrs. +) | ✓ | | | ✓ | | |
| 16 Shields (6 yrs. +) | ✓ | | | | | ✓ |
| 17 Kalmic and the Angry Alien (8 yrs. +) | ✓ | ✓ | | ✓ | | |
| 18 Cold Water Words (6 yrs. +) | ✓ | | | ✓ | | |
| 19 Grudge Jar (7 yrs. +) | | | | ✓ | | |
| 20 Anger Vocabulary (6 yrs. +) | | | ✓ | | | |
| 21 Swearing (6 yrs. +) | ✓ | ✓ | | ✓ | | |
| 22 Problem Solving (6 yrs. +) | ✓ | | | | | ✓ |
| 23 Aggroscenario (9 yrs. +) | ✓ | | | ✓ | | ✓ |
| 24 Anger in the World (10 yrs. +) | ✓ | ✓ | | | | ✓ |
| 25 We Can Make a Difference (10 yrs. +) | ✓ | | | ✓ | | ✓ |

Source: "Curriculum Integration," from *A Volcano in My Tummy: Helping Children to Handle Anger* (p. 17), by E. Whitehouse and W. Pudney (Gabriola Island, British Columbia, Canada: New Society Publishers). Copyright © 1996 by the Foundation for Peace Studies. Reprinted by permission.

**FIGURE 9.5** ▶Curriculum Integration

*after year she had become more and more concerned that her students were unable to use the skills they learned in her resource program in their general education classrooms. Co-teaching presented an opportunity to teach academic and social–emotional skills in the natural setting. Jenny shared Melissa's concerns, particularly as they related to her students' prosocial skills. Co-teaching would offer the advantage of two adults who together could model social–emotional skills and conduct role plays.*

Social–emotional skills instruction is a natural fit with *co-teaching* (Warger & Rutherford, 1993, 1996). After agreeing to co-teach, teachers can work together to

▶ select students to be taught,
▶ select skills to be taught,
▶ identify inappropriate behaviors (i.e., aggression, inattention) that have to be addressed,
▶ determine if the student cannot or will not perform the skill (see Chapter Two for a discussion of acquisition versus performance problems) so they can plan appropriate instruction. (Rutherford, Chipman, Di-Gangi, & Anderson, 1992)

In their program, *A Collaborative Approach to Teaching Skills,* Warger and Rutherford (1996) refined this model. Co-teachers work through three phases (shown as Figure 9.6) as they plan and deliver social–emotional skills:

*Phase One.* Co-teachers decide which skills to teach. Teachers can teach all or some of the 22 social–emotional skills related to success in the classroom identified by Warger and Rutherford, or they can choose skills from other programs. After skills are identified, the co-teachers identify the steps for each. They then decide if instruction will be given to an individual student, a small group of students, or the entire class. Finally, co-teachers develop an assessment plan.

*Phase Two.* Co-teachers decide how to teach each skill. Although teachers can rely on their creativity and personal teaching style, they should use this five-step model:

(1) Direct teaching of the social skill steps
(2) Modeling
(3) Practice
(4) Social reinforcement or feedback
(5) Self-control

For each skill, co-teachers identify all the times during the day that students can practice the skill. Co-teachers review the skill steps and prompt students to use newly acquired skills during appropriate times.

*Phase Three.* Co-teachers plan how they can help students to take responsibility for their own behavior.

Phase 1: *Develop Curriculum*
- ▶ Identify social skill to be taught
- ▶ Define social skill as observable behavior
- ▶ Determine performance based assessment

Phase 2: *Plan and Implement Instruction*
- ▶ Directly teach the social skill
- ▶ Provide for application

Phase 3: *Self-Control*
- ▶ Student monitors, evaluates, and provides self-reinforcement
- ▶ Evaluate instructional success

Source: "A Collaborative Approach to Teaching Social Skills Framework," from *A Collaborative Approach to Teaching Social Skills* (p. 21), by C. L. Warger and R. Rutherford, Jr. Copyright © 1996 (Reston, VA: Exceptional Innovations). Reprinted by permission.

**FIGURE 9.6** ▶Framework for a Collaborative Approach to Teaching Social Skills

A *teaming approach* to co-teaching of social–emotional skills emphasizes the need for careful instructional planning (Alsopp et al., 2000). Teacher teams

1. decide skills to be taught,
2. identify steps taken to perform a skill,
3. develop an instructional plan.

When developing the plan, teachers need to decide

- ▶ where skills will be taught,
- ▶ what types of groups (i.e., large versus small) will be formed,
- ▶ how children will be taught,
- ▶ how children will practice skills,
- ▶ types and amount of reinforcement to be used,
- ▶ how students will be taught to monitor and evaluate their use of the skill.

To be effective in any co-teaching situation, teachers need collaboration skills, time to plan, and support to include social–emotional skills instruction in the general education curriculum. In addition, parental support is important to reinforce skills at home and in the community. When co-teaching arrangements are not possible, we encourage teachers to consider how they can collaboratively teach social–emotional skills in their individual classrooms. When setting objectives for working with other school personnel, it can be helpful to create a planning sheet, including such topics as personnel to work with, objectives for collaborative work, and some areas to work on (Knapczyk & Rodes, 1996).

## Cooperative Learning

*The sixth-grade teacher, Vic, was seeing cooperative learning pay off in spades. Students' academic and social skills showed marked improvement. He had adopted* Learning Together *(D. W. Johnson & R. T. Johnson, 1975), which involved having heterogeneous groups complete assignment sheets individually and as a group. The group sheet was turned in and served as the basis for his evaluation. In addition, Vic gave each group and each member of the group specific feedback about how they were learning together.*

*The groups ran much more smoothly this year because Vic had taught his students essential prosocial skills, including cooperating, listening, giving positive and negative feedback, <u>before</u> the groups started to meet. In addition, students learned about group roles and were assigned a specific role during each cooperative learning activity. Vic smiled when he thought of how students jockeyed to assume the roles of "information seeker," "opinion seeker," "elaborator," "coordinator," "orienter," "evaluator," and "recorder" (Goldstein, 1999).*

*Cooperative learning* involves having heterogeneous groups of students work together to complete a task or project. Several models of cooperative learning are available. We recommend consulting D. W. Johnson and R. T. Johnson (1975) and Slavin (1983) for information about how to implement cooperative learning in the classroom.

Cooperative learning promotes social–emotional skills such as altruism and cooperation and offers opportunities for students to help and reinforce one another (Goldstein, 1999; Hawryluk & Smallwood, 1988). It also can lead to acceptance of students with disabilities by their nondisabled peers and encourage the development of cross-racial friendships (L. K. Elksnin & N. Elksnin, 1995). While students are engaged in cooperative learning activities, teachers can monitor and reinforce the use of skills and provide students with feedback.

For cooperative learning to be effective, students must be taught directly skills that will improve their academic productivity and social interactions. Social interaction and communication skills needed to participate in cooperative learning groups include the following (D. Johnson, R. Johnson, Holubec, & Roy, 1984; Whittaker, 1996):

▶ *Forming level skills:* using group members' names, avoiding "put-downs," keeping up with the group, using a quiet voice
▶ *Functioning level skills:* giving directions, requesting clarification, expressing support
▶ *Formulating level skills:* summarizing, elaborating
▶ *Fermenting level skills:* giving and accepting criticism, integrating divergent viewpoints, identifying conflict

Prater, Bruhl, and Serna (1998) found that students with learning disabilities benefited from direct instruction of essential cooperative learning skills. Students learned skills such as listening, problem solving, and negotiating much more readily if teachers identified skill steps rather than having students generate the steps. Kagan (1992) reported similar results, concluding that "many students lack the social skills needed to function successfully in a cooperative group. Deliberately teach these skills using discussion, modeling, and practice and provide for evaluation of them during a regular group processing time" (p. 37).

Several commercial programs are available that teach students how to cooperate in groups and to work effectively in teams. The Center for Research on Learning at the University of Kansas developed materials to teach cooperative thinking and teaming strategies. For example, the SCORE skills program (Vernon et al., 1996) teaches students strategies for sharing ideas, complimenting others, offering help/ encouragement, recommending changes nicely, and exercising self-control. The Teamwork Strategy (TEAMS) (Vernon, Deshler, & Schumaker, 1993) consists of these steps:

1. **T**alk about Tasks
2. **E**xecute Your Job
3. **A**sk and Share
4. **M**ake It Great
5. **S**urvey Your TEAM'S SCORE

Each step of TEAMS requires that students use previously mastered SCORE skills.

Goldstein (1999) offers exercises that teachers can use to teach students to cooperate in the PREPARE curriculum. He also devotes a chapter to how to teach older students about group processes in order to understand and use groups. Topics include how groups develop, resolving conflicts, group member roles, group climate, and power tactics.

To participate in groups, whether formal groups such as cooperative learning groups or informal groups such as play groups, children and youth must understand the "laws of group life" (Thompson et al., 2001):

> ▶ People want to be like their peers. The downside is that this law often promotes "group think." Group think makes it difficult for people to make independent, individual moral decisions.
> ▶ People would rather affiliate with a group, even one considered deviant or "uncool," than go it alone.
> ▶ People usually prefer to affiliate with individuals with whom they share common interests.
> ▶ People want to know "their place" in the social hierarchy.
> ▶ People play roles assigned by forces of the group.
> ▶ Groups punish people who break the rules of the group. Punishment includes teasing and name calling; exclusion, rejection, and "scapegoating;" bullying; and hazing. (Thompson et al., 2001)

Teaching children and youth about the realities of group life will enable them to make conscious choices about how and when to affiliate with a group.

Working in groups provides children and youth with opportunities to learn and practice social–emotional skills. Teachers and parents can structure environments to promote positive aspects of working in groups. For example, Forgan and Jones (2002) developed the Project Adventure curriculum to teach children about team-work. The curriculum incorporates outdoor education, experiential learning, and group counseling techniques. Children play adventure games according to Full Value Contract (FVC) rules, which require each child to

- ▶ work as a team member toward team goals;
- ▶ keep each other emotionally and physically safe;
- ▶ give and receive honest feedback (in a kind and unthreatening manner);
- ▶ refrain from devaluing anyone, including yourself;
- ▶ get over "it" (whatever may upset a team member during the activity). (p. 55)

After playing the game, the teacher debriefs students by asking how they liked the game, if they played according to FVC rules, what issues helped them improve their social–emotional skills, and how they could apply what they learned to the academic classroom.

Thompson et al. (2001) described how a music teacher involved everyone in the eighth grade in producing "You're a Good Man, Charlie Brown." By involving students, teachers, and staff members, the school became much more cohesive. Similarly, Dasho, Lewis, and Watson (2001) described how a "Family Science Festival," which turned a school into a hands-on science museum, created a spirit of camaraderie among teachers, parents, and children in the Oakland, California, schools in which half of the parents' first language was not English. The festival had a much more positive impact than the traditional competitive "Science Fair," which often included parent-made projects.

## Incidental, Co-Incidental, and Opportunistic Teaching

*Phil stood on the playground and watched his third graders. It was a beautiful spring day—warm, sunny, and breezy. The teacher observed Roger try to join a group of four boys who were shooting baskets.*

*"Can I play with you?" asked Roger.*

*The boys ignored his request. After asking two more times, Roger whined, "Why can't I play ball with you?"*

*Lenny stopped dribbling and turned to stare at Roger. "I'll tell you why. You can't shoot and you're a mama's boy."*

*Roger's face flushed, and he said, "I can shoot, and you can't stop me from playing. I'm going to tell Mr. Ogden, and he'll make you play with me!"*

*When Roger approached his teacher, Phil asked him to take a walk with him. Phil began to ask Roger some questions: "Okay, what did you want to happen when you talked to the boys? What went wrong? Why do you think Lenny acted the way he did?"*

*With the help of his teacher's questions, Roger began to analyze the events that led to his being rejected and decided that running to his teacher was not going to help him get along with his classmates.*

The terms *incidental teaching, co-incidental teaching,* and *opportunistic teaching* are all used to describe social–emotional skills instruction that takes advantage of "teaching opportunities" (Kohler et al., 2001). We prefer the term *incidental teaching.* Brown et al. (1991) defined incidental teaching as follows:

> Incidental teaching is different from more structured instruction in that it is conducted during unstructured activities for brief periods of time and typically when children show an interest in or are involved with materials, activities, or other children. (p. 36)

Brown et al. offer these suggestions when using incidental teaching:

▶ *Identify children who will benefit from incidental teaching* (i.e., *target children*). Children who tend not to socially interact often make good candidates.

▶ *Identify situations in which to use incidental teaching.* Likely situations include cooperative learning, on the playground, in the cafeteria, at the learning center, and so forth.

▶ *Plan how to encourage social interaction.* Examples include use of physical prompts, verbal prompts, and so forth.

▶ *Be sure that there is sufficient time to implement incidental teaching during unstructured activities.* For example, incidental teaching may take a backseat if the teacher's primary goal is to understand group dynamics through observing cooperative learning groups.

▶ *Anticipate potential problems.* For example, teachers may want to avoid assigning volatile students to the same group.

▶ *Be aware of potentially reinforcing situations.* For example, one child may like to use the art center, and another may enjoy doing science experiments.

▶ *Systematically encourage target children to interact with more socially proficient peers.* Encourage socially proficient peers to socially interact with target children.

▶ *Privately provide target children with specific, informative feedback following social interactions.* Tell the child precisely what he/she did well and not so well.

Incidental teaching promotes generalization of social–emotional skills because it can be used to address social–emotional issues *when they occur* at school or at home. Charney and Kriete (2001) described the day a teacher discovered the sixth-grade boys' list of "cool girls." The teacher recognized that the list had the potential for reinforcing existing class cliques. Rather than admonish the boys for creating the list, the teacher saw the situation as an opportunity and led the class in a conversation about dissemination of lists. When conducting class discussion, teachers can use Charney and Kriete's guidelines, given in Figure 9.7.

Another type of incidental teaching involves conducting a social skill autopsy. As you will recall from Chapter Four, when conducting an autopsy, children say what they said or did that resulted in a positive or negative social outcome, what happened when they said or did it, whether the social outcome was positive or negative, and what they will do when faced with a similar situation in the future.

---

▶ *Think about the situation and set up the meeting. Speak with individuals, groups, or the whole class before the meeting, if appropriate.*

Prepare the class for discussion and information that will help guide discussion. In a case like the "cool girls" list incident, the teacher could speak with authors of the list to discuss its potentially negative effects on the class and let the students know that she would like the entire class to discuss the list. She could approach girls who were and were not included on the list to understand their feelings.

▶ *Establish ground rules for discussion.*

Introduce these *guiding principles:*
  – Listen to what a classmate has to say.
  – Speak one at a time.
  – Respect opinions that are different from your own.
  – Remain open to changing your point of view.

▶ *Identify the topic.*

Describe the issue, and tell the class that you have set aside time in class to discuss it. For the list example, the teacher could tell the class that she saw a copy of the "cool girls" list and it made her think about how lists are used in general.

---

**FIGURE 9.7** ▶ Charney and Kriete's Guidelines for Conducting Discussion About Social–Emotional Issues

▶ *Ask questions not specific to the situation at hand.*

Ask questions that relate to the general nature of the issue at hand. General questions about lists could include: "What are some examples of lists?" "Why are lists created?" "When is it 'okay' to disseminate lists?" "What's the difference between private lists and public lists?" "Is it okay for celebrities to be on positive/negative lists (e.g., best/worst dressed, best/worst actor)?"

▶ Guide discussion and allow for different viewpoints.

Ask questions that will make students consider different perspectives on the issue. The teacher could ask, "Why was the 'cool girls' list created?" "How do you think people in class felt about the list?" "How did you feel about the list?" "Do you think it was a good idea?"

▶ *Help students to gain perspective.*

Ask questions that force students to think about the issue. For example, the teacher could ask, "How do we evaluate people?" "What external characteristics do we use to evaluate people?" "What internal characteristics do we use?" "Are there famous people who are 'cool' who were not 'cool' when they were younger?"

▶ *Help students come up with alternatives.*

Share personal experiences that illustrate how you came up with alternatives: "When we were younger, my parents asked me and my four brothers and sisters to write down each other's unique characteristics. We complained about it, but when we sat down and thought about each brother and sister, we identified some really interesting aspects of each person. My brother Tom was fearless. Sometimes this got him into trouble, but we each knew that Tom would defend us to the death. Kathryn was very shy but she was the most tenacious of all of us." Then ask questions that relate to the issue at hand, such as "What are ways we can acknowledge people's strengths/positive characteristics?"

▶ Use role reversals and strategies that promote role playing.

The teacher could say to the class, "Hey—want to see my list of the best kids in the class?"

Source: "Creating a Classroom Community Where Social Emotional Learning Thrives: The Case of the 'Cool Girls' List," by R. Charney and R. Kriete, in *Caring Classrooms/Intelligent Schools: The Social Emotional Education of Young Children* (pp. 77–84), edited by J. Cohen (New York: Teachers College Press, 2001).

**FIGURE 9.7** ▶(Continued)

## Teaching Self-Management Strategies

Our goal is for children and youth to use social–emotional skills when and where appropriate. Shifting responsibility for instruction and reinforcement from the teacher or parent to the child is an effective way to promote generalization and accomplish this goal (Warger & Rutherford, 1993). Self-management strategies include self-talk, self-monitoring, self-reinforcement, and self-recording. Schloss (1987) describes some of the advantages of self-management strategies:

> A youth with strong self-management skills is able to identify and alter potentially disruptive social behavior independently. The procedures he or she uses may be remarkably similar to those developed by the teacher. The major difference is that the youth develops and implements the procedures independently by selecting target behaviors, identifying provoking events, managing provoking events, learning coping skills, and arranging supporting consequences. (p. 40)

Children use *self-talk* to remind them to perform a social–emotional skill. For example, a youth taught to introduce himself might use self-talk when he goes to a party while visiting a cousin in another town.

*I'm going to be around a lot of people I don't know. It would be good if I remember to introduce myself by saying my name and where I go to school and telling the other people I'm glad to meet them. I probably shouldn't shake hands unless I'm meeting someone's parents. Kids would think shaking their hands was weird.*

*Self-monitoring* involves keeping track of one's own behavior. For example, a child might keep track of the number of times she compliments another student.

*I set a goal of giving five compliments today. I gave four compliments—one to my friend Stan about his new shoes, another to my sister for her new haircut, one to Ms. Starvos about her necklace, and another to Stan about winning the basketball game. I almost met my goal, and I think I did a good job of using the steps I learned in my resource class. I decided what I wanted to compliment the person for. I decided how I would compliment the person. I decided a good time and place to compliment the person. I was sincere when I complimented the person. Overall, I think I did a pretty good job, outside of missing my goal by one compliment.*

As shown in the above example, self-monitoring often involves *self-recording*, keeping a written record of social–emotional skills performed in a specific setting during a prescribed period of time; and *self-evaluation*, determining if social–emotional skill performance criteria were met. A self-recording form appears as Figure 9.8.

Name _____ Date _____

Social–Emotional Skill _____

Skill Steps:

1. _____

2. _____

3. _____

4. _____

5. _____

6. _____

7. _____

8. _____

Make a tally mark each time you use the skill:

I used this skill _____ times.

I would like to use this skill _____ times.

I can use this skill when:

1. _____

2. _____

3. _____

_____

Source: "Self-Recording Form," adapted from *Teaching Occupational Social Skills* (p. 50), by N. Elksnin and L. K. Elksnin (Austin, TX: Pro-Ed). Copyright © 1998 by Pro-Ed. Reprinted by permission.

**FIGURE 9.8** ▶Self-Recording Form

One reason that generalization of social–emotional skills is challenging is that children and youth may not be reinforced even after their behavior changes for the better (Scott & Nelson, 1998), and therefore are discouraged in using social–emotional skills over time and across settings. Teachers and parents can teach children to recruit reinforcement by pointing out their positive behavior to peers, teachers, and parents. Of course, care must be taken to be sure that kids do not over-use this strategy and turn into braggarts. *Reinforcement recruitment* will increase the probability that others will notice and compliment behavioral change. Another strategy is to teach children and adolescents to use *self-reinforcement,* a practice frequently used by adults (Brown & Odom, 1994). Teachers and parents can teach children to tell themselves vocally or mentally, "good job," "way to go," and so on.

### Assigning Homework

As with academic skills, social–emotional skills are more apt to generalize when children and youth practice using these skills in a variety of situations and settings. Homework formalizes practice opportunities. In some cases, expecting homework to be carried out at home is unrealistic because of lack of parental support or other factors. We use the term *homework* to refer to any social–emotional skill practice opportunity that occurs outside of the instructional setting, such as the cafeteria, playground, gym, hallway, classroom, workroom, and so forth. Homework assignments should be teacher-directed, planned extensions of classwork that focus on previously mastered skills (Heller, Spooner, Anderson, & Mims, 1988). *Every* homework assignment has to be evaluated by *someone* (i.e., a teacher, a paraeducator, a parent, or a classmate).

Many commercial curricula include a homework component, including ASSET (Hazel et al., 1996), the PREPARE curriculum (Goldstein, 1997), *Skillstreaming the Adolescent* (Goldstein & McGinnis, 1997), *Skillstreaming in Early Childhood* (McGinnis & Goldstein, 2003), and *Skillstreaming the Elementary School Child* (McGinnis & Goldstein, 1997).

Figures 9.9 and 9.10 are examples of forms that may be used when assigning homework. Figure 9.9 is an assignment sheet designed for younger children. The child writes down the skill steps, and the teacher checks for accuracy before the child leaves class. After performing the skill outside of class, the child evaluates his/her performance and records the outcome. Older children can use the form shown in Figure 9.10 to obtain feedback from teachers, parents, and classmates.

# Home–School–Community Collaboration

### Getting Parents Involved

We wrote this book for parents and teachers alike because social–emotional skills instruction is much more powerful when there is home–school collaboration (Elias

Name: *Sean Adams*        Date: *May 12*

Skill to be practiced:        *Dealing with Teasing*

Steps:        1.  *Stop and count to 5.*

        2.  *Think about choices:*
            a.  *Ignore.*
            b.  *In a nice way, tell the person how you feel.*
            c.  *Tell the person why to stop.*

        3.  *Do your best choice.*

Where I did it:        *At Cub Scouts*

How I did:        *Pretty good. Mike stopped.*

What happened:        *Mike stopped teasing me.*

Source: Adapted from "Teaching Social Skills to Students with Learning and Behavior Problems," by L. K. Elksnin and N. Elksnin, in *Intervention in School and Clinic, 33*, p. 137. Copyright © 1998 by Pro-Ed. Reprinted by permission.

**FIGURE 9.9** ▶Assignment Sheet for Younger Students

et al., 1997; L. K. Elksnin & N. Elksnin, 2000). Parents can become involved in the social–emotional learning (SEL) of their children in several ways. One way is to send home newsletters like the one shown in Figure 9.11, informing parents of the advantages of SEL and ways they can help support SEL at home. Several programs offer specific strategies parents can use to teach their children social–emotional skills. Mannix (1998) includes parent pointers for each social-emotional skill taught to adolescents, such as the following for "Being a Good Listener":

▶ When giving instructions, keep it short and simple. Ask for confirmation of what your child thinks he or she is supposed to do.

▶ Sometimes a simple "Got it?" might be enough to cue your child to quickly focus on what he or she is supposed to remember.

▶ Don't forget to use eye contact. When passing between errands and household, tasks don't rush so much that you and your child miss the moment of actually connecting!

Name _____

Date Assigned _____     Date Completed _____

*Assignment:* Perform the social–emotional skill three times outside of class. Before you perform the skill, ask a teacher, parent, or classmate to observe. After you perform the skill, ask the person to evaluate you by circling the best description of your performance.

Social–Emotional Skill _____

Social–Emotional Skill Steps

1. _____
2. _____
3. _____
4. _____
5. _____
6. _____
7. _____

Observer #1 Name _____ Location_____
☐ Excellent job (all steps performed)
☐ Good job (most steps performed)
☐ Needs improvement (steps left out and/or performed in incorrect order)

Observer #2 Name _____ Location_____
☐ Excellent job (all steps performed)
☐ Good job (most steps performed)
☐ Needs improvement (steps left out and/or performed in incorrect order)

Observer #3 Name _____ Location_____
☐ Excellent job (all steps performed)
☐ Good job (most steps performed)
☐ Needs improvement (steps left out and/or performed in incorrect order)

**FIGURE 9.10** ▶Assignment Sheet for Older Children

## Introducing the Program

## *Helping your child be successful!*

### The *Promoting Social Success* Program

Your child is beginning a new program at school. The *Promoting Social Success* program teaches children the social skills they need in order to be successful at school and at home. Teaching children social skills is very important. Social skills are essential for both academic success and healthy self-esteem.

Many children have difficulty making friends and may act out in ways that interfere with their learning. However, the *Promoting Social Success* program can help your child get along with others and control his or her behavior.

This program teaches children to

1. Better understand and deal with their emotions
2. Calm down when upset or overexcited
3. Accurately "read" social situations
4. Problem solve independently
5. Be a good friend

You will receive updates about what your child is learning and what you can do with your child to reinforce these skills at home.

I↑ is fun to have friend.

### The First Unit

After several introductory lessons, students will begin working on lessons about emotions and behavior. Lessons ask students to identify a variety of emotions (e.g., happy, sad, angry, frustrated, excited, confused) in both themselves and in others.

Being aware of their own emotions, and the emotions of others, helps children control their behavior. The first step to calming down is recognizing when you are upset! Students are taught three steps to help them calm down. The next newsletter will discuss each step.

Parents are a child's most important teachers! Your support of this program will benefit your child and his or her social development in countless ways. Thank you for your cooperation!

### What Can You Do?

With your child...

- Find a picture of someone who looks excited (or sad, angry, and so forth).

- Make a list of things to do when you are lonely.

- Read a book and identify the feelings of all the different characters.

- Draw a picture of something you love.

- Play Feeling Charades. Act out emotions and have the other person guess which one you are showing.

**FIGURE 9.11** ▶Newsletter to Parents

▶ Prove that you, too, are a good listener by repeating something important to your child that he or she mentioned earlier. Show that you noticed! (p. 3)

The *Ready-to-Use Social Skills Lessons and Activities* programs (Begun, 1995,
1996a, 1996b) include family training booklets. These booklets suggest family activities that support skills being taught in the classroom.

In addition to being involved at the classroom level, parents can make important contributions at the school or district level. For example, they can (Elias et al.,
1999)

▶ serve with staff and students as members of planning and management teams to
help identify, select, and develop SEL programs;
▶ actively participate in programs designed to encourage parents and students to
work together on specific projects;
▶ serve as instructors or co-instructors with teachers and other parents for specific
SEL curricular components and activities;
▶ provide logistical and material support in the form of fundraising efforts and
other material contributions that make SEL activities possible;
▶ mentor individual students or groups of students;
▶ act as SEL liaisons to community groups and agencies, representing the interests of the school and students, and gaining community support for SEL activities through creating newsletters and sponsoring SEL-related events. (p. 88)

## Schoolwide Social–Emotional Skills Instruction

For children and youth to master social–emotional skills, the skills must be taught
indirectly and directly throughout the school day. Schoolwide social–emotional
skills instruction offers the advantage of making SEL an integral part of school
life (J. Cohen, 1999; Elias, Arnold, & Hussey, 2003; Elliott et al., 2001; Weare,
2004).

Ten guidelines that school personnel can follow when designing schoolwide
SEL programs are (Pasi, 2001, pp. 10–13):

1. Social and emotional learning promotes intelligent decision making as the basis
of healthy, positive behavior.
2. Social and emotional education must provide students with experiences that
show the link between thinking, feeling, and behavior.
3. Effective social and emotional education programs incorporate direct and indi-
rect instruction into all areas of school life.
4. For an SEL program to be effective and take root, the school's and each classroom's climate must be characterized by caring and respect.
5. To promote social and emotional learning, students need opportunities to problem-solve with others and to examine what worked and did not work in those
interactions and collaborations.

6. Effective social and emotional education enhances a challenging academic program and promotes higher academic expectations for all.
7. A school committed to SEL must consider ways to involve parents in its social and emotional learning efforts.
8. The fact that evaluation of program success in the social/emotional area is less quantifiable than academic achievement should not be a deterrent to initiating a program.
9. No single course or program will answer every student problem.
10. When starting the social–emotional learning program, assure faculty that staff development opportunities in this area will be built into each year's professional development program.

J. Cohen (2001) recommends that the school first define social–emotional learning and then identify specific skill competencies that support the definition. School personnel must ensure that the SEL curriculum is developmentally appropriate by identifying relevant skills and competencies for early childhood, middle childhood, and adolescence. The final step is to create developmentally sequenced learning experiences that help students acquire essential social–emotional skills as they progress through the grade levels.

Jones et al. (1993) designed an SEL program that taught *all* school staff to use generalization procedures like those discussed in this chapter. Sixteen social–emotional skills considered critical by elementary teachers were sequentially taught to children who were considered at risk for interpersonal behavior problems:

1. Body basics of assertiveness
2. Following instructions
3. Problem solving
4. Decision making
5. Controlling your temper
6. Aggression replacement
7. "I" messages
8. Giving positive feedback
9. Accepting positive feedback
10. Asking permission/making requests
11. Feelings
12. Body language
13. Accepting negative feedback/teasing
14. Giving negative feedback
15. Initiating conversation/communication skills
16. Negotiation/compromise

Instructional procedures included reviewing previously taught skills, introducing the new skill through discussion and modeling, presenting skill steps, modeling positive and negative examples of the skill, practicing through role-playing, summarizing the lesson, and assigning homework to promote generalization.

To encourage students to use their newly acquired skills, school personnel attended two staff development sessions. The first hour-long session was an overview of the program, including its rationale, purpose, and objectives. The second session focused on teaching staff members instructional and generalization strategies. Booster sessions were presented throughout the year, and a planning meeting was held at the end of the year. A unique aspect of this program is that everyone was involved, including secretarial and cafeteria staffs. In addition, home-practice reports asked parents to report on the students' skill performance.

Another effective schoolwide prevention and intervention program is the Responsive Classroom (RC; Charney, 1992). Hundreds of schools use RC and report that students in the program showed higher social and academic gains than students who were not in the program. RC consists of six components:

1. *Morning meeting.* The tone is set for the day when teachers and students share academic and social skills.
2. *Classroom organization.* The classroom is set up in way that is responsive to students' social–emotional needs.
3. *Rules and logical consequences.* Children are taught self-control strategies that help them succeed academically and get along with classmates.
4. *Guided discovery.* Children are given choices about assignments.
5. *Academic choice time.* Choices include independent practice, cooperative research and study skills, showing work to classmates, creating a timeline for work completion, and so forth.
6. *Assessment and reporting.* Children's work is evaluated using traditional and nontraditional assessment.

The first 6 weeks of school are spent reviewing previously taught academic skills and teaching students how to behave appropriately and responsibly.

For schoolwide SEL programs to be effective, social-emotional skills instruction must be incorporated into all aspects of school life (Pasi, 2001):

> ▶ Faculty and staff understand the importance of modeling and providing examples.
> ▶ Expectations regarding students' interactions with each other (and staff) are made clear, and explicit disrespectful behavior is not ignored.
> ▶ Athletic coaches and moderators of extracurricular activities appreciate the school's SEL emphasis and recognize they must conduct themselves with students accordingly; students are expected to interact with each other in after-school activities with the same degree of respect they are challenged to bring to interactions during the school day.
> ▶ SEL principles are integrated into lessons across disciplines, in explicit and informal ways.
> ▶ Schoolwide initiatives, such as theme-based assemblies, reinforce SEL principles.

▶ Awards and honors include recognition of students who demonstrate outstanding social–emotional skills and attitudes. (p. 11)

## Creating Supportive Environments

Social–emotional learning requires a supportive school environment. Unfortunately, about 76% of children and youth do not feel that school is a caring, nurturing place (Bodine & Crawford, 1999). It is essential that we create socially–emotionally supportive classrooms that emphasize the following (Bodine & Crawford, 1999):

▶ *Cooperation.* Children learn to work together and trust, help, and share with each other.
▶ *Communication.* Children learn to observe carefully, communicate accurately, and listen sensitively.
▶ *Tolerance.* Children learn to respect and appreciate people's differences and to understand prejudice and how it works.
▶ *Positive emotional expression.* Children learn to express feelings, particularly anger and frustration, in ways that are not aggressive or destructive, and children learn self-control.
▶ *Conflict resolution.* Children learn the skills of responding creatively to conflict in the context of a supportive, caring community. (p. 53)

When building and maintaining a supportive school climate, several factors are essential (Fopiano & Haynes, 2001):

1. It is important to have a staff of nurturing adults, who serve as mentors, are respectful and trusting of students, and are available to help students solve problems.
2. Schools must create opportunities for students to establish positive peer relationships.
3. Respect for diversity and intolerance for bullying and violence must be clearly communicated to students.
4. Sensitive and responsive support services personnel such as counselors and psychologists must be available to students, and there must be coordination between school and community resource personnel.

Schools also develop classroom and schoolwide classroom management systems that support SEL. *The Well-Managed Classroom* (Connolly, Dowd, Criste, Nelson, & Tobias, 1995) is an excellent resource for developing a classroom management plan that links instruction in management and social–emotional skills. Topics addressed include student rights, building and maintaining relationships, problem solving, behavioral principles, and preventive teaching.

When developing a schoolwide management system, school personnel can begin by developing a constitution, like the one shown as Table 9.2, to identify essential rights, matched with essential responsibilities assumed by each person

**TABLE 9.2** ▶Constitution of Rights and Responsibilities

| Rights | Responsibilities |
|---|---|
| **I have the right:** | **I have the responsibility:** |
| To be treated with respect and kindness: no one will tease me, demean me, or insult me. | To treat all others with respect and kindness by not teasing, demeaning, or insulting them. |
| To be myself: No one will treat me unfairly because of looks, abilities, beliefs, or gender. | To honor individual differences by treating all others fairly regardless of looks, abilities, beliefs, or gender. |
| To be safe: No one will threaten me, bully me, or damage or remove my property. | To help make the environment safe by not acting dangerously, and by securing my property by not threatening or bullying others, and by respecting the property of others. |
| To be heard: No one will yell at me, and my opinions will be considered. | To listen to others, consider their opinions, and allow others to be heard. |
| To be free to express my feelings and opinions without criticism and to learn about myself through constructive feedback. | To express myself respectfully in ways that others can hear me, and to allow others to express themselves and provide constructive feedback. |
| To learn and to be given assistance to do so. | To accept assistance when given in the spirit of increasing my opportunity to learn and grow, and to unconditionally provide assistance to others whenever I can do so. |
| To expect that all rights will be mine in all circumstances and to receive assistance from those in charge when that is not the case. | To protect my rights and the rights of others by exercising my full responsibilities at all times and by helping others to do the same. |

Source: "Rights and Responsibilities," from *Developing Emotional Intelligence: A Guide to Behavior Management and Conflict Resolution in Schools* (p. 105), by R. J. Bodine and D. K. Crawford, 1999, Champaign, IL: Research Press. Copyright © 1999 by Richard J. Bodine and Donna K. Crawford. Reprinted by permission.

(Bodine & Crawford, 1999). After the constitution is written, a list of school rules is developed, which involves identifying behaviors that

- ▶ impact negatively on school climate, such as fighting, bullying, stealing, and harassment;
- ▶ support the constitution;
- ▶ are aligned with consequences.

The final list should include rules that are few in number and enforceable, with the understanding that rules may have to be changed.

## ▶ Chapter Summary

Building collaborative arrangements within a school and between the school and the home and community is of utmost importance (Haynes & Comer, 1996). Home–school–community partnerships increase the effectiveness of programs designed to teach children and youth social–emotional skills. Teachers and parents alike can adopt strategies to promote use of skills across individuals, settings, and situations. These approaches include linking social–emotional and academic skills instruction, having teachers co-teach and collaborate, using cooperative learning groups, teaching incidentally, teaching children self-management strategies, and assigning homework.

We encourage teachers and parents to think beyond individual classrooms and consider implementing schoolwide and districtwide SEL programs. Schools should develop specific strategies to create environments that support SEL.

APPENDIX A

# Books for Parents, Children & Youth, and Teachers & Administrators

## ► BOOKS FOR PARENTS

Bilodeau, L. (1992). *The anger workbook*. Center City, MN: Hazelden.

Cohen, C. (2000). *Raise your child's social IQ: Stepping stones to people skills for kids*. Silver Spring, MD: Advantage Books.

Cohen, L. J. (2001). *Playful parenting: A bold new way to nurture close connections, solve behavior problems, and encourage your child's confidence*. New York: Ballantine Books.

Duke, M. P., Nowicki, S., & Martin, E. A. (1996). *Teaching your child the language of social success*. Atlanta: Peachtree.

Eberly, S. (2001). *365 manners kids should know*. New York: Three Rivers Press.

Elias, M. J., Tobias, S. E., & Friedlander, B. S. (1999). *Emotionally intelligent parenting: How to raise a self-disciplined, responsible, socially skilled child*. New York: Harmony Books.

Frankel, F. (1996). *Good friends are hard to find: Help your child find, make and keep friends*. Los Angeles: Perspective Publishing, Inc.

Garbarino, J. (1995). *Raising children in a socially toxic environment*. San Francisco: Jossey-Bass.

Garrity, C., Baris, M., & Porter W. (2000). *Bully-proofing your child: A parent's guide*. Longmont, CO: Sopris West.

Glenn, H. S. (1989). *Raising self-reliant children in a self-indulgent world*. Orem, UT: Empowering People.

Gottman, J. (1997). *Raising an emotionally intelligent child*. New York: Simon & Schuster.

Greenspan, S. I. (1994). *Playground politics: Understanding the emotional life of your school-aged child*. New York: Perseus Book Group.

Greenspan, S. I., & Greenspan, N. T. (1994). *First feelings: Milestones in the emotional development of your baby and child*. New York: Penguin Books.

Kindlon, D., & Thompson, M. (1999). *Raising Cain: Protecting the emotional life of boys*. New York: Ballantine Books.

Marano, H. E. (1998). *"Why doesn't anybody like me?" A guide to raising socially confident kids*. New York: William Morrow.

Nowicki, S., & Duke, M. P. (1992). *Helping the child who doesn't fit in*. Atlanta, GA: Peachtree.

Shapiro, L. E. (1997). *How to raise a child with a high EQ: A parents' guide to emotional intelligence*. New York: HarperPerennial.

Shure, M. B. (1996). *Raising a thinking a child: Help your young child to resolve everyday conflicts and get along with others*. New York: Pocket Books.

Shure, M. (2000). *Raising a thinking child workbook: Teaching young children how to resolve everyday conflicts and get along with others*. Champaign, IL: Research Press.

Shure, M. B. (2000). *Raising a thinking preteen: The I Can Problem solve programs for 8- to 12-year-olds*. New York: Henry Holt.

Stein, S. J., & Book, H. W. (2000). *The EQ edge: Emotional intelligence and your success.* Toronto, Canada: Stoddart Publishing Company.

Thompson, M., Grace, C. O., & Cohen, L. J. (2001). *Best friends, worst enemies: Understanding the social lives of children.* New York: Ballantine Books.

Thompson, M. (2002). *Mom, they're teasing me: Helping your child solve social problems.* New York: Ballantine Books.

## ▶ BOOKS FOR CHILDREN & YOUTH

Brown, K., & Brown, M. (1998). *How to be a friend: A guide to making friends and keeping them.* Boston: Little, Brown, & Co.

Erlbach, A., & Espeland, P. (1995). *The best friends book: True stories about real best friends.* Minneapolis, MN: Free Spirit Publishing.

Espeland, P., & Verdick, E. (1998). *Making every day count: Daily readings for young people on solving problems, setting goals, and feeling good about yourself.* Minneapolis, MN: Free Spirit Publishing.

Garell, D. C. (1989). *Friendship and love.* New York: Chelsea House.

Herron, R., & Peter, V. J. (1998). *A good friend: How to make one, how to be one.* Boys Town, NE: Boys Town Press.

Herron, R., & Peter, V. J. (1998). *What's right for me: Making good choices in relationships.* Boys Town, NE: Boys Town Press.

Herron, R., & Peter, V. J. (1998). *Who's in the mirror: Finding the real me.* Boys Town, NE: Boys Town Press.

Johnson, J. T. (1992). *Making friends, finding love: A book about teen relationships.* Minneapolis, MN: Lerner Publications.

Karlsberg, E. (1991). *How to make and keep friends.* Mahwah, NJ: Troll Associates.

Packer, A. J. (1997). *How rude! The teenagers' guide to good manners, proper behavior, and not grossing people out.* Minneapolis, MN: Free Spirit Publishing.

Schneider, M. F. (1991). *Popularity has its ups and downs.* New York: Simon and Schuster.

Shapiro, L. (1995). *Sometimes I like to fight, but I don't do it much anymore: A self-esteem book to help children with difficulty controlling their anger.* Secaucus, NJ: ChildsWork/ChildsPlay.

Wirths, C. G., & Bowman-Fruhm, M. (1993). *Your circle of friends.* New York: Twenty-First Century Books.

Zimmerman, T., & Shapiro, L. (1996). *Sometimes I feel like I don't have any friends (but not so much anymore): A self-esteem book to help children improve their social skills.* King of Prussia, PA: Center for Applied Psychology Inc.

## ▶ BOOKS FOR TEACHERS & ADMINISTRATORS

Bocchino, R. (1999). *Emotional literacy: To be a different kind of smart.* Thousand Oaks, CA: Corwin Press.

Bodine, R. J., & Crawford, K. K. (1999). *Developing emotional intelligence.* Champaign, IL: Research Press.

Clark, R. (2003). *The essential 55: An award-winning educator's rules for discovering the successful student in every child.* New York: Hyperion.

Cohen, J. (1999). *Educating minds and hearts: Social emotional learning and the passage into adolescence.* New York: Teachers College Press.

Cohen, J. (2001). *Caring classrooms/intelligent schools: The social emotional education of young children.* New York: Teachers College Press.

Elias, M. J., & Clabby, J. F. (1992). *Building social problem-solving skills: Guidelines from a school-based program.* San Francisco: Jossey-Bass.

Elias, M. J., & Tobias, S. E. (1996). *Social problem solving: Interventions in the schools.* New York: Guilford.

Elias, M. J., Zins, J. E., Weissberg, R. P., Frey, K. S., Greenberg, M. T., Haynes, N. M., et al. (Eds.). (1997). *Promoting social and emotional learning: Guidelines for educators.* Alexandria, VA: Association for Curriculum and Development.

Elias, M. J., Arnold, H., & Hussey, C. S. (2003). *EQ + IQ = Best leadership practices for caring and successful schools.* Thousand Oaks, CA: Corwin Press.

Elksnin, L. K., & Elksnin, N. (1995). *Assessment and instruction of social skills.* San Diego: Singular Publishing Group.

Goleman, D. L. (1995). *Emotional intelligence: Why it can matter more than IQ.* New York: Basic Books.

Goleman, D. (1998). *Working with emotional intelligence.* New York: Bantam Books.

Pasi, R. J. (2001). *Higher expectations: Promoting social emotional learning and academic achievement in your school.* New York: Teachers College Press.

Weare, K. (2004). *Developing the emotionally literate school.* London: Paul Chapman Publishing.

# Children's Books
# Chosen by Children

## ▶ Children's Choices

When teachers and parents select books to teach social–emotional skills it is important to pick books that children find appealing. Begun in 1975, Children's Choices is a joint project of the International Reading Association (IRA) and the Children's Book Council (CBC). Each year 10,000 children and youth from all regions of the country are asked to read and vote for their favorite recently published books. For the 2002 list, children read and evaluated more than 700 books; 100 books published from 1998 to 2002 made the list (International Reading Association, 2002).

Dan T. Ouzts of The Citadel and Mark J. Palombo of the University of South Carolina—Beaufort compiled this list of 78 Children's Choice books that lend themselves to social–emotional skills instruction.

### Beginning Readers—Ages 5–6

| Title | Year | Author | Illustrator | Publisher |
|---|---|---|---|---|
| A Cat and a Dog | 2001 | Claire Masurel | Bob Kolar | North-South Books |
| Flip and Flop | 2001 | Dawn Apperly | Author | Orchard Books |
| Hoodwinked | 2001 | Arthur Howard | Author | Harcourt |
| Leon the Chameleon | 2001 | Melanie Watt | Author | Kids Can Press |
| Bear's Christmas Star | 2000 | Mireille D'Alliance | Author | Simon & Schuster |
| Dr. Duck | 2000 | H. M. Ehrlich | Laura Rader | Orchard Books |
| Good as Goldie | 2000 | Margie Palatini | Author | Hyperion Books |
| Max | 2000 | Bob Graham | Author | Candlewick Press |
| The Mouse That Snored | 2000 | Bernard Waber | Author | Houghton Mifflin |
| Quiet Wyatt! | 1999 | Bill Maynard | Frank Remkiewicz | Putnam |
| We Share Everything | 1999 | Robert Munsch | Michael Martchenko | Cartwheel/ Scholastic |
| Just Like Floss | 1998 | Kim Lewis | Author | Candlewick |
| Little Louie the Baby Bloomer | 1998 | Robert Kraus | Jose Aruego & Adrianne Dewey | HarperCollins |
| Shipwreck Saturday | 1998 | Bill Crosby | Varnette P. Honeywood | Scholastic |
| Ziggy Piggy and the Three Little Pigs | 1998 | Frank Asch | Author | Kids Can |

## Young Readers—Ages 6–8

| Title | Year | Author | Illustrator | Publisher |
|---|---|---|---|---|
| Franklin and Harriet | 2001 | Paulette Bourgeois | Brenda Clark | Kids Can Press |
| Giraffes Can't Dance | 2001 | Giles Andreae | Guy Parker-Reese | Orchard Books |
| The Great Gracie Chase: Stop That Dog! | 2001 | Cynthia Rylant | Mark Teague | Blue Sky |
| Sidney Won't Swim | 2001 | Hilde Schuurmans | Author | Whispering Coyote |
| Spike in the Kennel | 2001 | Paulette Bogan | Author | Putnam |
| Widget | 2001 | Lyn Rossiter McFarland | Jim McFarland | Farrer, Straus & Giroux |
| Aaron's Hair | 2000 | Robert Munsch | Alan & Lea Daniel | Cartwheel/ Scholastic |
| Mad Dog McGraw | 2000 | Myron Uhlberg | Lydia Monks | Putnam |
| Nothing Scares Us | 2000 | Frieda Wishinsky | Neal Layton | Carolrhoda Books |
| One Lonely Seahorse | 2000 | Saxton Freeman & Joost Effers | Authors | Scholastic |
| Wemberly Worried | 2000 | Kevin Hawkes | Authors | Greenwillow Books |
| The Ant Bully | 1999 | John Nickle | Author | Scholastic |
| Bad Habits! | 1999 | Babette Cole | Author | Dial Books |
| The Big Bug Ball | 1999 | Dee Lillegard | Rex Barron | Putnam |
| Cynthia Rylant | | Mark Teague Paulette Bourgeois | Brenda Clark | Scholastic |
| Good Job, Little Bear | 1999 | Martin Waddell | Barbara Firth | Candlewick |
| Herb, the Vegetarian Dragon | 1999 | Jule Bass | Debbie Harter | Barefoot |
| Hooway for Wodney Wat | 1999 | Helen Lester | Lyn Munsinger | Walter Lorraine Books |
| Impatient Pamela Asks: Why Are My Feet So Huge? | 1999 | Mary Koski | Dan Brown | Trellis Publishing |
| The Night Iguana Left Home | 1999 | Megan McDonald | Ponder Goembel | DK Ink |
| The Robobots | 1999 | Matt Novak | Author | DK Ink |
| A Bad Case of Stripes | 1998 | David Shannon | Author | Blue Sky |

## Young Readers—Ages 6-8 *(continued)*

| Title | Year | Author | Illustrator | Publisher |
| --- | --- | --- | --- | --- |
| The Boxer and the Princess | 1998 | Helme Heine | Author | Margaret K. McElderry Books |
| Chicken Soup for Little Souls: A Dog of My Own | 1998 | Lisa McCourt | Katya Krenima | Health Communications |
| Ebbie and Flo | 1998 | Irene Kelly | Author | Smith&Kraus |
| Elmer Takes Off | 1998 | David McKee | Author | William Morrow |
| Froggy's First Kiss | 1998 | Jonathan London | Frank Remkiewicz | Viking |
| How Leo Learned to Be King | 1998 | Marcus Pfister | Author | North-South Books |
| Pete's Pizza | 1998 | William Steig | Author | di Capua/ HarperCollins |
| The Pillow War | 1998 | Matt Novak | Author | Orchard Books |

## Intermediate Readers—Ages 8-10

| Title | Year | Author | Illustrator | Publisher |
| --- | --- | --- | --- | --- |
| Fat Commandos | 2001 | Daniel Pinkwater | Andy Rash | Scholastic |
| Fly High! The Story of Bessie Coleman | 2001 | Louise Borden & Mary Kay Kroeger | Teresa Flavin | Margaret K. McElderry Books |
| Judy Moody Gets Famous | 2001 | Megan McDonald | Peter Reynolds | Candlewick |
| One Puppy, Three Tales | 2001 | Karen Salmansohn | Author | Tricycle |
| The War | 2001 | Anais Vaulgelade | Author | Lerner |
| Who's in the Hall? A Mystery in Four Chapters | 2000 | Betsy Hearne | Christy Hale | Greenwillow Books |
| McBroom Tells the Truth | 1998 | Sid Fleischman | Amy Wummer | Penguin/Putnam |

## Advanced Readers—Ages 10–13

| Title | Year | Author | Illustrator | Publisher |
|---|---|---|---|---|
| Alice Alone | 2001 | Phyllis Reynolds Naylor | NA | Atheneum Books |
| Bad Girls Blues | 2001 | Sally Warner | NA | HarperCollins |
| Bad Girls | 2001 | Jacqueline Wilson | Nick Sharratt | Delacorte |
| Cirque du Freak | 2001 | Darren Shan | NA | Little Brown |
| Darkness Before Dawn | 2001 | Sharon M. Draper | NA | Atheneum Books |
| The Hostile Hospital | 2001 | Lemony Snicket | Brett Helquist | HarperCollins |
| Money Hungry | 2001 | Sharon G. Flake | NA | Hyperion |
| Note from a Liar and Her Dog | 2001 | Gennifer Choldenko | NA | Putnam |
| Say Goodbye (Wild At Hearth #5) | 2001 | Laurie Halse Anderson | Photos | Pleasant Company |
| Taking Chances (Heartland #4) | 2001 | Lauren Brooke | NA | Scholastic |
| You Don't Know Me | 2001 | David Klass | NA | Farrar, Straus & Giroux |
| The Body of Christopher Creed | 2000 | Carol Plum-Ucci | NA | Harcourt |
| Davis v. God | 2000 | Mary E. Pearson | NA | Harcourt |
| Don't Tell Anyone | 2000 | Peg Kehret | NA | Dutton |
| The Girls | 2000 | Amy Goldman Koss | NA | Dial Books |
| The Grooming of Alice | 2000 | Phyllis Reynolds Naylor | NA | Atheneum Books |
| Highs! Over 150 Ways to Feel Really, REALLY, Good . . . Without Alcohol or Drugs | 2000 | Alex Packer | Jeff Tolbert | Free Spirit |
| Skullcrack | 2000 | Ben Bo | NA | Lerner |
| Alida's Song | 1999 | Gary Paulsen | NA | Delacorte |
| Shelter Dogs: Amazing Stories of Adopted Strays | 1999 | Peg Kehret | Photos | Whitman |
| Sunny, Diary 3 (California Diaries, #12 | 1999 | Ann M. Martin | NA | Scholastic |

**Advanced Readers—Ages 10–13** *(continued)*

| Title | Year | Author | Illustrator | Publisher |
|---|---|---|---|---|
| Achingly Alice | 1998 | Phyllis Reynolds Naylor | NA | Atheneum |
| Angels Turn Their Backs | 1998 | Margaret Buffie | Florentina Bogdan | Kids Can |
| Bloomability | 1998 | Sharon Creech | NA | HarperCollins |
| Bradley and the Billboard | 1998 | Mame Farrell | NA | Farrar, Straus & Giroux |

# References

Achenbach, T. M. (1991a). *Manual for the child behavior checklist and 1991 profile.* Burlington: University of Vermont Department of Psychiatry.

Achenbach, T. M. (1991b). *Manual for the teacher's report form and 1991 profile.* Burlington: University of Vermont Department of Psychiatry.

Alberto, P. A., & Troutman, A. C. (2003). *Applied behavior analysis for teachers* (6th ed). Columbus, OH: Merrill Publishing Company.

Alex, N. K. (1982). *Bibliotherapy* (Report No. EDO-CS-93-05). Bloomington: Indiana University, Office of Educational Research and Improvement. (ERIC Document Reproduction Service No. ED 357 333)

Alsop, R. (2002, September 9). Playing well with others. *Wall Street Journal,* R11, R14.

Alsopp, D. H., Santos, K. E., & Linn, R. L. (2000). Collaborating to teach prosocial skills. *Intervention in School and Clinic, 35*(3), 141–146.

American Association on Mental Retardation. (1992). *Mental retardation: Definition, classification, and systems of supports* (9th ed.). Washington, DC: Author.

American Guidance Service. (1989). *Social skills on the job: A transition to the workplace for students with special needs.* Circle Pines, MN: Author.

American Psychiatric Association. (2000). *Diagnostic and statistical manual of mental disorders* (4th ed.). Washington, DC: Author.

American Psychological Association. (1993). *Violence and youth: Psychology's response.* Washington, DC: Author.

American Society for Training and Development. (1997). *Benchmaking forum member-to-member survey results.* Alexandria, VA: Author.

Anderson, P. L. (2000). Using literature to teach social skills to adolescents with LD. *Intervention in School and Clinic, 35,* 271–279.

Ang, R. P., & Hughes, J. N. (2001). Differential benefits of skills training with antisocial youth based on group composition: A meta-analytic investigation. *School Psychology Review, 31*(2), 164–185.

Antonello, S. J. (1996). *Social skills development.* Boston: Allyn & Bacon.

Arnold, M. E., & Hughes, J. N. (1999). First do no harm: Adverse effects of grouping deviant youth for skills training. *Journal of School Psychology, 37*(1), 99–115.

Asher, S. R., & Rose, A. J. (1997). Promoting children's social–emotional development with peers. In P. Salovey & D. Sluyter (Eds.), *Emotional development and emotional intelligence* (pp. 196–224). New York: Basic Books.

Barkley, R. A. (1990). *Attention-deficit hyperactivity disorder: A handbook for diagnosis and treatment.* New York: Guilford Press.

Barnhill, G. P. (2001–2002). Behavioral, social, and emotional assessment of students with ASD. *Assessment for Effective Intervention, 27*(1&2), 47–55.

Bar-On, R. (1997). *BarOn emotional quotient inventory: Technical manual.* Toronto, Ontario, Canada: Multi–Health Systems.

Bar-On, R., & Parker, J. D. A. (2000). *BarOn emotional quotient inventory: Youth version.* North Tonawanda, NY: Multi-Health Systems.

Baum, K. M., & Nowicki, S., Jr. (1998). Perception of emotion: Measuring decoding accuracy of adult prosodic cues varying in intensity. *Journal of Nonverbal Behavior, 22*(2), 89–107.

Baumgart, D., & Anderson, J. (1987). *Assessing and teaching job-related social skills.* Moscow: University of Idaho, Secondary Transition and Employment Project.

Beckman, P. J., & Lieber, J. (1992). Parent–child social relationships and peer social competence of preschool children with disabilities. In S. L. Odom, S. R. McConnell, & M. A.

McEvoy (Eds.), *Social competence of young children with disabilities: Issues and strategies for intervention* (pp. 65–92). Baltimore: Paul H. Brookes.

Begun, R. W. (1995). *Ready-to-use social skills lessons & activities for grades 1–3*. West Nyack, NY: Center for Applied Research in Education.

Begun, R. W. (1996a). *Ready-to-use social skills lessons & activities for grades preK–K*. West Nyack, NY: Center for Applied Research in Education.

Begun, R. W. (1996b). *Ready-to-use social skills lessons & activities for grades 4–6*. West Nyack, NY: Center for Applied Research in Education.

Begun, R. W. (1996c). *Ready-to-use social skills lessons & activities for grades 7–12*. West Nyack, NY: Center for Applied Research in Education.

Bender, W. N., Rosenkrans, C. B., & Crane, M. K. (1999). Stress, depression, and suicide among students with learning disabilities: Assessing the risk. *Learning Disability Quarterly, 22*(1), 143–156.

Bender, W. N., & Wall, M. E. (1994). Social–emotional development of students with learning disabilities. *Learning Disability Quarterly, 17*(1), 323–341.

Berk, L. E. (1989). *Child development*. Boston: Allyn & Bacon.

Berndt, T. J., & Keefe, K. (1995). Friends' influence on adolescents' adjustment to school. *Child Development, 66*, 1312–1329.

Berndt, T. J., Laychak, A. E., & Park, K. (1990). Friends' influence on adolescents' academic achievement motivation: An experimental study. *Journal of Educational Psychology, 82*, 664–670.

Bierman, K. L., & Montminy, H. P. (1993). Developmental issues in social-skills assessment and intervention with children and adolescents. *Behavior Modification, 17*(3), 229–254.

Bilodeau, L. (1992). *The anger workbook*. Center City, MN: Hazelden.

Bocchino, R. (1999). *Emotional literacy: To be a different kind of smart*. Thousand Oaks, CA: Corwin Press.

Bodine, R. J., & Crawford, K. K. (1999). *Developing emotional intelligence*. Champaign, IL: Research Press.

Bowers, F. E., McGinnis, C., Ervin, R. A., & Friman, P. C. (1999). Merging research and practice: The example of positive peer reporting applied to social rejection. *Education and Treatment of Children, 22*, 218–226.

Bowers, F. E., Woods, D. W., Carlyon, W. D., & Friman, P. C. (2000). Using positive peer reporting to improve the social interactions and acceptance of socially isolated adolescents in residential care: A systematic replication. *Journal of Applied Behavior Analysis, 33*, 239-242.

Boys Town Press. (1992). *Basic social skills for youth*. Boys Town, NE: Author.

Brazelton, T. B. (2001, November 20). How to raise a caring child. *Family Circle, 114*(15), 28–30.

Brion–Meisels, S., & Selman, R. L. (1984). Early adolescent development of new interpersonal strategies: Understanding and intervention. *School Psychology Review, 13*, 278–291.

Bromer, B. L. (1999). Who's in the house corner? Including young children with disabilities in pretend play. *Dimensions of Early Childhood, 27*(2), 17–23.

Brown, K., & Brown, M. (1998). *How to be a friend: A guide to making friends and keeping them*. Boston: Little, Brown & Co.

Brown, L., & Hammill, D. (1990). *Behavior Rating Profile* (2d ed.). Austin, TX: Pro-Ed.

Brown, W. H., McEvoy, M. A., & Bishop, N. (1991). Incidental teaching of social behavior: A naturalistic approach for promoting young children's peer interactions. *Teaching Exceptional Children, 24*, 35–38.

Brown, W. H., & Odom, S. L. (1994). Strategies and tactics for promoting generalization and maintenance of young children's social behavior. *Research in Developmental Disabilities, 15*(2), 99–118.

Bruininks R. H., Rynders, J. E., & Gross, J. C. (1974). Social acceptance of mildly retarded pupils in resource rooms and regular classes. *AAMD Journal, 78*, 377–383.

Bryan, T. (1974). Peer popularity of learning disabled children. *Journal of Learning Disabilities, 7*, 621–625.

Bryan, T. (1994). The social competence of students with learning disabilities over time: A response to Vaughn and Hogan. *Journal of Learning Disabilities, 27*(5), 304–308.

Bryan, T., Burstein, K., & Ergul, C. (2004). The social–emotional side of learning disabilities: A science-based presentation of the state of the art. *Learning Disability Quarterly, 27*, 45–51.

Bryan, T., Donahue, M., Pearl, R., & Sturm, C. (1981). Learning disabled children's conversational skills—The "TV talk show." *Learning Disability Quarterly, 4*, 250–259.

Bryan, T., Sullivan-Burstein, K., & Mathur, S. (1998). The influence of affect on social-information processing. *Journal of Learning Disabilities, 31*(5), 418–426.

Bullis, M. (1998). *Community-based social skill performance assessment tool.* Santa Barbara, CA: James Stanfield Co.

Bullis, M., Nishioka-Evans, V., Fredericks, H. D., & Davis, C. (1992). *Assessing job-related social skills of adolescents and young adults with behavioral disorders: Development and preliminary psychometric characteristics of two measures.* Monmouth: Western Oregon State College. (ERIC Document Reproduction Service No. ED 395965)

Bullis, M., Nishioka-Evans, V., Fredericks, H. D. B., & Davis, C. (1993). Identifying and assessing the job-related social skills of adolescents and young adults with behavioral disorders. *Journal of Emotional and Behavioral Disorders, 1*(4), 236–250.

Bullis, M., Nishioka, V., Fredericks, H. D. B., & Davis, C. (1997). *Scale of job-related social skill performance.* Santa Barbara, CA: James Stanfield Co.

Buysse, V., Goldman, B. D., & Skinner, M. L. (2002). Setting effects on friendship formation among young children with and without disabilities. *Exceptional Children, 68*, 503–517.

Calkins, C. F., & Walker, H. M. (1990). *Social competence for workers with developmental disabilities.* Baltimore: Paul H. Brookes.

Calloway, C. (1999). Promote friendship in the inclusive classroom. *Intervention in School and Clinic, 34*(3), 176–177.

Camp, B. W., & Bash, M.A.S. (1981). *Think aloud small group program—Increasing social and cognitive skills: A problem-solving program for children.* Champaign, IL: Research Press.

Camp, W. W., & Bash, M.A.S. (1985a). *Think aloud classroom program, grades 1–2.* Champaign, IL: Research Press.

Camp, W. W., & Bash, M.A.S. (1985b). *Think aloud classroom program, grades 3–4.* Champaign, IL: Research Press.

Camp, W. W., & Bash, M.A.S. (1985c). *Think aloud classroom program, grades 5–6.* Champaign, IL: Research Press.

Carnevale, A. P., Gainer, L. J., & Meltzer, A. S. (1990). *Workplace basics: The essential skills employers want.* San Francisco: Jossey-Bass.

Cartledge, G., & Kiarie, M. W. (2001). Learning social skills through literature for children and adolescents. *Teaching Exceptional Children, 34*, 40–47.

Cartledge, G., & Kleefeld, J. (1991). *Taking part: Introducing social skills to children.* Circle Pines, MN: American Guidance Service.

Cartledge, G., & Kleefeld, J. (1994). *Working together: Building children's social skills through folk literature.* Circle Pines, MN: American Guidance Service.

Cazden, C. B. (1988). *Classroom discourse: The language of teaching and learning.* Portsmouth, NH: Heinemann.

Celani, G., Battacchi, M. W., & Arcidiacono, L. (1999). The understanding of emotional meaning of facial expressions in people with autism. *Journal of Autism and Developmental Disorders, 29,* 57–66.

Center, D. B., & Wascom, A. M. (1987). Teacher perceptions of social behavior in behaviorally disorderd and socially normal children and youth. *Behavioral Disorders, 12,* 200–206.

Charney, R. S. (1992). *Teaching children to care.* Greenfield, MA: Northeast Foundation for Children.

Charney, R., & Kriete, R. (2001). Creating a classroom community where social emotional learning thrives: The case of the "cool girls" list. In J. Cohen (Ed.), *Caring classrooms/intelligent schools: The social emotional education of young children* (pp. 77–84). New York: Teachers College Press.

Cherniss, C. (2000). Social and emotional competence in the workplace. In R. Bar-On & J.D.A. Parker (Eds.), *The handbook of emotional intelligence* (pp. 433–458). San Francisco: Jossey-Bass.

Cherniss, C., & Goleman, D. (Eds.). (2001). *The emotionally intelligent workplace.* San Francisco: Jossey-Bass.

Christopher, J. S., Nangle, D. W., & Hansen, D. J. (1993). Social-skills interventions with adolescents. *Behavior Modification, 17,* 314–338.

Clark, R. (2003). *The essential 55: An award-winning educator's rules for discovering the successful student in every child.* New York: Hyperion.

Clement-Heist, K., Siegel, S., & Gaylord-Ross, R. (1992). Simulated and in situ vocational social skills training for youths with learning disabilities. *Exceptional Children, 58*(4), 336–345.

Cohen, C. (2000). *Raise your child's social IQ: Stepping stones to people skills for kids.* Silver Spring, MD: Advantage Books.

Cohen, J. (Ed.). (1999). *Educating minds and hearts: Social emotional learning and the passage into adolescence.* New York: Teachers College Press.

Cohen, J. (Ed.). (2001). *Caring classrooms/intelligent schools: The social emotional education of young children.* New York: Teachers College Press.

Cohen, L. J. (2001). *Playful parenting: A bold new way to nurture close connections, solve behavior problems, and encourage children's confidence.* New York: Ballantine Books.

Cohen, M., & Besharov, D. J. (2002). *The role of career and technical education: Implications for the federal government.* Washington, DC: U.S. Department of Education, Office of Vocational and Adult Education.

Coie, J. D., Dodge, K. A., & Coppotelli, H. (1982). Dimensions and types of social status: A cross-age perspective. *Developmental Psychology, 18,* 557–570.

Coleman, J. M., McHam, L. A., & Minnett, A. M. (1992). Similarities in the social competencies of learning disabled and low achieving elementary school children. *Journal of Learning Disabilities, 25,* 671–677.

Coleman, M., Wheeler, L., & Webber, J. (1993). Research on interpersonal problem solving training: A review. *Remedial and Special Education, 14*(2), 25–37.

Conners, C. K. (1997). *Conners' rating scale–Revised technical manual.* Toronto, Ontario, Canada: Multi-Health Systems.

Connolly, J. A. (1987). Sociometric status among disturbed adolescents in a residential treatment program. *Journal of Adolescent Research, 2,* 411–421.

Connolly, T., Dowd, T., Criste, A., Nelson, C., & Tobias, L. (1995). *The well-managed classroom: Promoting student success through social skill instruction.* Boys Town, NE: Boys Town Press.

Conroy, M. A., Langenbrunner, M. R., & Burleson, R. B. (1996). Suggestions for enhancing the social behaviors of preschoolers with disabilities: Using developmentally appropriate practices. *Dimensions of Early Childhood, 24*(1), 9–15.

Conte, R., & Andrews, J. (1993). Social skills in the context of learning disabilities definitions: A reply to Gresham and Elliott and directions for the future. *Journal of Learning Disabilities, 26,* 146–153.

Cooper, C. S., & McEvoy, M. A. (1996). Group friendship activities. An easy way to develop the social skills of young children. *Teaching Exceptional Children, 28*(3), 67–69.

Court, D., & Givon, S. (2003). Group intervention: Improving social skills of adolescents with learning disabilities. *Teaching Exceptional Children, 36*(2), 46–51.

Craighead, N. A. (1990). Mutual empowerment through collaboration: A new script for an old problem. In W. A. Secord (Ed.), *Best practices in school speech-language pathology* (pp. 109–116). San Antonio, TX: Psychological Corporation.

Craig-Unkefer, L. A., & Kaiser, A. P. (2002). Improving the social communication skills of at-risk preschool children in a play context. *Topics in Early Childhood Special Education, 22*(1), 3–13.

Damon, W. (1977). *The social world of the child.* San Francisco: Jossey–Bass.

Dasho, S., Lewis, C., & Watson, M. (2001). Fostering emotional intelligence in the classroom and school: Strategies from the child development report. In J. Cohen (Ed.), *Caring classrooms/intelligent schools: The social emotional education of young children* (pp. 87–107). New York: Teachers College Press.

DeGeorge, K. L. (1998). Friendship and stories: Using children's literature to teach friendship skills to children with learning disabilities. *Intervention in School and Clinic, 33*(3), 157–162.

Demaray, M. K., Ruffalo, S. L., Carlson, J. T., Busse, R. T., Olson, A. E., McManus, S. M., & Levinthal, A. (1995). Social skills assessment: A comparative evaluation of six published rating scales. *School Psychology Review, 24*(4), 648–671.

Denckla, M. (1986, June-July). The neurology of social competence. *ACLD Newsbriefs,* pp. 1, 16, 20, 21.

Deutsch, F. (1974). Female preschoolers' perceptions of affective responses and interpersonal behavior in videotaped episodes. *Developmental Psychology, 10,* 733–740.

Doctoroff, S. (1996). Supporting social pretend play in young children with disabilities. *Early Child Development and Care, 19*(1), 27–38.

Dodge, K. A. (1986). A social information processing model of social competence in children. In M. Perlmutter (Ed.), *Minnesota symposia on child psychology* (Vol. 18, pp. 77–125). Hillsdale, NJ: Erlbaum.

Donahue, M., & Bryan, T. (1983). Conversational skills and modeling in learning disabled boys. *Applied Psycholinguistics, 2,* 213–234.

Donahue, M., & Wong, B. Y. L. (2002). How to start a revolution. In B. Y. L. Wong & M. Donahue (Eds.), *The social dimensions of learning disabilities: Essays in honor of Tanis Bryan* (pp. 1–10). Mahwah, NJ: Lawrence Erlbaum.

Doty, G. (2001). *Fostering emotional intelligence in K–8 students.* Thousand Oaks, CA: Corwin Press.

Down, T., & Tierney, J. (1992). *Teaching social skills to youth: A curriculum for child-care providers*. Boys Town, NE: Boys Town Press.

Duan, D. W., & O'Brien, S. (1998). Peer-mediated social-skills training and generalization in group homes. *Behavioral Interventions, 13*, 235–247.

Duke, M. P., Nowicki, S., & Martin, E. A. (1996). *Teaching your child the language of social success*. Atlanta, GA: Peachtree.

DuPaul, G. J., Power, T. J., Anastopoulos, A. D., & Reid, R. (1998). *ADHD Rating Scale–IV*. New York: Guilford Press.

DuPaul, G. J., & Stoner, G. (1994). *ADHD in the schools: Assessment and intervention strategies*. New York: Guilford Press.

Dygdon, J. A. (1993). *CLASSIC: A program for socially valid social skills training*. Brandon, VT: Clinical Psychology Publishing.

Eberly, S. (2001). *365 manners kids should know*. New York: Three Rivers Press.

Eckert, S. P. (2000). Teaching the social skill of accepting criticism to adults with developmental disabilities. *Education and Training in Mental Retardation and Developmental Disabilities, 35*(1), 16–24.

Eisenberg, N., & Harris, J. D. (1984). Social competence: A developmental perspective. *School Psychology Review, 13*, 267–277.

Elias, M. J. (2004). The connection between social–emotional learning and learning disabilities: Implications for intervention. *Learning Disability Quarterly, 27*, 53–63.

Elias, M. J., Arnold, H., & Hussey, C. S. (Eds.). (2003). *EQ + IQ = Best leadership practices for caring and successful schools*. Thousand Oaks, CA: Corwin Press.

Elias, M. J., & Clabby, J. F. (1989). *Social decision making skills: A curriculum guide for the elementary grades*. Gaithersburg, MD: Aspen.

Elias, M. J., & Clabby, J. F. (1992). *Building social problem-solving skills: Guidelines from a school-based program*. San Francisco: Jossey-Bass.

Elias, M. J., & Tobias, S. E. (1996). *Social problem solving: Interventions in the schools*. New York: Guilford.

Elias, M. J., Tobias, S. E., & Friedlander, B. S. (1999). *Emotionally intelligent parenting: How to raise a self-disciplined, responsible, socially skilled child*. New York: Harmony Books.

Elias, M. J., Zins, J. E., Weissberg, R. P., Frey, K. S., Greenberg, M. T., Haynes, N. M., et al. (Eds.). (1997). *Promoting social and emotional learning: Guidelines for educators*. Alexandria, VA: Association for Supervision and Curriculum Development.

Elksnin, L. K. (1989). Teaching mildly handicapped students social skills in secondary settings. *Academic Therapy, 24*, 261–269.

Elksnin, L. K. (1994). Promoting generalization of social skills. *Learning Disability Forum, 19*(4), 35–37.

Elksnin, L. K. (1997). Collaborative speech and language services for students with LD. *Journal of Learning Disabilities, 30*, 414–426.

Elksnin, L. K., & Elksnin, N. (1995). *Assessment and instruction of social skills*. San Diego: Singular Publishing Group.

Elksnin, L. K., & Elksnin, N. (1996). Strategies for transition to employment settings. In D. D. Deshler, E. S. Ellis, & B. K. Lenz (Eds.), *Teaching adolescents with learning disabilities* (2d ed., pp. 525–578). Denver: Love Publishing.

Elksnin, L. K., & Elksnin, N. (1997). Issues in the assessment of children's social skills. *Diagnostique, 22*, 75–86.

Elksnin, L. K., & Elksnin, N. (1998). Teaching social skills to students with learning and behavior problems. *Intervention in School and Clinic, 33*(3), 131–140.

Elksnin, L. K., & Elksnin, N. (2000). Teaching parents to teach their children to be proso-cial. *Intervention in School and Clinic, 36*(1), 27–35.

Elksnin, L. K., & Elksnin, N. (2003). Fostering social–emotional learning in the classroom. *Education, 124*, 63–75.

Elksnin, L. K., & Elksnin, N. (2004). The social–emotional side of learning disabilities. *Learning Disability Quarterly, 27*(1), 3–8.

Elksnin, L. K., Elksnin, N., & Sabornie, E. (1994). Job-related social skills instruction of adolescents with mild mental retardation. *Journal of Vocational Special Needs Education, 17*(1), 1–7.

Elksnin, N., & Elksnin, L. K. (1991). Facilitating the vocational success of students with mild handicaps: The need for job-related social skills training. *The Journal of Vocational Special Needs Education, 13*(2), 5–11.

Elksnin, N., & Elksnin, L. K. (1998). *Teaching occupational social skills*. Austin, TX: Pro-Ed.

Elksnin, N., & Elksnin, L. K. (2001). Adolescents with disabilities: The need for occupa-tional social skills training. *Exceptionality, 9*(1&2), 91–105.

Elliott, S. N., & Gresham, F. M. (1991). *Social skills intervention guide: Practice strategies for social skills training*. Circle Pines, MN: American Guidance Service.

Elliott, S. N., & Gresham, F. M. (1993). Social skills interventions for children. *Behavior Modification, 17*, 287–313.

Elliott, S. N., Malecki, C. K., & Demaray, M. K. (2001). New directions in social skills assessment and intervention for elementary and middle school students. *Exceptionality, 9*(1&2), 19–32.

Elliott, S. N., Sheridan, S. M., & Gresham, F. M. (1989). Assessing and treating social skills deficits: A case study for the scientist–practitioner. *Journal of School Psychology, 27*, 197–222.

Ellis, E. (1991). *SLANT: A starter strategy for class participation*. Lawrence, KS: Edge Enterprises.

Elrod, G. F. (1987). Academic and social skills prerequisite to success in vocational training. *Journal for Vocational Special Needs Education, 10*(1), 17–21.

English, K., Goldstein, H., Kaczmarek, L., & Shafer, K. (1996). "Buddy skills" for preschoolers. *Teaching Exceptional Children, 28*(3), 62–66.

Erlbach, A., & Espeland, P. (1995). *The best friends book: True stories about real best friends*. Minneapolis, MN: Free Spirit Publishing.

Ervin, R. A., Johnston, E. S., & Friman, P. C. (1998). Positive peer reporting to improve the social interactions of a socially rejected girl. *Proven Practice: Prevention of Remediation Solutions for School Problems, 1*, 17–21.

Ervin, R. A., Miller, P. M., & Friman, P. C. (1996). Feed the hungry bee: Using positive peer reports to improve the social interactions and acceptance of a socially rejected girl in residential placement. *Journal of Applied Behavior Analysis, 29*, 251–253.

Espleland, P., & Verdick, E. (1998). *Making every day count: Daily readings for young peo-ple on solving problems, setting goals, and feeling good about yourself*. Minneapolis: Free Spirit Publishing.

Evenson, R. (1999). Soft skills, hard sell. *Techniques, 74*(3), 29–31.

Fopiano, J. E., & Haynes, N. M. (2001). School climates and social and emotional develop-ment in the young child. In J. Cohen (Ed.), *Caring classrooms, intelligent schools: The social emotional education of young children* (pp. 47–58). New York: Teachers College Press.

Forgan, J. W. (2002). Using bibliotherapy to teach problem solving. *Intervention in School and Clinic, 38*(2), 75–82.

Forgan, J. W., & Jones, C. D. (2002). How experiential adventure activities can improve students' social skills. *Teaching Exceptional Children, 34*, 52–58.

Forgan, J. W., & Gonzalez-DeHass, A. (2004). How to infuse social skills training into literacy instruction. *Teaching Exceptional Children, 36*(6), 24–30.

Forness, S. R., & Kavale, K. A. (1996). Treating social skill deficits in children with learning disabilities: A meta-analysis of the research. *Learning Disability Quarterly, 19*(1), 2–13.

Forness, S. R., Kavale, K. A., San Miguel, S. K., & Bauman, S.S.M. (1998). The psychiatric comorbidity hypothesis revisited. *Learning Disability Quarterly, 21*(3), 203–206.

Foss, G., Cheney, D., & Bullis, M. (1986). *Test of Interpersonal Competence for Employment.* Santa Barbara, CA: James Stanfield & Co.

Foster, S. L., Inderbitzen, H. M., & Nangle, D. W. (1993). Assessing acceptance and social skills with peers in childhood. *Behavior Modification, 17*(3), 255–286.

Foster, S. L., & Ritchey, W. L. (1979). Issues in the assessment of social competence in children. *Journal of Applied Behavior Analysis, 12*, 625–638.

Foxx, M., & McMorrow, M. J. (1983). *Stacking the deck: A social skills game for retarded adults.* Champaign, IL: Research Press.

Frankel, F. (1996). *Good friends are hard to find: Help your child find, make, and keep friends.* Los Angeles: Perspective Publishing.

Frederick, B. P., & Olmi, D. J. (1994). Children with attention-deficit/hyperactivity disorder: A review of the literature on social skills deficits. *Psychology in the Schools, 31*, 288–298.

Freeman, S.F.N., & Alkin, M. C. (2000). Academic and social attainments of children with mental retardation in general education and special education settings. *Remedial and Special Education, 21*(1), 3–18.

Frisch, M. B. (1988). Role-play training as a tool in social skills assessment. *Perceptual and Motor Skills, 67*, 483–490.

Fuchs, D., Fuchs, L. S., Mathes, P. G., & Martinez, E. A. (2002). Preliminary evidence on the social standing of students with learning disabilities in PALS and No-PALS classrooms. *Learning Disabilities Research & Practice, 17*(4), 205–215.

Fulton, L., & Silva, R. (1998). *The transitions curriculum: Vol. 1. Personal management.* Santa Barbara, CA: James Stanfield Co.

Gable, R. A., Strain, P. S., & Hendrickson, J. M. (1979). Strategies for improving the status and social behavior of learning disabled children. *Learning Disability Quarterly, 2*, 33–39.

Garbarino, J. (1995). *Raising children in a socially toxic environment.* San Francisco: Jossey-Bass.

Garell, D. C. (1989). *Friendship and love.* New York: Chelsea House.

Garrity, C., Baris, M., & Porter, W. (2000). *Bully-proofing your child: A parent's guide.* Longmont, CO: Sopris West.

Gibbs, J. C., Potter, G. B., & Goldstein, A. (1995). *The EQUIP program.* Champaign, IL: Research Press.

Glenn, H. S. (1989). *Raising self-reliant children in a self-indulgent world.* Orem, UT: Empowering People.

Goldstein, A. P. (1999). *The PREPARE curriculum: Teaching prosocial competencies* (rev. ed.). Champaign, IL: Research Press.

Goldstein, A. P., & McGinnis, E. (1997). *Skillstreaming the adolescent—revised edition.* Champaign, IL: Research Press.

Goleman, D. (1995). *Emotional intelligence: Why it can matter more than IQ.* New York: Basic Books.

Goleman, D. (1998). *Working with emotional intelligence.* New York: Bantam Books.

Goleman, D. (2001). An EI-based theory of performance. In G. Cherniss & D. Goleman (Eds.), *The emotionally intelligent workplace* (pp. 27–44). San Francisco: Jossey-Bass.

Goleman, D., Boyatzis, R., & McKee, A. (2002). *Primal leadership: Realizing the power of emotional intelligence.* Boston: Harvard Business School Publishing.

Gomez, R., & Hazeldine, P. (1996). Social information processing in mild mentally retarded children. *Research in Developmental Disabilities, 17*(3), 217–227.

Gonzalez–Lopez, A., & Kamps, D. M. (1997). Social skills training to increase social interactions between children with autism and their typical peers. *Focus on Autism, 12*(1), 2–14.

Gottman, J. (1997*). Raising an emotionally intelligent child.* New York: Simon & Schuster.

Greenan, J. P. (1983). *Identification of generalizable skills in secondary vocational programs. (Executive Summary).* Urbana–Champaign: Illinois State Department of Education.

Greenan, J. P., & Smith, B. B. (1981). *Assessing the generalizable skills of postsecondary vocational students.* Minneapolis: University of Minnesota, Minnesota Research and Development Center for Vocational Education.

Greenspan, S. I. (1994). *Playground politics: Understanding the emotional life of your school-aged child.* New York: Perseus Book Group.

Greenspan, S., & Granfield, J. M. (1992). Reconsidering the construct of mental retardation: Implications of a model of social competence. *American Journal on Mental Retardation, 96,* 442–453.

Greenspan, S. I., & Greenspan, N. T. (1994). *First feelings: Milestones in the emotional development of your baby and child.* New York: Penguin Books.

Gresham, F. M. (1981). Assessment of children's social skills. *Journal of School Psychology, 19,* 120–133.

Gresham, F. M. (1982). Misguided mainstreaming: The case for social skills training with handicapped children. *Exceptional Children, 48,* 422–433.

Gresham, F. M. (1990). Best practices in social skills training. In A. Thomas & J. Grimes (Eds.), *Best practices in school psychology–II* (pp. 695–709). Washington, DC: National Association of School Psychologists.

Gresham, F. M. (1992). Social skills and learning disabilities: Causal, concomitant or correlational? *School Psychology Review, 21*(3), 348–360.

Gresham, F. M. (1998a). Social skills training with children: Social learning and applied behavioral analytic approaches. In T. S. Watson & F. M. Gresham (Eds.), *Handbook of child behavior therapy* (pp. 475–497). New York: Plenum Press.

Gresham, F. M. (1998b). Social skills training: Should we raze, remodel or rebuild? *Behavioral Disorders, 24*(1), 19–25.

Gresham, F. M. (2001). Assessment of social skills in children and adolescents. In J. J. W. Andrews, D. H. Saklofske, & H. L. Janzen (Eds.), *Handbook of psychoeducational assessment: Ability, achievement and behavior in children* (pp. 325–355). San Diego: Academic Press.

Gresham, F. M., & Elliott, S. N. (1990a). *Social skills rating system—Elementary.* Circle Pines, MN: American Guidance Service.

Gresham, F. M., & Elliott, S. N. (1990b). *Social skills rating system—Preschool*. Circle Pines, MN: American Guidance Service.

Gresham, F. M., & Elliott, S. N. (1990c). *Social skills rating system—Secondary*. Circle Pines, MN: American Guidance Service.

Gresham, F. M., MacMillan, D. L., & Bocian, K. M. (1996). Learning disabilities, low achievement, and mild mental retardation: More alike than different. *Journal of Learning Disabilities, 29*(6), 570–581.

Gresham, F. M., Sugai, G., & Horner, R. H. (2001). Interpreting outcomes of social skills training for students with high-incidence disabilities. *Exceptional Children, 67*, 331–344.

Gresham, F. M., Watson, T. S., & Skinner, C. H. (2001). Functional behavioral assessment: Principles, procedures, and future directions. *School Psychology Review, 30*, 156–172.

Gronna, S. S., Serna, L. A., Kennedy, C. H., & Prater, M. A. (1999). Promoting generalized social interactions using puppets and script training in an integrated preschool. *Behavior Modification, 23*(3), 419–440.

Guevremont, D. (1990). Social skills and peer relationship training. In R. A. Barkley (Ed.), *Attention deficit hyperactivity disorders: A handbook for diagnosis and treatment* (pp. 540–572). New York: Guilford Press.

Gumpel, T. (1994). Social competence and social skills training for persons with mental retardation: An expansion of a behavioral paradigm. *Education and Training in Mental Retardation and Developmental Disabilities, 29*, 194–201.

Gumpel, T. P., & Golan, H. (2000). Teaching game-playing social skills using a self-monitoring treatment package. *Psychology in the Schools, 37*, 253–261.

Gumpel, T., & Wilson, M. (1996). Application of a Rasch analysis to the examination of the perception of facial affect among persons with mental retardation. *Research in Developmental Disabilities, 17*(2), 161–171.

Hagner, D., Rogan, P., & Murphy, S. T. (1992). Facilitating natural supports in the workplace: Strategies for support consultants. *Journal of Rehabilitation, 58*, 29–34.

Hallahan, D. P., & Kauffman, J. M. (2003). *Exceptional learners: Introduction to special education* (9th ed.). Boston: Allyn & Bacon.

Hartas, D., & Donahue, M. L. (1997). Conversational and social problem-solving skills in adolescents with learning disabilities. *Learning Disabilities Research & Practice, 12*(4), 213–220.

Hartshorne, T. S., & Johnston, D. W. (1982). The use of behavioral assessment. *Diagnostique, 7,* 212–220.

Hawryluk, M. K., & Smallwood, D. L. (1988). Using peers as instructional agents: Peer tutoring and cooperative learning. In J. L. Graden, J. E. Zins, & M. J. Curtis (Eds.), *Alternative educational delivery systems: Enhancing instructional options for all students* (pp. 371–389). Washington, DC: National Association of School Psychologists.

Haycock, K., & Huang, S. (2001, Winter). Are today's high school graduates ready? *Thinking K–16, 5*(1), 2–19.

Haynes, N. M., Ben-Avie, M., & Ensigh, J. (Eds). (2003). *How social and emotional development add up: Getting results in math and science education*. New York: Teachers College Press.

Haynes, N. M., & Comer, J. P. (1996). Integrating schools, families, and communities through successful school reform: The school development program. *School Psychology Review, 25*, 501–506.

Hazel, J. S., Schumaker, J. B., Sherman, J. A., & Sheldon, J. (1995). *ASSET, a social skills program for adolescents*. Champaign, IL: Research Press.

Healey, K. N., & Masterpasqua, F. (1992). Interpersonal problem-solving among children with mild mental retardation. *American Journal on Mental Retardation, 96*, 367–372.

Heller, H. W., & Spooner, F., Anderson, D., & Mims, A. (1988). Homework: A review of special education classroom practices in the Southeast. *Teacher Education and Special Education, 11*, 43–51.

Herron, R., & Peter, V. J. (1998a). *A good friend: How to make one, how to be one.* Boys Town, NE: Boys Town Press.

Herron, R., & Peter, V. J. (1998b). *What's right for me? Making good choices in relationships.* Boys Town, NE: Boys Town Press.

Herron, R., & Peter, V. J. (1998c). *Who's in the mirror? Finding the real me.* Boys Town, NE: Boys Town Press.

Heward, W. L. (2003). *Exceptional children: An introduction to special education.* Upper Saddle River, NJ: Merrill-Prentice Hall.

Hobson, R. P., & Lee, A. (1998). Hello and goodbye: A study of social engagement in autism. *Journal of Autism and Developmental Disorders, 28*, 117–127.

Hollinger, J. D. (1987). Social skills for behaviorally disordered children as preparation for mainstreaming: Theory, practice, and new directions. *Remedial and Special Education, 8*(4), 17–27.

Huggins, P. (1990–1994). *Teaching cooperation skills.* Longmont, CO: Sopris West.

Huggins, P., Manion, D. W., & Moen, L. (1993). *Teaching friendship skills—Intermediate version.* Longmont, CO: Sopris West.

Huggins, P., Moen, L., & Manion, D. W. (1993–1995). *Teaching friendship skills—Primary version.* Longmont, CO: Sopris West.

Hughes, J. N., & Baker, D. B. (1991). *The clinical child interview.* New York: Guilford Press.

Hundert, J., & Houghton, A. (1992). Promoting social interaction of children with disabilities in integrated preschools: A failure to generalize. *Exceptional Children, 58*(4), 311–320.

International Reading Association. (2002). Children's Choices of 2002. *The Reading Teacher, 56*(2), 139–153.

Jackson, D. A., Jackson, N. F., & Bennett, M. L. (1998). *Teaching social competence to youth and adults with developmental disabilities.* Austin, TX: Pro-Ed.

Jackson, D. A., Jackson, N. F., Bennett, M. L., Bynum, D. M., & Faryna, E. (1991). *Learning to get along.* Champaign, IL: Research Press.

Jackson, N. F., Jackson, D. A., & Monroe, C. (1983). *Getting along with others: Teaching social effectiveness to children.* Champaign, IL: Research Press.

Johnson, D. W., & Johnson, R. T. (1975). *Learning together and alone.* Englewood Cliffs, NJ: Prentice-Hall.

Johnson, D. W., & Johnson, R. T. (1990). Social skills for successful group work. *Educational Leadership, 47*(4), 29–33.

Johnson, D., Johnson, R., Holubec, E., & Roy, P. (1984). *Circles of learning: Cooperation in the classroom.* Alexandria, VA: Association for Supervision and Curriculum Development.

Johnson, J. T. (1992). *Making friends, finding love: A book about teen relationships.* Minneapolis, MN: Lerner Publications.

Jones, K. M., Young, M. M., & Friman, P. C. (2000). Increasing peer praise of socially rejected delinquent youth: Effects on cooperation and acceptance. *School Psychology Quarterly, 15*(1), 30–39.

Jones, R. N., Sheridan, S. M., & Binns, W. R. (1993). Schoolwide social skills training: Providing preventive services to students at-risk. *School Psychology Quarterly, 8*(1), 57–80.

Joseph, G. E., & Strain, P. S. (2003). Enhancing emotional vocabulary in young children. *Young Exceptional Children, 6*(4), 18–26.

Kagan, S. (1992). *Cooperative learning resources for teachers.* San Juan Capistrano, CA: Resources for Teachers.

Kamps, D. M., Kravits, T., Gonzalez-Lopez, A., Kemmerer, K., Potucek, J., & Harrell, L. G. (1998). What do the peers think? Social validity of peer-mediated programs. *Education and Treatment of Children, 21*(2), 107–134.

Kamps, D., Royer, J., Dugan, E., Kravits, T., Gonzalez-Lopez, A., Garcia, J., et al. (2002). Peer training to facilitate social interaction for elementary students with autism and their peers. *Exceptional Children, 68*, 173–187.

Karlsberg, E. (1991). *How to make and keep friends.* Mahwah, NJ: Troll Associates.

Kauffman, J. M. (2001). *Characteristics of children's behavior disorders* (7th ed.). Columbus, OH: Merrill.

Kavale, K. A., & Forness, S. R. (1996). Social skill deficits and learning disabilities: A meta-analysis. *Journal of Learning Disabilities, 29*(3), 226–237.

Kavale, J. A., & Mostert, M. P. (2004). Social skills interventions for individuals with learning disabilities. *Learning Disability Quarterly, 27*, 31–43.

Kellner, M. H. (2001). *In control: A skill-building program for teaching young adolescents to manage anger.* Champaign, IL: Research Press.

Kelly, A. (1996). *Talkabout: A social communication skills package.* Oxon, UK: Speechmark.

Kerr, R. (1999). *Self-discipline: Using portfolios to help students develop self-awareness, manage emotions and build relationships.* Markham, Ontario, Canada: Pembroke Publishers.

Kim, Y. A. (2003). Necessary social skills related to peer acceptance. *Childhood Education, 79*(4), 234–238.

Kindlon, D., & Thompson, M. (1999). *Raising Cain: Protecting the emotional life of boys.* New York: Ballantine Books.

Kinney, J., & Kinney, T. (2003). *Social standards at school.* Verona, WI: Attainment Company.

Klin, A., Volkmar, S. S., Sparrow, D. V., Cicchetti, D., & Rourke, B. P. (1995). Validity and neuropsychological characterization of Asperger Syndrome: Convergence with nonverbal learning disabilities syndrome. *Journal of Child Psychology and Psychiatry, 36*, 1127–1140.

Knapczyk, D. R., & Rodes, P. G. (1996). *Teaching social competence: A practical approach for improving social skills in students at-risk.* Pacific Grove, CA: Brooks/Cole.

Knapczyk, D., & Rodes, P. (2001). *Teaching social competence: Social skills and academic success.* Verona, WI: IEP Resources.

Knopf, H. M. (2001a). *The stop & think social skills program, preK–1.* Longmont, CO: Sopris West.

Knopf, H. M. (2001b). *The stop & think social skills program, 2–3.* Longmont, CO: Sopris West.

Knopf, H. M. (2001c). *The stop & think social skills program, 4–5.* Longmont, CO: Sopris West.

Knopf, H. M. (2001d). *The stop & think social skills program, 6–8.* Longmont, CO: Sopris West.

Kohler, F. W., Anthony, L. J., Steighner, S. A., & Hoyson, M. (2001). Teaching social inter-action skills in the integrated preschool: An examination of naturalistic tactics. *Topics in Early Childhood Special Education, 21*, 93–103.

Kolb, S. M., & Hanley-Maxwell, C. (2003). Critical social skills for adolescents with high incidence disabilities: Parental perspectives. *Exceptional Children, 69*(2), 163–179.

Korinek, L., & Popp, P. A. (1997). Collaborative mainstream integration of social skills with academic instruction. *Preventing School Failure, 41*(4), 148–153.

Kovacs, M. (1991). *The children's depression inventory (CDI)*. North Tonawanda, NY: Multi-Health Systems.

Kuhne, M., & Wiener, J. (2000). Stability of social status of children with and without learning disabilities. *Learning Disability Quarterly, 23*, 64–75.

Kurdek, L. A., & Rodgon, M. M. (1975). Perceptual, cognitive, and affective perspective taking in kindergarten through sixth-grade children. *Developmental Psychology, 11*, 643–650.

Kusche, C. A., & Greenberg, M. T. (1994). *The PATHS (promoting alternative thinking strategies) curriculum*. Seattle, WA: Developmental Research & Programs.

Ladd, G. W. (1990). Having friends, keeping friends, making friends, and being liked by peers in the classroom: Predictors of children's early school adjustment? *Child Development, 61*, 1081–1100.

Ladd, G. W. (1991). Family–peer relationships during childhood: Pathways to competence and pathology? *Journal of Social and Personal Relationships, 8*, 307–314.

Ladd, G. W., Kochenderfer, B. J., & Coleman, C. C. (1996). Friendship quality as a pre-dictor of young children's early school adjustment. *Child Development, 67*, 1103–1118.

LaGreca, A. M., & Stone, W. L. (1990). LD status and achievement: Confounding variables in the study of children's social status, self-esteem, and behavioral functioning. *Journal of Learning Disabilities, 23*, 483–490.

LaGreca, A. M., & Vaughn, S. (1992). Social functioning of individuals with learning dis-abilities. *School Psychology Review, 21*(3), 423–426.

LaFreniere, P. J., & Dumas, J. E. (1995). *Social competence and behavior evaluation—Preschool edition*. Los Angeles: Western Psychological Services.

Landau, S., & Moore, L. A. (1991). Social skill deficits in children with attention deficit hyperactivity disorder. *School Psychology Review, 20*(2), 235–251.

Lane, K. L., Wehby, J., Menzies, H. M., Doukas, G. L., Munton, S. M., & Gregg, R. M. (2003). Social skills instruction for students at risk for antisocial behavior: The effects of small-group instruction. *Behavioral Disorders, 28*(3), 229–248.

Lane, K. L., Givner, C. C., & Pierson, M. R. (2004). Teacher expectations of student behav-ior: Social skills necessary for success in elementary school classrooms. *Journal of Special Education, 38*(2), 104–110.

Larson, K. A. (2001, February). 12 secrets to raising popular kids. *McCall's, 94*, 100–101.

Lavoie, R. (Producer). (1994). *Social skills deficits and learning disabilities with Richard Lavoie: Last one picked . . . first one picked on*. Washington, DC: WETA.

Lee, J. W., & Cartledge, G. (1996). Native Americans. In G. Cartledge & J. F. Milburn (Eds.), *Cultural diversity and social skills instruction: Understanding ethnic and gen-der differences* (pp. 205–243). Champaign, IL: Research Press.

Leffert, J. S., Siperstein, G. N., & Millikan, E. (2000). Understanding social adaptation in children with mental retardation: A social–cognitive perspective. *Exceptional Children, 66*, 530–545.

Levine, M. (1994). *Educational care: A system for understanding and helping children with learning problems in home and school.* Cambridge, MA: Educators Publishing Service, Inc.

Lewis, T. J. (1994). A comparative analysis of the effects of social skill training and teacher-directed contingencies on social behavior of preschool children with disabilities. *Journal of Behavioral Education, 4,* 267–281.

Lieberman, A. F. (1993). *The emotional life of the toddler.* New York: The Free Press.

Little, S. S. (1993). Nonverbal learning disabilities. *Journal of Learning Disabilities, 24,* 439–446.

Lopez, M. F., Forness, S. R., MacMilllan, D. L., Bocian, K. M., & Gresham, F. M. (1996). Children with attention deficit hyperactivity disorder and emotional or behavioral disorders in primary grades: Inappropriate placement in the learning disability category. *Education and Treatment of Children, 19*(3), 286–299.

Loveland, K. A., Pearson, D. A., Tunali-Kotoski, B., Ortegon, J., & Gibbs, M. C. (2001). Judgments of social appropriateness by children and adolescents with autism. *Journal of Autism and Developmental Disorders, 31,* 367–376.

Lowenthal, B. (1995). Strategies that promote social skills in toddlers with special needs in the inclusive setting. *Infant Toddler Intervention: The Transdisciplinary Journal, 5*(1), 15–22.

Lowenthal, B. (1996). Teaching social skills to preschoolers with special needs. *Childhood Education, 72*(3), 137–140.

Mahoney, S. (2002, October). Healing the bully blues. *Better Homes & Gardens, 79*(10), 166, 168–169.

Mannix, D. S. (1986). *I can behave: A classroom self-management curriculum for elementary students.* Portland, OR: ASIEP Education Co.

Mannix, D. S. (1993). *Social skills activities for special children.* West Nyack, NY: Center for Applied Research in Education.

Mannix, D. S. (1995). *Life skills activities for secondary students with special needs.* San Francisco: Jossey-Bass.

Mannix, D. S. (1998). *Social skills activities for secondary students with special needs.* West Nyack, NY: Center for Applied Research in Education.

Marano, H. E. (1998a). Why friends matter. *Family Circle, 111*(13), Sept. 15, 30–33.

Marano, H. E. (1998b). *"Why doesn't anybody like me?" A guide to raising socially confident kids.* New York: William Morrow.

Marcus, R. F., & Sanders-Reio, J. (2001). The influence of attachment on school completion. *School Psychology Quarterly, 16,* 427–444.

Margalit, M. (1993). Social skills and classroom behavior among adolescents with mild mental retardation. *American Journal on Mental Retardation, 97,* 685–691.

Margalit, M. (1995). Effects of social skills training for students with an intellectual disability. *International Journal of Disability, Development, and Education, 42*(1), 75–85.

Margalit, M. (1998). Loneliness and coherence among preschool children with learning disabilities. *Journal of Learning Disabilities, 31*(2), 173–180.

Margalit, M., & Levin-Alyagon, M. (1994). Learning disability subtyping, loneliness, and classroom adjustment. *Learning Disability Quarterly, 17*(2), 297–310.

Marks, S. U., Schrader, C., Levine, M., Hagie, C., Longaker, T., Morales, M., & Peters, I. (1999). Social skills for social ills: Supporting the social development of adolescents with Asperger's syndrome. *Teaching Exceptional Children, 32*(2), 56–61.

Martin, R. P. (1988). *Assessment of personality and behavior problems.* New York: Guilford Press.

Mathews, R. M., Whang, P. L., & Fawcett, S. B., (1980). Development and validation of an occupational skills assessment instrument. *Behavioral Assessment, 2,* 71–85.

Mathews, R. M., Whang, P. L., & Fawcett, S B. (1981). Behavior assessment of job-related skills. *Journal of Employment Counseling, 18*(1), 3–11.

Mathews, R. M., Whang, P. L., & Fawcett, S. B. (1982). Behavioral assessment of occupational skills of learning disabled adolescents. *Journal of Learning Disabilities, 15,* 38–41.

Mathinos, D. A. (1991). Conversational engagement of children with learning disabilities. *Journal of Learning Disabilities, 24,* 439–446.

Mathur, S. R., & Rutherford, R. B., Jr. (1991). Peer-mediated interventions promoting social skills of children and youth with behavioral disorders. *Education and Treatment of Children, 14,* 227–242.

Matson, J. L. (1994). *Matson evaluation of social skills with youngsters* (2d ed.). Worthington, OH: International Diagnostic Systems.

Matson, J. L., & Ollendick, T. H. (1988). *Enhancing children's social skills: Assessment and training.* New York: Pergamon.

Matson, J. L., Sevin, J. A., & Box, M. L. (1995). Social skills in children. In W. O'Donohue & L. Krasner, *Handbook of psychological skills training: Clinical techniques and applications* (pp. 36–53). Boston: Allyn & Bacon.

Mayer, J. D. (2001). A field guide to emotional intelligence. In J. Ciarrochi, J. P. Forgas, & J. D. Mayer (Eds.), *Emotional intelligence in everyday life: A scientific inquiry* (pp. 3–24). New York: Psychology Press.

Mayer, J. D., Caruso, D., & Salovey, P. (1999). Emotional intelligence meets traditional standards for an intelligence. *Intelligence, 27,* 267–298.

Mayer, J. D., DiPaolo, M. T., & Salovey, P. (1990). Perceiving affective content in ambiguous visual stimuli: A component of emotional intelligence. *Journal of Personality Assessment, 54,* 772–781.

Mayer, J. D., Salovey, P., & Caruso, D. R. (2002). *Mayer–Salovey–Caruso emotional intelligence test.* North Tonawanda, NY: Multi-Health Systems.

McCarney, S. B. (1995a). *Attention deficit disorders evaluation scales–2d ed.: Home version technical manual.* Columbia, MO: Hawthorne Educational Services.

McCarney, S. B. (1995b). *Attention deficit disorders evaluation scales–2d ed.: School version technical manual.* Columbia, MO: Hawthorne Educational Services.

McFall, R. M. (1982). A review and reformulation of the concept of social skills. *Behavioral Assessment, 4,* 1–33.

McGann, W., & Werven, G. (1999). *Social communication skills for children.* Austin, TX: Pro-Ed.

McGinnis, E., & Goldstein, A. P. (1997). *Skillstreaming the elementary school child (rev.).* Champaign, IL: Research Press.

McGinnis, E., & Goldstein, A. P. (2003). *Skillstreaming in early childhood (rev.).* Champaign, IL: Research Press.

McIntosh, R., Vaughn, S., & Zaragoza, N. (1991). A review of social interventions for students with learning disabilities. *Journal of Learning Disabilities, 24*(8), 451–458.

McMahon, C. M., Wacker, D. P., Sasso, G. M., Berg, W. K., & Newton, S. M. (1996). Analysis of frequency and type of interactions in a peer mediated social skills intervention: Instructional vs. social interactions. *Education and Training in Mental Retardation and Developmental Disabilities, 31,* 339–352.

Mehrabian, A. (1968). Communication without words. *Psychology Today, 24*, 52–55.

Meichenbaum, D., & Goodman, J. (1971). Training impulsive children to talk to themselves: A means of developing self-control. *Journal of Abnormal Psychology, 77*, 115–126.

Merrell, K. W. (2002a). *Preschool and kindergarten behavior scales–2.* Austin, TX: Pro-Ed.

Merrell, K. W. (2002b). *School social behavior scales–2.* Eugene, OR: Assessment-Intervention Resources.

Merrell, K. W. (2002c). Social–emotional intervention in schools: Current status, progress, and promise. *School Psychology Review, 31*(2), 143–147.

Merrell, K. W. (2003). *Behavioral, social, and emotional assessment of children and adolescents* (2d ed.). Mahwah, NJ: Erlbaum.

Merrell, K. W., & Gimpel, G. A. (1998). *Social skills of children and adolescents: Conceptualization, assessment, treatment.* Mahwah, NJ: Erlbaum.

Meyer, J. A. (2001–2002). Cognitive patterns in autism spectrum disorders. *Assessment for Effective Intervention, 27*(1&2), 27–25.

Minskoff, E. M. (1994). *Technical-related and academic career competencies (TRACC).* Richmond: Virginia Department of Education and Virginia Department of Rehabilitative Services.

Moffatt, C. W., Hanley-Maxwell, C., & Donnellan, A. M. (1995). Discrimination of emotional, affective perspective-taking and empathy in individuals with mental retardation. *Education and Training in Mental Retardation and Developmental Disabilities, 30*, 76–85.

Montague, M. (1988). Job-related social skills training for adolescents with handicaps. *Career Development for Exceptional Individuals, 11*, 26–41.

Montague, M., & Lund, K. A. (1991). *Job-related social skills: A curriculum for adolescents with special needs.* Ann Arbor, MI: Exceptional Innovations.

Moreno, J. L. (1934). Who shall survive? *Nervous and Mental Disease Monograph* (No. 48). Washington, DC.

Moroz, K. B., & Jones, K. M. (2002). The effects of positive peer reporting on children's social involvement. *School Psychology Review, 31*(2), 235–245.

Morris, S. (2002). Promoting social skills among students with nonverbal learning disabilities. *Teaching Exceptional Children, 34*, 66–70.

Most, T., & Greenbank, A. (2000). Auditory, visual, and auditory–visual perception of emotions by adolescents with and without learning disabilities, and their relationship to social skills. *Learning Disabilities Research & Practice, 15*, 171–178.

Mugno, D., & Rosenblitt, D. (2001). Helping emotionally vulnerable children: Moving toward an empathetic orientation in the classroom. In J. Cohen (Ed.), *Caring classrooms/intelligent schools: The social emotional education of young children* (pp. 59–76). New York: Teachers College Press.

Myles, B. S., & Adreon, D. (2001–2002). Message from the guest editors: Assessment of children and youth with autism spectrum disorders [Special issue]. *Assessment for Effective Intervention, 27*(1 & 2), 3–4.

Nabuzoka, D., & Smith, K. (1995). Identification of expressions of emotions by children with and without learning disabilities. *Learning Disabilities Research & Practice, 10*, 91–101.

Naglieri, J., LeBuffe, P., & Pfeiffer, S. (1993). *Devereux behavior rating scale—School form.* San Antonio, TX: Psychological Corp.

Nelson, N. W. (1989). Curriculum-based language assessment, assessment, and intervention. *Language, Speech, and Hearing Services in Schools, 20*, 170–184.

Nelson, N. W. (1990). Only relevant practices can be best. In W. A. Secord (Ed.), *Best practices in speech–language pathology* (pp. 15–27). San Antonio, TX: Psychological Corp.

Newton, S. J., Olson, D., Horner, R. H., & Ard, W. R., Jr. (1996). Social skills and the stability of social relationships between individuals with intellectual disabilities and other community members. *Research in Developmental Disabilities, 17*(1), 15–26.

Nickerson, A. B., & Brosof, A. M. (2003). Identifying skills and behaviors for successful inclusion of students with emotional or behavioral disorders. *Behavioral Disorders, 28*(4), 401–409.

Nowicki, S., & Duke, M. P. (1992). *Helping the child who doesn't fit in*. Atlanta, GA: Peachtree.

Odom, S. L., & McConnell, S. R. (1993). *Play time/social time: Organizing your classroom to build interaction skills*. Tucson, AZ: Communication Skill Builders.

Odom, S. L., McConnell, S. R., & McEvoy, M. A. (1992). *Social competence of young children with disabilities: Issues and strategies for intervention*. Baltimore: Paul H. Brookes.

Odom, S. L., & Watts, E. (1991). Reducing teacher prompts in peer-mediated interventions for young children with autism. *Journal of Special Education, 25*, 26–41.

Olmeda, R. E., & Trent, S. C. (2003). Social skills training research with minority students with learning disabilities. *Learning Disabilities, 12*(1), 23–33.

O'Neill, R. E., Horner, R. H., Albin, R. W., Sprague, J. R., Storey, K., & Newton, J. S. (1997). *Functional assessment and program development for problem behavior: A practical guide*. Pacific Grove, CA: Brooks/Cole Publishing.

O'Reilly, M. F., & Glynn, D. (1995). Using a process social skills training approach with adolescents with mild intellectual disabilities in a high school setting. *Education and Training in Mental Retardation and Developmental Disabilities, 30*(3), 187–198.

Packer, A. C., & Brainard, S. (2003). Implementing SCANS. *The Highlight Zone, 10*, 1–10.

Packer, A. J. (1997). *How rude! The teenagers' guide to good manners, proper behavior, and not grossing people out*. Minneapolis, MN: Free Spirit Publishing.

Panacek, L. J., & Dunlap, G. (2003). The social lives of children with emotional and behavioral disorders in self-contained classrooms: A descriptive analysis. *Exceptional Children, 69*, 333–348.

Panella, D., & Henggeler, S. W. (1986). Peer interactions of conduct-disordered, anxious-withdrawn, and well-adjusted black adolescents. *Journal of Abnormal Child Psychology, 14*, 1–11.

Parello, N. (1996, October). Learning to be a friend. *Working Mother, 19*(10), 75, 78–79.

Pasi, R. J. (2001). Designing a program: The basic principles (pp. 10–13). *Higher expectations: Promoting social emotional learning and academic achievement in your school*. New York: Teachers College Press.

Pellegrini, A. D. (1992). Kindergarten children's social–cognitive status as a predictor of first-grade success. *Early Childhood Research Quarterly, 7*, 565–577.

Pianta, R. C. (1999). *Enhancing relationships between children and teachers*. Washington, D.C.: American Psychological Association.

Pierce, K., & Schreibman, L. (1997). Using peer trainers to promote social behavior in autism: Are they effective at enhancing multiple social modalities. *Focus on Autism and Other Developmental Disabilities, 12*(4), 207–218.

Porath, M. (2003). Social understanding in the first years of school. *Early Childhood Research Quarterly, 18*, 468–484.

Post, M., Storey, K., & Karabin, M. 2002. Supporting students and adults in work and community environments. *Teaching Exceptional Children, 34*, 60–65.

Prater, M. A., Bruhl, S., & Serna, L. A. (1998). Acquiring social skills through cooperative learning and teacher directed instruction. *Remedial and Special Education, 19*(3), 160–172.

Pray, B. S., Jr., Hall, K. W., & Marksley, R. P. (1992). Social skills training: An analysis of social behaviors selected for individualized education programs. *Remedial and Special Education, 13*(5), 43–49.

Quay, H. C., & Peterson, D. R. (1996). *Manual for the revised behavior problem checklist–PAR version.* Odessa, FL: Psychological Assessment Resources.

Quinn, M. M., Kavale, K. A., Mathur, S. R., Rutherford, R. B., & Forness, S. R. (1999). A meta-analysis of social skills interventions for students with emotional and behavioral disorders. *Journal of Emotional and Behavioral Disorders, 7*, 54–64.

Rahill, S. A., & Teglasi, H. (2003). Processes and outcomes of story-based and skill-based social competency programs for children with emotional disabilities. *Journal of School Psychology, 41*, 413–429.

Raskind, M. H., Goldberg, R. J., Higgins, E. L., & Herman, K. L. (2002). Teaching "life success" to students with LD: Lessons learned from a 20-year study. *Intervention in School and Clinic, 37*, 201–208.

Ratnesar, R. (1997, September). Teaching feelings 101. *Time, 150*(13), 62.

Reiff, H. B., & Gerber, P. J. (1990). Cognitive correlates of social perception in students with learning disabilities. *Journal of Learning Disabilities, 23*, 260–262.

Reisberg, L. (1998). Facilitating inclusion with integrated curriculum: A multidisciplinary approach. *Intervention in School and Clinic, 33*(5), 272–277.

Reynolds, C. R., & Kamphaus, R. W. (1992). *Behavior assessment system for children.* Circle Pines, MN: American Guidance Service.

Reynolds, C. R., & Richmond, B. O. (1985). *Revised children's manifest anxiety scale.* Los Angeles: Western Psychological Services.

Richardson, R. C. (1996a). *Connecting with others, K–2.* Champaign, IL: Research Press.

Richardson, R. C. (1996b). *Connecting with others, grades 3–5.* Champaign, IL: Research Press.

Richardson, R. C., & Evans, E. T. (1997). *Connecting with others, grades 6–8.* Champaign, IL: Research Press.

Richardson, R. C., & Meisgeier, C. M. (2001). *Connecting with others, grades 9–12.* Champaign, IL: Research Press.

Romer, L. T., Haring, N. G., & White, J. (1996). The effect of peer-mediated social competency training on the type and frequency of social contacts with students with deaf-blindness. *Education and Training in Mental Retardation and Developmental Disabilities, 31*(4), 324–338.

Rosenbaum, J. (2001). *Beyond college for all: Career paths for the forgotten half.* New York: Russell Sage Foundation.

Rosenbaum, J. E. (2002). *Beyond empty promises: Policies to improve transitions into college and jobs.* Washington, DC: U.S. Department of Education, Office of Vocational and Adult Education.

Rosenthal-Malek, A. L., & Yoshida, R. K. (1994). The effects of metacognitive strategy training on the acquisition and generalization of social skills. *Education and Training in Mental Retardation and Developmental Disabilities, 29*(3), 213–221.

Rourke, B. P. (1987). Syndrome of nonverbal learning disabilities: The final common pathway of white-matter disease/dysfunction? *Clinical Neuropsychologist, 1*, 209–234.

Rourke, B. P. (1989). *Nonverbal learning disabilities: The syndrome and the model.* New York: Guilford.

Rourke, B. P. (Ed.). (1991). *Neuropsychological validation of learning disability subtypes.* New York: Guilford.

Rourke, B. P., & Fuerst, D. R. (1991). *Learning disabilities and psychosocial functioning: A neuropsychological perspective.* New York: Guilford.

Rourke, B. P., & Fuerst, D. R. (1992). Psychological dimensions of learning disability subtypes: Neuropsychological studies in the Windsor Laboratory. *School Psychology Review, 21*(3), 361–374.

Rutherford, R., Chipman, J., DiGangi, S., & Anderson, K. (1992). *Teaching social skills: A practical instructional approach.* Ann Arbor, MI: Exceptional Innovations.

Saarni, C. (1999). *The development of emotional competence.* New York: Guilford.

Sabornie, E. J. (1994). Social–affective characteristics in early adolescents identified as learning disabled and nondisabled. *Learning Disability Quarterly, 17*(2), 268–279.

Sabornie, E. J., & Kauffman, J. M. (1985). Regular classroom sociometric status of behaviorally disordered adolescents. *Behavioral Disorders, 10*, 268–274.

Sabornie, E. J., Kauffman, J. M., Ellis, E. S., Marshall, K. J., & Elksnin, L. K. (1988). Bidirectional and cross-categorical social status of learning disabled, behaviorally disordered, and nonhandicapped adolescents. *The Journal of Special Education, 21*, 39–56.

Salovey, P., & Sluyter, D. J. (Eds.). (1997). *Emotional development and emotional intelligence: Educational implications.* New York: Basic Books.

San Miguel, S. K., Forness, S. R., & Kavale, K. A. (1996). Social skills deficits in learning disabilities: The psychiatric comorbidity hypothesis. *Learning Disability Quarterly, 19*(3), 252–261.

Sargent, L. R. (1988). *Systematic instruction of social skills.* Des Moines: Iowa Department of Education.

Sargent, L. R. (1991). *Social skills for school and community.* Arlington, VA: Division on Mental Retardation of the Council for Exceptional Children.

Sarkees-Wircenski, M., & Scott, J. L. (2003). *Special populations in career and technical education.* Homewood, IL: American Technical Publishers.

Schloss, P. (1987). Self-management strategies for adolescents entering the work force. *Teaching Exceptional Children, 19*, 39–43.

Schloss, P. J., Schloss, C. N., Wood, C. E., & Kiehl, W. S. (1986). A critical review of social skills research with behaviorally disordered students. *Behavioral Disorders, 12*(1), 1–14.

Schneider, M. F. (1991). *Popularity has its ups and downs.* New York: Simon and Schuster.

Schneider, M., & Robin, A. L. (1973). *Turtle manual.* Unpublished manuscript, Point of Woods Laboratory School, State University of New York, Stony Brook.

Schonert-Reichi, K. A. (1993). Empathy and social relationships in adolescents with behavioral disorders. *Behavioral Disorders, 18*(3), 189–204.

Schulze, K. A., Rule, S., & Innocenti, M. S. (1989). Coincidental teaching: Parents promoting social skills at home. *Teaching Exceptional Children, 21*, 24–27.

Schumaker, J. B. (1992). Social performance of individuals with learning disabilities: Through the looking glass of KU–IRLD research. *School Psychology Review, 21*(3), 387–399.

Schumaker, J. B., & Hazel, J. S. (1984). Social skills assessment and training for the learning disabled: Who's on first and what's on second? Part I. *Journal of Learning Disabilities, 17*, 422–431.

Schumaker, J. B., Hazel, J. S., & Pederson, C. S. (1988). *Social skills for daily living*. Circle Pines, MN: American Guidance Service.

Scott, T. M., & Nelson, C. M. (1998). Confusion and failure in facilitating generalized social responding in the school setting: Sometimes 2+2=5. *Behavioral Disorders, 23*(4), 264–275.

Scully, J. L. (2000). *The power of social skills in character development: Helping diverse learners succeed*. Port Chester, NY: Dude Publishing.

Secretary's Commission on Achieving Necessary Skills (1992). *What work requires of schools: A SCANS report for America 2000*. Washington, DC: U.S. Department of Labor. (ERIC Document Reproduction Service No. ED 332054)

Selman, R. L. (1980). *The growth of interpersonal understanding*. New York: Academic Press.

Selman, R. L., & Byrne, D. F. (1974). A structural-developmental analysis of levels of role taking in middle childhood. *Child Development, 45*, 803–806.

Shantz, C. U. (1975). The development of social cognition. In E. M. Hetherington (Ed.), *Review of child development research* (Vol. 5, pp. 257–323). Chicago: University of Chicago Press.

Shapiro, L. (1995). *Sometimes I like to fight, but I don't do it much anymore: A self-esteem book to help children with difficulty controlling their anger*. Secaucus, NJ: Childs Work/Childs Play.

Shapiro, L. E. (1997). *How to raise a child with a high EQ: A parent's guide to emotional intelligence*. New York: HarperPerennial.

Sheridan, M. K., Foley, G. M., & Radlinski, S. H. (1995). *Using the supportive play model: Individualized intervention in early childhood practice*. New York: Teachers College Press.

Sheridan, S. M. (1995–1996). *The tough kid social skills book*. Longmont, CO: Sopris West.

Sheridan, S. M., Hungelmann, A., & Maughan, D. P. (1999). A contextualized framework for social skills assessment, intervention, and generalization. *School Psychology Review, 28*(1), 84–103.

Shondrick, D. D., Serafica, F. C., Clark, P., & Miller, K. (1992). Interpersonal problem solving and creativity in boys with and boys without learning disabilities. *Learning Disability Quarterly, 15*, 95–118.

Shure, M. B. (1992a). *I can problem solve: Preschool*. Champaign, IL: Research Press.

Shure, M. B. (1992b). *I can problem solve: Kindergarten & primary grades*. Champaign, IL: Research Press.

Shure, M. B. (1992c). *I can problem solve: Intermediate elementary grades*. Champaign, IL: Research Press.

Shure, M. B. (1996). *Raising a thinking child: Help your young child to resolve everyday conflicts and get along with others*. New York: Pocket Books.

Shure, M. B. (2000a). *Raising a thinking child workbook: Teaching young children how to resolve everyday conflicts and get along with others*. Champaign, IL: Research Press.

Shure, M. B. (2000b). *Raising a thinking preteen: The I can problem solve programs for 8- to 12-year-olds*. New York: Henry Holt.

Shure, M. B., & Glaser, A. (2001). I can problem solve (ICPS): A cognitive approach to the prevention of early high-risk behaviors. In J. Cohen (Ed.), *Caring classrooms/intelligent schools: The social emotional education of young children* (pp. 122–139). New York: Teachers College Press.

Shure, M. B., & Spivack, G. (1971). *Solving interpersonal problems: A program for four-year-old nursery school children: Training script.* Philadelphia: Hahnemann Community Mental Health/Mental Retardation Center, Department of Mental Health Sciences.

Shure, M. B., & Spivack, G. (1978a). *A mental health program for kindergarten children: Training script (revised edition).* Philadelphia: Department of Mental Health Services, Hahnemann Community Mental Health/Mental Retardation Center.

Shure, M. B., & Spivack, G. (1978b). *Problem-solving techniques in childrearing.* San Francisco: Jossey-Bass.

Shure, M. B., & Spivack, G. (1980). Interpersonal problem solving as a mediator of behavioral adjustment in preschool and kindergarten children. *Journal of Applied Developmental Psychology, 1,* 29–44.

Sigler, G., & Fitzpatrick, D. K. (2000). *Playing a role: Real life vocational rehearsals.* Verona, WI: IEP Resources.

Silverman, R., Zigmond, N., & Sansone, J. (1981). Teaching coping skills to adolescents with learning problems. *Focus on Exceptional Children, 13*(6), 1–20.

Simpson, R. (1996). *Working with parents and families of exceptional children and youth.* Austin, TX: Pro-Ed.

Siperstein, G. N., & Bak, J. J. (1988). Improving social skills in schools: The role of parents. *Exceptional Parent, 18*(2), 18–22.

Siperstein, G. N., & Rickards, E. P. (2004). *Promoting social success: A curriculum for children with special needs.* Baltimore: Paul H. Brookes.

Skinner, C. H., Cashwell, T. H., & Skinner, A. L. (2000). Increasing tootling: Effects of a peer-monitored group contingency program on students' reports of peers' prosocial behaviors. *Psychology in the Schools, 37*(3), 263–270.

Slavin, R. E. (1983). *Cooperative learning.* New York: Longman.

Smith, S. W., & Gilles, D. L. (2003). Using key instructional elements to systematically promote social skill generalization for students with challenging behavior. *Intervention in School and Clinic, 39,* 30–37.

Sodac, D. (1997). Join the Amicus Club. Increasing high schoolers' social skills in an after-school program. *Teaching Exceptional Children, 29*(3), 64–67.

Soto, G., Toro-Zambrana, W., & Belfiore, P. J. (1994). Comparison of two instructional strategies on social skills acquisition and generalization among individuals with moderate and severe mental retardation working in a vocational setting: A meta-analytic review. *Education and Training in Mental Retardation and Developmental Disabilities, 29*(4), 307–320.

Spencer, P. (2003, July 8). Old friends, new friends. *Woman's Day, 66*(12), 108.

Spivack, G., & Shure, M. B. (1974). *Social adjustment of young children.* San Francisco: Jossey-Bass.

Spivack, G., & Shure, M. (1983). The cognition of social adjustment: Interpersonal cognitive problem-solving thinking. In B. Lahey & A. Kazdin (Eds.), *Advances in clinical child psychology* (Vol. 5, pp. 323–372). New York: Plenum Press.

Sprague, J., Sugai, G., & Walker, H. (1998). Antisocial behavior in schools. In T. S. Watson & F. M. Gresham (Eds.), *Handbook of child behavior therapy* (pp. 451–474). New York: Plenum Press.

Sprinthall, N. A., & Collins, W. A. (1988). *Adolescent psychology: A developmental view* (2d ed.). New York: Random House.

Stanovich, K. E. (1986). Matthew effects in reading: Some consequences of individual differences in the acquisition of literacy. *Reading Research Quarterly, 21,* 360–407.

Stanovich, K. E. (1988). Explaining the differences between the dyslexic and the garden-variety poor reader: The phonological-core variable-difference model. *Journal of Learning Disabilities, 21*, 590–604.

Stein, S. J., & Book, H. E. (2001). *The EQ edge: Emotional intelligence and your success.* Toronto, Ontario, Canada: Stoddart.

Stephens, T. M. (1992). *Social skills in the classroom.* Odessa, FL: Psychological Assessment Resources.

Stephens, T. M., & Arnold, K. D. (1992). *Social behavior assessment inventory.* Odessa, FL: Psychological Assessment Resources.

Stokes, T. F., & Baer, D. M. (1977). An implicit technology of generalization. *Journal of Applied Behavior Analysis, 10*, 349–367.

Stokes, T., & Osnes, P. (1986). Programming the generalization of children's social behavior. In P. Strain, M. Guralnick, & H. Walker (Eds.), *Children social behavior: Development, assessment, and modification* (pp. 407–443). Orlando, FL: Academic Press.

Stone, K. F., & Dillehunt, H. (1978). *Self-science: The subject is me.* Santa Monica, CA: Goodyear Publishing.

Stone, W. L., & LaGreca, A. M. (1983). Comprehension of nonverbal communication: A reexamination of the social competencies of learning-disabled children. *Journal of Abnormal Child Psychology, 12*, 505–518.

Storey, K., Danko, C. D., Strain, P. S., & Smith, D. J. (1992). A follow-up of social skills instruction for preschoolers with developmental delays. *Education and Treatment of Children, 15*(2), 125–139.

Storey, K., Lengyel, L., & Pruszynski, B. (1997). Assessing the effectiveness and measuring the complexity of two conversational instructional procedures in supported employment contexts. *Journal of Vocational Rehabilitation, 8*, 21–33.

Strain, P. S. (2001). Empirically based social skill intervention: A case for quality-of-life improvement. *Behavioral Disorders, 27*, 30–36.

Strain, P. S., & Odom, S. L. (1986). Peer social initiations: Effective intervention for social skills development of exceptional children. *Exceptional Children, 52*, 543–551.

Strain, P. S., & Smith, B. J. (1996). Developing social skills in young children with special needs. *Preventing School Failure, 41*(1), 24–27.

Sugai, G., Lewis-Palmer, T., & Hagan-Burke, S. (1999–2000). Overview of the functional behavioral assessment process. *Exceptionality, 8*(3), 149–160.

Sugai, G., & Lewis-Palmer, T. (2004). Overview of function-based approach to behavior support within schools. *Assessment for Effective Intervention, 30*(1), 1–5.

Sundel, S. (1994). Videotaped training of job-related social skills using peer modeling: An evaluation of social validity. *Research on Social Skills Practice, 4*(1), 40–52.

Swanson, H. L. (1996). Meta-analysis, replication, social skills and learning disabilities. *The Journal of Special Education, 30*(2), 213–221.

Swanson, H. L., & Malone, S. (1992). Social skills and learning disabilities: A meta-analysis of the literature. *School Psychology Review, 21*(3), 427–443.

Teglasi, H., & Rothman, L. (2001). STORIES: A classroom-based program to reduce aggressive behavior. *Journal of School Psychology, 39*(1), 71–94.

Telzrow, C. F., & Bonar, A. M. (2002). Responding to students with nonverbal learning disabilities. *Teaching Exceptional Children, 34*(6), 8–13.

Thompson, M. (2002). *Mom, they're teasing me: Helping your child solve social problems.* New York: Ballantine Books.

Thompson, M., Grace, C. O., & Cohen, L. J. (2001). *Best friends, worst enemies: Understanding the social lives of children.* New York: Ballantine Books.

Toro, P. A., Weissberg, R. P., Guare, J., & Liebenstein, N. L. (1990). A comparison of children with and without learning disabilities on social problem-solving skill, school behavior, and family background. *Journal of Learning Disabilities, 23*, 115–120.

Torrey, G. K., Vasa, S. F., Maag, J. W., & Kramer, J. J. (1992). Social skills interventions across school settings: Case study reviews of students with mild disabilities. *Psychology in the Schools, 29*(1), 248–255.

Tur-Kaspa, H., & Bryan, T. (1995). Teachers' ratings of the social competence and social adjustment of students with LD in elementary and junior high school. *Journal of Learning Disabilities, 28*(1), 44–52.

University of Pittsburgh. (1986). *School survival skills curriculum.* Pittsburgh: Author.

U.S. Congress, Public Law 108-446, *Individuals with Disabilities Education Improvement Act of 2004.*

U.S. Department of Education (1996). *Eighteenth annual report to Congress on the implementation of the Individuals with Disabilities Education Act.* Washington, DC: Author.

U.S. Department of Education. (2002). *Twenty-fourth annual report to Congress on the implementation of the Individuals with Disabilities Education Act.* Washington, DC: Author.

U.S. Department of Labor. (1992). *Learning a living: A blueprint for high performance—A SCANS report for America 2000.* Washington, D.C.: Author.

Vallance, D. D., Cummings, R. L., & Humphries, T. (1998). Mediators of the risk for problem behavior in children with language learning disabilities. *Journal of Learning Disabilities, 31*(2), 160–171.

Vaughn, S., Elbaum, B. E., & Schumm, J. S. (1996). The effects of inclusion on the social functioning of students with learning disabilities. *Journal of Learning Disabilities, 29*(6), 598–608.

Vaughn, S., & Haager, D. (1994). Social competence as a multifaceted construct: How do students with learning disabilities fare? *Learning Disability Quarterly, 17*(2), 253–266.

Vaughn, S., & Hogan, A. (1994). The social competence of students with learning disabilities over time: A within-individual examination. *Journal of Learning Disabilities, 27*(5), 292–303.

Vaughn, S., Zaragoza, N., Hogan, A., & Walker, J. (1993). A four-year longitudinal investigation of the social skills and behavior problems of students with learning disabilities. *Journal of Learning Disabilities, 26*(6), 404–412.

Vernon, A. (1989a). *Thinking, feeling, behaving: Children, grades 1–6.* Champaign, IL: Research Press.

Vernon, A. (1989b). *Thinking, feeling, behaving: Adolescents, grades 7–12.* Champaign, IL: Research Press.

Vernon, A. (1998a). *The passport program: A journey through emotional, social, cognitive and self-development—grades 1–5.* Champaign, IL: Research Press.

Vernon, A. (1998b). *The passport program: A journey through emotional, social, cognitive and self-development—grades 6–8.* Champaign, IL: Research Press.

Vernon, A. (1998c). *The passport program: A journey through emotional, social, cognitive and self-development—grades 9–12.* Champaign, IL: Research Press.

Vernon, D. S., Deshler, D. D., & Schumaker, J. B. (1993). *The teamwork strategy.* Lawrence, KS: Edge Enterprises.

Vernon, D. S., Schumaker, J. B., & Deshler, D. D. (1996). *The SCORE skills: Social skills for cooperative groups–revised edition*. Lawrence, KS: Edge Enterprises.

Vogel, S. A., & Forness, S. R. (1992). Social functioning in adults with learning disabilities. *School Psychology Review, 21*(3), 375–386.

Waksman, S. A. (1985). *The Waksman social skills rating scale*. Portland, OR: ASIEP Education Co.

Waksman, S., & Waksman, D. D. (1998). *The Waksman social skills curriculum*. Austin, TX: Pro-Ed.

Walker, H. M. (1983). *Walker problem behavior identification checklist–Revised*. Los Angeles: Western Psychological Services.

Walker, H. M., & McConnell, S. R. (1995a). *Walker–McConnell scale of social competence and school adjustment—Adolescent version*. San Diego: Singular Publishing.

Walker, H. M., & McConnell, S. R. (1995b). *Walker–McConnell scale of social competence and school adjustment—Elementary version*. San Diego: Singular Publishing.

Walker, H. M., McConnell, S., Holmes, D., Todis, B., Walker, J., & Golden, N. (1988). *The Walker social skills curriculum: The ACCEPTS program*. Austin, TX: Pro-Ed.

Walker, H. M., Todis, B., Holmes, D., & Horton, G. (1988). *The ACCESS program: Adolescent curriculum for communication and effective social skills*. Austin, TX: Pro-Ed.

Warger, C. L., & Rutherford, R. B., Jr. (1993). Co-teaching to improve social skills. *Preventing School Failure, 37*(4), 21–27.

Warger, C. L., & Rutherford, R., Jr. (1996). *A collaborative approach to teaching social skills*. Reston, VA: Exceptional Innovations.

Watson, T. S., & Gresham, F. M. (Eds.). (1998). *Handbook of child behavior therapy*. New York: Plenum Press.

Weare, K. (2004). *Developing the emotionally literate school*. London, UK: Paul Chapman Publishing.

Wehmeyer, M. L., & Kelchner, K. (1994). Interpersonal cognitive problem-solving skills of individuals with mental retardation. *Education and Training in Mental Retardation and Developmental Disabilities, 29*, 265–278.

Weisinger, H. (1998). *Emotional intelligence at work*. San Francisco: Jossey-Bass.

Wentzel, K. R. (1993). Does being good make the grade? Social behavior and academic competence in middle school. *Journal of Educational Psychology, 85*, 357–364.

Wentzel, K. R., Barry, C. M., & Caldwell, K. A. (2004). Friendships in middle school: Influences on motivation and school adjustment. *Journal of Educational Psychology, 96*(2), 195–203.

Wentzel, K. R., & Caldwell, K. A. (1997). Friendships, peer acceptance, and group membership: Relations to academic achievement in middle school. *Child Development, 68*, 1198–1209.

Whitehouse, E., & Pudney, W. (1996). *A volcano in my tummy: Helping children to handle anger*. Garbriola Island, British Columbia, Canada: New Society Publishers.

Whittaker, C. R. (1996). Adapting cooperative learning structures for mainstreamed students. *Reading & Writing Quarterly, 12*, 23–39.

Wiener, J., & Harris, P.J. (1997). Evaluation of an individualized, context-based social skills training program for children with learning disabilities. *Learning Disabilities Research and Practice, 12*(1), 40–53.

Wiener, J., & Sunohara, G. (1998). Parents' perceptions of the quality of friendships of their children with learning disabilities. *Learning Disabilities Research and Practice, 13*(4), 242–257.

Wiener, J., & Tardif, C. Y. (2004). Social and emotional functioning of children with learning disabilities: Does special education placement make a difference? *Learning Disabilities Research & Practice, 19*(1), 20–32.

Wiig, E. H. (1982). *Let's talk: Developing prosocial communication skills.* Columbus, OH: Charles E. Merrill Publishing.

Wiig, E. H., & Bray, C. M. (1983). *Let's talk for children.* Columbus, OH: Charles E. Merrill Publishing.

Wiig, E. H., & Bray, C. M. (1984). *Let's talk intermediate level.* Columbus, OH: Charles E. Merrill Publishing.

Wiig, E. H., & Harris, S. P. (1974). Perception and interpretation of nonverbally expressed emotions by adolescents with learning disabilities. *Perceptual and Motor Skills, 38,* 239–245.

Williams, G. J., & Reisberg, L. (2003). Successful inclusion: Teaching social skills through curriculum integration. *Intervention in School and Clinic, 38*(4), 205–210.

Wirths, C. G., & Bowman-Fruhm, M. (1993). *Your circle of friends.* New York: Twenty-First Century Books.

Yang, N. K., Schaller, J. L., Huang, T., Wang, M. H., & Tsai, S. (2003). Enhancing appropriate social behaviors for children with autism in general education classrooms: An analysis of six cases. *Education and Training in Developmental Disabilities, 38*(4), 405–416.

Youngs, B. B. (1995). *Problem solving skills for children ages 3–9* (2d ed.). Torrance, CA: Jalmar Press.

Yugar, J. M., & Shapiro, E. S. (2001). Elementary children's school friendship: A comparison of peer assessment methodologies. *School Psychology Review, 30*(4), 568–585.

Zigmond, N., & Kerr, M. M. (1985, April). *Managing the mainstream: A contrast of the behaviors of learning disabled students who pass their assigned mainstream courses and those who fail.* Paper presented at meeting of American Educational Research Association, Chicago.

Zimmerman, T., & Shapiro, L. (1996). *Sometimes I feel like I don't have any friends (but not so much anymore): A self-esteem book to help children improve their social skills.* King of Prussia, PA: Center for Applied Psychology.

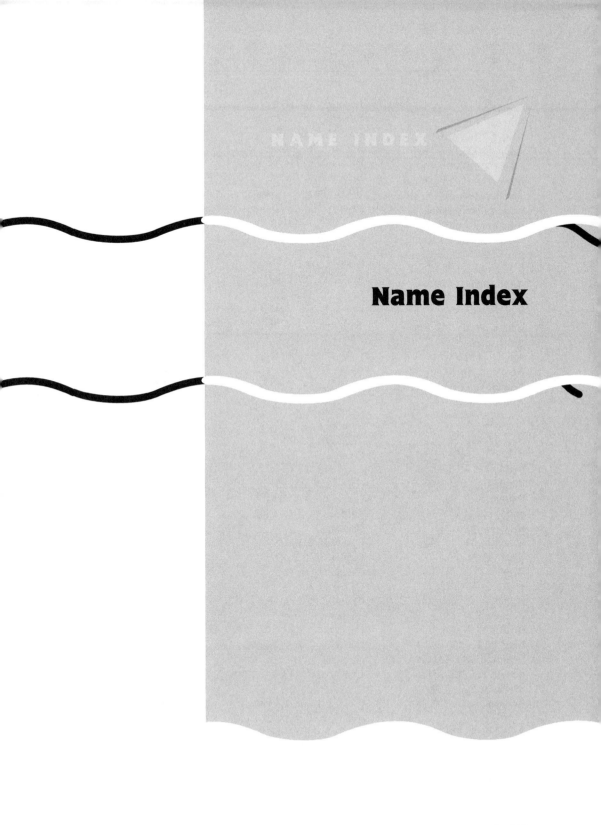

# Name Index

# Subject Index